The Holocaust in Hungary:
Sixty Years Later

Edited by

Randolph L. Braham and Brewster S. Chamberlin

The Rosenthal Institute for Holocaust Studies
Graduate Center of The City University of New York
Social Science Monographs, Boulder, CO

Distributed by
Columbia University Press

Published in association with the
United States Holocaust Memorial Museum

2006

EAST EUROPEAN MONOGRAPHS, NO. DCLXXVIII

Copyright 2006 by Randolph L. Braham
ISBN: 0-88033-576-9
(978-0-88033-576-8)
Library of Congress of Control Number: 2006922842

Published in association with the United States Holocaust Memorial Museum,
100 Raoul Wallenberg Place, SW; Washington, DC 20024-2126

Printed in the United States of America

Contents

Postwar

Historical/Sociological

Art and Literature

Foreword

The year 2004 marked the sixtieth anniversary of the deportation of Hungarian Jewry. Between May 15 and July 8, 1944, the Nazis and their Hungarian collaborators delivered more than 437,000 Hungarian Jews to Auschwitz, where the vast majority were murdered on arrival, with frightening efficiency. Until 1944 the historically vital and marvelously diverse Jewish community of Hungary, while subjected to prejudice and increasingly harsh discriminatory legislation during the Horthy regime, had remained largely intact physically. Then, in just a few months, expropriation, ghettoization, forced labor in excruciating circumstances, deportations to Auschwitz, and frenetic killing binges inside Hungary destroyed virtually the entire community outside Budapest—hundreds of thousands of innocents.

The murder of Hungarian Jewry starkly illustrates something that we have long come to accept. For the Nazis, the destruction of European Jews was an objective as important as military victory. It is more troubling to consider the fact that the Nazis' Hungarian collaborators pursued the destruction of their own countrymen—their friends, their neighbors, their clients, their schoolmates, their business partners, their life-associates—with fervor, urgency, and cruelty, at a time when it was clear that Hungary's war alongside Nazi Germany was going to be lost. And it is painfully disturbing that a world that understood by 1944 that European Jewry was being systematically murdered stood by and watched. For countries, as for individuals, doing nothing was not without its consequences. Inaction in the face of genocide empowers the perpetrators.

To commemorate this tragic history, the Center for Advanced Holocaust Studies of the United States Holocaust Memorial Museum, in partnership with the Rosenthal Institute of Holocaust Studies of the Graduate Center, City University of New York, organized a conference on "The Holocaust in Hungary: Sixty Years Later" in Washington and participated together with the Holocaust Documentation Center and Memorial Collection Public Foundation in a Budapest conference on the Holocaust. Our Museum also hosted visiting fellows from Hungary and participated in the dedication of Budapest's new Holocaust Museum.

It is important to confront, again and again, this dark page in the history of Hungary, of the Jewish world, and of humanity. We owe that to the murdered victims, to the survivors whose lives were forever changed, and to ourselves. The United States Holocaust Memorial Museum is proud to participate in this publication of presentations from the conference we hosted in 2004. In doing so we would also like to acknowledge the energy, guidance, and encouragement brought to this effort and many others by Professor Randolph Braham, survivor of the Hungarian Jewish forced labor battalions, preeminent scholar of the Holocaust in Hungary, Director of the Rosenthal Institute, and longtime member of the Academic Committee of the United States Holocaust Memorial Council.

Paul A. Shapiro
Director
Center for Advanced Holocaust Studies
United States Holocaust Memorial Museum

Introduction

This volume is an outgrowth of an international scholars' conference held in Washington, D.C. on March 16–18, 2004, under the auspices of the Center for Advanced Holocaust Studies of the United States Holocaust Memorial Museum and the Rosenthal Institute for Holocaust Studies of the Graduate Center of the City University of New York. Organized to coincide with the worldwide commemoration of the sixtieth anniversary of the Holocaust in Hungary, this conference—the third decennial scholars' conference of its kind—was coordinated with the conference "The Holocaust in Hungary: Sixty Years Later—A European Perspective" held in Budapest under the auspices of the Holocaust Documentation Center and Memorial Collection Public Foundation on April 16–18, 2004.

The conferences aimed, among other things, to promote international scholarly cooperation, present recent research findings, synthesize the results of the past decade's scholarly investigations relating to the Holocaust in Hungary, and explore the historical lessons of the Nazi era. They also provided an opportunity for experienced as well as younger scholars of the Holocaust to share their knowledge and insight into several important areas of investigation in their respective fields of specialization.

The volume opens with a foreword by Paul A. Shapiro, Director of the Center for Advanced Holocaust Studies United States Holocaust Memorial Museum; a Washington conference keynote by Nobel Laureate Elie Wiesel, and the keynote delivered by Randolph L. Braham at the Hungarian Academy of Sciences during the opening session of the Budapest conference. Both Braham and Shapiro attended the Budapest conference as representatives of the United States Holocaust Memorial Museum.

The contributions to this volume reflect increasing access to archival materials during the preceding decade, the expansion of disciplines that added new perspectives on the Holocaust in Hungary, and a better understanding of contemporary anti-Semitism, which is often coupled with the denigration, distortion, or actual denial of the Holocaust.

Several contributions provide new historical insights into areas that had not been sufficiently explored in the literature.

Many of these advances in the study of the Holocaust in Hungary have been, to a large extent, made possible by the archival acquisitions of the United States Holocaust Memorial Museum, thanks in part to the International Archival Programs Division of the Center for Advanced Holocaust Studies. The recently acquired archival materials have, among other things, permitted a more precise analysis of the fate of Jewish communities in Hungary, a situation reflected in several contributions to this volume.

The essays by Holly Case, Jean Ancel, and Zoltán Tibori Szabó address specifically the communities of Northern Transylvania. Case examines the Holocaust relationships between neighboring states in East-Central Europe, focusing on the historical conflict between Hungary and Romania over the issue of Transylvania. She demonstrates that the "Jewish policy" of the two countries hinged to a large extent on the issue of territorial revision. Ancel provides an overview of the plight of the Hungarian Jewish survivors from Northern Transylvania during the immediate postwar period, highlighting the various factors that influenced their decisions about relocation after liberation. Tibori Szabó analyzes the postwar situation of the Transylvanian Jewish community, relying on the Transylvanian Jewish press of the period, oral histories, and Romanian and Hungarian archival materials. His study examines problems of readjustment, intra- and inter-communal conflicts, and the community debates over the issue of responsibility for the Holocaust.

Other historical studies in this volume are more general in scope. László Karsai's essay focuses on the identification of 1942 as *the* fateful year in the history of the Holocaust. Relying on diplomatic dispatches by Hungarian consular officials stationed in the neutral and Nazi-dominated countries of Europe, he demonstrates that the leaders of Hungary, along with other officials and journalists, knew of the realities of the Final Solution as early as that year. Karsai also identifies some reasons why Prime Minister Miklós Kállay (March 1942–March 1944) consistently refused Hitler's demands for implementing the Final Solution in Hungary. Judit Molnár reviews the crucial role the Hungarian gendarmerie played in the Final Solution, as reflected in the postwar trials of individual gendarmes. Raphael Vago describes and analyzes the factors that determined the evolution of Israeli historiography on the Hungarian chapter of the Holocaust. Heightened interest in the tragedy that befell Hungarian Jewry stemmed from the Kasztner case that rocked Israeli society in the mid-1950s, and the capture and trial of Adolf Eichmann in the early 1960s. Gábor Kádár and Zoltán Vági document the political and ideological interests of the Hungarian rightist extremists in the expropriation of the Jews, focusing on the objectives the Döme Sztójay government pursued after the German occupation of Hungary on March 19, 1944. They make clear that by expropriating the Jews the quisling government aimed to balance the budget, meet the needs of the military establishment, relieve the social discontent that plagued the country, and broaden its public support through the distribution of Jewish wealth. Alice Freifeld identifies and analyzes the major dilemmas that confronted Hungarian Jewish survivors in general and those of Budapest in particular during the immediate postwar period. She demonstrates that many survivors had to confront major choices, especially the basic one of whether to re-assimilate and start anew within the context of a defeated Hungary, or to emigrate to Palestine or the West. The dilemma was particularly acute in 1947, when the Sovietization of Hungary became increasingly apparent.

Some of the essays in this volume draw on scholarship from other disciplines, thus adding fresh perspectives to the study of the Holocaust in Hungary. These include inquiries into the impact of gender during the Holocaust, the attitudes and reactions of the Christian churches, the activities of the righteous, and the reflection of the Holocaust in literature and the arts.

Focusing on the Hungarian city of Veszprém as a case study, Tim Cole's essay examines the impact that the recruitment of Jewish men of military age into labor service companies had on the city's Jewish community before the German occupation. It also analyzes the fate of the Jewish men and the Jewish women of the city after the occupation, highlighting the advantages for the men, who were conscripted for labor service, over the women, who ended up in Auschwitz. Paul Hanebrink reviews the public debate that developed in the immediate postwar years over the responsibility of Hungary's Christian churches for the anti-Semitic policies that made genocide possible in 1944. Daniel A. Lowy focuses on the rescue and/or support of Jews by both Hungarian and Romanian gentiles in Kolozsvár (Cluj in Romanian) as revealed by

Egység (Unity), the relatively short-lived postwar Hungarian Jewish daily in Transylvania.

Several authors address the issue of anti-Semitism, which in contemporary Hungary often is interlinked with the distortion or denial of the Holocaust. Ivan T. Berend analyzes the causes of anti-Semitism following the systemic change of 1989, emphasizing that the value vacuum created after the collapse of the Communist regime was partly filled by the revival of traditional Hungarian "tribal nationalism." He also reviews the evolution of anti-Semitism under the impact of the "national hysteria" that is deeply rooted in the history of the region. András Kovács presents the findings of his sociological survey conducted between March and November 1999. The survey, based on 2,015 interviews, reveals how Jews living in Hungary define anti-Semitism and examines the significant differences between Jews and non-Jews in the classification of certain phenomena or statements as being anti-Semitic. Attila Pók analyzes the historical, social, and political factors that led to the marginalization of two key issues—the relationship between traditional anti-Semitism and the Holocaust, and Hungarian society's responsibility for the Holocaust—in the historical debates that followed the systemic change of 1989. He focuses on factors such as the limited social impact of symbolic commemorations of the Holocaust, the half-hearted legal measures designed for financial compensation to the survivors, and the phenomena of latent and occasionally public manifestations of anti-Semitism. Michael Shafir studies the Jewish-Gentile clash of memories about the Holocaust and Communism. He identifies the post-Communist era mechanisms used in handling the legacy of the Horthy era and of the Holocaust, focusing on the differences in the attitudes of various governmental leaders. Victor Karády offers an overview of the incidence of death among the Jews of Budapest before, during, and after the Holocaust. His essay includes statistical-demographic data on the oscillation of death rates during three specific periods: the Nazi era and the concurrent anti-Jewish drive, the post-Holocaust turbulence, and the Communist period.

Several of the studies focus on literary and artistic reflections of the Hungarian chapter of the Holocaust. Ivan Sanders surveys post-1989 Hungarian literature on Jewish themes, pointing out differences—in approach, tone, and emphasis—between these works and literature on the same subject originating in the previous era. Sanders also examines

changing attitudes toward Jewish identity as reflected in Hungarian
literature, as well as some writers' continued rejection of the very notion
of Hungarian-Jewish literature. In this context he reviews the works of
Nobel Laureate Imre Kertész. Katherine Portuges's essay considers the
adaptation of Kertész's *Fateless* (*Sorstalanság*) from novel to film.
Assessing films directed by cinematographers who were themselves witnesses and survivors, Portuges compares them with movies based only
on memoirs, autobiographical novels, and historical accounts. Zsuzsanna
Ozsváth provides an in-depth analysis of some representative Hungarian
novels written between 1945 and 1989 under the impact of the Holocaust. She demonstrates that, despite the great psychological and political pressures to which they were subjected, many Jewish authors of the
period remained steadfast in their commitment to historical truth,
providing detailed and accurate accounts of the horrors they endured in
the camps and the labor service companies.

We owe a debt of gratitude to many individuals who made possible
the publication of this volume. First and foremost we would like to
express our thanks to the leaders and benefactors of the United States
Holocaust Memorial Museum, the Rosenthal Institute for Holocaust
Studies, and the J. and O. Winter Fund at the Graduate Center of the City
University of New York. We are grateful to Sara J. Bloomfield, Director
of the Museum, and Paul Shapiro, Director of the Center for Advanced
Holocaust Studies, for their support in hosting the International
Scholars' Conference in Washington and for their commitment to the
publication of its proceedings. We are indebted to Jack Rosenthal, the
mentor of the Institute that bears his name at the Graduate Center of the
City University of New York. We owe a special debt of gratitude to
Gábor Várszegi, the founder of the J. and O. Winter Fund at CUNY's
Graduate Center, for providing financial support for the conference and
this publication. Among the many other friends of the Rosenthal Insti-
tute, we are especially indebted to Gizella and Arie Edrich, Eva and
Norman Gati, Sheba and Jacob Gruber, Mimi Mautner, and Ann and
Gabriel Newmark.

We would like to express our thanks to the conference participants
who contributed updated versions of their papers to this volume. We are
particularly grateful to these scholars from various countries—Canada,
the Czech Republic, France, Germany, Hungary, Israel, Romania, the
United Kingdom, and the United States—for taking the time to share the

fruits of their research and scholarship with the world at large. For their valuable editorial assistance, we would like to express our appreciation to Elizabeth Braham, Aleisa Fishman and Nancy Tyson.

May 2005   *Randolph L. Braham*
                                                      Brewster S. Chamberlin

Keynote Address
by Elie Wiesel

I hope you know that I expect much from this very special Holocaust seminar. And I am sure you know why. It deals with events with which I am personally familiar—and yet many of its aspects remain either hidden from or unexplained to me. Will some of you, in your contributions here, answer questions that continue to haunt me for sixty years in all my studies and writings?

All that has been said and written about the tragic fate of European Jews can be applied to Hungarian Jews too—and more so.

Jews lived in relative tranquility in Hungary. In the early forties, Prime Minister Miklós Kállay refused to give in to Hitler's demands to deport the Jewish population to Germany. In 1941, so-called "alien" Jews had been sent across the Polish border to be shot and thrown into mass graves in Kamenets-Podolsk and Kolomea. But Hungarian Jews, proud of their citizenship, felt protected by their Hungarian government. Their naïveté resulted in excessive passivity, which had catastrophic consequences.

For now we all know that Hungarian Jewry was the largest Jewish community in occupied Europe still alive in April 1944. In one month, all the decrees were published, one following the other, one more cruel than the other: forbidden circulation, confiscation of stores, factories, and houses. The mass deportations began on May 15, 1944. What was meant to be the last phase of Germany's "Final Solution" proceeded uninterrupted. German armies occupied Hungary on March 19, 1944. Two days later, Adolf Eichmann was already at work in Budapest. His staff was amazingly small. Several Germans and scores of Hungarians. The team numbered less than two hundred persons, including secretaries, drivers, and cooks. Ten weeks after it was established, there were no more Jews left in the provinces. Never before had the abominable Final Solution been implemented with such efficiency. The average daily transport was twelve thousand. On June 1st the figure rose to twenty thousand.

I remember: four transports left my town in May. The entire operation was handled by Hungarian gendarmerie units. Only two Germans were present. One of them, I would discover later, was Adolf Eichmann. All the roads led to the flames over Birkenau. Did we know it then? No, we did not. The world knew; the victims did not. And my first question is: why didn't they? They could have been saved; why weren't they? In other words: why weren't they warned? The Red Army was so near my town, at night we could hear the thundering of its guns. It is with pain and anguish that I am saying to you these words: of all the Jews under Hitler's control, Hungarian Jews had the best chance of being saved. And they were not. When their sealed cattle cars stopped at a Polish railway station named Auschwitz, they had no idea what it meant.

Yet efforts had been made to warn them. They originated from inside the universe of ashes and despair. I understood when it was too late.

A quick recollection: a young teenager arrived in Birkenau from a little town in the Carpathian Mountains. In less than a minute, he was separated from his mother and sisters. As he and his father marched towards the shadows of eerie gigantic flames rising to the silent heavens, they were yelled at by inmates dressed in strange uniforms: "Idiots, why did you come here? Imbeciles, why didn't you stay home or run away? Why didn't you hide in rat holes rather than join us in this hell?"

For years and years I tried to understand their bizarre questions. I couldn't figure out their anger, which, at the time, I considered brutal and cruel. What did they think? That it had been a matter of choice for us? That all of us, men, women, and children, had volunteered to come to Auschwitz, as if it were, on vacation?

Later I understood. I read Rudolf Vrba's dramatic and harrowing account of his escape from Auschwitz. He and his friend Alfred Wetzler worked in the so-called Kanada Kommando whose members were better off than the rest of the inmates. Their work consisted of collecting and sorting out the belongings of new arrivals. At one point, in early 1944, they realized that new large installations were being made for many more huge transports. It didn't take much time for them to realize that Hungary was the only place where large Jewish communities were still alive. Vrba's conclusion? It meant that their turn had to come. And so he and his friend decided to do what governments of the free world had failed to do, namely intervene so as to alter the course of destiny. They decided to escape. More than to save their own lives, I want to believe, their goal was to save the lives of tens of thousands, correction: hundreds of thousands of Hungarian Jews. Few inmates tried to escape from Auschwitz and even fewer succeeded. Vrba and his friend were among the few. Their heroic adventure, published by Vrba decades ago, deserves to be read by more people, especially those who are interested in all that happened in those years. They managed to cross the border into Slovakia, met with Jewish representatives from Budapest and with high officials of the Catholic Church. They prepared a lengthy report on Birkenau with essential elements including maps and topographical material on the gas chambers and crematoriums: everything was all there. All that took place *before* the mass deportations began.

And nothing was done with the information and knowledge the report contained. Again, a question, the same as before: why not? And some follow-up questions: when and where did the meetings take place? Who were the Jewish representatives from Budapest? What did they do with the Vrba report? Did it reach the Vatican, London, and Washington? What were the reactions there?

Question number one: did those Jewish leaders who, in Budapest, together with Rudolf Kasztner dealt with Eichmann, often daily, know where we were being sent? And if so, why didn't they inform us? Was the Judenrat active in rescuing Jews? Did it represent a united front to the Germans? Are Raul Hilberg and Hannah Arendt right in declaring that it became a pawn in German hands?

In his testimony quoted by Eugene Lévai, Raul Hilberg, and Randolph Braham, Rudolf Kasztner declares,

> In Budapest we had a unique opportunity to follow the fate of European Jewry. We had seen how they had been disappearing one after the other from the map of Europe. At the moment of the occupation of Hungary, the number of dead Jews amounted to five million. We knew very well about the work of the Einsatzgruppen. We knew more than was necessary about Auschwitz.... We had as early as 1942 a complete picture of what was happening in the East with the Jews deported to Auschwitz and the other extermination camps....

But then why didn't he warn the Jews in my town to do everything possible and refuse to go on the train?

Many of us could have, would have found hiding places with Christian friends or in the surrounding mountains.

And what about the Allies? They must have known—in fact, now it has been documented that they knew quite a lot for some time. What did they do, in Washington, with their knowledge?

Incidentally, not everybody knew. On some levels people refused to know. Example: On March 19, 1944, the very day Germany invaded Hungary, Sir Cecil Hurst, of the United Nations Commission for the Investigation of War Crimes, officially declared that his Commission had no proof of Polish Jews being massacred by Germans....

Of course, there was proof. At the highest levels of government, in most allied and neutral capitals, the names Auschwitz and Treblinka evoked profound bewilderment, embarrassment, frustration, pain, and horror. By why didn't the leaders broadcast appeals to Hungarian Jews not to go to the railroad stations, not to rely on German promises that they would remain inside Hungary? Better yet: why didn't the Allies bomb, at least once, the railways going from Hungary to Birkenau? At that time, ten thousand men, women, and children were gassed every night: air attacks would have stopped the process, even for a few days, and sent a signal to Berlin that the civilized world cared....

Close to 440,000 Jews from the provinces were shipped off to Auschwitz in ten weeks. In Budapest, the process was slower. By then, FDR, the King of Sweden, and the Pope had issued appeals to Horthy to stop the deportations. A number of Jews were saved thanks to Raoul Wallenberg's audacious efforts. He will forever be remembered in Jewish history with admiration and gratitude. As will the Swiss Vice-Consul Carl Lutz and the Papal Nuncio Angelo Rotta, who offered shelters to thousands of frightened Jews.

Many of them were threatened not by German brutality but by Hungarian cruelty. Their chronicles of what the antisemitic 'Nyilas' thugs inflicted on Jews in Budapest are filled with details of their murderous activities. Many hundreds of Jews were arrested, tortured, and tied up together to be shot and thrown into the Danube River. The Hungarian novelist György Konrád describes what he had seen: "In a courtyard, piles of corpses were reaching the first floor." More were handed over to the Germans for deportation.

SS Colonel Walter Hagen related what he saw:

Without resistance and in submission, they marched by the hundreds in long columns to railway stations and piled into wagons. Only very few gendarmes were supervising the operations; it would have been easy to run away. In the Carpatho-Ruthenian province, which contained numerically the strongest Jewish settlements, the forbidding mountains and forests offered an opportunity for prolonged hiding. But few removed themselves from their doom.

But there was resistance in Budapest, Jewish resistance. Young Zionist boys and girls risked their lives snatching victims from the hands of the murderers. They too must be remembered—and remembered with gratitude.

However, what we retain from this chapter of history is a sense of frustration and sadness: Hungarian Jews could have been saved—and they weren't. As in so many other places over there, they were abandoned to the enemy. They were alone. They lived alone. Did they die alone? Did not something of some of us die with them?

Keynote Address
by Randolph L. Braham

I am honored to be here and to have the opportunity to reflect on some aspects of the Hungarian chapter of the Holocaust on this day, the 16th of April, Hungary's official day of Holocaust remembrance. I am particularly pleased that I can share some of my ideas with you in this magnificent citadel of learning—the Hungarian Academy of Science. This international scholars' conference on the Holocaust in Hungary is the second decennial conference being held in Budapest, this beautiful capital of the democratic Republic of Hungary. The 1994 international conference, the first and so far the only such scholarly gathering in the former Soviet-dominated world, was organized by the Graduate Center of the City University of New York in cooperation with the Institute of History of the Academy. I still remember with gratitude Professor Attila Pók's valuable contributions to assuring the success of that conference. This conference has been organized in coordination with the one that took place in Washington, D.C., last month. I would like to express my thanks and gratitude to my many friends and colleagues in Hungary and elsewhere for agreeing to participate in this conference and for sharing the fruits of their research. They are among the best and the brightest in Holocaust studies. I am especially grateful to Professor Judit Molnár for having borne the burdens of organization with skill and understanding.

This is a historic moment in the postwar commemoration of the Holocaust—this tragic chapter in the history of Hungarian Jewry, which is also one of the darkest chapters in the history of Hungary. Historians will probably record this conference and the commemorative events surrounding it as a possible turning point in the postwar history of Hungary. These commemorative events hopefully will ease, if not fully heal, the pains of the past. If continued by further acts of contrition, they may even pave the way to the national reconciliation desired by men and women of good will and help heal the wounds that scarred Jewish-Christian relations since 1938, if not 1919. And if this reconciliation takes place—and I fervently hope that it will—much of the credit will be shared by the governmental leaders who were responsible for the initiation, financing, and organization of these commemorative events. I am grateful to Prime Minister Péter Medgyessy for his leadership for the "múlt megvallása, megismerése, és megismertetetése." Toward this end he brought about the establishment of an international Holocaust Remembrance Committee—the first such action by a leader of the Hungarian government—and issued concrete directives for the proper remembrance of the martyrdom of the close to 600,000 Hungarian citizens of the Jewish faith.

As a survivor of the labor service system who lost his parents and many of his immediate and distant relatives in Auschwitz, I am also grateful to István Hiller, the Minister of Cultural Heritage, and his associates in the Ministry for *their* contributions to the cause of remembrance, including the establishment of the Holocaust Museum that was solemnly inaugurated yesterday. As a member of the Academic Committee of the United States Holocaust Memorial Museum I am also indebted to the Minister—and the Medgyessy administration—for signing the archival agreement with the United States Holocaust Memorial Museum in Washington—an agreement that will eventually place additional documentary materials at the disposal of those interested in the understanding and documentation of the history of Hungarian Jewry.

My retrospective analysis of the Holocaust in Hungary sixty years later reconfirms many of the conclusions I had reached decades ago. The destruction of Hungarian Jewry in 1944 represents the most controversial chapter in the tragedy that befell European Jewry during the Nazi era. Constituting the last chapter in the Nazis' war against the Jews, it is replete with paradoxes. Although deprived of their livelihood and many of their basic social and civil rights, the bulk of Hungarian Jewry survived the first four-and-a-half years of the war relatively intact. During this long period of the war, they felt basically secure under the physical protection of the conservative-aristocratic government. They felt so secure, in fact, that they became virtually oblivious to what was happening to the Jewish communities in the rest of Nazi-dominated Europe.

It is one of the sad ironies of history that after the German occupation of Hungary on March 19, 1944, it was this confident Jewish community that was subjected to the most ruthless destruction in the Nazis' Final Solution program. The Jews of Hungary—loyal and patriotic citizens who proudly identified themselves as Magyars of the Israelite faith—were destroyed on the eve of Allied victory when the secrets of

Auschwitz were already widely known to the leaders of the world, including the governmental and Jewish leaders of Hungary.

The mass murder of the Hungarian Jews was part and parcel of the Nazis' drive to annihilate European Jewry. The Final Solution was planned by the Nazis and carried out with the help of accomplices all over Europe in the broad daylight of the twentieth century. The murder of European Jewry took place while the civilized world remained basically passive or silent. The Allies, the neutral powers, the International Red Cross, and the Vatican were concerned with their own narrowly defined interests, caring little, if at all, about the tragedy befalling European Jewry. The ideals of the Judeo-Christian tradition, the ideas of the renaissance and the enlightenment, the conception of modernity with its emphasis on reason and pragmatism were, for the duration of the war at least, ignored or trampled upon.

While theologians and philosophers will continue to argue about the religious and moral implications of racism and the Final Solution, I believe that historians and other scholars empirically trained in the social sciences have solved the puzzle of the Holocaust. No other event in world history is as well documented as the Holocaust. We now have fully documented accounts of what happened and of how, when, and why it happened. Most of the parts constituting the puzzle of the Hungarian chapter of the Holocaust are clearly identifiable and fully documented. Obviously, I don't have the time to identify and analyze many of these parts; I shall select only a few for purposes of illustration.

Let me begin with a few "ifs." It is safe to assume that Germany's decision to occupy Hungary was to a large extent based on military considerations. The Nazi leaders were fully aware of Hungary's attempts to honorably extricate itself from the Axis Alliance, ever since the destruction of the Second Hungarian Army at Voronezh early in 1943. It is also safe to assume that in the absence of a German occupation, Hungarian Jewry would have survived the war, suffering "only" around 60,000 casualties, including those murdered at Kamenets-Podolsk and the Bácska. Over 40,000 of these casualties were suffered by Jewish males serving in the labor service system organized under the auspices of the Ministry of Defense. Commenting about this system, former President Árpád Göncz stated while in office: "This was the first Hungarian army in our history that called up and took men to the front in order to be killed by it."

It is further safe to assume that if, after the German occupation, the Horthy-appointed Sztójay government had refused to place the instruments of state power—the gendarmerie, police, and civil service—at the disposal of the relatively small Eichmann-Sondereinsatzkommando and instead adopted the stance of the Kállay government or of the Bulgarians and the Romanians, the Nazis—and their Hungarian accomplices—could not have implemented the Final Solution program.

The ease with which the Nazis and their Hungarian accomplices carried out the Final Solution was to some extent due to the illusions and rationalizations that characterized the thinking of the Jewish and governmental leaders of Hungary before and during the Second World War. In contrast to the illusions and rationalizations of the Jewish leaders and the unrealistic, if not quixotic, policies of the Hungarian governmental leaders, the Nazis and their Hungarian accomplices were realistic and resolute. They were resolved to carry out their racially and ideologically defined objective swiftly and unmercifully: the Final Solution of the Jewish question. Realizing that the Axis would lose the war, they were committed to winning at least the war against the Jews. Time was of the essence. The Red Army was fast approaching Romania, and the Western Allies, as the whole world expected, were planning their invasion of Nazi-dominated Europe.

Let me first briefly deal with the illusions that determined the attitudes and reactions of the central leadership of Hungarian Jewry. Nothing that I say in this context should detract from the ultimate responsibility the Nazis and their Hungarian accomplices must bear for the Holocaust. The attitudes and reactions of the Hungarian Jewish leaders during the interwar and wartime periods were to a large extent shaped during the so-called Golden Era in which they were born and raised. These leaders were convinced that the bonds they had forged with the governing conservative-aristocratic leadership of Hungary would safeguard Jews from the harm that had befallen their co-religionists in many other countries of Europe. As a consequence of the mutually beneficial symbiotic relationship that evolved between the two leadership groups, the Jewish masses in general felt ever more secure and became ever more patriotic and assimilated.

In the forefront of the Magyars' struggle for national independence in 1848–49, the Jews of Hungary had played an important role in the modernization of the country, in the flourishing of its culture, and, more importantly, in providing the slim political majority the basically feudal aristocratic-gentry class needed to rule in the multinational kingdom. Identifying themselves as "Magyars of the Jewish faith," chauvinistic Jewish elements even assumed a leading role in the government's drive for the Magyarization of the ethnic-national minorities. Grateful and ever more patriotic, the Jews in general and their leaders in particular were ready to overlook the fact that the conservative-aristocratic leaders of Hungary, enlightened as they appeared, were fundamentally undemocratic and reactionary, imbued with neither the principles of toleration nor the conceptions of pluralism.

The "social contract" between the ruling elite and the Jewish one was basically tenuous, one-sided, and short-lived. While the conservative-aristocratic elite formally adhered to this social contract as long as its political and economic interests required it, the Jewish leaders looked upon it as "binding," a guarantee of safety for the Jews. These leaders convinced themselves that the Magyars, civilized and chivalrous, would never forget the political, economic, and cultural services the Jews had rendered to the Hungarian nation since 1848.

The fact that the contract was one-sided and ephemeral was revealed almost immediately after the collapse of the Austro-Hungarian Empire in 1918. While the postwar Hungarian ruling elite unequivocally nullified it, the Jewish leaders continued to cling to it as still in effect, firmly adhering to their prewar patriotic posture. They looked upon the newly adopted numerus clausus law (the first anti-Jewish legislation in post–World War I Europe), the anti-Semitic outbursts that followed the short-lived Communist dictatorship, and the anti-Jewish rampages of the Horthy-led counterrevolutionaries as mere temporary aberrations. Clinging to their patriotic stance, they vehemently rejected the drive by some international Jewish organizations to have Hungary penalized for violating the peace treaties as a gross intervention in their country's internal affairs.

The national leaders of Hungarian Jewry continued to retain this posture even after Hungary, in emulation of Nazi Germany, began to carry out an increasingly severe anti-Jewish program in 1938. They tended to interpret the avalanche of ever more restrictive anti-Jewish laws as "reflections of the spirit of the time." They rationalized the adoption of some, if not all, of these anti-Semitic measures as both "understandable" and "necessary"—understandable in light of the inter-

xxvi							Keynote Address

national situation at the time and "necessary" in order to appease the Nazis abroad and the Nyilas at home. While they agonized over the many excesses that were committed in the name of the "New Order"—the Hungarians caused the deaths of around 60,000 Jews between 1941 and March 1944—the Jewish leaders continued to believe that what happened in Poland and elsewhere in Nazi-dominated Europe could not possibly happen in chivalrous Hungary.

Stunned and bewildered after the occupation, the Jewish leaders grasped at the last straw of hope. They were relieved when they heard that Miklós Horthy, the head of state, had decided to remain at the helm, convinced that, as commander in chief, he would continue to enjoy the allegiance and support of the military and state administration and thereby save the lives, if not the property, of the loyal "Magyars of the Jewish faith." Little did they know that the man on whom they had pinned their hopes had in fact consented, at his Schloss Klesheim meeting with Hitler on March 18, 1944, to deliver a few hundred thousand Jewish "workers" for "employment" in the Third Reich—an agreement the German and Hungarian Nazis successfully exploited for the speedy implementation of the Final Solution.

Let me now turn briefly to the wartime policies of the Kállay government, which precipitated the German occupation and the consequent destruction of Hungarian Jewry. The Hungarian leaders realized soon after the military debacle at Voronezh that the Axis powers would lose the war and began to look for an honorable way to extricate Hungary from that alliance. Caught in the vise of the two totalitarian states they loathed and feared—Nazi Germany to the West and the Soviet Union in the East—they tried to pursue their national and regime interests by finding a way of surrendering directly to the Western Allies. This objective was as quixotic in the context of 1943 as the many rationalizations they advanced in its support. They unrealistically assumed that the Western Allies—capitalist and anti-Bolshevik—would invade Nazi-dominated Europe from the Balkans so as to hit two birds with one stone: moving north toward the heart of East Central Europe, the Allies would not only crush the Nazis but also prevent the western penetration of Bolshevism. They also believed—falsely in retrospect—that the Germans would refrain from occupying Hungary, an ally whose resources and air space they desperately needed; finally, they hoped that by surrendering to the Western Allies, Hungary would be allowed not only to retain the territories it had acquired with the aid of the Third Reich between 1938 and 1941, but also to preserve the antiquated semi-feudal system.

After Italy's successful extrication from the Nazi Alliance in the summer of 1943, the Hungarian governmental leaders became increasingly resolved to follow suit. They established direct and indirect contacts with representatives of the Western Allies in Italy and Turkey without, however, taking any military contingency measures. Hitler, who was fully informed about the Hungarians' intentions, was determined to frustrate them. Driven primarily by strategic military interests of the Reich, he decided to occupy Hungary and replace the "Jewish-dominated" Kállay government with a more "reliable" one. He was determined to assure Hungary's continuing economic and military contributions to the joint war effort, to secure the uninterrupted flow of Romanian oil that fueled his war machine, and last but not least, to maintain the supply lines and possible escape routes of the German armies in the Balkans. It was this military decision, based on *Realpolitik,* that determined the occupation—an occupation that also made possible the achievement of the racially defined ideological goal: the Final Solution of the Jewish question in Hungary. It was Hitler's military decision that sealed the fate of Hungarian Jewry. It appears in retrospect that had Hungary continued to remain a militarily passive but politically vocal ally of the Third Reich instead of provocatively engaging in essentially fruitless, if not merely alibi-establishing, diplomatic maneuvers, which were not matched by any military preparedness, the German occupation might not have taken place and the Jews of Hungary might possibly have survived the war relatively intact.

In contrast to the illusions and rationalizations of the Jewish leaders and of the unrealistic pendulum-like policies of the Hungarian conservative-aristocratic elite, the Nazis and their Hungarian accomplices, enjoying the active support of the Sztójay government, lost no time in implementing the Final Solution program. For the first time in its history, Hungary, in clear emulation of Nazi Germany, embarked on a criminal campaign against its own citizens then classified as Jewish, transforming thievery and plunder into a state industry. Isolated, marked, expropriated, and incarcerated in ghettoes, the Jews—Hungarians of the Jewish faith, as well as the converts and Christians so identified under the racial laws then in effect—felt betrayed by the Magyars on whom they depended for their safety: Horthy secretly consented to the delivery of hundreds of thousands of Jewish "workers" to Nazi Germany; the Jews were told by the Hungarian officials they approached that "the demands of the Germans had to be obeyed"; the Sztójay government placed the instruments of state power at the disposal of the SS and their hirelings committed to the Final Solution; the heads of the Christian churches, who had supported many of the anti-Semitic measures of the succeeding governments, exchanged secret notes but never issued a pastoral letter; and the Christian population, intoxicated by years of anti-Semitic agitation, was at best largely passive. A large number of them gave vent to their rapacious instincts, eager to acquire the homes, wealth, shops, and professional offices of the Jews. There were a number of Christians who dared go against the tide, risking their lives to save Jews. Although relatively few in number, these Righteous Gentiles—active primarily in Budapest during the Nyilas era—contributed the brightest pages to the otherwise dark history of 1944 Hungary.

Here we are sixty years after these horrendous events and the peoples in the former Nazi-dominated world, including Hungary, are largely unaware of them. Misguided nationalists, eager to cleanse this dark chapter in their histories, have launched—starting almost immediately after the end of the Second World War—a veritable disinformation campaign, ignoring, denigrating, distorting, and actually denying the Holocaust. This is the case in Hungary as well as elsewhere. As I have often stated, I am not really concerned with the skinheads and the other charlatans who deny the Holocaust. They and their obscene ideas will eventually end up on the dung heap of history. I am more concerned about the respectable political, governmental, and military figures who, while acknowledging the realities of the Holocaust, are committed to absolving Hungary of any responsibility and to bringing about the rehabilitation of the Horthy era. They place almost exclusive blame for the Holocaust on the Germans and on some "misguided" Nyilas, ignoring the fact that the Final Solution was planned and implemented in cooperation with the SS by the constitutionally appointed Sztójay government while Miklós Horthy was Hungary's head of state. It is these respectable public figures who are in the forefront of the history-cleansing campaign today. They are the ones who are eager to make comparisons between Auschwitz and the Gulag, between the Holocaust and the evils of Communism, to identify the Jews with Bolshevism, to bring about the posthumous rehabilitation of men like Gömbös and Bárdossy, to erect statues to Teleki, organize exhibits on Szálasi, and resurrect the national-Christian principles of the Horthy era—to cite just a few of the recent disturbing developments. These history-cleansers fail to heed the admonition of men like former President Árpád Göncz or former Education Minister Zoltán Pokorni. According to the former president, Hungary "has so far been unable to confront—mercilessly confront—the past." The former minister of education echoed the same sentiments: "Who is responsible for everything that happened? We Hungarians will also have to come to grips with this question: what was the responsibility of the Hungarian state and of the citizens as a whole for the deportation of the Hungarian Jews and for their tragic fate?"

The questions were well posed but so far they have been left unanswered. Hungary has so far failed publicly and officially to come to grips with the Holocaust. It has so far failed to heed George Santayana's warning: "Nations who fail to learn the lessons of the past are doomed to repeat all the mistakes of the past." I look forward to the day when a head of state or head of government will do so in an official address to the nation, acknowledging Hungary's responsibility for the catastrophe that befell its Jewish citizens during the Second World War. If and when that time comes, history and historians will record that the first steps in that direction were taken by the governmental leaders who organized the current commemorative events, including this conference. Only the future will tell whether these steps were acts of expediency or acts of contrition. I salute these leaders in the name of the martyrs and of the survivors of the Holocaust.

I also salute the participants in this important conference and thank them in advance for their scholarly contribution to the documentation of the Holocaust. I am convinced that their papers will greatly enhance the field of Holocaust studies and induce the current and future generations to learn—in the spirit of Santayana—the historical lessons of the past and thereby contribute to the creation of a truly tolerant and pluralistic society in Hungary.

Antecedents

The Fateful Year: 1942 in the
Reports of Hungarian Diplomats

László Karsai

On December 2, 1942, Döme Sztójay, Hungarian minister in Berlin, had no choice but to hand over a firmly worded memorandum from his government to the German Foreign Ministry. The anti-Semitic minister[1] did not approve of his government's refusal to carry out the demands the Germans had made in Budapest on October 17. In the memorandum, the government of Miklós Kállay (March 9, 1942, to March 22, 1944) made it clear that they did not regard as possible either the introduction of the yellow star of David or the deportation of the Hungarian Jews, particularly when the Romanian and the Italian Jews were exempt from these demands.[2]

Below I shall endeavor to reconstruct why and on the basis of what information the Hungarian cabinet decided in late autumn of 1942 to defend "their own" Jews. One of the most important reasons for the decision was mentioned to Martin Luther, Under Secretary of State of the German Foreign Ministry, by Sztójay himself on October 5, 1942.[3] He mentioned, among other things, that he knew from his previous talks with Kállay that the Hungarian premier "was especially interested in whether the Jews deported to the East would be given the possibility for continuing existence. There were certain rumors circulating in connection with that, which he naturally did not believe, but which were slightly worrying Premier Kállay."[4] Actually, Sztójay not only "believed" that most of the Jews deported to the East were massacred in the death camps, but it was he who forwarded to Budapest most of the information related to the Nazi policies concerning the Jews. Sztójay was careful not to mention to Luther that he himself was one of the chief sources of the rumors "slightly worrying" the Hungarian prime minister.

On October 3, 1942, describing Hitler's speech of September 30, he reported to Kállay that, "Chancellor Hitler repeatedly, and with the strongest terms inveighed against the Jews, whose extermination he promised. This constantly recurring, firm, and extremist attitude leaves no doubt that there is much more than empty propaganda behind his words, and in any case there are facts to prove it."[5] It can even be established with relative certainty the date when the "well-informed" in Budapest knew that the Nazis were murdering all the Jews they could put their hands on. György Ottlik, editor-in-chief of *Pester Lloyd*, a German-language daily, which was close to the government, made a prolonged trip in Western Europe between August 18 and September 28, 1942. He visited Sztójay in Berlin, who, according to Ottlik,

> would rather Hungary did not wait until the urgent emergence of the issue [i.e., the Jewish question], but instead speed up the pace of the change of guard and deport a considerable portion of our Jewish population to occupied Russia. Our minister first mentioned 300,000 people, then, haggling with himself, lowered the number to 100,000. Upon my interspersed remark, he made no secret of the fact that this would mean not deportation but execution.[6]

Although this document was published nearly forty years ago, few have noticed what the conversation between the well-informed journalist from Budapest and the Hungarian minister in Berlin, who was even better informed than Ottlik in matters concerning the Holocaust, implied. It implied that in August 1942, at the latest, it was already a matter of common knowledge even in journalist circles in Budapest that if the Hungarian Jews were to be deported, that would mean their deaths.

What "facts" concerning the Jewish Holocaust did the Hungarian political leadership know and when prior to August 1942 did they know them? We shall attempt to answer these questions on the basis of the contemporary diplomatic reports to the Royal Hungarian Ministry of Foreign Affairs, a body of sources known by relatively few so far, and researched mainly by myself. Arranging these reports in chronological order allows us to reconstruct precisely when and what information Hungarian decision makers received in connection with the Holocaust. News from the eastern front of the carnages of the Einsatzgruppen, or of events in neighboring countries were brought or could be brought by intelligence agents, soldiers, gendarme detectives, and even private civilians. Thus far, no publication has treated the reports that came in from the Hungarian military police and other military organs operating in occupied Soviet territories.[7]

As the leader of the Yad Vashem Archives' (YVA) Hungarian Research Team, I have been researching the files of the Royal Hungarian Ministry of Foreign Affairs dating from 1938 to 1945. Our perspective might be that of the director of the Political Department of the Foreign

Ministry, who received all reports, including those marked "top secret," "confidential," "for your eyes only," and so on.[8] The amount of the extant Foreign Ministry files is considerable. In 1942, Hungarian diplomats were serving in thirty European cities, including the Vatican, excluding honorary consulates.[9] The Foreign Ministry was in the Castle of Buda, in the heart of the elegant government district, a few steps from the palace of the prime minister and the Ministry of Defense, and a stone's throw from the ministries of finance and the interior.[10] Hungarian diplomats serving in various European countries were highly trained, multilingual, much-traveled, and experienced men.[11] Every city from Athens to Sofia, from Berlin to Zagreb that played a major role with respect to the history of the Holocaust had Hungarian diplomats serving in them. These were people of different origin and outlook. In the Ministry on Dísz tér the more important departments were headed by men with titles of nobility if not aristocracy.[12]

There were no Jews, or persons of Jewish descent in the central apparatus at all, but the diplomats included quite a number of pro-Nazi anti-Semites, whose typical representative was Döme Sztójay, as well as liberals and philo-Semites. For example, László Velics, minister in Athens, or Péter Matuska, minister in Stockholm, belonged to the latter group.[13] According to what we know today it would seem that the political views of individual diplomats influenced what post they were given. Thus Sztójay was able to keep his post in Berlin from 1935 until March 1944, when he became prime minister of the collaborationist Hungarian cabinet after the German occupation of Hungary. László Velics, having represented Hungary in Geneva with the League of Nations for years, went on to serve in Athens from 1940 to 1944.

As we shall see, the diplomats acquired their information from a great variety of sources. They monitored the local press and radio, and kept in touch with their fellow diplomats and the local authorities. Hungarian diplomats also had access to valuable information at Arad, Temesvár, and in Bucharest through the local Jewish Councils. The ministries of defense and the interior maintained regular, daily working relations with the Foreign Ministry, sending each other copies of reports received concerning foreign affairs. Indeed, copies of such reports found their way to Berlin, Rome, and Bucharest not only to political decision-makers, but also to Jews who might have noted that during 1942 Hitler repeated several times his "prophecy," announced on January 30, 1939, "predicting" that the Jews would be destroyed in the world war. It was on January 2, 1942, in the manifesto he addressed to the German people from the Führer's headquarters that he first mentioned "the great front of national states," which was "engaged in a war with the Judeo-capitalist-bolshevik world conspiracy." However, he reassured his faithful, saying, "The Jew will not exterminate the nations of Europe, but on the contrary, he will fall victim of his own murderous attempt."[14]

The Hungarian diplomats and their superiors knew only too well that for Nazi Germany it was a cardinal question, the touchstone of alliance and friendship, how individual countries solved their own "Jewish questions." Berlin regarded a country as a reliable ally if it was ready to put all its human and natural resources at the disposal of the struggle against Bolshevism, and if, simultaneously, it took steps to radically solve the Jewish question. The German Reich regarded Hungary as one of its least reliable allies in both respects. It was with distrust mixed with incomprehension that Berlin received the news of the dismissal of Premier László Bárdossy, and Sztójay had a hard time convincing the Germans that Miklós Kállay, the new prime minister, would carry on the foreign policy of his predecessor.[15] During 1942 it became clear that the neighboring countries, Croatia, Slovakia, and Romania were following a much more radical line regarding the Jews than Hungary. Under such circumstances, Hungarian diplomacy was obliged to be permanently on the defensive concerning the Jewish question: they yet had to prove their unwavering loyalty as allies, but the Croatians, Slovakians, and Romanians had every right to say that they were Aryanizing Jewish property, deporting, and committing mass-murder, while hardly a hair of a Hungarian Jew's head was being touched in Hungary.

Based on a report dated January 26, 1942, from a "confidential person," that is, an intelligence agent or local undercover informant, the Ministry of the Interior informed the Foreign Ministry that in Bánát, part of the former Yugoslavia then under German occupation, extensive executions took place on January 9, and the Jews were "all carried away, so now there is not a single Jew there. Both the deportation of the Jews and the mass executions reported above were arranged by the Reich German authorities."[16] Lajos Bolla, Hungarian consul-general in Belgrade, mentioned the "dejewification" of Serbia in several reports. On February 3, 1942, he wrote, "the German occupying authorities have interned all the Jews both in Serbia and in Bánát without respect to citizenship.

Some of the women and children have been placed in the pavilions of the Belgrade International Fair, while the men are partly working in labor camps within Serbia, and partly have been transported to an unknown location."[17]

The Nazi Jewish policy in Serbia was completely in keeping with the "self-fulfilling prophecy" that Hitler repeated a second time that year in his January 30 speech: "I already declared in the Reichstag on September 1,[18] 1939—and I am not one given to rash predictions—that this war will not end the way the Jews imagine it will, that is, with them exterminating the Aryan peoples of Europe, but that the outcome of the war will be the destruction of Jewry."[19] At the end of February, Hitler repeated his prediction a third time.[20]

In early March 1942, when officials of the Foreign Ministry learned that the Jews in Slovakia were to be deported to the territory of the Generalgouvernement in occupied Poland, they immediately went into action. They asked the top officials in the Ministry of the Interior to reinforce the border guards because, according to information they had received, Jews were fleeing en masse into Hungary. Minister Lajos Kuhl in Bratislava was among the first to understand what fate awaited the deported. He wrote the following in his report of March 13:

> The Jews, threatened no longer only in their possessions but in their very lives, are doing everything to avoid being deported, which means nearly certain death, and their attention in that respect, for want of other possibilities, has turned unfortunately to Hungary.... I have received reports from several reliable sources in the last few days that the Jews here openly declare that they would rather spend their whole lives in detention centers or internment camps in Hungary than allow themselves to be deported....[21]

The development of the Jewish policy in Romania was always followed with close attention in Hungary. The Hungarian consul in Brassó (Brasov) reported that Romanian authorities, who were anti-Semitic but also hated Hungarians, sometimes warned the Hungarian inhabitants of Southern Transylvania that they would soon share the fate of the Jews. "This, naturally, causes panic among the population."[22] And that threat could frighten only people who had heard something about the fate of the Jews deported to Transnistria.

Around this time Lajos Kuhl learned about the plan for the Slovakian deportation bill, which contained the following comment: "Based on talks with competent German Reich authorities, the Republic of Slovakia will be able to get rid of all its Jews."[23] Before long, Budapest was informed under what circumstances the Jews of Slovakia were being deported. "According to reliable sources and eye-witnesses," Minister Kuhl reported, "the Hlinka Guards, charged with rounding up the Jews, rob the deportees of all their possessions save the clothes they are wearing, and transport them to their destination crowded in closed cattle-cars." Deportation was conducted so savagely that in some parts of the country the gendarmerie had to intervene because the Slovakian peasants turned against the Hlinka Guards, according to the information Kuhl received. At the end of his report he clearly placed the responsibility for the deportations on the Germans, noting, "the government of Slovakia was, upon orders from above, forced to undertake the experimental role of the first, completely Jew-free country."[24] The sad distinction of being the first "completely Jew-free country," however, went to Serbia, not Slovakia. The Hungarian Ministry of the Interior informed the Foreign Ministry, on the basis of information from a "confidential person," that "the situation of the Jews is the most intolerable in Serbia. As of today only two Jewish families are said to be living in Belgrade, the others have been killed or carried off to places unknown. In Bánát, all the remaining Jews, who had survived the bloodshed there, were carried to the interior of the country after the occupation to serve as forced laborers, their whereabouts and fate are unknown."[25]

Döme Sztójay listened to Hitler's every sentence, indeed, every gesture and word emphasis. As an eye-witness, he reported on the speech the Führer made in the Reichstag on April 26, 1942. He emphasized in his four-page, detailed analysis that Hitler dwelt at some length upon "Bolshevism under Jewish control," this "doubly deadly danger." Hitler, said Sztójay, used the word "Jew" twenty-eight times in his speech, "that is, more frequently than in his speeches so far, and also in a more energetic manner in his intonation."[26] Reading Hitler's speech, one can immediately understand what the Hungarian minister in Berlin meant when he wrote about "a more energetic manner" when speaking of the Jews. This time Hitler denounced the Jews in an even more hateful manner than previously.

Sometimes the submissions of private individuals yielded valuable information for the authorities with respect to what the "man in the street" knew about the fate of his deported relatives. Sándor Lieber turned to none other than the "Guardian Angel of Hungarian mothers," the wife of Regent Miklós Horthy, writing to her that his wife and daughter had been deported from Prague to Theresienstadt by the German authorities on April 5, although they were Hungarian citizens with Hungarian passports. He had been informed about this on April 14 and he immediately turned to the Hungarian Foreign Ministry, but to no avail. On July 21, his sickly wife notified him that "they were seriously in danger of being taken to Poland." Lieber was now praying for Her Serene Highness to save his wife and daughter from "death." In the Foreign Ministry, Miklós Kállay himself had given instructions on May 12 to secure the release of Mrs. Lieber and her minor child (Márta Lieber, born in 1927). On July 17, Márió Spányi, the Hungarian consul in Prague, informed the Foreign Ministry in a cipher telegram that, "the German authorities, for reasons of principle, refuse to return persons deported to internment camps."[27]

The only neighboring country with which Hungary managed to develop friendly relations during World War II, with the exception of the great German Reich, of course, was Croatia. As early as in the beginning of May the Foreign Ministry received information from confidential police sources that during the celebrations of the first anniversary of the foundation of the State of Croatia, "the persecution of Jews and Serbs of Greek Orthodox religion [had] relented to some extent, although during the festivities approximately one hundred thousand people were taken into custody. According to confidential information I have received, some one hundred and fifty thousand persons have been killed in the present territory of Croatia, most of them Jews and Serbs of Greek Orthodox religion."[28]

It was well known in Budapest in the spring of 1942 that certain death awaited the Slovakian deportees. In that situation, government officials, headed by Miklós Kállay, formulated two main goals: to save and bring to Hungary at least the property of those Jews who could prove their Hungarian citizenship, and to prevent Slovakian Jews from escaping en masse into Hungary. Premier Kállay, who was also foreign minister, turned to the Ministry of the Interior in the middle of May, saying that according to his information it was easy for the Jews in Slovakia to acquire certificates of Hungarian municipal residence, which in turn enabled them to legitimately apply for Hungarian passports. Kállay wrote, "It strikes one that Hungarian municipalities issue certificates of residence one after the other for Jews who have for years been living in the territory of Czechoslovakia and/or Slovakia, have even acquired citizenship there, and would never dream of returning to Hungary were it not for the risk of deportation." Kállay asked the officials of the Interior Ministry to order the competent sub-prefects to make the issuing of these certificates more difficult.[29] Kállay must have been aware that not only was his instruction to the Ministry of the Interior illegal, but it also risked the lives of the Jews in Slovakia who were otherwise entitled to apply for the recognition of their domicile in Hungary. Incidentally, dozens of examples show that such certificates of municipal residence were issued by the representative bodies of villages and towns after a close examination of land registers, tax records, and on the basis of clear evidence only.

In May, Consul Márió Spányi in Prague first reported that German "official practice had significantly changed with regard to the Jewish question."[30] That is, they had started to ruthlessly deport Jews from the Czech-Moravian Protectorate as well. In another report, which reveals that he basically agreed with the policy applied to the Jews in the Protectorate, Spányi wrote that there "the Jewish question will soon be resolved as a result of continuous large-scale deportations and other, relevant and useful measures...."[31]

Hungarian Ministry of the Interior intelligence agents reported in June 1942, with reference to information from "higher German circles," that "a plan is being prepared to ensure that the troops who have for a prolonged period of time been operating on the eastern front, and who have become accustomed to mass-murdering of Jews and other Russian populations not only on the front but in the rear areas as well, and who have grown coarse with regard to the respect of private property and law, will not be brought home at the end of the war."[32] A copy of the report found its way to Foreign Ministry officials as well. The Führer repeatedly talked with burning hatred about the Bolsheviks led by the Jews, and the soldiers of the SS and the Wehrmacht were committing mass murder—and there is no doubt that this was clear to informed circles in Budapest.

At the time, Bratislava also tried to exploit the fact that the Jewish policy Slovakia was pursuing was much more radical than that of Budapest. According to confidential information forwarded to the chief of the general staff, a closed meeting was held chaired by one of the leaders of the Hlinka Guards. The main point on the agenda was how the matter of the Slovakian Jews escaping to Hungary could be exploited by, for example, allowing Berlin to know that the Hungarian authorities were showing "very great forbearance" toward the refugees.[33]

The flow of information within the Hungarian diplomatic corps was, naturally, accurate. In one of his reports at the end of June 1942, Mihály Jungerth-Arnóthy, Hungarian minister in Sofia, wrote that the Jewish question would eventually be resolved in Bulgaria in the same manner as in Slovakia and Croatia. The main reason he adduced for this came from information that indicated the members of the Bulgarian cabinet thought that since "Bulgaria [was] not actually fighting in the battlefield, she should at least do her best to please the Axis powers in everything else, and act in the spirit of the new Europe."[34] In one part of the "new Europe," in the Protectorate, the responsible Nazis in Prague, as they themselves emphasized for Márió Spányi, did not deport the Jews with Hungarian citizenship living there "as exceptions...due to special consideration," despite the increased pace of the deportation of the Jews (*"Entjudung des Protektorates"*). Spányi made a point of stressing in his report that the German authorities had repeatedly emphasized to him that "the National-Socialist state regarded Jews as the number one enemy (*Staatsfeind Nr. 1*) regardless of their citizenship."[35]

From mid-June, the Slovakian authorities deprived their citizens who had been deported or fled abroad of their citizenship. It was with reference to that measure that they refused to take back the Slovakian Jews rounded up in Hungary and taken to the border to be expelled. The report of Minister Kuhl in Bratislava makes it clear that the Jews fleeing from Slovakia knew perfectly well that they would lose their citizenship, but they accepted this gladly. "Thus they can hope with some justice that no serious harm would come to them in Hungary; they might be locked up in internment camps at most, but they would be able to save their lives."[36]

During 1942, the Foreign Ministry on Dísz tér continuously received reports on Serbia and the Czech-Moravian Protectorate being rendered free of Jews (*Judenfrei*). In mid-August, László Bartók, *chargé d'affaires ad interim* at the Embassy in Zagreb, reported that the last of the Jews, the old, the sick, and women, had been transported from the Croatian capital to Lublin. According to Bartók's information, the "Italians" and the archbishop of Zagreb had protested in vain against the deportations.[37] By that time there were no more souls in the Hungarian Foreign Ministry innocent enough to believe that the Germans would provide careful medical treatment for the sick Croatian Jews, and the aged would be accommodated in a comfortably equipped senior citizens' home in Lublin (Majdanek).

The literature on the subject has yet to convincingly establish what reasons of foreign and domestic policy eventually prevented the deportation of Jews living in the Old Kingdom of Romania in September–October 1942.[38] With regard to this issue it is interesting to note that, according to information received by László Nagy, Hungarian minister in Bucharest, the statistics compiled by what he called "National Jewish Centre" indicated 274,000 Jews living in Romania. Nagy also knew that the August 8 number of *Bukarester Tageblatt* wrote about the planned deportation of the Romanian Jews. He said it was very "interesting" that Romanian-language newspapers had not written a word about it; "indeed, the Romanian government reproached the German paper for committing an indiscretion with its article publishing the still secret plans of the government."[39] Early in September even Tuka's assessment of the situation was that Hungary sooner or later would have to solve the Jewish question the same way as it was done in Slovakia. "First Romania will do that...and then Hungary will follow suit," Minister Kuhl quoted the words of the Slovakian prime minister.[40]

Incidentally, it was not only from Hitler's anti-Jewish outbursts delivered with prophetic furor that Hungarian officials could hear about the fate of European Jewry. With all the background knowledge to which they were privy, they surely understood perfectly well the situation of the Jews as described by the Berlin correspondent of the extremely right-wing daily *Új Magyarság*. "The Jews in Berlin are very pale. Their faces are the pallid color of wax, as if they were wearing death-masks, and when they pass by, I seem to hear their bones rattling."[41] Then, too, Hitler repeated his "Jew-murdering" prophecy for the fourth time within the year in his speech delivered in the Berlin Sports Palace.[42]

At the end of September, Chief of the General Staff Ferenc Szombathelyi learned from "National Jewish Centre" statistics that the Romanians had so far killed exactly 177,591 Jews, and that 30,000 of the remaining 272,409 had been deported to Transnistria.[43]

Probably the most important and most precise piece of information concerning the Holocaust was received by the Hungarian Ministry of the

Interior on October 7, 1942. According to the report of an unnamed professional detective,

> the German border guards issue one litre of warm water and one handful of bran as provisions for one day to Polish Jewish forced military laborers (the detective was present at the distribution). The Jews not assigned to forced labor service are given nothing at all to eat, and they feed themselves with roots and leaves of trees. According to what the Germans say, the Jews will be eliminated in Poland this year. The depositions of captured Jews confirm the above statements.[44]

Ten days later Dietrich von Jagow, German minister in Budapest, submitted to the Foreign Ministry a memorandum written by Martin Luther, in which the German government demanded the branding of Hungarian Jews with the yellow star of David and the preparations for their deportation. In a manner quite unusual in diplomatic practice, Premier Miklós Kállay replied to the German government five days later in public at a conference of the governing party, the Party of Hungarian Life (*Magyar Élet Pártja*). He announced that a special property tax would be levied on Jews, the issue of the flats of the Jews would be settled, the appropriation of the lands of the Jews would continue, and, finally, he promised that Jews liable to military service would be summoned to labor camps. However, he did not even mention that the yellow star would be introduced in Hungary, or that the Jews would be deported from Hungary. On the contrary, Kállay very firmly declared that "the government will stand up against not only the destruction of the Jews, but against those who see the Jewish question as the only problem in this country."[45] After this it could not have come as a surprise to the German government that in the memorandum that Döme Sztójay formally handed over in Berlin on December 2, 1942, mentioned in the introduction to this paper, the Hungarian government refused to fulfill the German demands.[46]

Conclusion

The anti-Semitic Hungarian politicians and leaders such as Regent Miklós Horthy and most of the members of the Kállay cabinet, more moderate in comparison to the Nazi mass-murderers, recoiled in 1942 from deporting the Hungarian Jews to their deaths. They had access to a great amount of fairly reliable data from various sources indicating that the fate of the deportees would be death. They regarded the resettlement of 800,000 Jews as unimaginable and extremely dangerous with respect to the continuity of (military) production. Foreign policy considerations were equally important: in formulating their Jewish policy, Hungarian officials kept their eyes not only on Berlin, but first of all on Rome, as well as on Bucharest and Vichy. As long as Mussolini refused to allow the deportation of Italian Jews, and when in October 1942 the *Conducator*, Marshal Ion Antonescu, stopped the deportation of the Romanian Jews, Hungarian leaders had precedents for their own action, or inaction. As Operation Torch shone increasingly bright in North Africa, and the Red Army exerted increasing pressure on the German forces at Stalingrad, Kállay and his colleagues regarded protecting their own Jews as a significant gesture toward the Western Allies.

Notes

1. Döme Sztójay noted when he delivered the memorandum that personally "he found this task very unpleasant, as he characterized himself as a 'pioneer' of anti-Semitism." Assistant Secretary of State of the German Foreign Ministry Memorandum of August 11, 1942, quoted by Christopher R. Browning, *The Final Solution and the German Foreign Office: A Study of Referat D III. of Abteilung Deutschland 1940–1943* (New York-London: Holmes and Meier Publishers, 1978), 105. Sztójay (1883–1946), a lieutenant general and Hungarian minister in Berlin from 1935 to 1944, became prime minister after the German occupation of Hungary. His government organized the deportation of 437,000 Hungarian Jews. Regent Horthy removed him on August 29. After the war he was indicted, tried by the People's Court, and executed.

2. For the text of the memorandum, see *A Wilhelmstrasse és Magyarország: Német diplomáciai iratok Magyarországról 1933–1944* (Wilhelmsrasse and Hungary: Papers of German diplomacy on Hungary 1933–1944) (Budapest, Kossuth K., 1968), 701–704 (hereafter *Wilhelmstrasse és Magyarország*).

3. Assistant Secretary of State Martin Luther represented the German Foreign Ministry at the Wannsee Conference on January 20, 1942. He had been head of Abteilung Deutschland since May 1940 and his responsibilities included relations with the SS, the police, and Jewish affairs.

4. Luther's notes on his talks with Sztójay, October 6, 1942 (*Wilhelmstrasse és Magyarország*), 697.

5. Hungarian National Archives (Magyar Országos Levéltár, hereafter OL) K63-Political Department of the Foreign Ministry – 1942-21-190/pol. 1942, Döme Sztójay to Miklós Kállay, October 3, 1942.

6. OL-K64-1942-41.-Vegyes-437. György Ottlik to Miklós Kállay, October 10, 1942. Elek Karsai, ed., *Vádirat a nácizmus ellen: Dokumentumok a magyarországi zsidóüldözés történetéhez* (Indictment against Nazism: Documents on the history of the persecution of Jews in Hungary) (Budapest: Magyar Izraeliták Országos Képviselete Kiadása, 1967), 64.

7. This is also the case with Sándor Szakály's *A magyar tábori csendőrség története 1938–1945* (A history of the Hungarian military police, 1938–1945) (Budapest: Ister K., 2000).

8. In 1942, Jenő Ghyczy held this position.

9. In alphabetical order: Amsterdam (consulate – c.), Ankara (embassy – e.), Arad (c.), Athens (e.), Belgrade (consulate general – cg.), Berlin (e.), Bern (e.), Brasov (c.), Brussels (c.), Bucharest (e.), Geneva (cg.), Helsinki (e.), Istambul (cg.), Cologne (cg.), Lisbon (e.), Madrid (e.), Milan (cg.), Munich (cg.), Paris (cg.), Bratislava (e.), Prague (cg.), Rome (e.), Stockholm (e.), Sofia (e.), Trieste (e.), Vatican (e.), Venice (c.), Vichy (e.), Vienna (cg.), Zagreb (e.).

10. Budapest, I. Ker. Vár, Dísz tér 2.

11. Sándor Hoffmann, counsellor at the Embassy in Berlin, met an old acquaintance, the former honorary consul of Norway in Belgrade, a Serbian reserve captain, at the residence of the former Swiss minister in Belgrade, representative in Germany of English and American interests, early in January 1942. OL-K63 –1942-16/7.-6/pol. 1942, Hoffmann to the Foreign Ministry, January 9, 1942. Péter Matuska-Comáromy, Hungarian minister in Stockholm, met Carl Ivan Danielsson, Swedish minister in Cairo, whom he had befriended during his service in Madrid. As he reported, it was possible that his friend would not return to Cairo, and his next post would probably be Budapest. His information proved correct, Danielsson served in Budapest until the end of the war. OL-K63-1942-17- 58/pol.-1942, Péter Matuska to Miklós Kállay, July 4, 1942.

12. For example, Jenö Ghyczy of Gicz, Assakürth, and Abláncz, et al.

13. Matuska was probably glad to report, as an instance typical of the mood of the public in Norway, that he had discovered an advertisement in a newspaper offering the collected works of the anti-Semite and pro-Nazi Knut Hamsun, winner of the Nobel Prize for Literature, for a song. Interested persons could have the books gratis. OL-K63-1942-31- 64/pol. 1942, Matuska to Kállay, July 27, 1942.

14. *Új Magyarság* (New Magyardom), January 3, 1942, 1–2.

15. OL-K83-Papers of Berlin Embassy-1942-48/pol. főn-1942, Döme Sztójay to Miklós Kállay, March 20, 1942. László Bárdossy (1890–1946) served as the Hungarian minister in Bucharest from 1934 to 1941, when in February he was appointed foreign minister. Following the suicide of Premier Pál Teleki (April 3, 1941), he became prime minister. Unable to prevent the extreme right from gaining strength, and finding himself in opposition to Regent Miklós Horthy over other issues of domestic policy, he was removed by Horthy on March 7, 1942. After the war he was tried before the People's Court and executed.

16. OL-K63-1942-21/7.-BM 7163/1942, VII. res. Information report for the Foreign Ministry, January 26, 1942.

17. OL-K63-1942-16-12/pol.-1942, Lajos Bolla to László Bárdossy, February 3, 1942.

18. In the following years Hitler, both in public and in private conversations, dated his "prediction" originally uttered on January 30, 1939, to September 1.

19. In a new Hungarian edition of Hitler's speeches, see Tibor Gede, ed., *Küzdelem a sátánnal* (Struggle with satan) (Budapest: Gede testvérek K., 2001), 429 (hereafter *Küzdelem a sátánnal*).

20. "My prediction that this war will annihilate not the Aryan humanity but the Jew shall be fulfilled. Whatever this struggle may bring, however long it should take, this will be the final outcome, and only then, only after the removal of these parasites will the long period of the mutual understanding of peoples, and with that of real peace come for the suffering world." *Új Magyarság*, February 26, 1942.

21. OL-K63-65-44/pol.-1942, Lajos Kuhl to Miklós Kállay, March 3, 1942.
22. OL-K63-27/7-87/pol.-1942, Zoltán Sztankay, consul at Brasov, to the Hungarian Embassy in Bucharest, March 13, 1942.
23. OL-K63-65-52/pol.-1942, Lajos Kuhl to Miklós Kállay, March 26, 1942.
24. OL-K63-65-59/pol.-1942, Kuhl to Kállay, April 9, 1942.
25. OL-K63-1942-16. BM 10.953/1942. VII. res. Strictly confidential report, April 10, 1942.
26. OL-K63-21-74/pol.-1942, Döme Sztójay to Miklós Kállay, April 30, 1942. For Hitler's speech, see *Küzdelem a sátánnal*, 437–54.
27. OL-K63-2/b-1943.-4508/7.
28. OL-K64-Papers of the Reserved Political Department of the Foreign Ministry. Royal Hungarian Police branch at Csáktornya. 39/1-1942, Report to the Chief of Police, May 1, 1942.
29. OL-K149-Papers of the Reserved Political Department of the Ministry of the Interior-581 res/10-1942, Kállay to Dept. VII (Public Security) of the Ministry of the Interior, May 15, 1942.
30. OL-K70-2/b-148/res.-1942, Márió Spányi to Miklós Kállay, May 20, 1942.
31. OL-K63-7-37/pol. 1942, Spányi to Kállay, May 20, 1942.
32. OL-K63-1942-21-BM-VII. res. Report No. 14.496 to Foreign Ministry, June 8, 1942.
33. OL-K149-BM 13.490-1942. VII. res. Note to Foreign Ministry, a copy of internal report of Ministry of Defense Vkf. 18.757/eln. 2.-1942. (June 14) attached.
34. OL-K63-5-II.-64/pol. 1942, Mihály Jungerth-Arnóthy to Miklós Kállay, June 30, 1942.
35. OL-K70-2/b-1942-198/res.-1942, Márió Spányi to Miklós Kállay, July 4, 1942.
36. OL-K63-65-116/pol.-1942, Lajos Kuhl to Miklós Kállay, July 15, 1942.
37. OL-K63-1942-67-92/pol.-1942, László Bartók to Miklós Kállay, August 14, 1942.
38. On this subject, see Jean Ancel, "The Suspension of the Plan to Deport Romanian Jews to Poland in September-October 1942 and the Transylvanian Issue" (Manuscript, 2004).
39. OL-K63-27-II-1942-291/pol.-1942, László Nagy to Miklós Kállay, September 3, 1942.
40. OL-K63-1942-65-142/pol.-1942, Lajos Kuhl to Miklós Kállay, September 4, 1942.
41. József Kárász, "Berlini nyár 1942" (Summer in Berlin), *Új Magyarság*, September 5, 1942.
42. *Küzdelem a sátán ellen*, 464. Sztójay commented on Hitler's speech in his report of October 3. See note 5.
43. OL-K99-1942-719, Information letter of the Foreign Ministry 6868/1942, to Minister Zoltán Máriássy in Rome, October 2, 1942.
44. OL-K149-20.722/1942, BM-VII. res. Report, October 7, 1942.
45. Miklós Kállay's speech was discussed in detail by the liberal *8 órai újság* (Eight o'clock paper), October 23, 1942.
46. See note 2.

The Holocaust and the Transylvanian Question in the Twentieth Century*

Holly Case

Introduction

This paper focuses on the Transylvanian question—the long-standing struggle between Hungary and Romania for control of Transylvania—and how attempts to resolve it affected the fate of the region's Jewish population during the Second World War. Thus conceptualized, the narrative emphasizes the multi-valent relationship between states engaged in an ongoing border dispute in which the identity and status of state-enfranchised nationalities both within and beyond the boundaries of the state, as well as of other minority groups such as the Jews, were constantly interpreted and reinterpreted under pressure from above and below the state level.

By navigating among three levels of inquiry—addressing the initiatives and responses of states, groups, and individuals to the events and pressures affecting and acting on them—while simultaneously examining a nexus of states around a common issue such as the Transylvanian question, this study aims not only to enrich the overall picture of the region's history, but also to challenge many of the assumptions upon which our understanding of the Holocaust are based. One such assumption is that examining the Holocaust in a "national" context is the best means by which to understand and explain how it came to be carried out in a given state. The result has been a mass of works focusing on the Holocaust in France, the Netherlands, Poland, Hungary, Romania, and so on. Such works are valuable and indeed necessary, specifically as

* This paper was prepared with the help of funding from the Yetta and Jacob Gelman Fellowship on the Holocaust in Romania at the Center for Advanced Holocaust Studies of the United States Holocaust Memorial Museum, support from the J. and O. Winter Fund, and research grants from the National Security Education Project and the American Council of Learned Societies. The author wishes to thank especially László Karsai and the staff and fellows at the United States Holocaust Memorial Museum for their thoughtful critiques and suggestions, and Vladimir Solonari for his invaluable help and kindness during the initial research phase of this project.

they address the issue of national culpability and responsibility vis-à-vis the victims of the Holocaust in these countries. Nevertheless, the emphasis on the Holocaust as it happened in individual states has left a fragmented and often ahistorical view of what took place, ironically failing in its primary mission of bringing states and societies closer to an honest confrontation with their wartime past. There are many reasons why the study of the Holocaust in the national context does not necessarily facilitate widespread engagement with the legacy of the Holocaust in these countries,[1] but the one historians are best equipped to address is the lack of contextualization that accompanies analyses of the Holocaust as "national" phenomena.

Writing histories of the Holocaust one state at a time—whether the state in question is occupied, puppet, or allied with the Axis—makes it possible for the less conscientious national historian to take advantage of the historical confusion precipitated by numerous border shifts to make inaccurate claims about the number and national identity of victims and perpetrators alike. Thus in 1990 we read the work of a Hungarian author who claimed that, "100,000 Romanian Jews were deported to Germany" from Northern Transylvania,[2] when in fact the overwhelming majority of those "Romanian" Jews were native speakers of Hungarian who considered themselves Hungarian, and who lived in a territory that had been re-annexed by Hungary in 1940.[3] Similarly, many Romanian historians, among them several authors of school history textbooks, continue to deny or ignore the fact that Romanian military personnel took part in the killing of over 200,000 Jews in the territories Romania conquered following the opening of the Russian front.[4] Furthermore, much of the historiography and popular sentiment on the Holocaust in Hungary and in Romania emphasize their subordinate position vis-à-vis Nazi Germany, concluding that the Germans were the real and only perpetrators.[5] This manipulation of statistical and factual information—the details of which will be outlined in more depth in a subsequent section—is by no means unique to the two cases examined here.[6]

Diplomatic history, although rightfully sapped of some credibility for its overemphasis on and reification of the power of political elites to mould and affect the lives of millions of seemingly helpless and passive individuals, nevertheless has the merit of shedding light on problems from a multi-national perspective. This perspective is too often lost in the country-oriented studies of the Holocaust, which tend to treat states as more or less self-contained entities whose ties with other countries are limited to subordination to a monolithic yet somehow abstract Nazi Germany, with a similarly nebulous Soviet Bolshevik menace flickering in the background. Meanwhile, the relationships of these states to their diasporas and neighboring states is largely overlooked, a particularly glaring oversight when we consider that not one of the countries of East-Central Europe survived the war without serious boundary shifts reflecting, on the whole, domestic territorial or secessionist aspirations that the Axis merely utilized to its own advantage.[7]

A related problem is the increasing divergence of the fields of Jewish studies and East European history following World War II. In the words of one historian, "Just as Israeli historiography emphasizes the successful Zionist project, neglecting the East European origins of Israeli politics, so Eastern European historiographies concentrate on statehood, often failing to give the Jews their due place."[8] Beyond offering a presentist and hence inaccurate view of both East European and Jewish history, this academic divergence has resulted in a sense that Jewish history and Eastern European history have taken separate paths *since* the Second World War, which is far from the truth. The involvement of Holocaust survivors in postwar Eastern Europe has taken many forms, and has influenced debates on a number of contemporary issues including European Union integration, relationships between states in the region, and relationships between minority and majority national groups within states. Furthermore, the political language of the World-War-II era, particularly of the Holocaust, has set the tone for legitimacy and historical dialogue both within and among the countries of Eastern Europe.

Another misconception fostered by a country-specific study of the Holocaust is that the Holocaust was primarily about state anti-Semitism shared and propagated by nationally enfranchised groups. In reality, the situation was much more complex, as the Jews were often used as proxies in battles with other states and state-enfranchised national groups. Thus in Poland, the Baltic states, and Bessarabia we see the Jews demonized as Soviet sympathizers, in Romania and Slovakia Jews were subject to "double" unwanted minority status as Jews and as Hungarians, in Hungary Transylvanian Jews were accused of collaborating with the interwar Romanian state, and in the Czech lands and Northern Bukovina Jews were even associated with the much-despised Germans.[9]

Furthermore, Jews were not the only victims of mass violence in these ongoing struggles, nor were Nazis the only perpetrators, as recent works on the Holocaust in Eastern Europe have revealed.[10] National Holocaust histories often obscure the murkiness and sprawl of persecution across communities, frequently ignoring the various strategies that lump the Jews together with other groups desirous of victim status in an effort to make use of the emotional and historical weight of the Holocaust to achieve contemporary political aims. Similarly, the oppressors of the Jews are lumped together with the oppressors of groups that would take advantage of Holocaust rhetoric to condemn their national enemies.

Finally, the emphasis on studies of the Holocaust in single states reinforces the perception of Jews as passive victims—devoid of any agency in affecting their own destiny—by ignoring instances in which Jews could and did take advantage of these national battles, civil wars, and boundary disputes to gain legal recognition, achieve personal goals, remain active in the local polity and/or cultural life, in rare cases even to save themselves from deportation, and ultimately to shape the legacy of the Holocaust in these countries.

The following historical analysis of the Holocaust in light of the Transylvanian question offers an alternative approach to the study of the Holocaust that will achieve Mark Mazower's objective of reintroducing "the role of historic contingency both in time—the catalytic impact of wars, civil wars, and other upheavals—and space—geopolitical location, the proximity of disputed borders" to the study of the Holocaust.[11]

Casualties of the War between Allies: 1940–1944

Following twenty-two years of Romanian control over Transylvania, the Transylvanian question took on a new life in late September 1938, when Nazi Germany carved up Czechoslovakia with the blessings of Britain, France, and Italy. As part of the dissection of Czechoslovakia in the Vienna Award of November 2, 1938, Hitler agreed to give part of southern Slovakia back to Hungary. This was the first of a series of border changes that were to take place in Eastern Europe during the course of the war. As a precedent, its significance cannot be underestimated. In orchestrating the annexation of the so-called Sudetenland, the creation of a Slovak puppet state, and a revision of the long-contested Treaty of

Trianon, Hitler demonstrated that Germany was the one force in Europe capable of effecting border shifts.

The Romanian administration at the time, and specifically Prime Minister Armand Călinescu, was concerned at the news of the First Vienna Award, noting the "aggressive attitude of the Hungarian press and the radio stations of Budapest [and] the concentration of masses of troops on the Romanian border." His response was to call up more men from the reserves, "completing therewith the forces necessary for securing the borders." Romania, he said, would defend her borders at all costs.[12]

But in the summer of 1940 the Soviet Union, with the Germans' consent, annexed Bessarabia and Northern Bukovina from Romania, thus showing that Romania's borders, too, were flexible. The most significant event of the war as far as Transylvania was concerned, however, took place shortly thereafter on August 30, 1940. It was then that the so-called Second Vienna Award, giving Northern Transylvania back to Hungary, was signed. This Award, the product of Axis arbitration between Hungary and Romania, was received with unprecedented euphoria in Hungary, while causing Romanian Foreign Minister Mihail Manoilescu to faint at the sight of the map showing the new borders.[13]

On the ground in Transylvania tens of thousands of Romanians demonstrated against the agreement in nearly all the major cities throughout what was left of the country. Meanwhile, many bureaucrats and officials working for the Romanian administration and educational institutions in Northern Transylvania prepared to leave. Most left their houses and property in the care of a legal overseer, hoping the new borders would prove temporary. At the same time, thousands of Hungarian families, as well as several hundred Hungarian-speaking Jews, left Southern Transylvania and moved north to be under Hungarian rule.[14]

Popular dissatisfaction with the Second Vienna Award threw Romania into political chaos. King Carol was forced to abdicate as the pariah who had brought upon Romania this national tragedy of unprecedented proportion. In his place a new leader emerged, General (later Marshal) Ion Antonescu. With members of the Fascist Iron Guard in his government, he took power on September 5, 1940, just seven days after the announcement of the Second Vienna Award.

Approximately 40,000 Jews remained in Southern Transylvania, most of whom were Hungarian-speaking. They suffered further discrimination and economic losses through their association with Magyardom. In 1941, the Jews of Southern Transylvania were categorized as foreign Jews, and as a result the titles to their rural properties were liquidated and they were forced into the cities.[15] The Hungarians of Southern Transylvania and the Romanian minority in Northern Transylvania were spared similar treatment due, on the one hand, to the allied status of Hungary and Romania, and by assurances of reciprocity if one state should harm a protected minority in any way.

Members of both nationalities and state administrations were frustrated by these restraints. In a report from the District Public Prosecutor of Turda (Torda in Hungarian) in March 1943, an official complained that the Romaniazation measures that took businesses and properties out of Jewish hands and turned them over to Romanians should not be limited to Jews, but should be extend also to ethnic Hungarians.[16] From another report on the "internal situation" prepared by the Romanian Ministry of Justice at the end of April 1942, we learn that the Romanian population of Brașov (Brassó in Hungarian) was incensed over the recent attacks by the Hungarians on the Romanian population of Northern Transylvania. Their anger was accompanied, the report said, "by disappointment with the reserved attitude of our government and dissatisfaction that these acts are not being reciprocated."[17] Even the Communist Party of Romania, in its September 1941 platform statement, had as its fourth program point "opposition to the Hitlerite Vienna Award [Diktat] regarding Transylvania, and support for the liberation of the people of Transylvania from Hitler's yoke, and support for their national liberation."[18] Antonescu was similarly eager to punish the Hungarians, but refrained from doing so for political reasons. "In order not to weaken our position in the West, let us close our eyes, be conciliatory, for if we do the same [as the Hungarians do], when it comes to a General Peace, the Hungarians will come and say that we have done the same to others. We must be prudent."[19] Hungary's leadership was equally aware of the danger of initiating a deterioration of relations between the two allies. Hungarian Prime Minister László Bárdossy commented in early September 1941 that, "our relations with Romania cannot be otherwise than those desired by Romania herself."[20]

Unlike the Hungarian and Romanian minorities in the two states, however, the Jews were protected by neither state, and since both states were Axis allies, targeting them was not only acceptable, but often encouraged. It is nonetheless significant that the Jews in both Southern and Northern Transylvania were not always targeted as Jews *per se*, but as members of or collaborators with the opposing national group (i.e., Hungarians or Romanians).

The Jews in Northern Transylvania under Hungarian rule were frequently criticized for their disloyalty to Magyardom during the interwar period. In June 1942, a representative of the Transylvanian Party, Baron Antal Braunecker, said in Parliament that, "the rank of Magyardom was abandoned first by the Jews of all the minorities. They negated any company with Magyardom and set off in the track of the enemy."[21] Another member of the Transylvanian Party, György Páll, voiced the conviction in a speech delivered in Kolozsvár (Cluj in Romanian) in the fall of 1942 that, "the Jews [of Transylvania] were never Hungarian and never will be Hungarian [...] they are not able to be assimilated."[22]

The Jews were even accused of deliberately contributing to the intensification of the struggle between Hungarians and Romanians. In one report distributed to regional police headquarters throughout Romania in 1942, officials claimed that the Jews of both Hungary and Romania had conspired to speak Hungarian in Romania and Romanian in Hungary. "Insofar as the conflicts between Hungarians and Romanians will multiply [as a result], so will the situation of [the Jews] improve, to the point where at a certain moment even the authorities will depend on the eventual aid of the Jews, be it material or moral."[23]

Besides raising tensions around the minority issue in the two states, the Second Vienna Award also affected the level of Hungarian and Romanian participation in the war. Since both countries were aware of the border-shifting power of Nazi Germany, Hitler could pit the two allies against each other in a struggle for greatest favor within the Axis. Romania under Antonescu, having already lost territory to three revisionist states (Hungary, the Soviet Union, and Bulgaria), had nothing to lose and everything to gain by contributing troops and resources to the Axis front against the Soviet Union in late June of 1941. The result was the re-annexation of Bessarabia and Northern Bukovina by Romania in September of that year. Still Romanian leaders made it quite clear to the Germans that territorial gains in the East would not shake their resolve to win back Northern Transylvania. In a 1942 report on southeastern Europe, Berlin economist Karl Janovsky observed that, "no nationally conscious Romanian would ever let go of Transylvania. An 'either-or' is mentioned as the only possible solution for the Transylvanian question."[24]

Antonescu, while vying for the favor of the Führer against Hungary, did not hide the fact that the re-annexation of Northern Transylvania was his ultimate goal. He took every opportunity to lobby for the return of Northern Transylvania during private audiences with Hitler. Paul Schmidt, Hitler's interpreter during the war, remembered one such audience in late November 1940:

> Before he saw Hitler, it was drummed into him that he must not say a word against the [Second Vienna] award. He spoke for two hours about nothing else [...] He made long speeches just like Hitler, usually starting off at the creation of Rumania, and somehow relating everything he said to the hated Hungarians, and the recovery of Transylvania.[25]

It was in part due to his fearlessness vis-à-vis Hitler that Antonescu was quickly becoming a favorite Axis ally.

Romania's favored status did not escape the attention of the Hungarian leadership. Hungary grudgingly agreed to send its forces to the Russian front, after which Janovsky reported that, in Hungary, "one has been forced to take part in the war, as it was high time to make some recompense for the massive, multiple re-annexations the country has enjoyed since 1939."[26] Hungarian Prime Minister Miklós Kállay was even more explicit in his *a posteriori* evaluation of the situation: "If we do not take part in the war against the Soviet Union like Romania, then Hitler will be forced [...] to change his position regarding the Transylvanian question to the Romanians' advantage."[27] Further, the Romanian Secret Intelligence Service reported in early September 1941 on claims made by the Secretary of the Hungarian Legation in Bucharest that, "the sacrifices being made by the Hungarian army in the war against the Bolsheviks will be repaid by Germany at a future peace conference when the territorial aspirations of Hungary will be radically and immediately realized."[28]

But just as Romania's early and enthusiastic involvement on the Eastern Front provoked, in part, more military engagement in the Axis cause by Hungary, it also gave pause to some Romanian officials who feared that, being so heavily invested in the East, Romania could not fend off a potential attack from Hungary in the West.[29] Commenting on a September 5, 1941, report stating that Hungarian Prime Minister

Bárdossy was withholding troops from involvement on the Soviet front, the Romanian Ministry of Internal Affairs concluded that, "Probably the Bárdossy government does not want to mobilize, but rather to keep its forces intact [for] entrance [...] into [Southern] Transylvania."[30] The Secret Intelligence Service also heard that the Hungarians in the region were talking about the "intensive preparations" Hungary was making for "a military action against Romania for the conquest of Southern Transylvania."[31]

The reports and suspicions of the Romanian Intelligence Service were not unfounded. Both the regent and prime ministers of Hungary, like Antonescu, took every opportunity to broach the subject of Transylvania with Hitler, as Hungary was by no means satisfied with the compromise of winning back only part of the region.[32] In a meeting between Hitler and Prime Minister Kállay in June 1942, Kállay supposedly made two "little requests" on behalf of Regent Miklós Horthy, the first of which was "that firstly the Lord God and secondly [Hitler] should turn a benevolent eye if the Hungarians started a fight with the Rumanians."[33]

The urgency of keeping Transylvania, and ideally winning all of it back in the end, was felt not only by the Hungarian and Romanian leadership, but at the time was a sentiment shared by many (probably most) Hungarians and Romanians, even many Jews. In a mid-May 1941 conversation between the Soviet and Bulgarian ambassadors stationed in Budapest, the Bulgarian ambassador, Toshev, concluded that, "Hungarians can be Anglophiles or Anglophobes, Germanophiles or Germanophobes, but they are all Romanophobes to the extent that even the Jewish population forgets about its anti-German feelings when it comes to revisionist aspirations."[34] Although Toshev's statement was certainly not true of all Transylvanian Jews, it is nonetheless the case that many Jewish families living in Southern Transylvania and the Regat (Old Romania) opted for Hungary following the announcement of the Second Vienna Award, and many also submitted claims under the famous 1440/1941 law by means of which Hungarian citizens could ask for property or compensation from Romanians who had exploited them during the interwar period.[35]

One of the most famous compensation cases was that of Jenő Janovics, who had been the director of the Hungarian theater in Kolozsvár during the interwar period. Under Romanian rule the Hungarian theater received no assistance from the state and Janovics sold some of his own real estate to sustain the struggling institution. When Hungarian rule returned, Janovics filed a claim against a Romanian couple who had bought one of his properties at half its appraised value in 1930.[36] He demanded compensation and legal expenses from the couple, who had in the meantime fled to Romania, on the grounds that his sacrifice had been made "because we needed money for the upkeep of the Hungarian theater in Kolozsvár." This claim was submitted just as the anti-Jewish legislation implemented in Hungary, and by extension in the re-annexed territories, forbid Jews to take part in the artistic life of the nation and Janovics and his wife, an actress, were forced to withdraw from involvement in the theater.[37] The Hungarian state thus allowed Jews to make claims against Romanians, because "correcting the injustices of the interwar period" was the primary element in the platform of the Transylvanian Party, but did not allow them to retain their positions in public life.

Further evidence of the paradox that simultaneously empowered and disenfranchised the Hungarian Jews of Northern Transylvania is offered by the Hungarian census of 1941. During the preparation of the census questions, Hungarian Prime Minister Pál Teleki, himself a native of Transylvania, predicted that, "in Hungary, as in Eastern and Central Europe in general, the sense of nationality does not differ from the mother tongue for the bulk of the population."[38] Insofar as Teleki's prediction was correct, the Hungarian-speaking Jews of Northern Transylvania could be counted on to bolster the official number of Hungarians in the region to a figure slightly higher than the number of Romanians. Yet although the 1941 census allowed, even encouraged Jews to declare themselves Hungarians, practically speaking they could not *become* Hungarian even by changing their names to Hungarian-sounding ones. Individuals with Christian backgrounds (Lutheran, Orthodox, Greek Catholic) and German or Romanian names, for example, could officially adopt Hungarian-sounding names, but Jews were denied this opportunity.[39] The field of recruitment for the national franchise thus included Romanians and Germans, but the traditional allies of Magyardom, the Jews, were permitted only part-time membership. Hungarian leaders were self-conscious about this shift, which put them in the unsavory position of lobbying for converts among their national enemies (Romanians and Germans) while alienating their only minority allies, the Jews.[40]

As Jews were being edged out of businesses and proprietary and management positions throughout Northern Transylvania, the justification voiced by the right-wing press, as well as the administration, was that the Transylvanian Jews had aided the Romanian regime in the oppression of Magyardom during the period of Romanian rule. One member of the Transylvanian Party commented in the fall of 1942 that, "under Romanian rule the majority of Transylvanian [...] Jews became extraordinarily rich, as did the Romanians. At the same time the Hungarians were driven to total poverty."[41] Furthermore, in a letter to Hitler, Regent Horthy confided that, "the Transylvanian Jews [...] were all satisfied with the Romanian regime, because they all figured out soon enough how much bribe money was needed, how much will be won in the course of a transaction, and whether it's worth it to make the trip to Bucharest."[42]

This statement was echoed in a daily newspaper article dated May 9, 1942, in the city of Kolozsvár. The article is a commentary on the exodus of Jewish shop owners following enforcement of anti-Jewish legislation that forbade the presence of Jewish merchants on the main square:

> Until now [...] the main square was ruled by the Grüns and the Cohens. The *nouveau riche* of the Romanian world, the occupying Romanian upper classes, were the most frequent visitors to these shops. The upper class women who came here from the Regat bought silk and fine "English" fabrics, fur coats, jewels, snakeskin shoes—the finest and most fashionable of everything. [...] That millions of Hungarian masses starved and went without at that time, while they weighed silk and jewels, was of no interest to them.[43]

From this passage it appears that forcing the Jews off the square was an extension of the same policy that forced the Romanian administration and many individual Romanians out of Northern Transylvania. Lumping targets together in this way, condemning by association, as it were, was a tactic victims could employ as well. Thus the Romanian leadership began linking the suffering of the Jews in Hungary to the suffering of Romanians, especially as the trajectory of the war increasingly favored the Allies.[44]

The treatment of their respective Jewish populations living abroad provided Hungary and Romania yet another area in which to compete. Not only did the two states keep close track of each other's domestic policies vis-à-vis the Jews, but they also compared the way other countries treated Jews from Hungary and Romania. In March 1942, for example, Romanian Jews living in Germany and Austria were required to wear the yellow star, whereas Hungarian Jews were not. This differential treatment incensed Romanian diplomats and officials, who protested to German authorities that Romanian Jews "should be treated as the equals of Jews from Hungary."[45] Again in the spring of 1943, Constantin Karadja, an official in the Romanian Ministry of Foreign Affairs, appealed to Mihai Antonescu, the Deputy Prime Minister of Romania and a distant relative of Ion Antonescu, to "instruct our legation in Berlin to insist that our citizens of the Israelite race be given treatment identical to that of Jews from other countries and, in the first instance, to those of Hungary." Karadja concluded his appeal with a tone of urgency, saying the matter should be addressed "promptly, otherwise it will be too late."[46]

But in the summer of 1942, when Nazi Germany was at the very peak of its power, both Hungary and Romania competed for Hitler's favor. Anti-Semitic policies—including the deportation of the Jews from both countries—were an important part of the competition. There was a very clear understanding within the German leadership that if the deportation of Jews from one country could be undertaken successfully, the other would soon commit to the same action.[47] Already in the late summer and early fall of 1942, the Antonescu government, at the suggestion of German political and military organs, had developed plans to deport Southern Transylvania's Jews. The Jews of this region were to be the first in a wave of deportations that would wipe out all of Romania's Jews.[48] In fact, the Undersecretary of State in the German Foreign Office, Martin Luther, was told in early autumn of 1942 that the evacuation of the Jews from Romania was already underway.[49] It is also noteworthy that, according to a separate Romanian plan for the deportation of the Jews formulated in September of 1942, the economic positions of the deported Jews were to be given to Romanians who had fled Northern Transylvania.[50]

Also in the fall and early winter of 1942, Mihai Antonescu began criticizing Kállay to the German leadership for his unreliability and relative friendliness to the Jews.[51] When it became clear in January 1943 that the Romanian leadership was also stalling on the deportations, Luther sent a note to the German embassy in Bucharest calling on the ambassador to "let the Romanian government know that [...] the positive stance of the Romanian Government with regard to the Jewish question to date has led us to hope that it will continue to act as a good example for our mutual interests."[52]

In the meantime, the German Foreign Ministry continued to pressure the Kállay government into going through with the planned deportation of the Jews from Hungary. On October 20, 1942, Secretary of State in the German Foreign Office, Ernst von Weizsäcker, had the Hungarian ambassador in Berlin, Döme Sztójay, in for a talk. Weizsäcker warned the ambassador that Germany was dissatisfied with the way in which Hungary was handling the Jewish question. He added, "the Romanians are committing everything they have to the present struggle against Bolshevism, while Hungary holds back a part of its forces for a conflict with Romania."[53] Hungary's self-centered politics again came under fire from Edmund Veesenmayer in a secret report composed some months later in April 1943. Veesenmayer, a brigadier-general in the SS, made a direct link between Hungary's Jewish policy and its flirtation with the Allies.

> [The Hungarian leadership] sees in Jewry a guarantee for the protection of "Hungarian interests," and believes it can prove with the help of the Jews that [Hungary] was forced to join this war on the side of the Axis powers, while in practice contributing to the cause of the enemies of the Axis with subtle and indirect acts of sabotage. [...] Kállay himself has recently offered proof of this, saying that, from the perspective of foreign policy, he will consider [...] all measures against the Jews as crimes against Hungary.[54]

There can be little doubt that the "Hungarian interests" Veesenmayer mentioned included territorial concerns.

At about the same time, the German Foreign Ministry sent a memorandum to the Hungarian government containing numerous accusations regarding Hungary's plans to extract itself from the war—and thereby from the Axis—and make contact with the Allies.[55] Among other things, the author of the memorandum gave the details of a contact made between a Hungarian professor and the American ambassador in Turkey. The message to the Allies from Prime Minister Kállay was that "he [Kállay] continually speaks against the Jews, but in fact does nothing, and was protecting 70,000 Jewish refugees in Hungary. He can follow no other political course at present, as Germany will otherwise occupy Hungary and all the Jews would be destroyed."[56]

Kállay's fears of German occupation were well founded. The Germans did indeed occupy Hungary less than a year later. One of their first demands to Horthy was that Kállay be dismissed and replaced by someone more amenable to the Reich's policies and interests. The choice fell on Sztójay. Once this was done, the plans for the deportation of Hungary's Jews were implemented almost immediately. The Jews of Northern Transylvania were among the first to be ghettoized and deported in May and June 1944.

By this time, many Jews in Transylvania and elsewhere knew what German occupation and deportation of the Jews meant. As a result, several hundred fled over the border into Romania to escape deportation. There they told stories of the anti-Jewish measures in Northern Transylvania.[57] In response, the Jews of Romania, encouraged by recent events that showed the Allies were winning the war on all fronts, started putting pressure on the Romanian leadership—specifically Antonescu—to not only protect the Hungarian Jewish refugees fleeing from Northern Transylvania, but to contact Hungary directly regarding the ruthlessness of the anti-Jewish undertakings in Transylvania: "[We] must show the [Romanian] government that it is in the political interest of Romania to give asylum to the Jewish refugees from Hungary just as the Hungarians are taking anti-Semitic measures."[58]

Antonescu proved amenable to these suggestions, but on his own terms. Initially, in response to German pressure, he agreed to have all Jews illegally crossing the border into Romania shot on sight, but the law remained un-enforced.[59] The Jews who crossed into Romania from Hungary were even treated as political refugees,[60] but Antonescu insisted they not stay in Romania. They were given transport to Palestine, many on ships tellingly named after the territories Romania had lost to Hungary and the USSR during its flirtation with the Axis,[61] showing that the Romanian leadership felt the Jewish question and the question of territorial revision were intimately linked.

Many Jews in Romania, particularly those in Southern Transylvania, apparently shared this belief. In a mid-May 1944 Romanian police report on the attitude of the Jews regarding the anti-Jewish measures being taken in Hungary, the reporting official asserted that the Jews of Alba Iulia (Gyulafehérvár in Hungarian) were talking about the ultimate victory of the Anglo-American forces over Germany. They were also purportedly spreading rumors that the measures taken by the Hungarian government would be avenged by the Allies at the conclusion of peace, and that the Jews would not forget the relatively "mild" treatment they had received at the hands of the Romanian state. As a reward, the rumor went, "Jewry from America would support the interests of Romania following an eventual American victory."[62] Another report from the same area prepared in July 1944 asserted that the Jewish intellectuals of the community were discussing the future of Transylvania: "After the end of the war, Hungary will not exist. Romania will get Transylvania up to the Tisza, or perhaps even up to the Danube, in exchange for giving Bessarabia and southern Moldova to Russia."[63] Yet another report from police officials in Aiud (Nagyenyed in Hungarian) related that the Jews there were of the opinion that, "if Germany loses the war, Hungary will be the definitive loser."[64]

Despite predicting an Allied victory, the Jews of Southern Transylvania also feared they may be next after the Hungarian Jews, should Germany decide to occupy Romania as well.[65] As a result, many Southern Transylvanian Jews sought a way out of Romania. According to the General Directorate of the Romanian Police, about 30,000 Hungarian Jews (presumably from both Southern and Northern Transylvania) had applied through the Turkish legation for permission to emigrate from Romania to Palestine by late July 1944.[66]

At the same time, the Romanian Consulate in Kolozsvár prepared a report on the "Situation of the Jews in Hungary." The author of the report commented on the ghettoization and deportation of the Jews. "The measures taken against the Jews were executed by local authorities mercilessly and in the most brutal manner. This brutality, otherwise characteristic of Hungarians, is nothing new for us Romanians; we have had numerous occasions to feel it every day since 1940."[67] Here the author is careful to link the suffering of the Jews to the suffering of the Romanians, an instance of lumping together the two groups as victims of Hungarian oppression. The Consul's valuation of the situation is complementary to the Hungarian administration's grouping of Jews and Romanians together as oppressors or subversive elements. Indeed, just as the Jews of Northern Transylvania were being ghettoized and deported, the Hungarian administration began sending Romanians (men and women) either to the front, or to work in Hungary or Germany. They purportedly justified this move to the Germans by declaring that the Romanians in question "had worked hand in hand with the Jews."[68]

Meanwhile, the rhetoric of victimization by association with the Jews is further evident from a May 1944 report submitted by the Romanian border police stationed outside Kolozsvár. The agent reported that, "among the ethnically Hungarian inhabitants of Kolozsvár, it is said that after they finish sending the Jews to the camps, they will send the Romanians."[69] A report from the Romanian Consulate in Nagyvárad (Oradea in Romanian) from about the same time points out that the Jews from the territories formerly under Romanian state control were treated with particular cruelty, not only during the deportations, but since the Second Vienna Award in August 1940. Of particular interest is the conclusion of the report:

> [It is] incontestable that the attitude of the Hungarian government toward the Jews of Northern Transylvania was dictated not by anti-Semitic considerations, but by well-known political motives, in close connection with the future destiny of Transylvania and of the Romanians from Transylvania.[70]

Another response of the Romanian administration to the deportation of the Jews from Northern Transylvania took the form of accusations regarding the misrepresentation of nationality statistics. Noticing that there were 18,000 Jews in the ghetto in Kolozsvár, Romanian military headquarters pointed out that the Hungarian administration had shown the number of Jews to be considerably lower, making the number of Hungarians by the same measure higher. "It is widely known that in support of their territorial aspirations over Northern Transylvania, the Hungarians have always used false statistical data, showing the majority of Jews to be Hungarians. Current information reveals the truth with regard to the number of Hungarians in Kolozsvár, which is much less than was claimed."[71]

The Romanian leadership in Bucharest and its diplomatic personnel abroad were also acutely aware of the links between the Jewish question and the Transylvanian question. The Romanian ambassador to Switzerland, Vespasian V. Pella, saw in Hungary's intensified persecution of the Jews a window of opportunity for reopening the Transylvanian question. In a message to the Ministry of Foreign Affairs in Bucharest, Pella argued that:

> With the means now at our disposal we should undertake a special action
> to protect the Jews of Northern Transylvania. [...] In this way we could
> attract the sympathy both of the world Jewish organizations and of the
> Anglo-Americans, while in the same stroke consolidating our rights to the
> territories lost with the so-called Second Vienna Award. Of course in
> order to achieve the best results from this action, it [...] should appear to
> be initiated, or at least favored by the Romanian government.[72]

That the laws empowering border officials to shoot Jews crossing illegally into Romania on sight remained un-enforced is indicative of how
greatly the Antonescu regime had changed its Jewish policy. German
leaders were quick to scold Romania for these changes, suspecting—
correctly, as it turned out—that this change in policy foreshadowed
Romania's withdrawal from the Axis alliance.

On August 23, 1944, King Michael of Romania arrested Antonescu
and effected the country's defection to the side of the Allies. But it was
not until November 7, 1944—months after the Jews of Northern
Transylvania had all been deported, and weeks after the Northern Transylvanian city of Kolozsvár had been liberated by combined Red Army
and Romanian troops—that the Romanian government sent a note to the
Hungarian government via Switzerland. The note criticized the Hungarian government for targeting, in cooperation with German forces, the
Jews of Northern Transylvania, the "Romanian" Jews living in Hungary,
and the Romanians in Germany and Hungary.[73] The note threatened to
target, in turn, Hungarians and Germans living in Romania if the oppression of the three above-named groups continued.

In response to the note, the Hungarian Foreign Office denied the
accusations of mistreatment of Jews and Romanians from Romania and
Northern Transylvania, but made a couple of very telling comments. The
first, in connection with the Jews in Northern Transylvania, was an
expression of surprise at the sudden concern for the fate of the Jews, "for
whom only now the Romanian government has shown any interest."[74]
The response concluded with the following paragraph:

> The Royal Hungarian Government cannot escape the impression that all
> of the accusations and threats brought forth from the Romanian side are
> to serve merely as pretexts to publicly justify the previously planned and
> partially already carried out anti-Hungarian measures in Transylvania,
> and to distract the attention of the interested governments and

organizations away from the desperate state of the Transylvanian Hungarians.[75]

In case there was any doubt as to the identity of the "interested governments and organizations," the final clue is a document issued by the American government, also through the Swiss Embassy, in late October 1944 warning the Hungarian government not to mistreat the Jews. The note further explained that such atrocities would not go unpunished.[76]

That the threats issued by the Allies were taken seriously by the Hungarian leadership is evident from a report on the progress of the deportations in Hungary by Veesenmayer from early July 1944. Sztójay was purportedly "left cold" by the accusations and threats of the Anglo-American legations. "He explained to me that he would see the matter as uninteresting if we were to be victorious, but if not his life is over."[77] Sztójay communicated to Veesenmayer that Regent Horthy, in collusion with the Hungarian government, had put a stop to the deportation of the Jews. By that time, all but the Jews of Budapest and those in labor service companies had already been deported from Hungary. Sztójay outlined the reasons why the Hungarian government had decided to put a halt to the deportations. His first two reasons are telling indeed. First, the Hungarian government had discovered that "in Romania no particular measures were being taken against the Jews there." The second related reason was that Slovakia had also begun to protect the Jews remaining there.[78] That the Hungarian government was so closely following the policies of these two countries in particular with regard to the Jewish question is a further indication of the tightly woven links between territorial concerns and treatment of the Jews.

By late summer 1944, though the Allies were winning and the Red Army had advanced into Romania, German-occupied Hungary took one last opportunity to win back Southern Transylvania. The Hungarian army moved into Southern Transylvania in September of that year. Several dozen Romanians and Jews in some of the occupied towns and villages were massacred.[79] When the Romanian army re-entered the area, and later Northern Transylvania with the Red Army in October, these atrocities were reciprocated, this time against the Hungarians.

The confidence of the Romanian Army was high in late October 1944 as the territory of Northern Transylvania came under its control. A general proclamation from the minister of war, Mihai Racoviţă, dated

October 26, reads: "Holy Transylvania, the beloved cradle of the Romanian people, snatched away by an odious *Diktat*, generously offered to
the Hungarian magnates for the completion of their estates by the dicta-
tors of Europe, has returned today, through a just struggle and worthy
sacrifice, to the country from which it was torn."[80]

Although the region was not formally returned to Romania until
August 23, 1947, on the third anniversary of the successful King
Michael coup, in the fall of 1944 another exodus from Northern Transylvania had already begun, this time of Hungarian officials, educators,
and others who did not feel comfortable living under Romanian rule.

Conclusion

This paper has traced the history of Hungary and Romania during
the war through the Transylvanian question. The above narrative shows
that the two states constantly tracked each other's policies with an eye
toward winning the favor of powerful, victorious allies, and thereby
ensuring their respective claims on the region of Transylvania. That
questions of national and ethnic identity, treatment of minorities, and
diplomatic relations with other countries were, in large part, determined
by these goals is no less obvious. The two countries' inconsistent Jewish
policies reveal the multiplicity of roles and functions the Jews of Transylvania played in this territorial struggle. At times enfranchised, at
others persecuted, at times protected, at others subject to the harshest
restrictions, the Transylvanian Jews never enjoyed a stable status either
as national allies or national enemies. This fact belies many valuations of
anti-Semitism in the region, which define it as uniquely tied to a sense of
the threat Jews pose to the nation as Jews. Native, essentialist anti-
Semitism certainly influenced the character of various forms of popular
sentiment and state policies vis-à-vis the Jews, but it would be incorrect
to assume that the persecution of Jews in Hungary and Romania was a
product merely of indigenous, popular anti-Semitism. Treatment of the
Jews in the two states was also determined by another, more immediate
concern to the leaders and inhabitants of these countries; namely, the
question of territorial revision and a resolution of the longstanding
conflict surrounding the future of Transylvania and its state-enfranchised
nationalities, the Hungarians and Romanians.

Hungary's and Romania's varying ties with Germany, their contributions to the Axis war effort, the relationship they had with one

another, as well as the ebb and surge of anti-Jewish legislation were all factors these countries' leaders felt could influence the territorial reshuffling that would inevitably follow close on the heels of the peace. As such they watched each other's moves very closely and acted according to their assessment of who would win the war, and by extension, who would have the power to effect territorial revision in their own favor following the peace.

Notes

1. For instance, studies of the Holocaust are perceived by many as efforts to hijack the historical consciousness of relatively new and struggling sovereign states. One notorious right-wing politician in Hungary, István Csurka, complained in 1991 that, "For 45 years we have had to live as guilty nation, losers, last satellite, humiliated servant-nation." Two years later in Romania, a sympathizer of the infamous Party of Greater Romania, which won an astonishing 27% of the votes in the last Romanian elections, commented on the occasion of the opening of the United States Holocaust Memorial Museum attended by Romanian President Ion Iliescu that "The President of Romania is humiliating himself in a wholly unacceptable manner by participating in the festivities of [...] a museum in which [...] Romania is presented as a highly anti-Semitic country. [...] The act of holding the whole Romanian people culpable [for the events of the Holocaust] is absolutely un-quantifiable." Cited in Vera Ranki, *The Politics of Inclusion and Exclusion: Jews and Nationalism in Hungary* (New York: Holmes & Meier, 1999), 243; István Török, "Holocaust Denial in Romania's Post-Communist Period" (Budapest, Central European University, MA Thesis, 1999), 60–1.

2. Cited in László Karsai, "A Shoah a magyar sajtóban, 1989–1991" (The Shoah in the Hungarian press), in *Zsidóság, identitás, történelem* (Jewry, identity, history), eds. Mária Kovács, et al. (Budapest: T-Twins, 1992), 70.

3. More specific census data on the identity of the Transylvanian Jews will be provided in a subsequent section.

4. See Felicia Waldman, "A zsidókérdés és a holocauszt a román tankönyvekben, 1998–2002" (The Jewish question and the Holocaust in Romanian textbooks), *Regio: Kisebbség, politika, társadalom* (Region: Minority, politics, society), 2 (2003), 150–65.

5. Randolph L. Braham, *The Politics of Genocide: The Holocaust in Hungary* (New York: Columbia University Press, 1994), 1358. In 1990, a member of the Hungarian Parliament, György Gadó, went so far as to declare that "the majority of Hungarian public opinion still allows itself to believe that [the Holocaust] was the crime solely of the German occupiers." Cited in Karsai, "A Shoah a magyar sajtóban," 72.

6. Indeed Deborah Lipstadt comments on a related phenomenon that she calls "the numbers game," a common tactic employed by deniers of the Holocaust. Deborah Lipstadt, *Denying the Holocaust: The Growing Assault on Truth and Memory* (New York: Plume, 1994), 58–60.

7. Such states (or would-be independent states) include Bulgaria, Croatia, Slovenia, Romania, Hungary, Poland, and Slovakia.

8. Timothy Snyder, *The Reconstruction of Nations: Poland, Ukraine, Lithuania, Belarus, 1569–1999* (New Haven: Yale University Press, 2003), 7.

9. Bela Vago, "The Destruction of the Jews of Transylvania," in *Hungarian-Jewish Studies*, ed. Randolph L. Braham (New York: World Federation of Hungarian Jews, 1966), I, 181. Following the war, even Czechoslovak President Edvard Benes "declared that the Jews had been willing tools of the Germans and that, to deserve equal rights, they should have fought for the liberation." Wilma Abeles Iggers, ed., *The Jews of Bohemia and Moravia: A Historical Reader* (Detroit: Wayne State University Press, 1992), 347–48. For Bukovina, see Albert Lichtblau and Michael John, "Jewries in Galicia and Bukovina, and Lemberg and Czernowitz: Two Divergent Examples of Jewish Communities in the Far East of the Austro-Hungarian Monarchy," in *Jewries at the Frontier: Accommodation, Identity, Conflict*, eds. Sander L. Gilman and Milton Shain (Urbana: University of Illinois Press, 1999), 57–60.

10. The most famous example is the controversial book by Jan Gross on the Polish town of Jedwabne, where Poles participated in, arguably orchestrated, the mass killing of Jews in the town. Jan Gross, *Neighbors: The Destruction of the Jewish Community in Jedwabne, Poland* (Princeton, NJ: Princeton University Press, 2001). More recently, Timothy Snyder linked the perpetrators of the "Final Solution" in Volhynia to the perpetrators of the slaughter of Poles from that region. "Withal we observe the lines of continuity: from the Final Solution to partisan cleansings to communist cleansings to the establishment of communist rule." Snyder, *The Reconstruction of Nations,* 8.

11. Mark Mazower, "Violence and the State in the Twentieth Century," *American Historical Review* (October 2002): 1160.

12. *23 August 1944, Documente* (Bucharest: Editura Stiinţifică şi Enciclopedică, 1984), doc. 10, I, 11–12.

13. Paul Schmidt, *Hitler's Interpreter* (New York: The Macmillan Company, 1951), 189.

14. *Martiriul evreilor din România, 1940–1944: Documente şi mărturi* (The martyrdom of the Jews in Romania, 1940–1944, documents and testimonies) (Bucharest: Editura Hasefer, 1991), 256; and Vago, "The Destruction of the Jews of Transylvania," 178.

15. United States Holocaust Memorial Museum Archives (henceforth USHMM), RG-25.017, Selected Records of the Cluj Branch of the Romanian National Archives, 1934–1952, Roll 3, Inspectoratul de Poliţie Cluj, 1916–1948, fond 209, nr. inv. 399, dos. 44/1940–1942, f. 25. Categories 1/a and 3/a were targeted under law Nr. 2650 from 1940. These categories included Jews who came to Romania after December 30, 1918, and the Jews of Transylvania respectively. For specific restrictions and description of categories, see ibid., Roll 4, dos. 54/1940, f. 75–6.

16. Ibid., Roll 7, Parchetul General Cluj, 1919–1952, fond 137, nr. inv. 35, dos. 34/1943, f. 78.

17. Ibid., dos. 31/1942, f. 18.

18. *23 August 1944,* doc. 224, I, 303.

19. *Stenogramele şedintelor consiliului de ministri: Guvernarea Ion Antonescu* (Minutes of the meetings of the Council of Ministers: The Ion Antonescu governance), vol. VI. CM 3 February 1942 (Bucharest: Mica Valahie, 2002), 214.

20. USHMM, RG-25.013M, Preşedinţia Consiliului de Miniştrii–Cabinet Militar, 1940–1944, Roll 14, dos. 402/1941, f. 38.

21. USHMM, RG-25.004M, Romanian Information Service Records, 1936–1966, Roll 73, 40027, Ministry of Internal Affairs, vol. 11, f. 14.

22. György Páll, "A zsidókérdés Magyarországon" (The Jewish question in Hungary), in *Erdélyi kérdések—magyar kérdések* (Transylvanian questions—Hungarian questions) (Kolozsvár: Minerva, 1943), 38–9.

23. USHMM, RG-54.001M, Moldova National Archives, Chisinau, Roll 9, fond 679, nr. inv. 1, dos. 6293, f. 565. See also ibid., Roll 5, fond 696, nr. inv. 1, dos. 84, f. 150.

24. Hoover Institution on War, Revolution and Peace Archives, Stanford, CA, Karl Janovsky, "Lagebericht 1942 über die Verhältnisse in Südost," 10.

25. Schmidt, *Hitler's Interpreter*, 206.

26. Janovsky, "Lagebericht 1942 über die Verhältnisse in Südost," 17.

27. Miklós Kállay, *Magyarország miniszterelnöke voltam, 1942–1944* (I was Hungary's Prime Minister, 1942–1944) (Budapest: Európa História, 1991), 91.

28. USHMM, RG-25.013M, Preşedinţia Consiliului de Miniştrii–Cabinet Militar, 1940–1944, Roll 14, dos. 402/1941, f. 60.

29. USHMM, RG-25.017, Roll 7, Parchetul General Cluj, 1919–1952, fond 137, nr. inv. 35, dos. 31/1942, f. 50.

30. USHMM, RG-25.013M, Roll 14, dos. 402/1941, f. 113. From the beginning of 1943, "In Ungaria se vorbeşte ca odata cu primavara se va pornii compania contra Romaniei" (They're saying in Hungary that come spring the campaign against Romania will begin), USHMM, RG-25.017, Roll 7, Parchetul General Cluj, 1919–1952, fond 137, nr. inv. 35, dos. 34/1943, f. 254. On Hungarian plans to move into Southern Transylvania while the Romanians were disorganized, see ibid., dos. 32/1944, f. 350, 467.

31. USHMM, RG-25.013M, Roll 14, dos. 402/1941, f. 203.

32. The Hungarians' dissatisfaction with the Second Vienna Award solution was clear to Janovsky, as well, who noted that both sides had an all-or-nothing stance as regards the fate of Transylvania. Janovsky, "Lagebericht 1942 über die Verhältnisse in Südost," 10.

33. *Hitler's Table Talk, 1941–1944: His Private Conversations* (London: Phoenix Press, 2000), 516.

34. T. V. Volokitina, T. M. Islamov, and T.A. Pokivailova, eds., *Transilvanskii vopros: Vengero-rumynskii territorialnyi spor i SSSR. 1940–1946 gg. Dokumenty rossiiskikh arkhivov* (The Question of Transylvania: The Hungarian-Romanian Dispute and the USSR, 1940–1946. Documents from the Russian Archives) (Moscow: Rosspen, 2000), 157.

35. *Martiriul evreilor din România*, 255–56. See also Janovics case. 4,333 such claims were submitted by the end of 1941 in Northern Transylvania. ASFJC, Biroul de cenzură Cluj-Turda, nr. 1/1940–1942. f. 311.

36. Ibid., f. 341.

37. Dániel A. Lőwy, *A télglagyártól a tehervonatig: Kolozsvár zsidó lakosságának története* (From the brickyard to the freight train: The history of the Jews of Kolozsvár) (Kolozsvár: Erdélyi Szépmíves Céh, 1999), 176.

38. E. Árpád Varga, *Fejezetek a jelenkori Erdély népesedés történetéből* (Chapters from the contemporary history of population growth in Transylvania) (Budapest: Püski Kiadó, 1998), 38.

39. Arhivele Judeţului Cluj, Primăria mun. Cluj, "Reg. de intrare," Inv. 386/1942, Nr. 19276, 19275, 19635, 24578, 29178, 29534, 33016, 34157. Jews in Hungary were denied the right to change their names to Hungarian-sounding ones starting in 1938. Viktor Karády and István Kozma, *Családnév és nemzet: Névpolitika, névváltoztatási mozgalom és nemzetiségi erőviszonyok Magyarországon a reformkortól a kommunizmusig* (Family name and nation: Name-politics, name-changing movement, and nationality conditions of power in Hungary from the age of reform to that of communism) (Budapest: Osiris Kiadó, 2002), 244.

40. Kállay in particular was concerned that if Hungary got rid of its Jews, there would have to be a higher rate of assimilation of the Germans. *Judenverfolgung in Ungarn, Dokumentensammlung* (Frankfurt am Main: United Restitution Organization, 1959), 121.

41. Páll, "A zsidókérdés Magyarországon," 38–9.

42. Miklós Nagybányai Horthy, *Horthy Miklós titkos iratai* (The secret papers of Miklós Horthy) (Budapest: Kossuth Könyvkiadó, 1972), 221–22.

43. "Kolozsvár főtérréről május elsejétől eltünnek a zsidó kereskedők" (Beginning with May 1, the Jewish merchants will disappear from Kolozsvár's main square), *Magyar Nép* (Hungarian People), (May 9, 1942): 295.

44. See *Martiriul evreilor din România,* 255–56, 259–61.

45. Radu Ioanid, *The Holocaust in Romania: The Destruction of Jews and Gypsies Under the Antonescu Regime, 1940–1944* (Chicago: Ivan R. Dee in association with the United States Holocaust Museum, 2000), 262–63.

46. Ibid., 267.

47. In a December 1942 note from Himmler to Ribbentrop, we read: "Es wäre außerordentlich erfreulich, wenn es uns gelänge, die [Judenfrage] auch in Ungarn aus der Welt zu schaffen, zumal meines Erachtens hierdurch zweifellos auch die Rumänische Regierung zur Aufgabe ihrer zaudernden Haltung, die sie im Hinblick auf den endlichen Beginn der Judenevakuierung an den Tag legt, gezwungen wird." *Judenverfolgung in Ungarn,* 120.

48. Vago, "The Destruction of the Jews of Transylvania," 198–99.

49. *Judenverfolgung in Ungarn,* 93.

50. USHMM, RG-25.013M, Roll 30, dos. 560/1942, f. 12.

51. Bela Vago, "Germany and the Jewish Policy of the Kállay Government," in *Hungarian-Jewish Studies*, ed. Randolph L. Braham (New York: World Federation of Hungarian Jews 1969), II, 193.

52. *Judenverfolgung in Ungarn,* 127

53. Ibid., 106.

54. Ibid., 147.

55. Lajos Kerekes, ed., *Allianz Hitler-Horthy-Mussolini: Dokumente zur ungarischen Aussenpolitik, 1933–1944* (Budapest: Akadémia Kiadó, 1966), 346–50.

56. Ibid., 347–48.

57. Jean Ancel, ed., *Documents Concerning the Fate of Romanian Jewry during the Holocaust* (New York: Beate Klarsfeld Foundation, 1986), VIII, 63.

58. Ibid. By May 18, 1944, Romanian officials reported that around 300 Jews had fled from Hungarian territory. USHMM, RG-25.017, Roll 5, Inspectoratul de Poliție Cluj, 1916–1948, fond 209, nr. inv. 399, dos. 157/1944–1945, f. 19.

59. *Martiriul evreilor din România,* doc. 136, 253.

60. Ibid., doc. 141, 262. See also Randolph L. Braham, ed., *The Destruction of Hungarian Jewry, A Documentary Account* (New York: Pro Arte, 1963), doc. 316, II, 680. The Germans at this time became aware of the fact that the policy vis-à-vis the Jews in Romania became increasingly typified by "increasing tolerance and significant negligence of originally strong measures." Ibid., doc. 318, 684.

61. *Martiriul evreilor din România,* doc. 142, 262–63.

62. USHMM, RG-25.017, Roll 5, Inspectoratul de Poliție Cluj, 1916–1948, fond 209, nr. inv. 399, dos.157/1944–1945, f. 21.

63. Ibid., f. 77.

64. Ibid., Roll 6, dos., 410/1944–1945, f. 57.

65. Ibid., Roll 5, dos.157/1944–1945, f. 36, 79, 92, 105. The Germans of Romania (Saxons, Swabians, representatives of the G.E.G.) indeed hinted that the occupation of

Romania could be imminent, and was, as far as they were concerned, desirable. Ibid., dos.154/1944–1945, f. 172; dos. 157/1944–1945, f. 71-72.

66. Ibid., dos. 157/1944–1945, f. 96.

67. *Martiriul evreilor din România,* doc. 138, 255.

68. USHMM, RG-25.017, Roll 6, dos. 403/1944–1945, f. 172. See also ibid., dos. 605/1943–1944, f. 13–14.

69. Ibid., Roll 5, dos. 605/1943–1944, f. 119.

70. *Martiriul evreilor din România,* doc. 139, 256–60.

71. *Martiriul evreilor din România,* doc. 135, 252.

72. Sergiu Stanciu, et al., eds., *Evreii din România între anii 1940–1944* (The Jews of Romania during the years 1940–1944), vol. IV, *1943–1944: Bilanțul tragediei–renașterea speranței* (The balance sheet of the tragedy – the rebirth of hope) (Bucharest: Editura Hasefer, 1998), xx.

73. Braham, *The Destruction of Hungarian Jewry,* doc. 354, II, 750–51.

74. Ibid., doc. 355, 752–53.

75. Ibid., 754.

76. Ibid., doc. 406, II, 828.

77. Toviah Friedmann, ed., *Vor 50 Jahren 1944–1994, Das SS-Sonderkommando Eichmann in Budapest und die Vernichtung der Juden Ungarns-Rumäniens* (Haifa: Institute of Documentation in Israel for the Investigation of Nazi War Crimes, 1994), doc. 677, 3–4. The document was written before July 10, 1944.

78. Ibid., 1–2.

79. Vago, "The Destruction of the Jews of Transylvania," 200–201.

80. *23 August 1944,* doc. 900, II, 833.

Wartime

A Gendered Holocaust?[1]
The Experiences of "Jewish"[2]
Men and Women in Hungary, 1944

Tim Cole

Just before stepping into the elevator that begins the Permanent Exhibition, visitors to the United States Holocaust Memorial Museum are invited to collect an identity card from two boxes labeled "male" and "female." The victim featured on the card accompanies the visitor on their tour of *The Holocaust*, and with each turn of the page further information on their fate is revealed. In the original design for the Permanent Exhibition, the plan was to assign an identity card of both a similar age and gender to the visitor.[3] However, today's visitors choose only on the basis of gender, tending to take an identity card of the same sex as themselves.[4] It would seem that not only the museum's designers, but also we the visitors, assume gender to be a—if not the—significant category for those who visit the museum. But what difference did gender make during the historical event that we know as the Holocaust, and in the case of the Hungarian Holocaust in particular?

Over the last couple of decades, a growing number of writers have stressed the significance of gender in understanding the experiences of Holocaust victims. Beginning with the seminal conference on "Women Surviving the Holocaust" organized in 1983 by Joan Ringelheim and Esther Katz,[5] the suggestion that "Jewish" men and "Jewish" women experienced the Holocaust differently has, by and large, been accepted within the academy, if not always outside of it.[6] In an essay published at the end of the 1990s, Ringelheim, whose scholarship on the subject spanned the 1980s and 1990s, summarized what can perhaps be seen as an emerging consensus on the question of the gendering of the Holocaust:

> For Jewish women the Holocaust produced a set of experiences, responses, and memories that do not always parallel those of Jewish men…. If in the gas chambers or before the firing squads all Jews seemed alike to the Nazis, the path to this end was not always the same for women and men. The end—namely, annihilation or death—does not describe or explain the process.[7]

Whilst emerging as a consensus of sorts, this position has been critiqued in more penetrating ways than simply reactionary outbursts. In a fascinating essay, which argues for the need for sensitivity to the gendered narratives of the Holocaust, Pascale Rachel Bos suggests that the ways in which Nazi policy towards the "Jews" was gendered was in reality much more limited than many who have written on gender and the Holocaust have argued. Shifting focus to the gendered nature of memory, Bos argues that what were shared experiences can be remembered and recounted differently by "Jewish" men and women. For Bos, only three major elements of an essentially shared Holocaust process were gendered at the point of implementation:

> First, the Nazis selected mostly men for the (relatively privileged) positions of Jewish leadership. Second, because Jewish men were more often selected to work than women, women were more often killed immediately. Finally as is to be expected, women were especially vulnerable with respect to their sexuality and reproductive function. Yet women's sexuality could work both to their advantage and disadvantage. Women were at risk of being assaulted...but sometimes women were in a position to barter sex for food rations, an option that could prove life saving.[8]

The second gendered difference highlighted by Bos—labor—is one of particular significance in the case of Hungary. However the relationship between "Jewish" men and labor was not as simple as Bos suggests. The labor potential of "Jewish" men in Holocaust Europe in general—and in Holocaust Hungary in particular—could "work both to their advantage and disadvantage."

There is evidence that labor offered "Jewish" men a degree of privilege. As Joan Ringelheim argued, the fact that the Nazis saw "Jewish" women "as persons less valuable than men because of the curious and damaging sexual division of labor,"[9] had an impact on Jewish Council attempts at adopting a policy of "rescue through work,"[10] and offered limited possibilities for "Jewish" men to escape immediate death through labor. Looking at the sheer statistics of Schindler's list, with its 1000 "Jewish" men and 200 "Jewish" women makes it "easy to see why women had less of a chance to survive than men."[11] The end result was, Ringelheim suggested, that "Women and children often suffered a killing rate faster than that of men because the Nazis had even less use for

Jewish women than for Jewish men. All in all, genocide was not neutral about gender. Gender was a coordinate in the process of destroying the Jewish populations."[12]

However, the same patriarchal assumptions that saw "Jewish" men as a potential means of labor, could—and did—also see "Jewish" men as a potential threat. As a result, Nazi thinking was ambivalent about "Jewish" men. As Nechama Tec has suggested, given the dominant assumptions of patriarchy, "Jewish men were viewed as a potentially greater threat to the Nazi political system than Jewish women. Inspired by this kind of reasoning, the Nazis set out to eliminate Jewish men first."[13] Tec implicitly suggests a need to think chronologically about the gendered implementation of the Holocaust. At least initially, "Jewish" men can be seen as subjected to harsher measures. Chronologically, the first victims of the Holocaust tended to be overwhelmingly male. Whilst "in the final tally, women were most probably more than half of the dead," Raul Hilberg suggests that "men died more rapidly."[14]

> The phenomenon of men dying first WAS not confined to the ghettos. The shootings in the occupied USSR began with the killing of men. The same procedure was followed in Serbia.... Men in the Hungarian labor service companies were among the first casualties from Hungary. "Labor" in the east was the German explanation for deportations from France, and the first six transports from that country consisted almost wholly of men.[15]

As Hilberg suggests, the labor potential of "Jewish" males—at least in these initial years—was far from advantageous. However, once mass deportations to death camps commenced, then labor could—and did— mean something different. Hilberg argues that

> the comparative advantage afforded to women was limited to the labor recruitment and expansion drives of 1940, 1941, and 1942. With the onset of deportation there was a reversal of fortunes. Labor became numerically the most important reason for deferment or exemption during roundups. More women than men could now be considered "surplus."[16]

With this shift, labor did offer to "Jewish" men a means of reprieve from immediate gassing. The result was, Hilberg suggests, that in the death camps "fewer women than men were spared from immediate gassing."[17]

"Jewish" Men, the Holocaust, and Labor:
The Impact of Gendered Policy in Veszprém, Hungary

This shifting chronology of gendered labor as a potential danger in the early 1940s, and a potential means of reprieve once mass deportations commenced, is particularly marked in the case of Hungary. With the entry of Hungary into the war on the side of the Axis powers on June 27, 1941, plans for separate "Jewish" labor battalions were put into action. "Jewish" men aged 20–42 years were called up to serve for a period of two years in auxiliary labor service units, which were deployed to the Eastern Front alongside the Hungarian army divisions fighting there. Randolph Braham notes that here they suffered especially harsh conditions and higher casualty rates than the "non-Jewish" male military divisions.[18] Indeed Braham suggests that prior to the German occupation of Hungary in March 1944, some 42,000 labor servicemen died.[19]

Placing "Jewish" males of military age in labor battalions meant that an entire generation of "Jewish" men was removed from the "Jewish" community in Hungary. The demographic impact of this plan can be seen in the surviving lists of "Jewish" communities submitted to the authorities in the spring of 1944. In Veszprém, in western Hungary, the list of the "Jewish" community drawn up in early May 1944 revealed a significant drop in the "Jewish" population of the town from the census statistics gathered three years earlier.[20] At the time of the 1941 census—prior to mass mobilization—887 "Jews" of Jewish faith and ninety-nine "Jews" not of Jewish faith were living in Veszprém.[21] After the German occupation, the registration recorded 608 "Jewish Jews," forty-three "Christian Jews," and twenty-three "Christian Jews" in mixed marriages. Of the 674 "Jews" of varying classification in Veszprém in spring 1944, 401 were female (59.5%) and 273 were male (40.5%).[22] Breaking down the male and female populations into age groups reveals that this marked predominance of females was due in large part to the call-up of "Jewish" males into labor battalions during the preceding three years. Missing from the town is a significant element of the labor battalion generation—men aged 18–42.

Table 1. "Jews" Registered in Veszprém, May 2, 1944

Age Group	Female	Male		
0-9	30	19		
10-17	41	43		
18-29	38	17		
30-42	81	30		
43-49	56	43		
50-59	67	50		
60-69	42	40		
70-79	30	17		
80+	11	9		
	396	268		
	+5 (no d.o.b.)	+ 5 (no d.o.b.)		
Total	401	273	=	674 "Jews"

The lists reveal a small number of "Jewish" men explicitly noted as not currently residing in Veszprém because of being posted elsewhere on labor service.[23] However, what the lists show more by dint of implicit absence rather than explicit presence are the numbers of "Jewish" men of military-service age absent from the town. And it is clear that a number of those missing from the May 1944 list were already dead. On November 21, 1942, a twenty-seven-year-old "Jewish" labor battalion member from Veszprém, Dr. Sziklai Imre, was buried at Jablocsnoje, leaving a wife and seven-year-old son in the city.[24] In January 1943, at the time of the Battle of the Don, a host of labor battalion members from Veszprém were reported missing.[25] During these years—1942 and 1943—when all Hungarian "Jews" were subjected to a number of anti-Jewish laws, which amounted in particular to an economic onslaught,[26] it was only "Jewish" men in their 20s, 30s, and early 40s who were dying. In short, the first victims of the Hungarian Holocaust were adult males. [27] All of this changed in 1944.

Following the occupation of Hungary by Nazi Germany on March 19, 1944, the newly formed Sztójay government introduced a raft of anti-Semitic measures. At the beginning of April 1944, Hungarian "Jews" were compelled to wear a yellow star on their outer clothing when in public places. At the end of April, the process of crowding the country's "Jews" into ghettos began: a process that was completed nationwide by the end of June. On May 15, mass deportations of Hungarian "Jews" from these newly established ghettos to Auschwitz-Birkenau commenced. Throughout the early summer of 1944, "Jews" from all ghettos apart from Budapest were transported out of the country.

In the context of the implementation of ghettoization and mass deportations, service in labor battalions offered a degree of gendered advantage for Hungarian "Jewish" men of military age. In the ghettoization decree issued at the end of April 1944, Jewish labor battalion members on active service were explicitly exempted from being placed into ghettos.[28] However it was not only men already serving who were exempt from ghettoization. Rather, as ghettoization was being implemented, new conscription of "Jewish" men took place, to the exasperation of Gendarmerie Lieutenant Colonel László Ferenczy who was in charge of the concentration and deportation of the "Jews." Ferenczy informed László Endre—one of the two undersecretaries of state in the Interior Ministry who oversaw anti-"Jewish" measures—in his May 10 report that draft papers were being delivered to the newly established transit camps. His comments pointed to a degree of contestation over "Jewish" male lives (seen as a more valuable commodity than "Jewish" women) between the Hungarian Army and the German Security Police.[29] He reported an order of mass conscription by the former, whilst the latter claimed Ministry-of-Defense agreement that "Jews" could not be called up for labor service in areas where they were being rounded up and placed into transit camps and ghettos. In view of what he termed "two contradictory directives," Ferenczy informed the Interior Ministry of his decision to halt "the delivery of draft notices to the camps until instructions are received from higher authorities."[30] In his May 29 report, Ferenczy complained about the freedom of movement being enjoyed by labor battalion members, and pointed to the continuing delivery of call up notices to "Jews" in transit camps and ghettos.[31] A few weeks later, on June 12, he reported "new attempts to call Jews up for labor service."[32]

The conscription of "Jewish" men aged 18–48 during the early summer of 1944 meant that men were not only being removed from ghettos and transit camps, but were also therefore being spared from the mass deportations to Auschwitz-Birkenau. As Randolph Braham has reflected, "it is one of the ironies of history that the Ministry of Defense, which had been viewed as one of the chief causes of suffering among

[male] Jews during the previous four to five years, suddenly emerged as the major governmental institution actively involved in the saving of Jewish lives."[33] The motives behind the conscription campaign of early summer of 1944 are, Braham suggests, "not absolutely clear" but certainly mixed.[34] He suggests that, "it is safe to assume that many local commanders, aware of the realities of the ghettoization and deportation program and motivated by humanitarian instincts, did everything in their power to rescue as many Jews as possible," but also that "Hungarians were also probably motivated to save able-bodied Jews because of the manpower shortage from which the country was suffering at the time."[35] At this stage in the war, the Hungarian administration arguably saw "Jewish" male lives as a more valuable commodity than "Jewish" female lives, given assumptions about their greater potential for performing labor. It was not "Jewish" women, children, or the elderly who were being fought over in early summer 1944, it was "Jewish" men aged 18–48. Only in the fall of 1944, when the Arrow Cross (*Nyilas*) government was increasingly desperate for labor, were "Jewish" women living in Budapest called up en masse.[36]

The impact of the waves of conscription of "Jewish" men in May and June 1944 can be seen in the city of Veszprém in western Hungary, where deportations were not scheduled until early July 1944. On May 20, thirty-seven Veszprém "Jewish" men ranging in age from 18 to 49 were drafted.[37] On June 4, eleven "Jewish" men from Veszprém county, ranging in age from 25 to 46 were drafted.[38] On June 12, a further seventeen "Jewish" men from Veszprém ranging in age from 23 to 48 were drafted.[39] By mid June 1944, the city ghetto in Veszprém had already been established. It is clear that men were called up in Veszprém not only before the community was concentrated in the ghetto, but were also called up once they were in the ghetto itself. Aware that this situation would occur, the vice president of the Jewish Council in Veszprém wrote to the deputy mayor on May 23, 1944, requesting that those 21–48 year old men awaiting their call-up for labor service be permitted to take a backpack of additional clothing and equipment into the ghetto with them.[40]

The impact of these—and other—drafts upon the gender balance of the two ghetto populations in Veszprém was marked.[41] Of the total population of 627 in the main city ghetto in mid June 1944, 434 (69.2%) were female and 193 (30.8%) male.[42] With the renewed mobilization of

"Jewish" men for labor service, this clear female majority within the
ghetto more generally was most visible within the adult population.
Whilst there were 187 women aged 18–49 living in the ghetto, there
were only thirteen men of the same age.

Table 2. "Jews" in the Horthy Miklós u. Ghetto, Veszprém, June 1944

Age Group	Female	Male		
0-9	35	26		
10-17	45	43		
18-29	41	2		
30-42	88	6		
43-49	58	5		
50-59	70	41		
60-69	50	41		
70-79	35	20		
80+	11	9		
	+1 (no d.o.b.)			
Total	434	193	=	627 "Jews"

A similar picture emerges when the other ghetto in Veszprém is
examined—the Komakuti ghetto—which housed "Jews" gathered from
surrounding villages. Of the 447 Jews concentrated in this second ghetto,
316 (70.7%) were female and 131 (29.3%) were male. As with the
ghetto housing the city's "Jews," the clear female majority was most
visible within the adult population. There were 129 women aged 18–49
living in the Komakuti ghetto, but only eight men of the same age.

Table 3. "Jews" in the Komakuti Ghetto, Veszprém, June 1944

Age Group	Female	Male		
0-9	21	26		
10-17	17	20		
18-29	35	1		
30-42	55	1		
43-49	39	6		
50-59	62	29		
60-69	36	28		
70-79	37	15		
80+	14	5		
Total	316	131	=	447 "Jews"

The fact that the inmates of the Hungarian ghettos were predominantly female corresponds to the situation throughout central and eastern Europe, where women comprised a majority of ghetto populations.[43] However, the predominance of "Jewish" women—and specifically "Jewish" women aged 18–49—in Hungary is particularly marked given the history of the mass mobilization of "Jewish" men for labor service. To give only one example, in the Warsaw ghetto—where women made up 57.3 percent of the ghetto population in January 1942—women outnumbered men most markedly in the 20–29 year old age group (where they accounted for 65%) and the 30–39 year old age group (where they accounted for 58.5%).[44] Such figures are dwarfed by those from the two ghettos in Veszprém. In the Horthy Miklós u. ghetto—where women made up 69.2 percent of the ghetto population in June 1944—women accounted for 97.4 percent of 20–29 year olds and 90.8 percent of 30–39 year olds. In the Komakuti ghetto—where women made up 70.7 percent of the ghetto population in June 1944—women accounted for 96.7 percent of 20–29 year olds and 97.4 percent of 30–39 year olds.

As such figures suggest, there is a need to consider the intersections of gender and age when examining just who was placed in the ghettos in this Hungarian city in the early summer of 1944. The absence of men serving in labor battalions did not simply mean the absence of men, but the absence of men *of working age*. There was not simply a striking gender imbalance in the ghetto populations, but also an age imbalance. The result was that the two ghettos in Veszprém were effectively populated by women, children, and the elderly.

Both ghettos proved to be short-lived. After less than a month, the women, children, and elderly from Veszprém's two ghettos were taken to Pápa and on to Auschwitz-Birkenau.[45] From what we know of the selections at Auschwitz-Birkenau, there can be little doubt that, given the demographic breakdown of the "Jews" deported from Veszprém, a very high proportion of those deported would have been selected for immediate gassing and cremation. The three groups most vulnerable to immediate gassing at Auschwitz—pre-adolescent children, the elderly, and mothers accompanying children under the age of fourteen[46]—dominated the 1074 "Jews" transported from the two ghettos in Veszprém.[47]

Table 4. "Jews" in the Two Veszprém Ghettos, June 1944

Age Group	Total number of "Jews" in Horthy Miklós u. ghetto	Total number of "Jews" in Komakuti ghetto
0-9	61	47
10-19	91	43
20-29	40	30
30-39	66	38
40-49	91	63
50-59	111	91
60-69	91	64
70-79	55	52
80+	20	19
	+ 1 (no d.o.b.)	
	627	447 = 1074 "Jews"

Conclusions: Three Families' Stories

Clearly, the experiences of Veszprém's Jews were not shaped by gender alone. For children and the elderly in Veszprém, gender differences were of much lesser significance than for those aged roughly 18–49. But, for "Jews" from Veszprém aged 18–49, gender was of primary importance after ethnicity ("Jewishness") in determining what happened before and during the fateful early summer of 1944. Prior to 1944, "Jewish" men aged 18–42 from Veszprém were targeted with mobilization in labor battalions. By the time ghettoization was implemented in June 1944, a number of these men were already dead, killed in particular when the Hungarian Army was devastated at Voronezh during the disastrous Battle of the Don in January 1943. However, with the implementation of ghettoization in June 1944 and the subsequent deportations to Auschwitz-Birkenau at the start of July 1944, conscription—and in particular the waves of conscription in the summer of 1944—provided "Jewish" men aged 18–49 with a reprieve from deportation to Auschwitz-Birkenau at least, even though they still faced labor service during the final year of the war.[48] Three families' stories—families that lived a short walk from each other in Veszprém—reveal something of the impact of the intersections of age and gender in shaping differing experiences of the Hungarian Holocaust.[49]

Shopkeeper Simon Füzes, aged seventy-three in 1944, lived on Szent Imre út with his sixty-year-old wife Róza. They had already felt the impact of the mobilization of "Jewish" men for labor service well before the registration and ghettoization of Veszprém's "Jews" in the summer of 1944. Just under a year and a half earlier, their son György, aged forty-three, was reported missing at Kamenka.[50] In June, Simon and his wife moved into the ghetto. However their younger son, László—a factory worker aged thirty-five in 1944—did not remain with them in the ghetto for long. On June 12, he was among the seventeen local men mobilized for labor service.

Also mobilized for labor service in the early summer of 1944 was nineteen-year-old carpenter László Krebsz. He lived with his forty-five-year-old mother Irén, his seventeen-year-old brother Zoltán—a glazier—and his sixteen-year-old sister Irma—a seamstress—on Cserhát u. László was one of the thirty-seven men mobilized for labor service on May 20, 1944, thus he did not join his mother and younger brother and sister when they were taken into the nearby ghetto a week or so later. Whilst László was old enough to be called up for labor service, his brother Zoltán was just a year too young.

Living on the next street—Völgyikút u.—was the day laborer Dénes Salzberger, aged forty-five in 1944, his wife Ilona aged thirty-eight, and their children György (eighteen)—an apprentice—Éva (sixteen), and László (eight)—both students. Like László Krebsz, Dénes Salzberger and his oldest son György were drafted in May 1944.[51] Just over a week later, his wife Ilona was forced to move, along with her daughter Éva and youngest son László, into the ghetto created in the nearby synagogue and "Jewish" community buildings. Joining them was Ilona's seventy-three-year-old mother, Adolfné Neu.

A month later, the ghetto was liquidated and the entire population transferred to the transit camp in Pápa, and then on to Auschwitz-Birkenau. There, teenagers Irma Krebsz and Éva Salzberger were chosen for labor and sent to the concentration camp at Stutthof.[52] However for the rest of Éva Salzberger's family—a seventy-three-year-old woman, and a thirty-eight-year-old mother accompanying an eight-year-old son—Auschwitz-Birkenau was a lethal place.

These are, of course, only three families' stories.[53] However, the stories reflect the differing experiences of male and female, and young and old "Jews" from Veszprém prior to and during the months of May,

June, and July 1944. The experience of "Jews" from that city suggests that the implementation—and not simply the experience—of the Holocaust in this particular city can clearly be seen as gendered, and that this situation influenced not only the process, but also the end.[54] What happened in Veszprém in 1944 cannot be taken as representative of the entire Hungarian experience, let alone the Holocaust more generally, because the specifics of time and space are crucial.[55] However, it would seem that the experience in Veszprém suggests what was happening in the early summer of 1944 in at least some areas of Hungary.

In the regional archives, a letter addressed to the chief administrative officer of Körmend from the Szombathely army headquarters survives and calls for the Jewish Council to gather "Jewish" men—both converts and of Jewish faith—born between 1896 and 1926 (aged 18–48) in the ghetto early on the morning of June 12 for recruitment.[56] The instructions contained in this letter of June 8 were implemented by the chief administrative officer the next day. He wrote to the Körmend Jewish Council instructing them to oversee the compulsory gathering of all "Jewish" men of the relevant ages, and arranged for municipal clerks, doctors, and gendarmes to be present for the call-up.[57] Although this is the only such letter that appears to have survived, clearly it was not the only form-letter sent from Szombathely army headquarters implementing a Defense Ministry decision.[58] And it is also clear that this Defense Ministry decision was advertised much more broadly than in the Szombathely district. Certainly, in the southern Hungarian city of Szeged, the local press reported the national decision that "those men considered Jewish, born between 1896 and 1926" were "obliged to enlist for (noncombatant) military service on June 4 and 5," and called for Szeged "Jewish" men to comply with this requirement.[59] This call-up in early June was one that Szabolcs Szita suggests took place not only in the gendarmerie district—Szombathely—which included Veszprém and Körmend, but also in the Budapest, Székesfehérvár, and Miskolc gendarmerie districts.[60]

The case study of Veszprém is thus not entirely exceptional. Indeed, the age and gender profile of the "Jews" in the Körmend ghetto[61] is almost identical to that of the "Jews" in Veszprém. Such evidence surely points to the need for gender to be much more central to the research agenda regarding the implementation and impact of the Holocaust in Hungary. At the very least, we would do well to end sterile debates over whether gender is an appropriate or inappropriate category with which social historians of the Holocaust should work. Atina Grossman, in a review essay on recently published works on gender and the Holocaust, noted the irony that,

> despite the vast archival, memoir, and testimonial evidence they have accumulated, scholars who insist upon gender's relevance in the Holocaust still operate on the defensive. They feel compelled to note the obvious: that to explore difference does not imply hierarchizing or trivializing suffering; on the contrary, the aim is to hear the voices of the victims and survivors in such a way as to deepen our understanding of events that defy comprehension.[62]

Her conclusion, "If the Holocaust is available for scholarly analysis, rather than occupying a sacred dark void in which awed silence must reign, then gender analysis of the Holocaust is as legitimate as it is for any other historical inquiry,"[63] is perhaps particularly relevant—given the somewhat exceptional nature of the Hungarian experience—for those of us who research the Holocaust in Hungary. Not only is there room for gender to assume much more importance within the historiography of the Hungarian Holocaust, but also for the Hungarian experience to be much more central to the broader literature on gender and the Holocaust.

Notes

1. The author thanks the Center for Advanced Holocaust Studies at the United States Holocaust Memorial Museum and the Resnick family for their generous support through the granting of the Pearl Resnick Post-doctoral Fellowship in 1999–2000 and the Leverhulme Trust for their generosity in granting a research fellowship in 2003–2004.

2. On my use of quotations to stress the constructed nature of the category "Jew" in wartime Hungary, see my more general theoretical comments in Tim Cole, "Constructing the 'Jew,' Writing the Holocaust: Hungary 1920–45," *Patterns of Prejudice* 33:3 (1999): 19–27; and Tim Cole, *Holocaust City: The Making of a Jewish Ghetto* (New York: Routledge, 2003), 44–8. The use of quotations when referring to the "Jews" in Veszprém seems necessary given that the May registration makes a clear distinction between "Jewish Jews," "Christian Jews," and "Christian Jews in mixed marriages."

3. Edward T. Linenthal, *Preserving Memory: The Struggle to Create America's Holocaust Museum* (Harmondsworth: Penguin, 1997), 187.

4. Anna Reading, *The Social Inheritance of the Holocaust: Gender, Culture and Memory* (Houndmills: Palgrave, 2002), 115–16.

5. Esther Katz and Joan Ringelheim, eds., *Proceedings of the Conference on Women Surviving the Holocaust* (New York: Institute for Research in History, 1983).

6. See in particular the critical comments leveled against gender analysis of the Holocaust by the editor of *Commentary*, Gabriel Schoenfeld, in his "Auschwitz and the Professors," *Commentary* 105:6 (June 1998), 42–6, and the flurry of letters from academic and non-academic respondents in the August 1998 issue.

7. Joan Ringelheim, "The Split between Gender and the Holocaust," in *Women in the Holocaust*, eds. Dalia Ofer and Lenore Weitzman (New Haven: Yale University Press, 1998), 350.

8. Pascale Rachel Bos, "Women and the Holocaust: Analyzing Gender Difference," in *Experience and Expression: Women, the Nazis, and the Holocaust*, eds. Elizabeth R. Baer and Myrna Goldenberg (Detroit: Wayne State University Press, 2003), 32–3.

9. Joan Ringelheim, "Thoughts about Women and the Holocaust," in *Thinking the Unthinkable: Meanings of the Holocaust*, ed. Roger S. Gottlieb (Mahwah NJ: Paulist Press, 1990), 146.

10. Ibid., 148. Ringelheim suggests that the Jewish Council policy of "rescue through work" presumed that usefulness to the Nazis would save the lives of Jews. But the strategy did not benefit women. If it benefited anyone, it was Jewish men. The skills the Nazis needed were those of men, not women. Ghetto Chief Jacob Gens of the Vilna Ghetto summed this up most succinctly: "I want to avert the end through work. Through work by healthy men. Thanks to that the ghetto exists…. The Germans wouldn't keep a ghetto for women and children for very long: they wouldn't give them food for one extra day."

11. Joan Ringelheim, "Women and the Holocaust: A Reconsideration of Research," in *Different Voices: Women and the Holocaust*, eds. Carol Rittner and John Roth (New York: Paragon House, 1993), 399, notes that, "In another labor camp, Debica, there were 10 women and 300 men. None of these numbers can make us sanguine about the possibilities for either Jewish women or Jewish men to survive. But they add to the growing impression that Nazi policy allowed for the possibility of more Jewish men than Jewish women to survive; and that the Jewish Councils, either through ignorance or acknowledgement of the situation, decided to save Jews—which often meant the saving of Jewish men."

12. Ibid., 392.

13. Nechama Tec, *Resilience and Courage: Women, Men, and the Holocaust* (New Haven: Yale University Press, 2003), 11.

14. Raul Hilberg, *Perpetrators Victims Bystanders: The Jewish Catastrophe 1933–1945* (London: Secker & Warburg, 1995), 127.

15. Ibid., 129. See the same chronology as noted in the case of Liepāja, Latvia, in Edward Anders and Juris Dubrovskis, "Who Died in the Holocaust? Recovering Names from Official Records," *Holocaust and Genocide Studies* 17:1 (2003): 131–32, who argue "In Liepāja in the summer of 1941 the Y chromosome suddenly became lethal, and men were killed regardless of personal qualities and skills. By fall it was equally dangerous to be old. By winter, it was fatal to be a Jew of either sex and any age, unless one had certain occupational skills. In Riga in 1943/44 it was fatal to be old, or a mother with a young child."

16. Hilberg, *Perpetrators*, 128–29.

17. Ibid., 130.

18. On the labor service system, see Randolph Braham, *The Hungarian Labor Service System, 1939–1945* (New York: Columbia University Press, 1977); and Randolph Braham, *The Politics of Genocide: The Holocaust in Hungary* (New York: Columbia University Press, 1994), I, 294–380 (hereafter Braham, *Politics*).

19. Braham, *Politics*, II, 1298. The military General Staff gave the following figures for "Jewish" labor battalion casualties in 1943: 2158 deaths, 716 injured, 18843 missing, and 1591 captured—see Szabolcs Szita, "A zsidó munkaszolgálat" (The Jewish labor service), in *The Holocaust in Hungary: Fifty Years Later,* eds. Randolph Braham and Attila Pók (New York: Rosenthal Institute for Holocaust Studies, Graduate Center of the City University of New York; Budapest: Institute of History of the Hungarian Academy of Sciences: Europa Institute; Boulder CO: Social Science Monographs, 1997), 339.

20. For the May 2, 1944, registration, see United States Holocaust Memorial Museum Archives (USHMM), RG-52.001M, "I collection" (hereafter I), Reel 116.

21. József Kepecs, ed., *A zsidó népesség száma településenként 1840–1941* (The number of Jews by settlement, 1840–1941) (Budapest: Központistatisztikai Hivatal, 1993), 340–41.

22. In Hungary the figure of a "Jewish" population made up of 52.08% women in 1930, roughly matched the proportions in other national communities: Poland—52.08% in 1931; Germany—52.24% in 1933; Czechoslovakia—50.81% in 1930; Lithuania—52.08% in 1923; Latvia—53.68% in 1930; Ukraine—53.70% in 1939; Byelorussia—53.25% in 1939. See Hilberg, *Perpetrators*, 127.

23. Four men are explicitly listed as serving in labor battalions: two in Budapest and one in Zombor.

24. Gavriel Bar Shaked, ed., *Nevek: Munkaszázadok veszteségei a keleti Magyar hadmüveleti területeken* (Names: The losses of labor service companies in the Hungarian eastern front lines) (New York and Paris: Beate Klarsfeld Foundation, 1992), II, 592.

25. Ferenc Deutsch was reported missing—aged 38—leaving a mother and older sister in Veszprém, ibid., I, 158; György Füzes was reported missing—aged 43—leaving a father, mother and younger brother in Veszprém, ibid., I, 321; János Kaszas was reported missing—aged 23—leaving a widowed mother and older sister in Veszprém, ibid., II, 18; Rezsõ Pollák was reported missing—aged 35—leaving a father and mother in Veszprém, ibid., II, 334; Andor Rosenfeld was reported missing—aged 30—leaving a mother in Veszprém, ibid., II, 389; Imre Szántó was reported missing—aged 27—leaving a father, mother and wife in Veszprém, ibid., II, 580. Unfortunately *Nevek* does not reproduce the place of residence of the next of kin, which is information included on the files from the Department for Missing Persons in the Hungarian Ministry of Defense. However place of birth and mother's maiden name are reproduced making it possible to compare *Nevek* with the registration and ghetto lists from Veszprém.

26. Nathaniel Katzburg, *Hungary and the Jews: Policy and Legislation 1920–1943* (Ramat-Gan: Bar Ilan University Press, 1981).

27. Two points are worth bearing in mind here. First, the exception to this general rule was the expulsion—and subsequent execution—of some 20,000 "Jews" in 1941 (see Braham, *Politics*, I, 205–22). Second, non-"Jewish" men of military age were also conscripted during this period and suffered heavy losses at the Battle of the Don in January 1943. Tom Kramer, *From Emancipation to Catastrophe: The Rise and Holocaust of Hungarian Jews* (Lanham, MD: University Press of America, 2000), 120, notes that the mortality rate of Jewish labor service conscripts attached to the Second Hungarian Army was over 85% in comparison to a mortality rate of 65% for non-"Jewish" Hungarian combat troops, and points to "the fundamental dichotomy between these two figures: whereas the Hungarian Second Army was decimated by enemy action in the theatre of battle, the Jewish Labor Service casualties resulted largely from the deliberate actions of nominally friendly forces."

28. 1.610/1944. M.E. sz, *Budapesti Közlöny* (Gazette of Budapest) 95 (April 28, 1944), paragraph 8, no. 4.

29. On earlier "friction" between the German and Hungarian authorities over "Jewish" labor servicemen, see Braham, *Politics*, I, 323–24.

30. USHMM, RG-52.009.04/1. Ferenczy report of May 10, 1944, 16/1944, paragraph 2.

31. Ibid., RG-52.009.04/2. Ferenczy report of May 29, 1944, 16/1944, paragraph 7, see also paragraph 12.

32. Ibid., RG-52.009.04/1. Ferenczy report of June 12, 1944, 16/1944, paragraph 5.

33. Braham, *Politics*, I, 352. See also ibid., II, 1122, where Braham notes that, "the institutional approach... was more effective in saving Jewish lives. Among the agencies of the government that contributed toward this end were the Ministry of Defense, which recruited able-bodied Jewish males into the labor service system..." See also Randolph Braham, ed., *The Wartime System of Labor Service in Hungary: Varieties of Experiences* (New York: Columbia University Press, 1995), vii–viii, where Braham notes the irony that "when the Final Solution program was launched...the labor service system became refuge for many thousands of Jewish men. While the newly established quisling government of Döme Sztójay virtually surrendered control over the Jews to the SS, the labor service system continued to remain under the jurisdiction of the Hungarian Ministry of Defense. As a result the labor servicemen were not subjected to the ghettoization and deportation that took place during April–July 1944."

34. Braham, *Politics*, I, 352. See also ibid., I, 356. Szita, "Zsidó," 340, notes the problem of a lack of sources to determine exactly what lay behind Ministry of Defense mobilizing of "Jews" in the aftermath of the Nazi German occupation.

35. Braham, *Politics*, I, 352–53.

36. Ibid., 357–58, "Jewish" men between the ages of 16 and 60 and "Jewish" women between the ages of 16 and 40 were called up "for national defense service" on October 26, 1944. "Jewish" women aged 16 to 50 who knew how to sew were called up on November 2. Although see also Elek Karsai, ed., *Vádirat a Nácizmus Ellen: Dokumentumok a Magyarországi zsidóüldözés történetéhez* (Documents on the persecution of Jews in Hungary), III (Budapest: A Magyar Izraeliták Országos Képviselete Kiadása, 1967), 53–4, which refers to the call-up of 18–30 year old "Jewish" and "non-Jewish" women in Budapest in July 1944.

37. USHMM, RG-52.001M, I 171, May 20, 1944, list of "Jews" enlisted for labor service.

38. Ibid., June 4, 1944, list of "Jews" enlisted from the Komakuti Jewish camp.

39. Ibid., June 12, 1944, list of enlisted Veszprém "Jews." Note that fifteen of the seventeen men on the list are from Veszprém, with one each from the surrounding communities of Nemesvámos and Városlöd.

40. A Veszprémi Zsidó Hitközség Gyüjteménybõl, letter of May 23, 1944, reproduced in Csaba Králl, ed., *Holocaust Emlékkönyv: A vidéki zsidóság deportálásának 50 évfordulója alkalmából* (Memorial Book: On the fiftieth anniversary of the deportation of Jews from the provinces) (Budapest: TEDISZ, 1994), 388.

41. For the two ghetto lists, see USHMM, RG-52.001M, I 171. These lists can also be found in *Töredék: Fejezetek a veszprémi zsidó közösség történetéből* (Fragmentary chapters from the history of the Jewish community of Veszprém) (Veszprém: Veszprémi Zsidó Örökségi Alapítvány, 2001), 73–90, 93–105.

42. The Horthy Miklós u. ghetto included "Jewish Jews" and "Christian Jews" from Veszprém (some of whom were not included on the earlier May registration list) and fifty-one "Jews" brought in from surrounding villages.

43. For Lódz, see Michael Unger, "The Status and Plight of Women in the Lódz Ghetto," in *Women*, eds. Ofer and Weitzman, 123, who notes that in Lódz a prewar predominance of women over men in the "Jewish" community (52.3% cf. 47.7% in 1931) was heightened in the ghetto. He suggests that in 1940 the ghetto population was 54.4% female and 45.5% male and that this disparity increased due to higher mortality rates amongst men and the labor transports of men. At the end of December 1941, Hilberg, *Perpetrators*, 129, notes that the Lódz ghetto population was 57% female and 43% male. Once deportations from the ghetto commenced in January 1942, women were a majority of those deported. However despite this, women continued to be a majority of the ghetto population, with the ghetto population in December 1942 being 56.6% female and 43.4% male (Unger, "Status," 127). Ringelheim, "Women," 398, argues that, "Women formed the majority of the population (both indigenous and refugee populations) of the Lódz ghetto, and they were chosen for deportation in greater numbers and percentages than their representation in the population: overall 62% of those transported were women and 38% were men. Gender differences must be a critical factor in the analysis of the transports." For Warsaw, see Dalia Ofer, "Gender Issues in Diaries and Testimonies of the Ghetto: The Case of Warsaw," in *Women*, eds. Ofer and Weitzman, 145, who notes that a pre-war predominance of women in the "Jewish" community (the "Jewish" population of Warsaw in 1939 was 54% female and 46% male) was heightened in the ghetto, with a ghetto population in January 1942 that was 57.3% female and 42.7% male. With the onset of mass deportations in the summer of 1942, a majority of those deported were women, leading, Hilberg, *Perpetrators*, 129, suggests, to a minority (44%) of women in the registered ghetto population post-deportations. Ringelheim, "Women," 398, comments that, "there are far fewer statistics for Warsaw than for Lódz. However, in those that are available, the numerical pattern is similar: there are more women than men in the population; fewer women than men die in the ghetto of disease; more women are available for deportations; and more women are sent to the camps.... At the beginning of 1942 there were more women than men in the ghetto by a ratio of 4:3. After the deportations, the ratio was reversed...." For the rather different case of Theresienstadt, see Ruth Bondy, "Women in Theresienstadt and the Family Camp in Birkenau," in *Women*, eds. Ofer and Weitzman, 313, who notes that, "from May 1942, when the transports of old people started to pour in from Germany and Austria, until the liberation, the number of women in the ghetto always exceeded the number of men...." In January 1944, the ghetto population was 60% female, and "after seventeen thousand people left with the transports of autumn 1944, Theresienstadt was a city of women. The only men remaining were most of the prominents, all the Danish Jews, and others privileged in German eyes."

44. Ofer, "Gender," 145. See Unger, "Status," 123–24, who notes that in the case of the Lódz ghetto in June 1940, "for Jews between ages 20 and 45—those in the fertile years and their physical prime—the [gender] disparity was even greater: of the 64,430 members of this group, 27,281 were men and 37,149 were women. Thus women comprised 57.7% of this age group."

45. Veress Csaba, "Adatok a zsidóság Veszprém megyében a II: Világháború idején lejátszódott tragédiájához" (Data on the tragedy of Jews in Veszprém County during the second world war), *Töredék*, 23.

46. See Carol Rittner and John Roth, "Prologue: Women and the Holocaust," in *Different*, eds. Rittner and Roth, 3, who note that, "At Auschwitz...the Jewish women

selected for labor were mainly in their late teens and early twenties and without children. Auschwitz selection policy kept children, usually those under fourteen, with their mothers. Along with older women, those mothers were typically dispatched to the gas chambers on arrival." See also Debórah Dwork, *Children with a Star* (New Haven: Yale University Press, 1991), xix, who argues that, "Women alone had a chance for a temporary stay of execution, but mothers and their children were sent to death imediately."

47. Based on lists drawn from USHMM, RG-52.001M, I 171. Csaba, 'Adatok', 24, suggests that only fifty of the 750 Veszprém "Jews" returned from the camps and that for Veszprém county as a whole, the figure was 640 from a total of 4106 "Jews" deported.

48. On the experience of labor battalion members during the final year of the war see Braham, *Politics*, I, 349–65 and II, 969–71 and 1368–370.

49. These families' stories draw upon the registration, ghetto, and conscription lists found in USHMM, RG-52.001M, I 116 and I 171.

50. *Nevek* (1992), I, 321.

51. Ibid.

52. Gavriel Bar Shaked, ed., *Nevek: Magyar zsidó nők a stutthofi koncentrációs táborban* (Names: Hungarian Jewish women in the Stutthof concentration camp) (New York and Paris: Beate Klarsfeld Foundation, 1995), 331, 474. As Hilberg notes, *Perpetrators*, 3, "at Auschwitz...the Jewish women selected for labor were mainly in their late teens and early twenties and without children."

53. Tec, *Resilience*, 8, rightly notes that, "Unrepresentative figures about deportations or mass killings cannot prove whether more women perished than men. At best, they indicate that in specific places, at specific times, either men or women were more likely to be deported, that in particular environments either men or women may have had a better chance to survive. Evidence about the death rates of men and women is so scattered, so incomplete, that definitive answers are impossible. The most we can say is that we don't know: the exact figures are missing." However the evidence from Veszprém while fragmentary and by definition essentially unrepresentative, does afford the opportunity for at least suggestive—if not definitive—conclusions. As anyone engaged in historical research knows all too well, fragmentary sources are what we inevitably end up working with. The critical issue is recognition of the limitations of our source material, and a consciousness of not extrapolating wildly from a limited source base.

54. See Braham, *Politics*, II, 1300–301, who notes that compared to Budapest, "in the countryside, where the losses among the labor servicemen were somewhat lighter and the deportations affected the entire Jewish population, the male-female ratio of the survivors was considerably better. In 1946 there were 24,604 male survivors and 22,520 female survivors. In the vital 20 to 60 age group, the number of males (19,619) exceeded that of females (16,685) by 2,934. The exact ratio, of course, varied from community to community."

55. Braham's passing comments on Veszprém perhaps suggest that he viewed the situation in this town to be exceptional. See Braham, *Politics*, II, 764, who notes that, "according to one report approximately 170 Jewish men escaped deportation because they had been called up for labor service." The report he mentions is presumably the Jewish Council report reproduced in Jenő Lévai, *Zsidósors Magyarországon* (Jewish fate in Hungary) (Budapest: Magyar Téka, 1948), 421, which notes that close to 170 were absent from Veszprém, excluding the war dead.

56. USHMM, RG-52.001M, I 99, 24.534 sz. M III m.o. 1944.

57. Ibid., I 99, 2767/1944.

58. It is clear that this is a form letter, which has been tailored to the specific circumstances of Körmend. See the addition of the date of the call up (June 12) in a separate type. See also the signature is not that of Ujvárossy—his name is simply given in type at the end of the letter.

59. *Szegedi Uj Nemzedék* (New generation of Szeged) (June 2, 1944), 5.

60. Szita, "Zsidó," 340, notes in the case of the Miskolc gendarmerie district that 18–48 year old "Jewish" men were being called up out of ghettos "from Losonc to Gyöngyös."

61. Based on lists drawn from USHMM, RG-52.001M, I 99

62. Atina Grossmann, "Women and the Holocaust: Four Recent Titles," *Holocaust and Genocide Studies* 16:1 (2002): 94.

63. Ibid.

Interviews with Survivors of the
Hungarian Forced Labor Service: An Evaluation

Dan Danieli

Introduction

Interviews with Jewish survivors of the Hungarian proto-Fascist government's forced labor service system (*Munkaszolgálat*) constitute only a small part of all Holocaust survivor interviews. Nevertheless, these interviews are a valuable research tool because, although much has been written about the labor battalions, only fragmentary information about the history and fate of company-level battalions exists.[1] The question then arises: with the wealth of information available, how can we evaluate the historical validity of these interviews in reference to the labor service?

Researchers have written histories about one or another specific unit, and others have paid tribute to the roles of rescuers by researching the archives of the Hungarian government and Yad Vashem. One example of such projects is the work about the commanding officer of the 101/359th labor company, Captain László Ocskay, whose actions saved approximately 2000 Jews.[2]

This paper is based on work completed at the Survivors of the Shoah Visual History Foundation (hereafter "the Foundation") and on 180 interviews, some with survivors of the Hungarian forced labor service system, done for the same organization. Hundreds of videotaped interviews in Hungarian, English, Hebrew, German, and French were viewed in order to clarify the validity of statements in the survivor's narrative and to pinpoint geographic locations with their correct names (when mispronounced, spelled phonetically, or when a colloquial designation was used). Hundreds of handwritten pre-interview questionnaires were examined to assure historical and geographical accuracy. In the end, a small percentage of interviews with former labor servicemen were chosen to form the statistical basis for this paper.

Limitations

A formal evaluation of the interviews conducted with former labor servicemen and servicewomen would require extensive reference to a multitude of sources, including statistics, quotations from authorities on the subjects discussed, and in some cases audio-visual aids. Because the primary sources are the interviews conducted at the Foundation, this conventional manner of supporting findings is not possible. The interviews collected and archived by the Foundation are available for public view under strictly controlled circumstances and/or as a part of educational aids published by the Foundation. Thus, except for a few statistics available for public dissemination, this evaluation is the result of the writer's work with the relatively small sample of interviews noted above.

To clarify the quantitative aspect of the interviews collected by the Foundation and their relevance to the subject of this paper, the following figures assembled from an internal report titled *Indexing and Cataloging Statistics by Language,* disseminated periodically within the Foundation, may be helpful. The report from which the following figures have been extracted is dated May 7, 2004:

Total number of interviews conducted: 51,752;

Total number of interviews indexed: 28,747, remaining: 23,005;

Total number of interviews catalogued: 47,446, remaining: 4,306

The term "indexing" refers to the provision of index terms to one-minute segments. The term "cataloguing" refers to entering basic information from the Pre-Interview Questionnaire (PIQ) into a database.

From all the indexed interviews, the Foundation's Education Department prepared an extract listing the interviews that fulfilled the following criteria regardless of the language in which the interview was conducted:

- The survivor was born in Austria-Hungary, Hungary, Czechoslovakia, Romania, or Yugoslavia, and
- the interview included a term or terms indicating that the survivor was a member of a Hungarian forced labor battalion or company, labored on military fortifications, was forced into military labor as a civilian or as a previous member of the military, and mentioned Hungarian forced labor supervisors or military guards.

A search of the database resulted in a list of 1,348 interviews.

Methodology

The interviews upon which this evaluation is based were conducted in a rigorously formatted environment with little left to the interviewer's discretion as the interviewing proceeded throughout the world since 1995. Several stages of quality control were built into the Foundation's procedures; these were well documented and updated several times. Probably by coincidence, the interviewing procedures defined in the Foundation's internal guides follow very closely the pertinent guide used by the U.S. Army.[3]

The Foundation did not select the interviewees, but accepted those who volunteered to be interviewed without prior knowledge of the questions to be asked or the specific areas of Foundation interest. As such, they should be considered a random sample of the survivors, even taking into consideration the possible exceptions noted by professional statisticians. The content of each interview is obviously anecdotal evidence, as is all oral history to some degree.

The Foundation accepted volunteer interviewers based on their own descriptions of their backgrounds, regardless of previous interviewing experience or of specific wide-ranging Holocaust-related knowledge. The Foundation offered a short instructive seminar and selected the interviewers after testing them very briefly. Most interviewers had no specific historical knowledge of the Hungarian labor service system, except that some may have personally been part of that service. It is clear that such specific knowledge would have been important when conducting the interviews, but it was also clear that too much knowledge of that history could have biased the interviewer. As stated in a relevant study: "There is no doubt that the single most important factor in the constitution of an interview is the questions posed by the interviewer. Inevitably derived from a set of assumptions about what is historically important, the interviewers' questions provide the intellectual framework for the interview and give it direction and shape."[4]

The material used here derives from the interviews in their original unedited format. The interviews were videotaped with the questions and responses clearly audible; no editing of the tapes was allowed. The only additional interaction between the interviewer and the survivor occurred before and after the taping and during a very short window of time when the interview was stopped for the change of the videotape in the recorder. A Pre-Interview Questionnaire was used in preparation for the interview: the interviewer filled out the form either during a telephone conversation or during a meeting with the survivor and included biographical information on the survivor and his/her family in addition to abbreviated chronological and movement data.

For this paper, I used the PIQ forms intensively, even more so than the actual tapes. The interviews for which I was the interviewer provided the most material for this evaluation, but the total number of interviews that passed through my hands during the research phase was approximately 1,500. Only a small percentage of those interviews came from survivors of the Hungarian labor service system and during my routine research for the Foundation, several aspects of the survivors' experience pertaining to labor service came into focus. The salient points of interest were:

- Dates: which dates seem to have been of sufficient and lasting interest to the survivor and how do such dates coincide with historical data?

- Locations: geographically correct identification of places in which the survivor was located during his/her service;

- Routing or movement between locations;

- Perception of the survivor in reference to his/her own experience and/or in reference to generally held beliefs;

- Women survivors' perception of their role in forced labor units; and

- Prewar education, social status, and geographic origin as determinants for the survivors experience.

The narratives of the survivors of labor service companies were evaluated in order to:

1. Establish a point of reference as to the place and value of this anecdotal information within the framework of established and still evolving Holocaust history;

2. Ascertain if there was a need for a concentrated effort to research and write the history of individual Hungarian forced labor companies; and

3. Arrive at some conclusion as to differences, if any, between the specific Hungarian forced labor service related interviews and other interviews pertaining to the Holocaust.

Dates in the Testimonies

The date uniformly mentioned correctly, with very few exceptions, was March 19, 1944—the occupation of Hungary by German forces. However, the day of the week, Sunday, was recalled only by some. The overwhelming majority of survivors did not remember the date they were called up for labor service. Very few survivors, mostly those with an advanced education, kept diaries either during their service or put their recollections on paper shortly after their liberation or discharge from service. It is clear that for the most part conditions during their service were not conducive to keeping records, nor did the educational background of most survivors provide an incentive for writing down their experiences.

Considering that much of the survivors' time was spent marching or being transported, the dates mentioned in the narratives are mostly guesses and many times fall within a very wide time frame. An especially broad range of dates occurs when referring to unit movement on the eastern front, particularly when comparing those date ranges with testimonies concerning unit movement within Trianon Hungary. It is interesting to note that the memory of dates was especially chaotic among the survivors of units within the reoccupied areas of Slovakia (*Felvidék*), Carpatho-Ruthenia (*Kárpátalja*), and Romania (*Észak Erdély,* that is Northern Transylvania). On the other hand, many survivors who had served in units within the Yugoslav areas, and especially the survivors of Bor, retained vivid memories about when, where, and how they moved.

Although the transfer of Hungarian labor service companies to German jurisdiction on the way to and into Austria is clearly narrated in many interviews, seldom was the exact date mentioned.[5]

Geography, Locations, and Routing

In evaluating the narratives, one aspect closely linked with the question of establishing dates is the correct identification of geographic locations inside and outside of Hungary where the survivors of the labor service units were deployed. Obviously this is not unique to the survivors discussed in this presentation; it was a problem for Jews of many nationalities speaking many languages, moving through unfamiliar areas, and trying to understand unfamiliar languages and to remember names and locations never encountered. The Hungarian units included not only

Hungarian-speaking Jews, but also many born or living outside of Trianon Hungary, who spoke the languages of the Austro-Hungarian monarchy, and who were thrown into the language cauldron of Eastern Europe during the war. Thus, even those labor servicemen who had been stationed in or had been moved within Hungary may not have been able to identify geographic locations correctly.

For a Yiddish-speaking person, for whom Hungarian may or may not have been the second language, identifying and remembering the name of a Hungarian village could have been daunting. The narrators' problems of identification were compounded by pronunciation, by colloquial and sometimes local-usage names, and by the interviewers' understanding and correctly transcribing the location names during the pre-interview. The problem of transliteration was compounded exponentially for interviews conducted and documented in Hebrew. This situation often resulted in phonetic spellings that could have a large number of variants.

In order to re-create a valid history of individual labor service units, one must know where the units operated, where they started and where they ended up, and when and how they were routed. There are several valuable routing sources for the mass movement of Jews during the Holocaust,[6] but none specifically pertain to the movement of Hungarian labor service companies. It is clear that comparing the resources used to compile various inclusive studies of forced movements during the Holocaust, such as the *Auschwitz Chronicles,*[7] with existing data about movements of labor companies would be unfair. An exact compendium of movements of even as large a forced labor battalion headquarters such as Jászberény does not exist in published form.

Some memoirs published by former labor servicemen do have information pertaining to geography and routing, but even some well-written memoirs are extremely sketchy when it comes to details that would allow the tracing of movements. For example, one memoir clearly lays out the location of a certain labor service company, but indicates the identification number of the company as 110/2 on a photograph and later mentions the number 14/110 (probably 110/14) in the narrative without any clear connection between the two units.[8] A second memoir mentions the identification number III/4 on one photograph, but gives no details of the company's history in the text.[9] Thus, a large number of memoirs have been published by former labor servicemen, but unfortunately many, perhaps most, lack the exact particulars that would allow the reconstruction of the historical record.

The same problem arises when attempting to correlate survivors' testimonies with data published in some valuable investigative documentation. A clear example is a book—used when preparing for interviews—that contains exhaustively researched material, but that cannot establish the history of individual labor companies.[10] Another well-organized source—frequently used before and after the interviews to clarify the matter of origin-routing-destination—while very detailed, fails to provide clear and unequivocal information.[11] It is obvious that neither the authors of academic studies, nor the writers of relevant memoirs had sufficient material available to them or they were not interested in the re-creation of the history of the forced labor service companies. As for the interviews conducted by the Foundation, the focus was not on establishing history at all, but rather to recall the individual experience of survivors. Forced labor service was a detail within the Holocaust experience and the interviewer's knowledge or lack of knowledge of that specific subject resulted in questions and responses that for the most part failed to illuminate the history of the specific forced labor service company in which the survivor had served.

While survivors originating from relatively large urban areas were able to define rather clearly the geographic parameters, including administrative and political boundaries, those of rural origin often could not provide exact information. The most confusion existed in the testimonies pertaining to Austria, Czechoslovakia, northern Hungary, Carpatho-Ruthenia, Transylvania, Romania, southern Hungary, Yugoslavia, Poland, Russia, and Ukraine. This confusion is easily explainable by the changing political boundaries of Eastern Europe between 1918 and 1945, especially within the memories of survivors from non-urban areas, with elementary or less education, or educated in parochial schools. Some survivors from areas ceded by Greater Hungary to neighboring countries, especially from the northeastern parts, had problems describing such locations as being in Hungary, Czechoslovakia, or Romania. Some resolved the matter by using commonly understood names as they existed in the Austro-Hungarian Empire prior to 1918. On the other hand, some of the more educated survivors of urban origin who were moved around with the labor service companies expressed serious doubts about their own recollection of their routing in Eastern Europe and in Austria.

Perceptions of the Survivors

The interviewed survivors' perceptions of the labor service system and its relationship to survival is particularly interesting. It is possible that the debate that started in Hungarian academic and lay circles shortly after liberation received its impetus not from the research into documents and court proceedings, but from the actual perception of the survivors. Arguments persist and will continue concerning the existence of the labor service system as either an instrument of the "Final Solution" or as a camouflage, after the German occupation of Hungary, to *save* Jews from the Final Solution, and this paper will not attempt to direct the argument in any direction. However, it should be noted that these perceptions are influenced not only by postwar research or input from external sources, such as newspaper articles, memoirs, or conversation with other survivors, but also by the survivors' own experiences. Even so, it is not easy to distill perceptions from interviews that were collected more than fifty years after the war, during which period external influences had sufficient time to penetrate the consciousness of the survivors.

Discussion of the purpose and objective of the labor service system can be found only in a limited number of testimonies. The survivors' place of origin and their experience with Hungarian authorities apparently influenced their perceptions to a large degree. Those survivors who came from territories reoccupied by Hungary, such as Southern Slovakia (the *Felvidék*), Northern Transylvania, Northeastern Slovakia (*Kárpátalja*), and Northern Yugoslavia (*Délvidék*) experienced mostly harsh encounters with the authorities and probably as a result later viewed their induction into the labor service system as an attempt to exterminate them. Those whose families were ghettoized and deported under the most inhumane conditions had a similar view, while those who relate cases of escape, hiding, or being saved mostly consider their own survival a direct result of their work in a labor service company. No firm categories can be established in this respect—perceptions can be mixed or unclear—but as a generalization these are the views that emerged from the survey. Even the differences in mother tongue among Hungarian-speaking survivors and those born with the languages of the post-Trianon non-Hungarian areas and Yiddish created in many cases divergent perceptions. Most survivors who spoke Hungarian viewed the labor service system in a more favorable light than those who did not. One reason was surely the easier contact with guards and camp administrators. Listening to the testimonies of former labor servicemen offers one a different perspective from historians' explanations and reasoning. Most survivors evaluate and judge the existence and objectives of the labor service system through their own experience, or are influenced by their friends' and relatives' experiences. In the interviews evaluated for this research only one survivor had an absolute and firm opinion pertaining to the labor service systems' objectives: he and his company were assigned to the company commander's bakery to bake and distribute bread to the neighboring military units, not far from Budapest, with ample supplies directed to his labor service company. This company's exceptional circumstances included weekend passes for home visits. It is therefore understandable that this survivor perceived the labor service system as a savior of Jews, not only those in his own company, but *per se.*

It is also clear from the survivors' stories, and supported by available historic records, that there were good commanders and bad ones, benevolent and sadistic guards (*keret legénység*) with differences even between neighboring units, and vastly different conditions between units and between periods of time served. The existence of good commanding officers and guard personnel emerge from testimonies of survivors and from the archives of Yad Vashem together with details in pertinent memoirs and scholarly publications.[12] At the same time, the cruelty and murderous intent of other military personnel is just as obvious in the interviews and in the large number of post-liberation trial documents. Thus it is obvious that no uniform perception could be expected under such dissimilar conditions.

Women Survivors of the Forced Labor Service

Because of the rather confusing variety of testimonies from women survivors, their interviews must be considered separately.

It is important to briefly indicate the position of certain Hungarian scholars in post-1945 research. Professor Randolph L. Braham, for example, assessed it as follows:

> In 1943, the women served under the central administration of the National Superintendent of Labor Service for Women (*A Női Munkaszol-gálat Országos Felügyelője*). Following the reorganization of the labor service system in 1944,...they were placed, like all other labor service personnel, under the jurisdiction of the Labor Organization of National Defense. During the recruitment drive of 1944, priority was given to the call-up of women between 18 and 30 years of age who had been employed in Jewish enterprises.[13]

Regardless of the ongoing controversy over the role of the Hungarian military establishment or at least of individual officers, such as Colonel János Heinrich, to use the labor service companies as a means to save rather than to destroy Jewish men and women,[14] the fact that many women were a part of the labor service system is indisputable. Those women were not included in the tens of thousands of women rounded-up, ghettoized, deported, and forced into slave labor inside and outside of Hungary.

Listening to women survivors' testimonies a picture emerges about the confusion in recollections regarding the structure of the labor service system and the female survivors' place in that organization. While none of the interviewees included in our survey mentioned having received an actual and formal call-up by the Hungarian authorities, many of them referred to "being called-up." Some mentioned call-ups by age groups published in newspapers, others associated their induction with official orders posted on walls in the streets. A number of survivors related their experience of being rounded up in the street, dragged from their homes, arrested on trains and trams, and of other methods not associated with regular military call-up procedures. A number of female survivors described being marched to the west from Budapest and at a certain point forced from the column into a group that from then on constituted a Hungarian forced labor company under military guard. Although descriptions of identifiable attributes of a labor service company do occur quite frequently, none of the accounts include a company or battalion identification number. Even women survivors who were taken over the border into Austria as part of a labor company working on fortifications, construction, or other non-agricultural work, did not mention such a number.

Considering the frenzied times in Hungary, especially after March 19, 1944, and even more so the last few months of 1944 until the liberation in 1945, this plethora of experiences can be attributed to the chaotic situation and not to confusion in the memories of the survivors. While there is no doubt that many were actually part of a labor service company, others performed forced labor for ad-hoc military, para-military, police, gendarme, or Arrow Cross units. It is understandable that many women's perceptions of their organizational affiliation did not crystallize during their service, and neither did it constitute an important part in the recollection of their experiences.

Prewar Status of the Survivors

The prewar level of education, the geographic origin, the political borders, and the different urban or village life experiences—all were determinants of the survivors' perception of their experiences. These determinants obviously refer not only to the survivors of the Hungarian labor service system, but to all survivors of the Holocaust, or, for that matter, to all participants in oral history projects. This fact is well stated in the following:

> What the narrator says, as well as the way the narrator says it, is related to that person's social identity (or identities). Who the narrator is becomes a cognitive filter for their experiences. Recognizing the differing social experiences of women and men, feminist historians have noted that women more so than men articulate their life stories around major events in the family life cycle, dating events in relation to when their children were born, for example. Men, on the other hand, are more likely to connect their personal chronologies to public events like wars....[15]

Relating the above to observations pertaining to the interviews surveyed for this paper, it can be stated that the survivors' prewar identities strongly influenced their perceptions and the story they had to tell as much as their postwar identity did.

Summary

Although I intended in this paper to evaluate the interviews with survivors of the Hungarian labor service system, most of my conclusions reflect all interviews with Holocaust survivors, and by extension most oral history projects. The very large number of interviews conducted by the Foundation allows for a substantially fair comparison between the history of the Holocaust as written in countless books and articles by scholars and the oral stories that emerged from the words of the survivors. On the whole, it seems that oral history, at least as it pertains to the Holocaust, stands up to "real" historical research based on documents and other authentic sources.

How do the survivors' stories resolve the arguments concerning the positive and negative effects of the labor service system? Is there overwhelming evidence in favor of those who say the service was nothing but a tool in the hands of those who wanted to bring about the Final Solution? Or does the evidence show that in the final analysis the labor service system was intended as respite from the Final Solution? Numerical analyses of mortality rates and other hard facts resulting from research will ultimately have to produce overwhelming evidence for one side or for the other.

At the beginning of this paper, I posed the question about the need to reconstruct the history of individual forced labor units. Histories of wartime military units are abundant in the official literature and in memoirs. Memoirs, history texts, and internet websites include a large number of historical recollections and research pertaining to individual units of the Allied armies and of the German military, but very little exists about the individual labor service companies. Some data can be found in fiction, in memoirs of questionable authenticity, and in historical documents where certain fractional details exist. An important reason for the lack of such histories emerges from listening to the survivors who stated that very little postwar cohesion existed among members who served in the same unit due to their wide geographic dispersal after the war. Additionally, many survivors would rather forget that period of their life and not dwell on it. The chaos of wartime and the postwar period made it difficult for survivors to reconstruct their stories in the correct chronological and geographical order. This presents a serious and perhaps insurmountable obstacle to the writing of the history of the many individual units.

It is possible that the next conference, "The Holocaust in Hungary–Seventy Years Later," will permit a further expansion of the evaluation of the interviews with survivors of the Hungarian forced labor service. At the end of May 2004 there were still 726 Hungarian language interviews ready to be indexed and 242 interviews to be catalogued in the archives of the Survivors of the Shoah Visual History Foundation; in addition many interviews in languages other than in Hungarian may be pertinent to this subject.

Notes

1. Randolph L. Braham, ed., *The Hungarian Jewish Catastrophe: A Selected and Annotated Bibliography.* 2nd rev. & enlarged edition (New York: Columbia University Press, 1984); and Randolph L. Braham, ed., *The Holocaust in Hungary–A Selected and Annotated Bibliography: 1984–2000* (New York: Columbia University Press, 2001).

2. Dan Danieli, *Captain Ocskay, a Righteous Man* (Riverdale, NY: D. Danieli, 1996).

3. Stephen E. Everett, *Oral History: Techniques and Procedures* (Washington, DC: U. S. Army Center of Military History, 1992); also available on the internet at: http://army. mil/cmh-pg/books/oral.htm (10/29/2003).

4. Linda Shopes, "Who Is the Interviewer?" in *Making Sense of Oral History* (History Matters: The U.S. Survey on the Web, n.d.). Available at: http://historymatters.gmu.edu/ mse/oral/question2.html (10/29/2003).

5. In stark contrast to this, see the valuable study by Eleonore Lappin, "The Death Marches of Hungarian Jews through Austria in the Spring of 1945," *Yad Vashem Studies* 28 (2000): 203–42, which gives a large number of exact dates when groups of Jews were moved, but does not identify individual labor service units. (Also available on the internet at: http://www.yad-vashem.org.il/download/about_holocaust/studies/lappin_full.pdf).

6. See for example, Martin Gilbert, *Atlas of the Holocaust* (New York: Morrow, 1993); and United States Holocaust Memorial Museum, *Historical Atlas of the Holocaust* (New York: Macmillan Publishing Company, 1996).

7. Danuta Czech, *Auschwitz Chronicles 1939–1945* (New York: Henry Holt, 1997).

8. Hilel Danzig, *Bazel Susim* (In the shadow of horses) (Israel: Beit Lohamei Haghettaot, 1976).

9. T.W. Tibby Weston, *The Vision—A Candid Autobiography of a Survivor of Nazi and Communist Oppression* (New York: Xlibris Co., 2000).

10. Szabolcs Szita, *Utak a Pokolból: Magyar deportáltak az annektált Ausztriában 1944–1945* (Ways out of hell: Deported Hungarians in Austria, 1944–1945) (Budapest: Metalon Manager Iroda KFT, 1991).

11. Elek Karsai, ed., *"Fegyvertelen Álltak Az Aknamezőkö..."* ("Without arms, they stood in the minefields..."), in *Dokumentumok a munkaszolgálat történetéhez Magyarországon* (Budapest: A Magyar Izraeliták Országos Képviselete Kiadása, 1962), II, 769–79.

12. For example, see Martin Gilbert, *The Righteous—The Unsung Heroes of the Holocaust* (New York: Henry Holt, 2003), 381–405.

13. Randolph L. Braham, *The Politics of Genocide: The Holocaust in Hungary*, revised and enlarged edition, 2 vols. (New York: Columbia University Press, 1994), I, 356–57, and II, 1367.

14. Szabolcs Szita, "A hadsereg és a zsidókérdés," in *Nagy Képes Milleneumi Hadtörténet*, ed. Rácz Árpád (Budapest: Rubicon-Aquila-Könyvek, 2000), 424.

15. Linda Shopes, "Who Is Talking?" in *Making Sense of Oral History* (History Matters: The U. S. Survey on the Web, n.d.). Available at: http://historymatters.gmu.edu/ mse/oral/question1.html (10/29/2003)

The Economic Annihilation of the Hungarian Jews, 1944–1945

Gábor Kádár and Zoltán Vági

Between the two world wars the ruling conservative-right political force and its extreme right opposition agreed on the need for "repressing the Jewish influence" in Hungary. After the Jewish Laws were issued (1938–1942), the "changing of the guard" had sped up, although it was not fast and effective enough for the race-protectionist right wing. Not only pro-German circles supported the anti-Jewish legislation, many Hungarian citizens and significant parts of the Gentile Hungarian intelligentsia approved of the measures taken at the expense of Jewish property. German pressure played an insignificant role in these processes before 1944, and its impact remained marginal even after the German occupation.

With the arrival of the German army in the spring of 1944, the long-held aim of total expropriation of Jewish wealth and use thereof in promotion of the "national interest" was at last within reach: confiscation of Jewish property provided the collaborating Hungarian government with a wide array of political and economic options. It had four main objectives through the confiscation of this huge source of revenue: to restore a balanced national budget, to cover increasing military expenditures, to relieve social discontent, and to broaden the government's base of support through the distribution of the Jewish wealth.

Minister of the Interior Andor Jaross did not attempt to veil the government's intentions when he made the following statement during the inauguration ceremony of the new prefect in Nagyvárad in May 1944: "I underscore the fact that all assets, wealth, and valuables, which Jewish greed was able to amass during the liberal era, no longer belongs to them—it is now the property of the Hungarian nation."[1] In a speech delivered at a government ceremony, Minister of Finance Lajos Reményi-Schneller also deemed Jewish assets to be "national property."[2] This notion was not uniquely Hungarian: every collaborating government administration in Europe considered Jewish wealth to have become part of the national domain.

These motivations are reflected in the draft bills created by the government. Although these laws did not come into force, they precisely demonstrate the intentions of the Sztójay government. In May 1944, Minister of Justice István Antal introduced a draft bill about "generating national wealth." The intent of this proposed legislation was to "eliminate the Jewish presence in Hungarian public and economic life."[3] The bill would have enabled the administration to "utilize Jewish assets to cover military expenditures and revitalize the Hungarian economy through the long-term government bonds"; any remaining sources "would then be used to provide displaced Jews with a minimal subsistence and to finance their eventual expatriation." In other words, according to the bill Jews would receive compensation for their expropriated assets in the form of government subsidization of their confinement to the ghetto and subsequent deportation. Thus the bill was designed to implement the idea of "self-financing genocide." Antal also attempted to establish the legal foundation for the collaborating government's deportation of Hungarian Jews in the same paragraph: "The ministry is furthermore authorized to conclude agreements with foreign states in order to expedite the expatriation of Jews and to take any other necessary measures to accomplish this objective."

A draft decree introduced at the end of July went even further: "All Jewish assets...will be considered ceded to the Hungarian state with the promulgation of this decree."[4] In theory, the decree offered government compensation to the divested Jews in the form of an annual repayment amounting to 3 percent of the estimated value of all expropriated property and wealth. (At this rate, it would have taken thirty-three years for the expropriated to obtain total restitution for their arbitrarily appraised assets.) The draft guaranteed that Jews would not receive a penny in compensation: "Jews residing abroad are not eligible to receive compensation during the period of their absence. Moreover, debts to Jews who have left the country for good are officially and permanently nullified." In light of the fact that the government of Döme Sztójay, which advanced this draft, was working feverishly to ensure that all Hungarian citizens declared to be Jewish would be compelled to "leave the country for good" and that approximately 300,000 Jews had already disappeared without a trace, this nominal program of compensation entailed no risks for the régime.

Despite the work of drafting this legislation, which would have legalized the seizure of Jewish property, the collaborating government was unable to achieve its objectives. The implementation of the long-existing plans was chaotic and fragmentary for several reasons.

The Time Factor

In Nazi Europe, Aryanization and nationalization had been a time-consuming process, involving the temporary sealing by various governments of millions of fully furnished flats and houses; the blocking of the contents of hundreds of thousands of bank accounts and safe deposit boxes; and the appropriation of the assets and stocks, current accounts, and goods of hundreds of thousands of shops and companies owned by millions of Jews across Europe, then re-channeling them into the economy after having allocated them to new owners. The process took years. In Hungary, however, one year after the German occupation, the Red Army ruled the country. The last third of this twelve- to thirteen-month period was nothing less than agony for the state. Therefore, there were only eight to nine months for the Aryanization of Jewish assets in Hungary. It was impossible to confiscate, appraise, and reintroduce into the economy the assets of approximately 760,000–780,000 people in such a short period. The collaborating government failed to inject the majority of confiscated Jewish assets (the countless shops and companies, the thousands of tons of immovable property, and the huge amount of real estate property) into the Hungarian economy. This failure did not mean of course that the looting of Jews did not take place. On the contrary, it did happen, and there can be no doubt about its totality. There was enough time to seize the catch, but not enough time to "digest" it.

As a result of the efficient cooperation between Eichmann-Sondereinsatzkommando and the "deportation trio" of the the Ministry of the Interior (state secretaries of the Ministry of the Interior László Endre and László Baky, Gendarmerie Lieutenant Colonel László Ferenczy), Jews from the Hungarian countryside were deported at a pace unprecedented in the history of the Holocaust. The plundering of Jewish assets could not keep up with the process of ghettoization and deportation. Let us not forget that in the space of a few weeks following the German occupation of Hungary on March 19, 1944, the most important anti-Jewish decrees were introduced and all Hungarian Jews were confined to ghettos, internment camps, and "yellow star houses." Then, in only fifty-six days starting with May 15, 437,000 people from the countryside (everyone with the exception of 15,000 who were taken to Strasshof, Austria) were deported to Auschwitz-Birkenau. The systematic removal of hundreds of thousands of people from their homes (including herding the Jews living in Budapest into yellow-star houses) began before a central operational concept was drawn up from the multitude of plans concerning the seizing, handling, storage, and subsequent fate of the enormous pool of assets that would be left behind; thus, the regime lacked a framework that could have controlled this huge task from seizure to redistribution. By the time the processing and the redistribution of confiscated Jewish assets could have begun in earnest in the late summer and the early autumn of 1944, the military situation had begun to deteriorate rapidly. Fighting erupted in Hungary and total collapse was only a few months away.

Lack of a Homogenous Legislative Framework

The first comprehensive law on Jewish property was the Prime Minister's Decree 1600/1944 on the "declaration and seizure of the wealth of Jews." It was dated April 14 and became effective on April 16, ordering Jewish citizens to report to the state all their movable and immovable property, which the state then sequestered.[5] During the next few months this decree became the "legislative basis" for robbing the Jews of their wealth, since ministerial decrees regulating minor issues related to the treatment of Jewish assets falling under their control were, as a rule, made in reference to and based on Decree 1600/1944. The implementation of the decree was hindered by several obstacles. In April there was hardly any consultation occurring between the Ministry of Finance and the Ministry of the Interior about their plans, and the confusion was further heightened because—while the secret decree of the Ministry of the Interior on the ghettoization issued on April 7 ordered securities, precious metal, and cash in Jewish ownership to be surrendered at branches of the Hungarian National Bank (HNB)[6]—Decree 1600/1944 designated different financial institutions for the same purpose. Thus only two HNB branches were willing to accept Jewish assets from the authorities acting in accordance with the plan adopted by the Ministry of the Interior, because they were supposed to be acting in accordance with the concept adopted by the Ministry of Finance.[7] But the delay in adopting Decree 1600/1944 was a much bigger problem: ghettoization in Carpatho-Ruthenia started on the same day as Decree 1600/1944 became effective, that is on April 16, so there was nothing left to do but to go ahead with rapid looting as ordered by the secret decree of the Ministry of the Interior. But even if the police, the gendarmerie, and public administration authorities had wanted to respect the new decree, Jews who had been forcibly removed from their homes, forced to leave their valuables behind, and crowded into ghettos would have been physically unable to carry it out, in other words, they were in no position to make an inventory, appraise, deposit, and declare their own assets. The authorities could not offer adequate protection for the assets left behind, and many of these were simply stolen or destroyed. The fiasco could not be concealed. At the June 1, 1944, meeting of the Council of Ministers, Minister of Finance Lajos Reményi-Schneller said,

> Most of these [ghettoized] Jews could not declare their wealth at all, and on the other hand the assets (valuables and movable property) that were left at the flats, shops, warehouses, etc., of Jews who had been relocated from their homes were left uncared-for and unattended, and so some of these—according to the reports of various financial directorates—perished.[8]

Once the process of ghettoization and deportation began, Hungarian and German soldiers began to move into Jewish houses and apartments without any authorization, while the looting of abandoned property became commonplace among the general public throughout the country.[9] The state financial administration network (the institutional network of the so-called financial directorates), which was the only official apparatus possessing the personnel and organizational structure capable of performing an orderly and efficient confiscation of Jewish property and assets, was assigned only the duty of collecting registration forms for the Jewish assets. The Council of Ministers decided only at the beginning of May to invest in the Board of Excise oversight of Jewish property and assets confiscated in the course of ridding the country of its Jews. On May 15, State Secretary of the Ministry of the Interior László Endre instructed all agencies subordinate to his Ministry to report all Jewish property in their custody to the nearest financial directorate headquarters and to initiate the process of delivering them to the appropriate authorities.[10] On the same day, the minister of finance issued two, characteristically contradictory decrees regarding the handling of Jewish property and assets.[11] According to the first decree, inventories were to be taken, then the confiscated items sorted by category and placed in the appropriate warehouse; any cash and stocks were to be deposited temporarily in secured accounts opened under the name of the person from whom these had been expropriated, in the case of stocks, to the Financial Institution Center. Theoretically, objects of high value were to be transported to Budapest as soon as possible, while money of unknown origin was to be deposited in a separate postal savings bank, to account number 157,875: "Deposit Account for Cash of Unknown Individuals, Budapest."

Reményi-Schneller's second decree of that day reflected the confusion that permeated the entire process of confiscation and liquidation of Jewish assets: in order to prevent state financial agencies from becoming overwhelmed with the burden of this task, he instructed officials under his jurisdiction to take delivery of only the most valuable assets, leaving the rest under the supervision of local administrative authorities, who were also charged with the task of preparing the inventories. Financial officials were only to conduct spot checks on the entire procedure.[12] It is not difficult to identify the impetus behind the flurry of decrees that emanated from the two ministries on May 15: this was the date on which the mass deportation of Jews began. These two ministries, as those most responsible for this undertaking, were aware that the some 200,000 policemen, gendarmes, civil servants, and state financial officials involved nationwide in the operation had to manage the seized Jewish property in accordance with contradictory and/or inadequate decrees.

On May 20, Endre once again pressed local administrators for their cooperation; as a result, by the end of the month it looked as if central government authorities had finally caught up with the ghettoization of Jews that had been taking place on the ground for several weeks. An efficient division of labor had apparently emerged: the police and gendarmerie took responsibility for maintaining law and order, while state financial administrators supervised the delivery and handling of Jewish assets and property. Law enforcement organizations provided assistance to state administrators when the latter proved unable to contend with the growing influx of expropriated Jewish wealth. In reality, during the months of April and May, city and village officials, local police officers, and gendarmes did as they pleased with confiscated Jewish property.

This patchwork system, which sometimes varied from deportation zone to deportation zone, county to county, city to city, and even village to village, often produced a fait accompli, which subsequent legislation simply could not standardize. Progress toward the ultimate objective nevertheless continued unabated: Jews were identified, rounded up, segregated, deported, and fleeced of their possessions. However, the chaotic and inconsistent manner in which this was accomplished made it unlikely that confiscated Jewish assets and property could retain its previous degree of economic and financial potential.

Rivalry among Different Government Authorities

The successful fulfillment of the government's plans was significantly hindered by the clashes of competence among different authorities from the highest levels (ministries) to the lower echelons (local administrative bodies and law enforcement agencies). A good example of this phenomenon is the formation and the operation of the so-called Turvölgyi-bureau. In order to restrain the chaos at last, and to coordinate the work of different ministries, Reményi-Schneller proposed to the Council of Ministers in early June to set up a government commissioner's office to "implement solutions concerning the material and financial affairs of Jews in accordance with a standard set of principles," and to give it control over Jewish assets. According to Reményi-Schneller it was necessary to "make it possible for ministers to delegate those tasks, which up until now constituted the exclusive competence of individual ministers pursuant to the relevant statutes."[13] It is not surprising that the Minister of Finance wanted the new government organization to be supervised by his Ministry: in effect Reményi-Schneller wanted to ensure that he would be in charge of the Aryanization process. Therefore, he nominated one of his subordinates as the government commissioner. This was Albert Turvölgyi, who was previously in charge of Aryanization measures in the liquor industry and had extensive experience in expropriation matters. The government accepted both the nomination and the report. But virtually nothing happened for nearly two months. Rival ministers became active and began to sabotage cooperation. Even though by mid-June Turvölgyi had already addressed some cases concerning Jewish wealth,[14] work of the Government Commissioner's Office to Solve the Material and Financial Affairs of the Jews did not essentially begin before mid-August. The decree meant to regulate the scope of the government commissioner's responsibilities did not become effective before July 23.[15]

Reményi-Schneller could not have been satisfied with the establishment of the new commission, since it precluded the realization of his plan to organize a supreme, supra-ministerial agency to deal with the issue of Jewish assets: as a rule, the commissioner was invested with the power to act only upon such matters placed under his authority by a competent governmental minister. In other words, Reményi-Schneller's proposal for a comprehensive concentration of powers had not been accepted. The opposition of certain ministries to initiatives emanating from the Ministry of Finance ultimately produced the feeble compromise of a new governmental commission with severely circumscribed authority.[16] The Turvölgyi Office began to function in earnest during the second half of August, though documentary evidence indicates that it became truly active only in September and October. However, even during these months this office possessed no real authority, ministerial agencies, local administrative offices, and, following the Arrow Cross seizure of power in October 1944, party organizations served as the source of all genuine decision-making regarding Jewish assets. Therefore, the commission led by Turvölgyi was a key player in theory, but in practice ended up a marginal participant in the economic annihilation of the Jews.

The other competent government body was called the Government Commissioner's Office for the Registration and Preservation of the Confiscated Works of Art of the Jews, and the painter Dénes Csánky was appointed to lead it. This commission was responsible for seizing and processing works of art owned by Jews and the decree establishing it provided a rather broad scope of authority for the fulfillment of its task.[17] Once again, however, practice departed from the theory and Csánky's commission regularly lost the clashes of authority it fought with rival bodies among the financial and military authorities.[18]

German Intentions

The fact that the significant Jewish wealth had also whetted the appetites of the Nazis greatly impeded the Hungarian government in its attempt to expropriate Jewish property. Despite the fact that the Germans did not intervene in the details of the state-organized looting, they seized every opportunity to divest Jews of their property, and despite their limited opportunities, the Germans gained direct access to a disproportionately large amount of expropriated Jewish assets. The leading characters of the looting were the members of the Eichmann-Sondereinsatzkommando and Himmler's personal emissary, *SS-Obersturmbannführer* Kurt Becher. The most blatant and large-scale example of the Nazis' organized expropriation of Jewish wealth was their seizure of the Weiss Manfréd Works, Hungary's largest industrial complex. This gambit, which provoked a Hungarian government crisis was committed by Becher. The Weiss Manfréd affair was not the only example of Becher's looting the Hungarian Jewish wealth. In the course of his activity in Budapest he seized Jewish assets representing $1–3 million. After the Arrow Cross Party came to power in October 1944, in the framework of the Nazi "evacuation," that is, the wholesale robbing of the Hungarian economy, approximately 600,000 tons of crops, commodities, industrial equipment, vehicles, livestock, and raw materials flowed into the Reich, about one fifth of which was originally Jewish property.[19] The organized plunder of Jews was the source of much greater conflict between the Hungarian and German authorities than was the deportation and extermination of a half million human beings.

We have to add that contrary to the intentions of the collaborating government the deportations resulted in serious problems for the economy, the public welfare, and health-care. Even before the start of the deportations, Minister of Industry Lajos Szász identified the primary concern of his government: "An exhaustive and permanent resolution of the Jewish question will not and cannot be allowed to damage the Hungarian economy. The government considers issues relating to productivity and the continuity of productivity to be of greater importance than resolution of the Jewish question."[20] The deportation of Jews nonetheless crippled the economy in certain areas of the country. Minister of the Interior Andor Jaross wrote the following to Minister of Trade and Transportation Antal Kunder: "The closing of Jewish shops in Carpatho-Ruthenia has caused serious disruption to the provision of basic consumer goods, because a significant portion of the merchants operating in the region are Jews."[21] At an April 26 meeting of the Board of Directors of the Financial Institution Center, one board member stated that as a result of the ghettoization of Jews in Gendarmerie District VIII (Kassa), "the economy [in the region] has ground to a halt."[22] The problems could not be concealed from the Germans either. At the end of July, Plenipotentiary of the Greater German Reich and Minister in Hungary

Edmund Veesenmayer reported the following to the Wilhelmstrasse: "Generally speaking, production figures have dropped due to the elimination of the Jews, to different degrees in the various sectors."[23] The various economic hardships (which we do not detail here due to lack of space) did not effect only those territories in which the number of the Jewish population was high. In Carpatho-Ruthenia, the number of Jewish inhabitants reached 9.1 percent in 1941, that is, almost twice as high as the national average (4.9%).[24] In Jász-Nagykun-Szolnok County, Jews made up only 1.8 percent of the whole population; however, the ghettoization and deportation of the relatively small community resulted in significant economic and production difficulties.[25]

In spite of the above-mentioned hardships, the government was able to redistribute a small part of the Jewish wealth. However chaotic the process of redistribution, huge piles of clothes, furniture, other personal belongings, numerous apartments, houses, large stocks of merchandise, and so forth were allocated by different central and local authorities to the Gentile population throughout Hungary. Receipt of Jewish property from these governing bodies was only one way to acquire such assets. Many people took advantages of the Jewish owners' absence and the government's incapability to safeguard the assets to expropriate the "unclaimed" property. In spite of the fragmentary central redistribution of the Jewish wealth, within a few short months hundreds of thousands of Gentiles increased the amount of property and valuables in their possession. In some cases this redistribution led to serious tensions after the war between returning survivors and the Gentile population. In addition to the tragic economic situation of the destroyed country this could be considered one of the main reasons why the restitution of the Jewish assets did not occur immediately after 1945. It is probably also one of the obstacles that hindered the Hungarian society and intelligentsia from facing the past and the realities of the Holocaust.

Notes

1. The May 17 report of the *Kolozsvári Estilap* (Evening paper of Kolozsvár) on Jaross's speech is cited by Jenő Lévai, *Zsidósors Magyarországon* (Jewish fate in Hungary) (Budapest: Magyar Téka, 1948), 138 (hereafter Lévai, 1948).

2. Letter of Archbishop Jusztinián Serédi to the bishops, July 9, 1944. Elek Karsai, ed., *Vádirat a nácizmus ellen* (Indictment against Nazism), vol. 3 (Budapest: Magyar Izraeliták Országos Képviselete, 1967), 118 (hereafter Karsai, 1967).

3. Bill on the exclusion of Jews from the Hungarian public and economic life, May 19, 1944. Ilona Benoschofsky and Elek Karsai, eds., *Vádirat a nácizmus ellen* (Indictment against Nazism), vol. 2 (Budapest: Magyar Izraeliták Országos Képviselete, 1960), 69–75 (hereafter Benoschofsky and Karsai, 1960).

4. Draft decree on the exclusion of the Jews from the Hungary's economic life, June 2, 1944 (Benoschofsky and Karsai, 1960, 152–55).

5. Prime Minister's Decree 1600/1944 on the declaration and seizure of the wealth of Jews, April 14, 1944. *Budapesti Közlöny* (Official journal of the Hungarian government) (April 16, 1944).

6. Minister of the Interior's Secret Decree 6163/1944 on the designation of the place of residence of the Jews, April 7, 1944. Ilona Benoschofsky and Elek Karsai, eds., *Vádirat a nácizmus ellen* (Indictment against Nazism), vol. 2 (Budapest: Magyar Izraeliták Országos Képviselete, 1958), 124–27 (hereafter Benoschofsky and Karsai, 1958).

7. Memorandum of the Legal Department of the Hungarian National Bank, October 19, 1946. The document is in the possession of the Jewish Heritage of Hungary Public Endowment. See also János Botos, *The History of the Hungarian National Bank* (Budapest: Presscon, 1999), 269–70.

8. Minutes of the meeting of the Council of Ministers, June 1, 1944 (Benoschofsky and Karsai 1960, 145).

9. A few selected examples: Head of the Excisemen's General Commissioner's District Sándor Madarász in Balassagyarmat reported 800 local residents to the police for looting properties left behind by Jews. Árpád Tyekvicska, ed., "Adatok, források, dokumentumok a balassagyarmati zsidóság holocaustjáról" (Data, sources and documents on the Holocaust of the Jews in Balassagyarmat), in *Nagy Iván Történeti Kör évkönyve* (Yearbook of the Iván Nagy historical society) (Balassagyarmat: Nagy Iván Történeti Kör, 1995), 111. The general commissioner of the excisemen of Csorna was forced to lock up the most valuable Jewish properties in a separate warehouse "due to frequent break-ins occurring in the ghetto." Report by General Commissioner of the Excisemen of Csorna Jenő Takács, January 13, 1945, in *Dokumentumok a zsidóság üldöztetésének történetéhez* (Documents on the history of the persecution of the Jews), ed. Ágnes Ságvári (Budapest: Magyar Auschwitz Alapítvány – Holocaust Dokumentációs Központ, 1994), 24. The uncontrolled looting in Beregszász was conspicuous even for the Germans. The report sent to Berlin by Plenipotentiary of the Greater German Reich and Minister in Hungary Edmund Veesenmayer on June 27, 1944, contained information obtained from Hungarian police sources and reported that the local population had broken into and looted 80–100 of the 800 real estate properties owned by Jews in Beregszász. Randolph L. Braham, ed., *The Destruction of Hungarian Jewry. A Documentary Account*, 2 vols. (New York: World Federation of Hungarian Jews, 1963), I, 615. When stocktaking officials began to appraise Jewish properties in Munkács, they often found empty rooms with chattels (furniture, bedclothes, furnishings, and personal belongings) already removed by neighbors (Lévai, 1948, 102). In June, the chief notary of Huszt complained that "staff numbers at the Excise Board are insufficient, therefore, inventorying and the emptying of flats will require at least another six months, during which time there will be a vast number of thefts and break-ins. A huge number of flats have been burglarised already. The gendarmerie is continuously receiving reports of break-ins, but they are unable to respond due to insufficient staff numbers" (Letter from the Huszt chief notary to the governor's Commissioner of Carpatho-Ruthenia. Magyar Országos Levéltár (Hungarian National Archives – HNA), I-series, Reel 11).

10. Minister of the Interior's Secret Decree 31.100/1944 XXI. res. May 15, 1944. HNA, I-series, Reel 11.

11. Minister of Finance's Decree 147.310/1944 VI on the taking over of the Jews' movables seized by the administrative authorities and the inventory of the abandoned Jewish apartments, shops, warehouses, May 15, 1944. HNA I-series, Reel 143. See also Minister of Finance's Decree 147.379/1944 VI on the safeguarding of the property of Jews isolated and allocated in collection camps, May 15, 1944. HNA, I-series, Reel 11.

12. Ibid.

13. Minutes of the meeting Council of Ministers, June 1, 1944 (Benoschofsky and Karsai, 1960, 146).

14. Summary Regarding the Government Commissioner's Office to Solve the Material and Financial Affairs of the Jews (Hungarian Jewish Museum and Archives, I 8/4).

15. Minutes of the meeting of the Council of Ministers, July 19, 1944 (Karsai 1967, 218–21).

16. Prime Minister's Decree 2650/1944 on regulating of certain aspects of the Jewish wealth, July 21, 1944. *Budapesti Közlöny* (July 23, 1944).

17. Prime Minister's Decree 1830/1944 on the registration and the preservation of the confiscated works of art the Jews, May 22, 1944. *Budapesti Közlöny* (May 25, 1944).

18. For details, see Gábor Kádár and Zoltán Vági, "Művészet és népirtás: A Műkincskormánybiztosság működése és a magyar zsidó műtárgyak elrablása, külföldre hurcolása, 1944–1945" (Art and genocide: The operation of the commission on works of art and the plundering and carrying off of works of art owned by Hungarian Jews), in *Küzdelem az igazságért: Tanulmányok Randolph L. Braham 80. születésnapjára* (Struggle for the Truth: Studies on the occasion of Randolph L. Braham's 80th birthday), eds. László Karsai and Judit Molnár (Budapest: Mazsihisz, 2002), 317–55 (hereafter Karsai and Molnár, 2002). See also Christian Gerlach and Götz Aly, *Das letzte Kapitel: Realpolitik, Ideologie und der Mord an den ungarischen Juden, 1944–1945* (Stuttgart: Deutsche Verlags-Anstalt, 2002), 186–239.

19. For the activity of Becher and the evacuation, see Gábor Kádár and Zoltán Vági, *Self-Financing Genocide: The Gold Train, the Becher Case and the Wealth of Hungarian Jews* (Budapest-New York: Central European University Press, 2004), Part II.

20. As quoted in the investigative material of Mátyás Matolcsy in Történeti Hivatal (Office of history), Budapest, V-117.742

21. Jaross to Kunder, June 7, 1944 (Benoschofsky and Karsai, 1960, 151).

22. Minutes of meeting of the Financial Institution Center, April 26, 1944. HNA, Reel 24.463.

23. Veesenmayer's report to the German Ministry of Foreign Affairs, July 29, 1944. Gyula Juhász, Ervin Pamlényi, György Ránki, and Loránt Tilkovszky, eds., *A Wilhelmstrasse és Magyarország: Német diplomáciai iratok Magyarországról 1933–1944* (Wilhelmstrasse and Hungary: German diplomatic documents from Hungary 1933–1944) (Budapest: Kossuth, 1968), 895.

24. József Kepes, ed., *A zsidó népesség száma településenként, 1840–1941* (The Jewish population by settlements, 1840–1941) (Budapest: Központi Statisztikai Hivatal, 1993), 30–31.

25. For the details see László Csősz, "Őrségváltás? Az 1944-es deportálások közvetlen gazdasági-társadalmi hatásai" (Changing of the guard? The direct economic and social consequences of the 1944 deportations), Karsai and Molnár, 2002, 75–98.

Ordinary Deaths in Times of
Genocide and Forced Assimilation:
Patterns of Jewish Mortality in Budapest (1937–1960)

Victor Karády

Studies dedicated to the Jewish catastrophe in Hungary rarely consider the demographic consequences of anti-Jewish laws and Nazi rule, except for the estimation of the global losses in local Jewry.[1] I have several times attempted to look into problems of the specific development of Jewish mortality as compared to that of non-Jews in the country before and even after the Shoah.[2] Rather than summarizing the results of these analyses of comparative historical socio-demography, this study will focus exclusively on inner-Jewish patterns of mortality as recorded in some published but hitherto unexplored data and large number of documents in the records of the Budapest Neolog (Conservative) Community, in addition to, cursorily, in archival records of other Jewish communities in the city or its suburbs. Unfortunately the records of the relatively small—but by itself sizable—Autonomous Orthodox Jewish Community could not be consulted for my study. Thus, all data cited from inter-Jewish sources represent an underestimation of between 3 and 6 percent of the facts to which they refer.[3]

Though the dreadful balance sheet of the Shoah in the Hungarian capital looms large in my discussions—notably as to the utter unreliability (that is, crass under-registration) of the numbers of victims—the thrust of this study will lie in the sociological interpretation of data derived from various registrations available. By their quantitative scope and qualitative contents, death records are indeed by far the richest serial testimony about the victims and the survivors, as well as the constrained living conditions to which the latter were subject following their liberation. And this constitutes the central topic of my study: the relative 'quasi-normality' of Jewish mortality patterns up to 1944 and, after the tragic break during the months of Arrow Cross mob rule, their paradoxically increasingly aggravated "distortion" determined by trends of post-Shoah emigration and the pressure of the Communist Party's assimilation program.

Ordinary Deaths and the Shoah

Table 1 offers an overall outline of the evolution of mortality in Budapest. These religion-specific data indeed appear to indicate a slight growth of the number of Jewish deaths during the first years of the anti-Semitic legislation as compared to the years immediately preceding. The trend is manifest both in the official statistics and in the community records and—as in the last column of Table 2—in the number of burials attested. But this growth hardly continued in 1943 according to the same calculations, and certainly not in terms of the proportion of Jewish deaths among all the deceased (rising from 16.7 percent in 1935–38 to 18.9 percent in 1939–42, and to 18.2 percent in 1943). Still, these figures do suggest some agitation, even if not decisively, during the post-1938 period if we consider two extra-demographic factors significantly diminishing the number of Jews in the capital's population. First the high numbers of the conversion movement must be mentioned. Centered in Budapest, conversion removed some 3,089 people from Judaism in 1935–39; 9,685 in 1938–39; and 7,126 in the following four years— totaling 19,900 people.[4] Thus, close to one tenth of the Jewish popula- tion was withdrawn from those exposed to the risk of dying in the capital city. Here we have the main reason why the Jewish share in the popula- tion decreased by exactly 10 percent from 1930 (204,371) to 1941 (184,453).[5] Furthermore, the 1941 census of Christians identified 17 per- cent (mostly recent converts) as legally qualified as Jewish by the 1939 Second Jewish Law.[6] But Jewish numbers were further diminished by the periodic mobilization of Jewish males into forced labor service as well, mostly in the provinces or on the Russian frontline, resulting, in the latter case, in an enormous number of fatalities. The "drafting effect" must have been felt among non-Jews sent to the front as well, hence the much lower number of deaths after 1939 in the Gentile population as compared to former years.

As for Jews, the decreasing numbers of those in the city and the growing numbers of the dead recorded in Budapest clearly bear the mark of ever-worsening living conditions under discriminative legislation up to 1943. But there was no dramatic increase until 1944. Hereafter, though, our data obviously fail to reflect the dire reality. Indeed, monthly death records of both the Chevra Kadisha (burial society) services and the city administration demonstrate the relative normality of Jewish death rates until March 1944, followed by four months of an ever-growing number of deaths. The trend was reversed in August, which saw a temporary relaxation of danger for surviving Budapest Jews.[7]

Among other things, this situation was due to significant political and military changes. The deportations had been officially halted in early July, the number of exemptions from anti-Jewish measures granted by government services[8] was extended, the approach of the Red Army promised forthcoming liberation, all the more so given that Romania had changed sides on August 23, 1944. The government had already shed some of its radically anti-Semitic members on August 7, and on August 29 a new government took office, charged with negotiating a peace treaty. The decrease in the number of Jewish deaths appeared to be particularly relevant for those committing suicide, a sensitive indicator of situational mortality.[9] But August was also the last month for which public death records provide information (community data being available for September as well).

The overall yearly data officially gathered later show a real increase in deaths during the two last war years, equal to a doubling of both Jews and non-Jews, but also—and much more notably—a crass under-representation of Jews among the dead (with only 22 percent of Jews among those in 1944 and a mere 17 percent in 1945). Manifestly, this is only a pale reflection of the devastations staged by Arrow Cross (*Nyilas*) murder squads, the horrendous existence of survivors in the Budapest Ghetto, and the siege of Budapest. Many fatalities of these months (whether Jewish or Gentile) disappeared without proper burial, and if formally buried, many escaped any recording in the absence of operational administrative services. Under-registration of casualties must have been apparently the rule in late 1944 and early 1945, before the reestablishment of municipal and community administrations in charge of death records. Still these data are not completely disconnected from reality. One can presume that the majority of losses suffered by Budapest Jewry were actually deportees, especially the victims of death marches to the West under SS or Arrow Cross guards in late 1944.

In any case, the data for 1946 appear to provide a much more realistic picture of the new situation. Significantly enough, the number of deaths for Gentiles (more than 15,000) was at the level of the years preceding the collapse of the old regime. This implies, not surprisingly, a considerably increased mortality since at that time the global population had been considerably diminished from its prewar size due to the war losses, expatriations, state-organized flights from the Soviet army, and the prolongation of the captivity of many prisoners of war.[10] In the meantime, Jewish deaths recorded for 1946—among them many casualties of the Shoah subsequently inscribed in Chevra Kadisha books—hardly exceeded one half of the pre-1944 numbers. Since there are no precise estimates about the real size—obviously in constant flux[11]—of the Jewish cluster concerned, it is impossible to determine the population base of the count of recent deaths. Though actual Jewish death rates may have increased as well, as in the general population, as compared to times of peace, the dramatic decrease in the annual number of Jewish deaths in the city convincingly renders the tragic fact—confirmed by other testimonies[12]—that the Jewish population in Budapest had been reduced globally (not denomination specific) to half its former size due largely, if not exclusively, to the Shoah. By 1946 indeed the ultimately negative outcome of various migration trends following liberation (return of surviving deportees, concentration of provincial survivors in Budapest, emigration to Palestine, departures to the West) weighed heavy in the demographic balance sheet of surviving Jewry in the capital.

From 1947 onward only Neolog Chevra Kadisha data systematically record the development of Jewish mortality in the capital, while global counts of deaths also continued to be published (with an interruption only during the worst years of the Stalinist terror). Now these figures for Jews appear to be surprisingly high, so that we must attempt to interpret their remarkable continuity. It is indeed much easier to account for the regular though modest rising global numbers of the dead. This must simply reflect the combined outcome of the fast growth of the city population (from 1,590,000 in 1949 to 1,805,000 in 1960[13]) owing both to the administrative extension of its territory in 1950 and the pressure of forced urbanization of large rural masses implemented by the Communist planners, as well as the continued but much slower general decrease of mortality rates.

Thus, the number of burials arranged by the Chevra Kadisha, instead of declining (as expected, under Communist pressure) during the first decade of Communist rule (after 1948), indeed *significantly exceeded* (by some 15 percent) the numbers recorded before the final takeover (1947–48). The 1947–48 postwar bottom level was reached again only in 1960.

It is legitimate to ask whether these figures indicate a deterioration of living conditions for surviving Jewry. However, the data on increased Jewish death rates contradict other data related to mortality in these years, indicating that the general population benefited from the extension and even the improvement of sanitation and medical care achieved by the new regime. The issue of whether the Jewish population increased during those years is more controversial and may yield some, if only partial, clues to explain the rising death figures. On the one hand legal and illegal emigration to Israel and the West before 1950 and following the 1956 uprising obviously decreased the Jewish population in Budapest as in the country as a whole. On the other hand, however, immigration to the city from the provinces and even from former Hungarian territories (Transylvania and Slovakia, above all) continued to boost the local Jewish population. Thus the number of Jews may not have undergone further global losses as a consequence of these contradictory movements, or may even have somewhat grown since 1960—at least in the extended sense inclusive of affiliated groups.[14] But this latter hypothesis remains uncertain pending further research.

In any case, while all other indices of Jewish community affiliation display a brutal collapse in the early Communist years, the number of deaths handled by the Chevra Kadisha tended to stay on its post-Shoah level or even to increase. Thus, in a way, Chevra Kadisha records offer the richest (if not the best) set of information about Jews in the capital who survived and remained in their homeland. However, if sheer numbers continue to be comparable, all other indicators suggest that the collective profile of those buried by Chevra Kadisha services differed vastly from other Jews identifiable in the post-Shoah period.

A technical difference, perhaps a major one, concerns the scope of the geographical provenance of the dead. The destruction of most provincial communities in the Shoah, due to the much more severe losses in life endured by Jews as a consequence of full-scale deportations, generated an intensive migration of many survivors from the provinces to Budapest (and out of the country) observable in the late 1940s, the 1950s, and even after 1956. In addition there were frequent transfers of provincial deceased to one of the Budapest Jewish cemeteries, which continued to operate,[15] especially when there was a demand for ritual burial. Most of the Jewish cemeteries in the provinces were abandoned following the disappearance of communities, hence the frequency of such transfers.

This hypothetical connection seems to be indirectly confirmed by the fact that the proportion of those born in Budapest among the deceased recorded in Chevra Kadisha files, though it varied somewhat with a peak in 1946, did not significantly grow from 1937 to 1960 and remained on the whole rather low (see Tables 3A and 4), in spite of the otherwise probable increase of the locally born or indigenous Jewish population. In 1930, Jews constituted by far the most "locally rooted" part of the Budapest population (44.4 percent against only 36 percent of Gentiles born in the city).[16] Up to the Shoah there is no reason to hypothesize any decrease of this proportion. After 1944, we have no data on the dead in this respect, but records on married couples do not show any diminution of the proportion of those of local origin. Among brides and bridegrooms enrolled on marriage registers of the Budapest Neolog Community in 1946, 43 percent were born in the city. A couple of years later, in 1950–66 the comparable figure jumped up to 54.4 percent.[17] It is reasonable to suppose that the same trend of "inrootedness" applied to the cluster of those ritually buried during these years. If this is true, the persistently low proportion of Budapest-born deceased of the total taken care of by the Chevra Kadisha must be attributed to provincial dead to whom the last honors were paid in a Jewish cemetary of the capital. But the most spectacular differences appear to be linked to the sharply increasing age of those buried by the Chevra Kadisha.

Those in the burial society's records tended to be old, indeed ever older with the passage of time. Even before the Shoah a very small and declining number (from 8 to 4 percent between 1937 and 1943) of deceased below thirty years of age were taken care of by the Chevra Kadisha. At the same time the share of those above seventy grew from less than one third to more than two fifths among the buried (see Table 3A) This was in clear contrast to general trends, since the comparable proportions were much higher among Gentiles: in 1937 as much as 29 percent for the young, but a mere 20 percent for the post-seventy age group.[18] The year 1946 represents an exception with an unprecedented high proportion of young Jewish dead and a low ebb of the elderly. This probably transitory reversal of the trend may be imputed to the dual impact of the provisional freedom regained by surviving Jews to assert identity unimpeded by Nazi pressures and yet not influenced by Communist pressures, as well as the need to bury belatedly many victims of the Shoah by mourning families, irrespective of their actual degree of traditionalism or commitment to Orthodoxy.

Ritual burial in such cases could signify the liberation from oppression and a symbolic satisfaction to honor those who had been murdered for simply being Jewish. But the ageing process of the ritually buried continued much more drastically under Communism, so that by the 1950s the absolute majority (56 percent in 1954 and 67 percent in 1960) of the Chevra Kadisha clientele belonged to the over seventy group, while the younger cluster below thirty, let alone the infants, practically disappeared. Once again this stood in stark contrast to the general trend, which in 1960 still comprised 7 percent of all dead in the cluster below thirty and only 46 percent in the cluster beyond seventy.[19]

The soaring percentage of Chevra Kadisha burials after 1948 may indeed more directly be linked to various socio-demographic factors of the ageing process, such as the continued fall of birth rates, selective emigration, and age-specific Communist assimilationist pressures (affecting mainly the politically mobilized youth, but largely leaving aside the elderly) or, even more specifically, absence or weakness of anti-clerical (or anti-religious) drive in the control of burials (as against other strategic rites of passage).

Ageing entered into the collective destiny of post-Shoah Hungarian Jewry because of the long-term demographic depression due to declining birth rates, which had been ongoing since the nineteenth century. The anti-Jewish laws since 1938 immediately resulted in the sharp further collapse of Jewish fertility, especially in Budapest, with an annual number of births of 1,060 in 1939–44 as against 1,540 in 1938. [20] Thus the age pyramid of surviving Jewry was older in 1946 than ever before, with 19 percent of those above sixty years (following a reasonable estimation) as against 17 percent in 1941 and 13 percent in 1930. "Natural" ageing must have continued during the years of Stalinism, since the rare estimations of the number of births after 1945—a period of compensatory "recuperation" of "postponed" births and other demographic losses—hardly exceeded the low levels preceding Nazification (before 1939).[21]

But other 'non-natural' circumstances must have also contributed to the distortion of the age pyramid to the benefit of the elderly. Emigration before 1950 and after 1956 drew probably, as is usual in "strategic" population movements, more on the younger than the older generations.

More importantly, Communist assimilation, another strategic movement of social mobility, identity change, and collective self-assertion, must have also preferentially attracted Jews of the younger generation, conducive as it was to the rejection of Jewish ways, including obviously the public observance of community rituals, such as a burial by the Chevra Kadisha. Such display of religious identity and respect for confessional rules would not only contradict the often sincerely proffered secular convictions of Jewish Communists, but would also occasionally make public their Jewish connections and background, which they often did their best to delete from their lives. Thus, if the global Jewish cluster concentrated in Budapest, as defined by traditional or social criteria, did not experience a specifically drastic ageing process, those with families accepting or requiring a ritual burial (i.e., the most observant Jews) most probably did so.

Similarly, the ageing of the deceased on Chevra Kadisha records had to do with the different treatment of various rites of passage when they represented the end of life as compared to those oriented toward the future. Religious birth and marriage rituals came to be often most severely condemned, controlled, and occasionally castigated or stigmatized because they involved young people expected to contribute to the Communist constituency, not betray it by way of acceding to the call of "outmoded traditions," regarded as alien from or even hostile to Communist customs. The same inquisitorial rigor did not fully apply to burials. The deceased had in life often been inactive people beyond the reach of ideological control. No expectations could be raised about their political convictions and activities. Burials (unlike marriages) could be arranged without much publicity, escaping ideological qualifications. The supposed "infamy" in the Communist perspective of the recourse to ritual burials for relatives of Communist Party cadres could be easily shifted to the respect of old-fashioned desires of the deceased. For such adepts of the Communist faith the very attachment to ritual observance could also help to demonstrate the obsolete nature of religion (the famous Marxian "opium of the people"), inasmuch as it involved only the elderly; hence the relaxation of ideological vigilance and resistance against ritual burials by Jewish Communists and their Gentile political acolytes.

If ageing is such a central category for the study of post-Shoah mortality, this is because it commands directly most other socio-demographic characteristics observable about the dead inscribed into Chevra Kadisha files. Because of ageing it is hazardous to compare collective features of the dead in a chronological sequence, just as it is highly problematic to identify these features, which derive, let us not forget, from by far the most abundant source of information on surviving Jewry in their home country, with those of all survivors. The problem of interpretation of Chevra Kadisha data is due to the fact that the ageing of the dead may be attributed to at least three completely different factors: the natural ageing of the basic population owing to the decline of fertility or the emigration of the young, the normal demographic process of the shift of dying over the aged generations (extension of life expectancy) in the course of the modernization process, and—maybe most importantly in the historical juncture under scrutiny—the desertion from the community and its rituals (including burial services) by the young who grow up and make their career in the new regime hostile to (if not repressive against) religious affiliation. All these factors may have concomitantly influenced the ageing process observed in Chevra Kadisha books. Because we lack detailed information offering clues about their specific importance, we cannot propose here more than a tentative interpretation of the global socio-demographic characteristics of those cared for by the Budapest Chevra Kadisha services, grounded though as it may occasionally be on working hypotheses with some empirical foundations.

Table 2 offers the most direct and indeed most striking confrontation between the contents of various community and (until 1946 or 1950) public records (the latter being published only until 1946) as to rites of passage. Three important observations deserve to be stressed here.

The first one is of a purely demographic nature. The comparison of vital statistics displayed here presents a crude picture of a sharp demographic decline of Budapest Jewry from the time of the interwar years. (It is well known that the decline started in the early twentieth century in the cities and reached the whole of Hungarian Jewry by the mid 1920s.[22]) Yearly numbers of Jewish marriages and births, whatever registration one uses, hardly reached half of the annually buried in the first lines of Table 2. The demographic decline was clearly aggravated during the anti-Semitic legislation, let alone the year following the 1944–45 emergency situation. If there is a short period (1946–48) of recuperation, the resumption of the decline is again recorded in the data for the following years. Because the exodus of the young continued in

1956–57 and later, there is no reason to think that the trend has changed much ever since. Hungarian Jewry continued to retain the dubious privilege of remaining in the vanguard of "demographic modernization," which would definitely prevail in the whole country in the 1960s.

Second, Chevra Kadisha records are undisputedly the richest of all data mustered here, since they cover the whole period under scrutiny and their numbers, as mentioned above, remain high, indeed without any sizable decline from 1947 to 1960. This is much in contrast to other community records, where enrollments tended to disappear for births and marriages. In the decade after 1950 community records registered only a small proportion (one-seventh to one-tenth) of those in the post-war years. This can be clearly imputed to Communist assimilation, the first stage of which from the very beginning was secularization and the refusal to indulge in traditional community rituals, especially when they included some commitment for the future, as in births and marriages.

But, third, our data most strikingly demonstrate the well-proven historical experience of the secularization process. Far from being a Communist invention, it had been placed high on the agenda of Jewish life. Here again differences between death and other vital records are manifest. Contrary to the two other existential events referred to in Table 2, almost all Jewish deaths appear in both public and Chevra Kadisha records for each year. This is true even if we know that our data disregard Jewish deaths registered by the other communities in Budapest (those of Buda, Óbuda, and the Orthodox)—an under-representation of Jewish mortality in the capital, which was possibly compensated by some deaths from outside (occurring in the suburbs or even in provinces lacking Jewish cemeteries) and buried ritually by the Budapest Chevra Kadisha. For 1944 the numbers recorded by the Chevra Kadisha considerably exceeded those in public records. Though both evidently under-represented the real number of fatalities, the relatively inflated Chevra Kadisha numbers were caused by the belated registration of many deaths. Such belated registrations can be found in later years, too. On the whole, until the post-Shoah years, the refusal of ritual burial (dissimulation) remained marginal in Budapest Jewry, much in contrast to other vital events. Almost half of newly wed Jewish couples and children born before 1944 in the capital escaped any registration by the community. If we take into account other local community records, we can calculate this proportion as an estimation to three-fifths of the cases concerned.

Thus dissimulation was already far-reaching in the final years of the old regime. It attained, understandably, its maximum in 1944–45, the months of Nazi rule being unfavorable for the religious publicity of Jewish family events. Although there is some upsurge of the proportions of community recorded marriages and (though much less) births in the years following liberation, the dissimulation of such events continued henceforth to be the rule rather than an exception and, after the establishment of the Stalinist regime in 1948, the presence of such entries in community records became increasingly rare. The Communist taboo on matters Jewish held fast, especially when those matters concerned young people who were expected to make their way through the turmoil of Stalinism, the post-Stalinist thaw, Revolution, and the post-1956 predicament. Official secularism manifestly prevailed for these generations, even if all their members were not necessarily subdued by the mirage of Soviet-imposed socialism (and many even changed sides and faiths after 1953).

A number of other socio-demographic features of those registered in the Chevra Kadisha books are worthy of note. The gender distribution of the recorded dead has progressively switched from a clear male majority of two-thirds to a no less clear female majority. This cannot be simply explained by the prevailing sex ratios since there was already a slight female majority before the war (109 women for one hundred men in 1930 and 1941), though this imbalance increased considerably following the Shoah. In 1949 there were in the Jewish population of Budapest 146 women for one hundred men.[23] But the female majority among the deceased may have been connected to the usual trend of unequal ageing as well. Women living longer and ever longer, due to their lower mortality in all ages, may have made possible the growing difference between mean ages of men and women and resulted in a higher global rate of mortality of women (most of the dead being concentrated in the oldest generations of which women made up the large majority). Indeed, following Table 4, the proportion of elderly deaths (those beyond sixty years) was always significantly larger among women throughout the decades under scrutiny.

But the imbalance of sexes may have had equally to do with Communist practice partly imputable to the more intense secularization and assimilation of men. Until the end of the old regime, male adults were significantly more often professionally active than women. Thus, they could not avoid adjusting their life strategies to outside pressures, among them official secularism, hence the trend that more female than male deaths were reported to community authorities. Differences in degrees of assimilation between the two sexes are manifest in the far larger proportions of men with Magyarized names, as compared to women (Table 4). By 1960, close to two-thirds of men on Chevra Kadisha records bore Magyar surnames, while only one-tenth of women did so.[24]

The last remark leads us to the evaluation of the clientele of ritual burials regarding their absolute (though only presumable) level of "assimilation" or/and "modernization" via empirical indicators constructed to this effect. The survey's findings suggest the rather obvious conclusion, that those seeking ritual burial belonged to the relatively less "modernized" sectors of surviving Jewry. The very ageing process they display, with the quasi absence of young deceased after 1946, can implicitly be interpreted in this sense. The consistently low proportion of those born in Budapest, whether men or women, as compared to the much higher estimates of the ever growing general proportions of "indigenous" Jews also leads to the same conclusion, since urban affiliation (birth, residence) ranks among general factors of radical assimilation following all other indices available in this matter, such as mixed marriages, baptism, surname nationalizations, secular elite schooling, and so on.[25] In Table 4 the high proportions with Magyar names among Jewish couples married in 1949 show striking differences as compared to those enrolled in Chevra Kadisha files around this year. The gap between women and brides in Chevra Kadisha files appears to be particularly striking. Age differences between the dying and the married must obviously also be taken into account in the interpretation of such disparities, since most of the newlyweds are among the younger age groups, but the discrepancy between the two groups remains paramount.

Some differences, though far from being decisive ones, may also be observed between the occupational status of the ritually buried and that of the rest of surviving Jewry, the latter being illustrated by the professional distribution of Jewish men married to Jewish women in 1949 (Table 3C). More than a third of bridegrooms were indeed manual workers compared with one quarter or less among the deceased. Such differences may be of course also be in part due to the effect of ageing. Careers in middle-class occupations required time to be achieved, so that they were connected more often than not to an advanced age, especially under Communism, which forced in its initial stages a large-scale déclassement and otherwise disastrous social degradation of various formerly middle-class brackets. One can presume that such degradation concerned the young and the middle aged even more frequently than the elderly, who were often pensioners by that time. A similar process may have involved craftsmen and traders—who appear in much more sizable proportions in Chevra Kadisha files than among the bridegrooms: the Communist drive against such "economically independent" (stigmatized as "petty capitalists") obviously touched more intensely those still active than the older generation liable to become a client of the Chevra services.

It is curious to observe that the consequences of Communist-type social mobility of Jews in the public sector are hardly perceptible in our data. The share of civil servants among the ritually buried as among the bridegrooms is equally low, and not decisively higher among survivors as compared to those dying during the old regime. Age differences may also have affected the share of intellectuals and professionals, equally high (one-sixth to close to one-fifth) in both compared clusters. This certainly did not apply to members of the capitalist bourgeoisie, a significant proportion (over 10 percent) among the dead during the old regime, who practically disappeared for understandable reasons (whatever their age) from among the dead or the bridegrooms after 1946. Finally, ageing may be also connected to the high proportion of old age pensioners and other economically inactive groups (last two lines of Table 3) among those on Chevra Kadisha records.

Curiously, there is neither significant evolution in the residential distribution of those in the Chevra Kadisha files, nor a major gap between addresses of the post-Shoah dead and the newlyweds in 1949 (Table 3B). District VII of Budapest, which included the ghetto in late 1944, remained by all indications considered here the biggest Jewish quarter with around one-third of all registered on community files. Districts VI and VIII came second in almost all records, while Districts V and XIII remained generally somewhat less represented. This situation appears to rather strongly contradict the retrospective identification of addresses of Jewish homes following the 1991 survey. District XIII (Újlipótváros) emerged after 1948 as the most populous Jewish residential area of the capital. In 1951, only half of the local Jewish population apparently lived in the four central "old Jewish" districts and in 1970 only 38 percent,[26] as against 60 percent of Chevra Kadisha clients in 1954 or as much as 73 percent of those seeking ritual marriage in 1949 or 65 percent of couples ritually married in the following years. Though such dispersed data deserve further exploration in conjunction with the mobilization of other relevant comparisons, the residential distribution of those in community records remained more often concentrated in the old Jewish quarters than others. The most faithful to their community remained faithful, as a rule, to the traditional Jewish living quarters as well. This can be interpreted as much on the strength of their probable lesser social mobility and inclination to Communist assimilation as, concurrently, their attachment to places of worship consecrated by ancestors whose memory, whether victims of the Shoah or the passage of time, could not be disengaged from the streets where they had lived.

Lastly, the singular issue of the causes of death recorded in Chevra Kadisha and public files must be raised (as in Table 3D). The space is lacking here to analyze all the details that merit closer scrutiny in this context, all the more so because the relevant rich confession-specific data collection available until 1943 for Budapest could not be consulted. The comparison for 1946 of Jewish and Gentile mortality patterns, however, offers some interesting discrepancies, which should in a broader study also be related to differences of the age pyramid and the occupational structure of the two clusters. Both the two main sources of fatalities, heart diseases and cancer, appear to have been more prevalent among Jews than among Gentiles (33–43 percent as against 30 percent in 1946 according to various records), while infectious diseases occurred less frequently among Jews (15 percent as against 21 percent in 1946). The relatively better protection of Jews against the major health calamity of the age before antibiotics, tuberculosis, a quasi-permanent feature of Jewish mortality patterns even in earlier periods, is also particularly important in this context.

A provisional conclusion of this rather unusual investigation cannot but confirm the importance of further exploration of community archives containing precious untapped sources on patterns of collective behavior, which cannot be properly interpreted on the strength of other testimonies. As to more substantial results, Chevra Kadisha data show that a population such as Budapest Jewry was able to mobilize reserves even under the oppression of brutally discriminative legislation, unaffected, at least immediately, by a rapidly rising death toll, except when repression became—as it did in the winter months of 1944–45—properly murderous. But previous trends continued largely to prevail during the post Shoah transition, before Communist assimilation and secularization started to influence the relationship of the Jews to their community. Still, surviving Jews remaining in their homeland appeared much more often faithful to their community when dying than while alive, as far as other vital records of the Budapest Jewish community bear witness of their conduct. The Communist taboo left clearly its mark on the experience of the "remnants" as shown in the statistical data presented here.

Table 1

Yearly Number of Deaths by Religion in Budapest
(1935–1960, selected years and yearly averages)

	Non-Jewish		Jewish		
	All[27]	Budapest[28] Inhabitants	All[29]	Budapest[30] Inhabitants	in *Chevra Kadisha* records[31]
1935-38	16,218	12,966	3,252	?	2,764
1939-42	14,936	11,407	3,454	3,158	3,106
1943	15,526	12,108	3,460	3,235	3,138
1944	20,227	?	5,628	?	7,608 (5,174[32])
1945	41,059	37,281	8,305	8,747	6,440
1946	15,217	12,351	1,836	1,774	1,870
1947	15,673[33]				1,481
1948	15,785				1,457
1949-55	15,856				1,709
1956-59	16,121[34]				1,659
1960	16,677				1,487

Table 2

Jewish Existential Events and Rites of Passage in Budapest Public Records and Community Registers (1933-1960)[35]

	births			marriages			deaths			
	1	2	3=2/1[36]	4	5	6=5/4[37]	7	8	9=8/7[38]	10
	public rec.[40]	comm. rec.[41]		public rec.[42]	comm. rec.[43]		public rec.[44]	comm. rec.		burials[39]
1933-37	1,673	1,001	59.8	1,745	950	54.4	3,081	2,714	88.1	3,178
1938-43	1,126	582	51.7	1,427	779	54.6	3,422	3,039	88.8	3,537
1944	1,164	350	30.1	1,184[45]	251	21.2[46]	5,628	7,608	135.2	
1945	529	109	20.6	1,261	370[47]	29.3	8,305	6,440	77.5	
1946	1,401	504	36.0	2,304	1,658[48]	72.0	1,836	1,807	98.4	1,973[49]
1947	1,590[50]	569	35.8	1,793[51]	839	46.8		1,481		
1948	1,507	481	31.9	1,527	734	48.1		1,457		
1949	1,123	319	28.5	1,133	485	42.8		1,650		
1950	777	203	26.4	182[52]	183			1,700		
1951-60		75			65			1,658		

Table 3

Socio-Demographic Characteristics of Jewish Dead in Budapest (1937-1960, selected years in percentages)[53]

A. Demographics

	1937	1943	1946	1954	1960
men	62.6	55.5	51.9	41.1	43.0
with Magyar surname	17.1	15.2	26.7	27.7	21.8
below thirty years of age	7.6	4.2	14.2	1.4	0.8
above seventy years of age	31.3	42.4	26.6	55.5	66.5
before one year of age	2.3	1.4	3.5	0.8	—
those born in Budapest	25.3	21.7	32.6	27.6	25.7

B. Address in Budapest

	1937	1943	1946	1954	1960	Jewish marriages	
						1949[54]	1950-1966[55]
V. District	14.0	10.5	11.1	6.6	7.7	15.0	5.7
VI. District	14.4	11.0	14.1	17.4	16.0	16.5	13.7
VII. District	27.9	37.3	31.9	22.0	29.3	31.5	30.0
VIII. District	10.4	7.1	11.9	13.4	8.6	10.8	15.6
XIII. District	2.4	6.4	7.3	12.9	15.2	1.5	8.2
XIV. District	5.1	5.2	5.3	4.8	7.1	3.1	3.8
Other	25.8	22.5	18.4	22.1	16.1	21.6	23.0
all	100.0	100.0	100.0	100.0	100.0	100.0	100.0

Table 3

Socio-Demographic Characteristics of Jewish Dead in Budapest (1937-1960, selected years in percentages)

C. Occupational Status	1937	1943	1946	1954	1960	Married,[56] Jewish men, 1949[57]
Manual worker	10.4	19.1	18.4	22.1	26.4	334.1[57]
Craftsman, artisan	10.4	12.8	10.4	20.8	18.6	7.9
Trader (petty)	26.6	22.8	26.7	9.7	15.4	11.5
Employee[58] (industry, trade)	15.6	12.7	14.8	24.2	18.2	19.4
Civil servant	4.8	5.0	7.5	6.9	3.2	5.9
Intellectual, professional	19.0	14.7	15.9	14.5	16.4	18.7[59]
Capitalist, entrepreneur	12.5	10.8	5.0	1.0	0.9	2.4
Rabbi, cleric	0.7	2.1	1.2	0.7	0.9	—
All	100.0	100.0	100.0	100.0	100.0	100.0
N	289	702	479	289	220	252
N = in whole the survey	342	1,393	904	801	638	258
inactive	5.5	4.7	45.0	34.1	37.1	
pensioners	9.9	44.9	1.8	29.5	28.4	

Table 3

Socio-Demographic Characteristics of Jewish Dead in Budapest (1937-1960, selected years in percentages)

D. Main Causes of Death[60]	1937	1943	1946	1954	1960	1946[61] Jews	1946[61] non-Jews
War, persecution	–	0.3	15.5	–	–	–	–
Suicide	2.5	3.6	2.2	1.4	1.7	2.4	2.2
Heart diseases	19.4	20.0	21.1	25.7	16.7	28.6	20.0
Cancer	14.2	10.0	12.3	17.8	22.0	14.7	9.5
Pneumonia	11.4	3.0	8.3	5.1	3.6	5.9	8.6
Weakness	6.1	9.6	10.0	5.8	7.4	6.1	6.8
Tuberculosis	5.7	7.5	6.2	1.6	2.2	7.7	12.3
Apoplexy	5.5	5.1	8.6	13.2	7.6	6.6	5.6
Arteriosclerosis	5.1	1.1	3.9	7.1	10.7	1.8	0.8
Thrombosis	3.7	0.2	2.7	6.7	7.9	?	?
Accident	1.8	2.7	2.2	2.5	3.3	4.1	6.8
Kidney	5.6	2.3	4.3	3.0	5.0	2.8	2.0
Liver	0.4	0.7	1.0	1.9	2.4	0.9	1.1

Table 4
Some Gender Specific Characteristics of Jewish Dead in Budapest[62]
(in percentages)

		1937	1943	1946	1953	1960	married couples 1949[63]
sixty years	men	55.8	66.7	48.1	77.6	84.7	
and over	women	62.6	70.7	53.4	80.2	89.0	
born in	men	28.4	21.9	37.1	31.8	28.7	41.1
Budapest[64]	women	24.8	24.4	34.7	29.2	27.0	52.7
with Magyar	men	23.0	23.6	35.2	34.2	38.2	52.7
surname	women	7.0	5.3	16.2	10.8	9.3	28.8

Notes

1. For a demographic balance sheet of the Shoah in Hungary, see Tamás Stark, *Zsidóság a vészkorszakban és a felszabadulás után 1939–1955* (Jewry during the Holocaust and after liberation) (Budapest: MTA Történettudományi Intézet, 1995).

2. "Les Juifs sous les lois antisémites: Etude d'une conjoncture sociologique," *Actes de la Recherche en Sciences Sociales* 56 (March, 1985): 3–30; "Patterns of Apostasy in Surviving Hungarian Jewry after 1945," in *History Department Yearbook 1993* (Budapest: Central European University, 1993), 225–63; "Desperation and Resistance under the Rise of Fascism and Nazi Rule: Paradoxes of Jewish Mortality in Budapest, 1938–1945," in *Küzdelem az igazságért: Tanulmányok Randolph L. Braham 80. születésnapjára* (Struggle for the truth: Studies on the occasion of Randolph L. Braham's 80th birthday) (Budapest: Mazsihisz, 2002), 357–66; "A halálozási kockázat egyes felekezeti összetevői Magyarországon a második világháború előtt és alatt" (Some denominational components of the chances for death in Hungary before and during World War II), in *Kisebbségkutatás* (Minorities research) (Budapest, 2003); as well as relevant chapters in my book, *Túlélők és újrakezdők: Fejezetek a magyar zsidóság szociológiájából 1945 után* (Survivors and the beginners anew: Chapters from the sociology of Hungary Jewry) (Budapest: Múlt és Jövő, 2002).

3. If the records of the Budapest Neolog and Orthodox communities are totaled, registrations of births among the Orthodox for the years 1921–31 were 8.7%. The similar percentage for marriages was a mere 2.3%. But there were at that time three other smaller Israelite communities, which retain some of their records, within city limits in Buda, Óbuda, and Kőbánya, to which the much larger Újpest community was added after 1945 (IV. District). Thus data related to the Neolog community may constitute approximately 85–90% of the relevant information concerning law abiding religious Jews in the Hungarian capital.

4. See the yearly numbers with related data in my study, "Patterns of Apostasy in Surviving Hungarian Jewry after 1945," 225–63, especially 232.

5. *A zsidó népesség száma településenként, 1840–1941* (The number of Jews by settlement, 1840–1941) (Budapest: KSH, 1993), 26.

6. Ibid., 27.

7. For details of monthly death rates, see my "Desperation and Resistance," 363–64.

8. See "Egy naív ember bársonyszékben: Interjú Mester Miklóssal" (A naïve man in an armchair: An interview with Miklós Mester), *Valóság* (Reality) 10 (1981): 56–67.

9. Ibid., 364.

10. This can be gathered from the 1949 census data. In spite of vast movements of urbanization occurring since the very first years of the economic recovery organized by the new regime, Gentile sectors of the Budapest population (especially the Catholics) remained in 1949 (globally 1,489,000) and below their size in 1941 (globally 1,501,500). See *Magyarország településeinek vallási adatai, 1880–1949* (Data on religion for Hungarian settlements, 1880–1949) (Budapest: KSH, 1997), I, 14.

11. In the years after 1944 witnesses report a constant coming and going of deportees and émigrés, especially between DP (Displaced Persons) camps, Palestine, the West, and the home country, the overall trend being a departure from Hungary and also, for many surviving deportees, a refusal to return.

12. In the present territory (enlarged as compared to 1941) of Budapest, including many suburbs, the number of Jews recorded in the 1949 census was 101,252 as against 211,311 in 1941, a decrease of more than one half. These data disregard converts and those victims of Nazi persecutions who would not declare themselves as members of a Jewish religious community.

13. See *Budapest Lexikon* (Budapest: Akadémiai, 1993), II, 194.

14. Such as, for example, partners in mixed marriages and their offspring. In his 1999 survey, András Kovács found for the 66–75 year-old group as much as 49% of married Jews in mixed couples; that is, those whose mean date of marriage fell by and large in the first decade of Communist rule. See András Kovács, ed., *Zsidók Magyarországon: Az 1999-ben végzett szociológiai felmérés eredményeinek elemzése* (Jews in Hungary: Analysis of the results of the sociological survey of 1999) (Budapest: Múlt és Jövő, 2002), 19.

15. There were four Jewish burial grounds in Budapest before the Shoah—those at Salgótarjáni Road, Óbuda, Farkasrét in Buda, and Kozma Street in Pest. After intense activity in 1945 (more than a thousand burials) Salgótarjáni úti was closed down, while all the others continued to be used until the 1990s, though the bulk of Jewish deceased (well over 90%) were henceforth put to rest in the Neolog and Orthodox cemeteries at Kozma Street. (Data from the Chevra Kadisha services.)

16. *Budapest Székesfőváros statisztikai évkönyvei* (Statistical yearbooks of the capital) (*BSZSÉ*) *1933*, 61.

17. Survey results from community records. Even in the much smaller Buda community the proportion of newly ritually wed Jews born in Budapest was 45%, following similar survey results.

18. *BSZSÉ 1938*, 117–19.

19. See *Magyarország népesedése 1960* (Hungary's population growth 1960) (Budapest: KSH, 1962), I, 68.

20. See the detailed presentation and the sources of these data in *Túlélők és újrakezdők,* 86–89.

21. Ibid., 86–87.

22. In 1921–25, 9.8 marriages and 15.4 births were recorded per thousand as against 13.8 deaths per thousand. By 1926–30 the proportion of Jewish deaths decreased to 13.5 per thousand, but those of births decreased to a mere 12.9 and those of marriages to 8.8 per thousand. See data in *Magyar statisztikai szemle, 1936/9* (Hungarian Statistical Review, 1936/9), 765.

23. See my *Túlélők és újrakezdők,* 71.

24. On the general nature of such gender specific imbalance in matters of surname changes see my recent book written with István Kozma, *Családnév és nemzet: Névpolitika, névváltoztatási mozgalom és nemzetiségi erőviszonyok Magyarországon a reformkortól a kommunizmusig* (Family name and nation: Name-politics, name-changing, movement, and nationality conditions of power in Hungary from the age of reform to the age of communism) (Budapest: Osiris, 2002).

25. On all these connections between urbanization and modernization many examples are cited in my following studies, *Zsidóság, asszimiláció és polgárosodás* (Jewry, assimilation, and embourgeoisement) (Budapest: Cserépfalvi, 1997); *Zsidóság és társadalmi egyenlőtlenségek, 1867–1945* (Jewry and social inequalities, 1867–1945); *Történeti-szociológiai tanulmányok* (Historical-sociological studies) (Budapest: Replika könyvek, 2000); and above all *Önazonosítás és sorsválasztás: A zsidó csoportazonosság történelmi alakváltozásai Magyarországon* (Self-identification and the historical changes in group identification in Hungary) (Budapest: Új Mandátum, 2001).

26. See the study by János Ladányi, in *Zsidók a mai Magyarországon,* ed. Kovács, 83.

27. From the *BSZSÉ,* especially retrospectively for 1940–46 in *BSZSÉ 1944–46,* 32.

28. Ibid., regarding deaths occurring in Budapest or in the provinces.

29. As above in note 27.

30. As above in note 28.

31. Until 1944 the death records of the Budapest (Neolog) Israelite community were held in the Ritual Department (*Szertartási osztály*) of the Community Office. Post-1945 statistics are provided by the Chevra Kadisha services in the Community Office. I herewith extend my thanks for the access to both of these precious archival sources to the acting director of the Budapest Community Office and to the director of the Chevra Kadisha services.

32. Chevra Kadisha records.

33. Data for 1947–55 are found in *Magyarország népesedése 1956* (Hungary's population growth) (Budapest, KSH, 1958), 87. Overestimation by the subtraction of Chevra Kadisha data from the global number of deaths recorded during the period. (No religion-specific data is available.)

34. Data for 1956–60 in *Magyarország népesedése 1961* (Budapest, KSH, 1963/4), 136. Overestimation as in the preceding note.

35. Rounded yearly averages.

36. In percentages.

37. In percentages.

38. In percentages.

39. As registered in Jewish cemeteries in *BSZSÉ* till 1943.

40. From *BSZSÉ,* unless otherwise indicated.

41. Combined records of the Pest and the Buda (Neolog) communities, kept separately until 1948. There are no entries in the Buda community registers after 1948.

42. Homogamous Jewish marriages only (where both partners were Jewish). From *BSZSÉ,* unless otherwise indicated.

43. Only for the Neolog Pest community, unless otherwise indicated.

44. Dead registered in *BSZSÉ* prior to 1946.

45. For January–August 1944 and Jewish men in homogamous marriages only (*Budapest Székesfőváros Statisztikai havifüzetei* (Monthly statistical journals of the capital), 1944).

46. Estimation.

47. For the combined Pest (Neolog), Buda, and Újpest communities.

48. For the Pest (Neolog) and the Buda communities.

49. Combined overall data on burials for the Autonomous Orthodox Community in Budapest as well as for the other Jewish communities in the capital, including those of Pest, Buda, Óbuda, Újpest, and Kőbánya.

50. Manual count in the archival birth records of the Budapest municipal administration for 1947, 1948, 1949, and 1950 (until the end of April only for this year). Religion is not indicated in the records for later periods. Births of children with two Jewish parents only.

51. For 1947–50 by manual count from the marriage records of the Budapest Municipal Archives (homogamous Jewish marriages only).

52. Prior to the end of April 1950 only, with the inclusion of data for Újpest (IV. District).

53. Codification of data from community death records and Chevra Kadisha registries.

54. Survey data from the marriage records in the Budapest Municipal Archives. Homogametic Jewish marriages only, according to the address of the bridegroom.

55. Survey data from the marriage records of the Pest (Neolog) Community.

56. Survey results from the marriage records of the Budapest Municial Archives. Homogamous Jewish married couples only.

57. Includes a few farmers.

58. Includes employees with unspecified job catagories (*hivatalnok*).

59. Includes students.

60. In percentages of all deaths, calculated in each column separately for the year concerned. Only causes responsible for more than 2% of deaths are recorded in one of the years under survey.

61. Data from *BSZSÉ* 1948, 38.

62. Data from the codification of community records and Chevra Kadisha registers.

63. Survey results from the marriage records of the Budapest Municipal Archives. Homogamous Jewish marriages only.

64. Includes those born in the suburbs outside city limits.

Christian Help Provided to Jews of Northern Transylvania during World War II: As Revealed by the Jewish Weekly *Egység* (May 1946–August 1947)

Daniel A. Lowy

Introduction[1]

Most accounts of Christian help provided to persecuted Hungarian Jews during World War II relate to Trianon Hungary. A significant number of these studies, diaries, memoirs, and recollections are dedicated to the activity of diplomats accredited in Budapest, such as Raoul Wallenberg, Per Anger, Carl I. Danielsson, Valdemar Langlet, and Lars Berg of Sweden; Carl Lutz, Harold Feller, Ladislaus Kluger, and Péter Zürcher of Switzerland; Sampayo Garrido, Carlos Branquinho, and Gyula Gulden of Portugal; George Mandel-Mantello of El Salvador; Papal Nuncio Angello Rotta of the Vatican; Angel Sanz-Briz of Spain; and the self-proclaimed Spanish diplomat, in reality an Italian, Giorgio (Jorge) Perlasca.[2]

Diplomatic rescue did not, however, have much impact on Northern Transylvania and the province in general, as it almost exclusively took place in Budapest, where the legations of neutral countries were located. A few exceptions are Mihai Marina, the Romanian consul and his deputy, Ion Isaiu, in Nagyvárad (Oradea in Romanian), who were involved in rescue activities and informed the Swiss Red Cross about the inhuman living conditions in the ghetto of Nagyvárad.[3] Claudon Blanchart, the French consul in Kolozsvár (Cluj in Romanian), hid two Jewish women: high school teacher Lili Székely and her mother.[4] According to inconsistent sources, Colonel Mihai Guru,[5] the Romanian military attaché in Kolozsvár, offered his official car to transport dozens of Jews to the Romanian side of the border, but the journalist Ernő Marton is the only person known to have benefited from this service.[6]

Szabolcs Szita, a Hungarian scholar of the Holocaust, reviewed—in chronological order—the civil, diplomatic, and military rescue of Jews in 1944–45, providing a limited number of examples from Northern Transylvania.[7] He also gives accounts of Jews who had previously relocated from Transylvania to Trianon Hungary where they benefited from Christian help. Examples include Béla Purjesz, professor of medicine in Szeged, who started his career at Ferenc József University in Kolozsvár, and the Jewish wife of Áron Tamási, a noted writer from Transylvania.[8] Randolph L. Braham's monumental work, *The Politics of Genocide* (published in Hungarian as *A népirtás politikája*), includes several chapters on Christian help extended to Jews.[9] "Droplets in the Sea" is the evocative title of László Karsai's paper in which he reviewed the rare cases of rescue and Christian support throughout all of Hungary;[10] only a few cases, however, pertained to Hungarian-ruled Northern Transylvania.[11] In a 1998 study, Gábor Kádár and Zoltán Vági[12] researched the DEGOB[13] depositions and examined various forms of Christian help and solidarity. Of these, only a few relate to Northern Transylvania. Two cases focus on Szatmárnémeti (Satu Mare in Romanian), another two recall help offered to Jews in the ghetto of Nagyvárad, while the deposition of a thirty-one-year-old Jewish technician states that he arrived from the ghetto of Bárdfalva (Berbesti in Romanian) at the railway station of Máramarossziget (Sighetu Marmatiei in Romanian) where an unidentified man offered to hide him.[14] Six additional DEGOB testimonies describe the humane attitude of commanding officers of labor service companies: Imre Raksay, commander of a labor service company stationed in Szászrégen (Reghin in Romanian); Károly Kammermayer from Budapest; Lieutenant Pálmay, commander of Labor Service Company No. 109/319; József Gönczi from Nagybánya; Gálfy, a school teacher from Szatmárnémeti; and Ensign Ignác Nagy "from Transylvania."[15]

A relatively large number of reports emphasize the role played by Christian church leaders,[16] including several Transylvanians: Bishop Áron Márton, head of the Roman Catholic Church in Alba Iulia (Gyulafehérvár in Hungarian),[17] and Protestant Minister Andor Járosi of Kolozsvár.[18] Only rarely do the reports mention the names of Transylvanian clergyman acting independently, such as Lajos Szabó, a minister of the Reformed Church, and Roman Catholic Chaplain János Ópalotay, both in Nagyvárad, who provided pre-dated baptismal documents.[19] In the same city, Virgil Maxim, a professor at the Greek-Catholic Seminary, and Gheorghe Mangra, the principal of the seminary, hid young Jews.[20] Sources biased by postwar Romanian historiography describe the solidarity of Greek Catholic Bishop Iuliu Hossu and his secretary,

Canon Vasile Aşteleanu (who later became an Orthodox bishop), and several Greek Catholic clergymen such as Titus Moga, priest of Apahida, and minister Florea Mureşanu. Among these, Aşteleanu and Mureşanu forged baptismal certificates.[21]

There are several accounts of activities in which people were saved with the participation of the International Committee of the Red Cross (ICRC)[22] supported by outstanding clergymen such as Protestant Minister Gábor Sztehló, assisted by Emil Koren in Budapest,[23] who together rescued a significant number of Jewish children. The ICRC, however, did not extend its humanitarian activities to Northern Transylvania. A number of documents relate to missionary nun and politician Margit Slachta's interventions on behalf of the Jews from the Széklers' Land during fall 1940 (September–December) and in summer 1942.[24] Slachta's efforts were supported by Pál Gábor, a lawyer from Csíkszereda, who served as a deputy of the Transylvanian Party (*Erdélyi Párt*) in the Parliament in Budapest.[25] Yad Vashem has recognized many of these people as Righteous Among the Nations.

Little is known, however, about the "anonymous" rescuers, everyday people who had the courage to go against the stream, defying the official policy of hatred. They were intellectuals (medical doctors, attorneys, engineers, clerks, high-school teachers and university professors, priests, aristocrats, and even high-ranking officers) and less-educated people (factory workers, tailors, delivery-service drivers, salespersons, storekeepers, home owners, waiters, hairdressers, confectioners, janitors, nurses, nannies, housewives, peasants, and soldiers). Jenő Lévai wrote an early account on the subject,[26] and Uri Asaf has recently published one of the most comprehensive studies on Christian support for Jews in Hungary during the Holocaust.[27] Asaf reviewed almost 600 cases of Christian help, classifying them under the following nine categories: individuals, military personnel in the Hungarian labor service system (*munkaszolgálat*), officials of Christian churches, clergymen acting independently, representatives of neutral countries, international organizations, Hungarian government officials, members of the Hungarian resistance, and individual non-Hungarians.[28]

In Asaf's study, however, only twenty-three examples relate to the righteous from Northern Transylvania, a figure that corresponds to 4 percent of the total. These people were active mainly in Kolozsvár, Szatmárnémeti, Nagybánya (Baia Mare in Romanian), Dés (Dej in

Romanian), and Sepsiszentgyörgy (Sfântu Gheorghe in Romanian). They hid Jewish children from Transylvania in Budapest, or intervened as officials on behalf of Jews from Transylvania.[29]

Relying primarily on postwar periodicals and oral histories, a chapter in my history of the Jews of Kolozsvár deals with the rescue activities of exceptional "ordinary" people.[30] Additional cases of the righteous in Northern Transylvania also are cited in the *Geographic Encyclopedia of the Holocaust in Hungary*, edited by Randolph L. Braham.[31]

This current study covers the cases of fifty-four additional righteous Christians, and examines articles published in the Hungarian-language Jewish weekly, *Egység* (Unity). Launched in spring 1946, this periodical is a valuable and not yet completely explored resource, containing narratives of Christian help. Uri Asaf did not access this periodical, and so far I have addressed in Hungarian only the cases that referred to Kolozsvár. Although *Egység* did not publicize any rescue of Jews by clergymen, aristocrats, or state functionaries, and it typically did not emphasize the favorable attitude shown Jews by some high-ranking military officers, the weekly did publish accounts of a large number of rescue cases that have not been disclosed to a wider audience until now.

Christian Rescue as Revealed by Egység

Egység was published from May 1946 to March 1949 in Cluj-Kolozsvár, the most important cultural center of Transylvania, which after World War II was put under Romanian rule. Initially, the publication defined itself as the "central periodical of Transylvanian Jewry," becoming after November 5, 1948, a pro-Communist "democratic Jewish weekly." Its first editor was Sándor Neumann (May–August 1946), followed by György Rózsa (October 1946–August 1948).[32] A short note in the fifth issue refers to Christian help given to persecuted Jews during World War II. Signed with the initials *f. e.* (most likely Ernő Fischer),[33] it requested that readers share their own true stories on how "non-Jews offered help to Jews, who were the most severely hit victims of Fascism." This introductory article announced a follow-up on the topic, and it requested the cooperation of readers in developing the subject into a series titled "Lehetett így is!" (This possibility existed!). This study summarizes the articles according to the *type* of rescue or other help provided to Jews under the following headings: rescuing children, hiding

Jewish individuals or families, feeding Jews before and after the ghettos were established, safeguarding Jewish property and/or valuables, intervening on behalf of Jews, providing a moral response as a protest against the persecution of Jews, and assisting labor servicemen. Cases within each category are listed in alphabetical order by location, and then in alphabetical order by the surnames of the rescuers.

Rescuing Children

Ilona Jagamos. In May 1944, when the ghetto was established in Kolozsvár, Ilona Jagamos, a journalist, assumed responsibility for a young Jewish child, hiding her until the liberation of the city.[34] (In contrast, the names of Melánia Szilánszky, Irén Kosári, and Pálné Kolozsi are also listed; they denounced some of the few Jewish children who initially escaped the round-up and went into hiding.)[35]

In her own apartment, Mrs. Jagamos hid Ilona Dávidovics from Kolozsvár and two labor servicemen from other cities: István Grosz and Miksa Léb. All three survived the war. Ilona Jagamos also provided forged police forms to a woman and her child, and arranged for them to be hidden in a village close to Kolozsvár.[36] Furthermore, Mrs. Jagamos loaned her own and her husband's Christian identity papers to a man[37] and his wife, living in Budapest, who were under threat of deportation.[38] After the war Ilona Jagamos resumed writing articles until 1960 when the Communists banned her from publication.[39] She died in 1983, and as of 2005 she has not received Yad Vashem's recognition as a Righteous Among the Nations.

Károlyné Lakatos. Some of the former staff of the Jewish Hospital (*Zsidó Kórház*) were not deported, and on August 7, 1944, a Jewish nurse gave birth to a child. Mrs. Lakatos, who was working at the Hungarian Railways Hospital (*MÁV-Kórház*), took the child into her care.[40]

Lászlóné (Elsie) Németi. At the time when ghettoes were established in Northern Transylvania, Mrs. Németi, a visual artist, was living in Budapest. When she learned that her Jewish friend, Elemérné Bokor, had given birth to a child, Ms. Németi traveled to Kolozsvár, took the baby girl from the hospital and returned to the capital. There she raised the girl together with her own new-born son. Following the war, the little girl was safely returned to her parents.[41] Elsie Németi settled in New York and in 1994 she was recognized as a Righteous Among the

Nations.[42] After the war, the Bokor family lived in Marosvásárhely (Târgu Mureş in Romanian).

János Treibner and **Gerőné Boczánczy**. Acting together, the two assumed responsibility and hid the child of foundry owner János Hirsch. Though denounced repeatedly and intimidated by police officer Eördögh, Treibner, an assistant professor, and Mrs. Boczánczy refused to divulge the whereabouts of the child. As a result, the child survived the war. The two Christians who saved him suffered no legal consequences.[43]

József Tóth. After typographer Pál Hegedűs returned from labor service, he was immediately deported. As a Christian, Hegedűs's wife was not required to wear the yellow star. During the roundup of the Jews of Kolozsvár she was able to remain at home and to hide their two teenage sons. Shortly after her husband was deported, Mrs. Hegedűs died. Cadet-Sergeant József Tóth took the two teenagers into custodial care and hid them over an extended period.[44] Tóth intervened at a crucial moment, offering shelter to the two brothers, first in his house, and later in an air-raid-safe basement. The two boys survived the war. József Tóth became a professor of business and economics at the University of Kolozsvár and in 1994 he was recognized as a Righteous Among the Nations.[45]

Romanian peasants. A number of Romanian peasants living in villages close to Nagybánya hid Jewish children. Named in the weekly are Grigore Breban and his wife, Ilie Haidu, Maria Haidu, Domnica lui Ştefan, and Nicolae Cherecheş and his wife, Dumitru Lenghel and his wife. At a 1946 commemoration of those who had been deported, all the peasants listed above were invited to the stage where they held in their arms the children they managed to save.[46]

Hiding Jewish Individuals or Families

Few Christians possessed the appropriate conditions and surroundings for accommodating one or more people forced to wear the yellow star. Nevertheless, a few professors of medicine were able to save large number of Jews by housing them as patients in their clinics.

Irma Juhos. During the days of Hungarian occupation of Arad,[47] when members of the pro-Nazi Arrow Cross Party initiated a manhunt against the Jews, Mrs. Juhos, a clerk, hid Jewish families in her home. She was not intimidated by the authorities' threat to shoot anyone who helped Jews. Though aware of the consequences, Irma Juhos took on the responsibility and all the members of six Jewish families were saved.[48]

István Czikora. When Baron Lamoral Braunecker, warden of the prison in Kolozsvár, reportedly prevented detainees from receiving packages, Czikora, the penitentiary's chief guard, allowed packages to be mailed to his home address and he then delivered them to the jail. On June 6, 1944, Warden Braunecker—according to the account in *Egység*, "on his own initiative"[49]—handed over the Jewish prisoners to the gendarmes. They were taken to the railway station and put into freight cars to be sent to Auschwitz. Upon Czikora's intervention at the military headquarters, the lead seals on the wagon doors were removed, and 150 Jews were returned to the prison. From June through September 1944 they were kept in detention under Czikora's protection. When the German and Hungarian forces decided that detainees should be sent to Sopronkőhida in western Hungary, again Czikora disobeyed the order. He released the prisoners and they were able to go into hiding until the city was liberated.[50]

Without questioning István Czikora's merits, one should recognize that this account is biased by the spirit of the postwar era. According to my own research, Baron Lamoral Braunecker showed goodwill toward political prisoners detained for Communist activities. My conclusions disagree with the *Egység* report that he beat prisoners, particularly the Jews, with a dog whip and took the initiative that would have led to their deportation and almost certain death. Furthermore, it seems unlikely that Czikora, a low-ranking officer, would have been able to bypass his superior and contact the military headquarters to reverse orders.

István Herkel. Over four weeks, from September 1944 through the liberation of Kolozsvár,[51] Herkel, an employee of the council of Kolozsvár, hid three Jews after they completed their sentence and were released from the political prison. (As examples of those who not only did not help Jews, but who acted against them, the names Balogh, Lázár, and Bede are cited.)[52]

Dr. Dezső Klimkó. At the surgical hospital of Kolozsvár, the Szeged-born Dr. Dezső Klimkó[53] saved the lives of several Jews. He moved to the city in 1940 from Trianon Hungary[54] and after the war (1945–1947) he organized and directed the surgical clinic in Marosvásárhely. After his later return to Hungary, Dr. Klimkó continued his activity as both a surgeon and a university professor.[55]

Dr. Dezső Miskolczi[56] and **Dr. Wilhelm Prach**.[57] Professor Dezső Miskolczi, with the help of Assistant Professor Wilhelm Prach, hid eighteen Jewish patients at the psychiatric clinic of Kolozsvár. The two doctors resisted the authorities' pressure to release the patients and they arranged for an underground hiding place to which the patients could retreat whenever patrols came to the clinic.

Tivadar Müller. In the basement of his house, Tivadar Müller, a waiter in Kolozsvár, hid Jenő Teszler and his family in the hope that eventually these Jews would able to flee to Romania. Unfortunately, János Szaniszló, a brazier, denounced the Teszler family; the Gestapo arrested, interrogated, and beat them. Tivadar Müller also tried to help Olga Moskovits of Kolozsvár by loaning her Mrs. Müller's Christian police form. Willing to escort Moskovits to Debrecen, Tivadar Müller purchased two railway tickets, but unfortunately it was too late: the next morning she was taken to the ghetto.[58]

Marioara Olpreteanu. Until the liberation of the city, Olpreteanu, a factory worker in Kolozsvár, hid two young Jewish women who had managed to escape from the ghetto of Kolozsvár. Her brave and humane action is contrasted to that of Vadas,[59] István Kerényi, Vilmos Horák, and Lajos Ormos.[60] Of these four names, only one can be identified: Vilmos Horák, a furrier in Kolozsvár, who, in his capacity as street supervisor (*utcabiztos*), denounced to the Gestapo two Jewish families in hiding. As a result, the members of the Sándor Schwartz and Miksa Schönhaus families were rounded up.[61] After the war a People's Court sentenced Vilmos Horák to ten years in prison.[62]

Lajos Péter. Péter, a shoemaker in Kolozsvár, hid a Jewish person from May until the liberation of the city on October 10, 1944. He was assisted in his rescue efforts by the Reinfeld family (see below). Moreover, beginning in September 1944, Péter provided shelter to six political prisoners. As in *Egység*'s other articles, Mr. Péter's actions are compared to that of three denouncers, in this case, Sándor Oláh, Zoltán Osváth, and Gusztáv Sarkady.[63] The "Jewish person" saved by Péter was later identified as Jenő Neumann, a lawyer and a leading intellectual in Kolozsvár. His colleague, János Demeter, a lawyer, journalist, and editor, who after war became the vice-president of Bolyai University, made the necessary arrangements for hiding Neumann.[64]

Ştefan Pop-Silaghi. In June 1944, Ştefan Pop-Silaghi, a manager in Kolozsvár, hid Gábor László, a chemical engineer, and László's widowed mother, Gyuláné, in his apartment. When their situation became critical, Pop-Silaghi provided them with his own and a relative's Christian papers and moved them to Budapest, where they survived the war. Had they been deported, they surely would have perished because Mrs. László was too elderly to have been perceived as a potentially good worker and her son was physically handicapped.[65] After the war, mother and son returned to Kolozsvár, where Gábor László published articles and invented and patented a large number of processes.[66]

Péter Rebreanu. Over a period of several weeks, Rebreanu, a lawyer in Kolozsvár, hid his colleague, Jenő Kertész, an important politician of the Károlyi era (1918–1919), together with Mrs. Kertész. Later the husband and wife decided to cross the border to Romania. Unfortunately, they were caught by guards, and taken to Germany. Jenő Kertész never returned.[67] Rebreanu also offered to hide to a journalist who subsequently decided not to accept because he could not bear to be separated from his parents. That journalist was deported along with his entire family.[68]

Sándor Reinfeld. Reinfeld, an engineer in Kolozsvár, and his family provided important assistance to Lajos Péter, playing a large role in hiding the lawyer Jenő Neumann. As a mixed Christian-Jewish family, the Reinfelds assumed great risk; the family members could have been easily rounded up and taken to the ghetto.[69]

Gyula Sulyai-Sulyánszky. A warden at the military prison in Kolozsvár, Sulyai-Sulyánszky refused the order to transfer sixty-five Jews from the penitentiary to the ghetto. Moreover, he hid one of his former prisoners who had been released after completing his sentence: this person would have been taken to the ghetto but was saved from deportation through Sulyai-Sulyánszky's action. After the Jews of the city had been deported, he sent packages to the detainees and when some of them were transferred to Budapest, the warden purchased food for them out of his own funds. His brave actions, including his refusal to obey orders, did not have any legal consequences for him. (The contrary attitudes and actions of several other officers are cited in the publication, including Colonel Géza Körmendy, Major General (*vezérőrnagy*) István Kozma, as well as György Kugler-Füleki, József Gecse, Péter Czeisperger, and József Harácsek.[70])

Rózsi Morányi. Defying the orders of Major General Károly Rajnay, the prefect of Bihar County,[71] Rózsi Morányi, a storekeeper in

Nagyvárad, hid a Jewish family of four in her store at 2 Bessenyei György Street. Later, four additional Jewish civil defense servicemen joined them, so that she managed to hide and feed a total of eight people for an entire week. Denounced by someone, Ms. Morányi succeeded in distracting the attention of the gendarmerie detectives during their search of her store so they did not discover the eight Jews hiding behind the counter.[72]

Feeding Jews before and after the Ghettos Were Established

Gábor Bakó. A tailor in Kolozsvár, Bakó smuggled food to his neighbor's wife, Ferencné Öszterreicher and her child in the ghetto, and also forwarded the postcards sent to his wife by Ferenc Öszterreicher, who was serving in a forced labor service unit. Though questioned twice by the police, Bakó did not stop his humanitarian efforts.[73]

János Bindász. From May through October 10, 1944, Bindász, a hairdresser in Kolozsvár, not only fed salesman Náthán Mór and his three family members, but repeatedly prevented the roundup of these Jews by forging Mór's World War I military declarations that entitled him to an exemption from deportation. Bindász could not prevent the family from eventual arrest and imprisonment, but immediately following their unexplained release and hospitalization, Bindász provided them with an appropriate hiding place that did prevent their deportation.[74]

János Mátrai. A journalist in Kolozsvár, Mátrai offered help to Jews exempted from deportation and allowed to remain in Kolozsvár. Local officials refused to grant food ration cards to these few Jewish families, but Mátrai intervened on their behalf. After the war, Mátrai served as the editor of an independent publication.[75]

Jeromosné Melik. After the roundup of the Jews in the city, Mrs. Melik, a resident of Kolozsvár, drove around in a hackney carriage to collect food supplies for those Jews detained in the ghetto and intervened on behalf of several Jews to secure their release from the ghetto.[76]

Margit Piroska. A nurse, Piroska forwarded packages to former staff members of the Jewish Hospital (*Zsidó Kórház*) who managed to remain in the city after the deportations. She also coordinated mail delivery between the Jewish medical staff and their family members in forced labor service. The police repeatedly interrogated her about these actions, but apparently she was not arrested.[77]

János Krausz. A financial clerk in Zilah, Reserve Lieutenant Krausz was the second-in-command of a Jewish labor service company. At one point, he received a large sum of money from his commanding officer. Suspecting that the origin of the money was not quite above board, he used it to feed Jewish political prisoners and continued to provide the detainees with food after the initial funds were spent.[78]

Safeguarding Jewish Property

József Pozsonyi. A confectioner in Érmihályfalva (Valea lui Mihai in Romanian), Pozsonyi safeguarded the valuables of ten Jewish families. After the war he returned everything to the surviving family members.[79]

Mária B. Gima. A resident of Gyalu (Gilau in Romanian), Gima conveyed Pinkas Pfeffermann's property to her own name and administered it during the war. When the family returned to the village she returned the property to them as its rightful owners.[80]

Ferenc Krejcsi. While serving in the army, Krejcsi, a tailor in Kolozsvár, helped his Jewish neighbor (who used to be his fellow soldier during WWI) by picking up luggage filled with valuables from his colleague's home and hiding it. After the war he returned the property with a complete inventory.[81]

Ferenc Weress, Jr. Prior to the roundup of the Jewish population, Dr. Weress, a physician in Kolozsvár, offered to hide Ibolya Albert. When she refused to go into hiding, he moved a truckload of her household goods to his basement and walled them off. Although Dr. Weress lost most of his own property in the war, he returned to Albert all of hers when she returned from deportation. After the war, he was appointed professor at the School of Medicine of Bolyai University in Marosvásárhely.[82]

Intervening on Behalf of Jews

Mária Kolumbán. Relying on her connections at the health inspectorate (*egészségügyi főfelügyelőség*), Dr. Kolumbán, a physician in Kolozsvár, made the necessary arrangements for several of her Jewish medical doctor colleagues to be drafted into the labor service rather than taken to the ghetto. At that time, the labor service constituted a unique alternative to deportation, and in many cases saved Jewish lives. In addition, she provided financial help and food to Jewish doctors and safeguarded many of their properties. Even after the decrees prohibited Christian physicians from ministering to Jewish patients, she continued to provide them with attentive care.[83] (In the publication, Dr. Kolumbán's humanitarian attitude is contrasted to that reported of other medical doctors, such as Kálmán Parádi, Árpád Gyergyai, Dr. Koleszár, and Dr. Koronka, who apparently refrained from providing any help to their Jewish colleagues.)

Moral Response as a Protest against the Persecution of the Jews

János Jósika. The prefect of Szilágy County, Baron Jósika refused to associate himself with the Sztójay regime and resigned.[84] In the article published in *Egység,* Jósika is weighed against other "homini regis," who did not quit their positions, such as Inczédy-Joksmann, Kálmán Borbély, and Gábor Szentiványi.[85]

Lajos Tárkány. A municipal officer in Kolozsvár, Tárkány refused to participate in the roundup of Jews, declaring that he was not an executioner. Fortunately for him, his firm stance did not have any legal consequences and he was not even put on probation. (Once again, the publication contrasts the conduct of other reportedly reprehensible people, but the surnames supplied—Tar, Cser, Pirkler, and Boldizsár—are difficult or impossible to identify since their given names are not provided.)[86]

In another account, someone who is likely to be this same municipal officer is referred to as *Tárkányi* (although no given name is recorded). According to this article, at the time of the roundup, Tárkányi allowed salesman Náthán Mór and three members of his family, whom we have already met, to remain in their home.[87]

Dezső Vaska. Defying the *numerus nullus* regulation, Vaska, the director of the school of commerce (*Kereskedelmi Iskola*) in Kolozsvár, not only admitted Olivér Lustig to his school as a regular first-year student, he also offered the young Jewish man a complete tuition waiver.[88]

Assisting Labor Servicemen

These cases are typically the least defined; they refer to commanding officers or lower-ranking military personnel to whom many Jewish labor servicemen (*munkaszoláglatosok*) owe their lives. However, the names, professions, and residences of most of them are uncertain.

Gyula Bercse. On June 29, 1942, Labor Service Company No. 110/15, a penal unit, was transferred from Szinérváralja (Seini in Romanian) to the Don River area in the Ukraine. The officer in charge, Lieutenant Cselényi, reportedly attempted literally to annihilate the Jewish labor servicemen under his command. Fortunately, in less than six months, in early December 1942, Lieutenant Bercse took over the command and he arranged appropriate accommodations for the labor servicemen in the houses of Ukrainian peasants. Bercse organized medical care for the labor servicemen, had them disinfected, and set up an infirmary for them. After the Soviet counter-offensive began on January 23, 1943, Bercse ordered a retreat and he provided forged identity documents to sixty Jewish labor servicemen so that they could return home safely.[89]

Csomor and **Gyula Dravesz**. When Labor Service Company No. 107/12 was transferred from Vigov-Krasnopolje to First Lieutenant Csomor's company in Rovno, the Ukraine, nineteen Jewish labor servicemen from Transylvania and one Jewish medical doctor from Budapest were in very bad condition, weighing an average fifty kilograms each. Lieutenant Csomor, an architect from Balassagyarmat, and Reserve Lieutenant Dravesz, an internal revenue officer from Pesterzsébet, nourished, dressed, and provided medical care for them and, after a retreat was ordered, the officers defied their orders and arranged motor-vehicle transportation for the still weak men.[90] (In DEGOB-deposition No. 3507 reference is made to First Lieutenant Gyula Csomor, commanding officer of a Jewish labor service company in Rimaszombat [during 1942–43] who approved all possible requests from his men, including vacation leave. Though the latter time frame possibly overlaps with that of the Ukraine service reported in *Egység*, it is likely that the two accounts refer to the same commanding officer.[91])

Kálmán Gálffy. As commanding officer of Labor Service Company No. 110/67, First Lieutenant Gálffy, a former school inspector from Szatmárnémeti, provided forged discharge letters to a number of the 250 Jewish men under his command, these documents to be used after the Szálasi takeover. At the same time, he hid and fed some of the men. Gálffy saved the life of Ákos Keppich when the latter escaped from a nearby prison. In the area where company 110/67 was stationed, 700

Jews were discovered hiding in a bombed building and Gálffy issued orders to feed these people out of his company's rations.[92] Later, Gálffy was accused of eighteen different offenses; he evaded severe legal consequences by requesting to be transferred to the frontlines.[93] (DEGOB-deposition No. 3074 probably refers to the same officer, identified as "vitéz" (valiant) Gálffy, a teacher from Szatmárnémeti, who in 1944 commanded Civil Defense Company No. 101/33. Late in the war, Gálffy fed the Jewish women who were being marched to Hegyeshalom and he also procured Swiss documents to protect his men.)[94]

Gulácsy. An officer in charge of military provisions, First Lieutenant Gulácsy, commanding officer of a Jewish labor service company stationed in the Ukraine, provided food and clothing to forty-seven starving, bedraggled labor servicemen, restoring their faith in the possibility of survival. Later, when stationed in Sumsk, the Ukraine, Gulácsy learned about twenty-four hidden Ukrainian Jews and ordered two bags of foodstuffs to be delivered to them. Gulácsy's initiatives were wholeheartedly supported by Sergeant Varga.

Mihály Humayer. As commanding officer of a Jewish labor service company, Reserve Lieutenant Humayer treated his men compassionately, granting them furloughs of seven to ten days. After deportations started, this officer did not keep his people from establishing contact with deportees in freight cars passing through their territory. Consequently, his men were able to get food and water into the sealed railroad cars. Lieutenant Humayer disobeyed the order to surround the men's work area with a barbed-wire fence, as if their area were a detention camp.[95]

István Morik. As commanding officer of a Jewish labor service company, First Lieutenant Morik behaved in a humane and caring manner with his charges. In the publication his attitude and behavior are contrasted to that of Lieutenants Polgár and Pomázi.[96]

Imre Reviczky. As commander of Labor Service Battalion No. X, headquartered in Nagybánya, Lieutenant Colonel Reviczky rescued thousands of Jews, drafting them for labor service, often prior to their twentieth birthday, which was the official draft age. Thus, many Jewish boys managed to avoid deportation. He took action against brutal guards and he disbanded the punitive labor service units.[97] In early July 1946 Reviczky was invited to Transylvania on the initiative of former labor servicemen he had saved. He was celebrated in Nagyvárad and

Kolozsvár.[98] Later, the new Hungarian authorities denied Reviczky's pension, and allowed him to be employed only at physical labor. In 1967, he was posthumously recognized by Yad Vashem as a Righteous Among the Nations. Four streets in Israel were named after him and inscriptions were placed in his honor in Budapest and in Nyíregyháza.[99]

Lajos Schronk. A lawyer from Marosvásárhely who was the commanding officer of Romanian Labor Service Company No. 10/49, stationed at Dédabisztra (Deda in Romanian), Schronk protected the Jewish physician assigned to the division by defying orders to assign his medical doctor heavy physical labor. At his transfer from the company, Schronk advised the new commander that he should consider it a duty to protect the Jewish surgeon.[100]

Tibor Szigeti Szöllősi. As second-in-command of Labor Service Company No. 108/57 stationed at Kolomea, the Ukraine, Szigeti Szöllősi treated the labor servicemen very humanely. Recognizing that the work assigned to Jewish laborers could not be completed with the provisions supplied to them, Szigeti Szöllősi doubled their food rations. This brave officer convinced his company commander, László Gergely, not to oppose his actions.[101]

Pál Veress. *Egység* published two accounts about Captain Veress. In the first, Veress is referred to as a first lieutenant in charge of the company stationed in Csík County; in the second, he is identified as a retired school inspector from Kolozsvár, and as commanding officer of Labor Service Company No. 110/27 stationed in Csík County, then in Baja. Possessing a charitable character, he arranged humane living conditions for the men under his command. Furthermore, after gendarmes arrested Benő Wieder while the Jew was on leave from the company, Veress declined to turn him over to the military courts. Whenever he learned about upcoming inspections during which his men would be searched for their valuables, he collected and secured their money and other items, later returning everything to the owners.[102] At the time when the ghettoes were established in the province, Pál Veress is mentioned as a captain commanding a company stationed in Baja, where his people had the benefit of good quality food and were allowed to receive uncensored letters. Upon the request of Major Tivadar Maros, also serving in Baja, Veress took under his protection thirty Jewish men, women, and children, assigning them household and laundry work. Despite this assistance, they eventually were rounded up and deported.

Veress filed a petition at the headquarters of Labor Service Battalion No. V in Szeged requesting that the families of labor service men not be taken to the ghetto. His request was denied. After Szálasi's assumption of power on October 15, 1944, the withdrawal of the company was ordered on October 17, 1944, the captain purposely delayed executing this order until the Soviet army liberated his men. By doing so, Pál Veress saved the lives of 230 Jewish men, many of them from Transylvania. According to the article in *Egység*, after the war, Veress returned to Baja where he and his family barely survived on the small pension he received. His former servicemen expressed their gratitude to Veress by initiating action to bring him to Transylvania.[103]

Change in the Name and the Decay of Egység

The successor of *Egység*, the weekly *Új Út* (New route), revealed an increasingly powerful Communist influence in both its title and contents. The series *Lehetett így is!...* was discontinued shortly after the name change. I did, however, discover one last article published under the same series title, although it is completely different from the scope and initial goal of the series and is unrelated to the fate of Jewry in Northern Transylvania. Published in summer 1949, the story is signed by Eusebiu Camilar,[104] a writer from the Old Kingdom of Romania. It is part of his novel titled *The Fog*, originally written in Romanian and awarded the Creangă Prize of the Romanian Academy of Science in 1949.[105] The published excerpt tells how a Romanian soldier, Costan Cimpoieşu, rescues Yitzhak Blonder, a Jew probably from Moldavia.

Conclusions

Following its promising start in June 1946 with the series of articles on Christians who saved Jews, *Egység* gradually came under Communist influence. Little by little, political reasons determined which rescuers could and could not be written about. As a result the periodical generally did not report on help provided to Jews by aristocrats, such as writer and theatre director Baron János Kemény, who continuously supported a group of Jewish actors who had been fired from the Concordia Jewish Theatre in Kolozsvár.[106] Except for the case of Baron János Jósika referred to above, the publication did not report the moral responses of prefects and deputy prefects who resigned as a protest against the persecution of Jews. Among these were Count Béla Bethlen and Count János Schilling, prefect and deputy prefect of Szolnok–Doboka County;[107] László Mikó Oroszfáji, prefect of Maros–Torda County; and Endre Hlatky, prefect of Bihar County. Nor did the weekly mention István Soós, mayor of Nagyvárad, who refused to execute the ghettoization order and turned in his resignation.[108] Nor was any mention made of rescue actions undertaken by officials of the state administration, for example, Miklós Mester, undersecretary of state for religion and education, and Sándor Vita, deputy of the Transylvanian Party (*Erdélyi Párt*), both of whom arranged for exempting approximately seventy Jewish families in Northern Transylvania from the anti-Jewish regulations, and high-ranking officers such as Baron Lamoral Braunecker, commander of the military prison in Kolozsvár. (Although the article in *Egység* depicted him in negative terms—an assessment likely biased by the spirit of the Communist era—as revealed above Baron Lamoral Braunecker showed goodwill toward political prisoners.) In general, credit is given to medical doctors, such as professors Dezső Miskolczy and Dezső Klimkó, and to Dr. Wilhelm Prach. Therefore, it is difficult to understand the lack of recognition of Professor Imre Haynal, dean of the College of Medicine in Kolozsvár, who defied the prohibition to provide medical care to Jewish patients, and who hid at his clinic several Jewish women and children, and even men who had evaded labor service.[109] One explanation would be that for his military merits Haynal received the "vitéz" title, a rough equivalent of the knight's rank, introduced by the Horthy regime.[110] Another possible reason for not citing him is that, as a Hungarian citizen, Haynal was banished from Romania in 1946 and had to return to Budapest. In 1999 he was posthumously recognized by Yad Vashem as a Righteous Among the Nations.[111] On the whole, the articles published in *Egység* reveal a clear proclivity to recognize less-educated people, rather than intellectuals.

Although political considerations affected the content and credibility of some of these accounts, the *Egység* series, discontinued in May 1947, constitutes a primary resource that can be used as a starting point for further research on the rescue of Jews in Northern Transylvania.

Notes

1. I would like to express my thanks to Ilona Balla, Lucian Blaga Central Library of Babes-Bolyai University in Cluj-Napoca, for her valuable help in providing documentation, and to Ellen Ficklen, an editor and journalist, for her critical reading of the manuscript and for her valuable suggestions.

2. For bibliographical references to these rescuers, consult Randolph L. Braham, comp. and ed., *The Hungarian Jewish Catastrophe: A Selected and Annotated Bibliography* (New York: Columbia University Press, 1984); and Randolph L. Braham, comp. and ed., *The Holocaust in Hungary: A Selected and Annotated Bibliography, 1984–2000* (New York: Columbia University Press, 2000).

3. Mózes Teréz, *Váradi zsidók* (Jews of Nagyvárad) (Nagyvárad: Literátor Könyvkiadó, 1995), 221.

4. The two women lived in the building of the French Consulate in Kolozsvár. See Daniel Lőwy, *A Kálváriától a tragédiáig* (From the calvary to the tragedy) (Kolozsvár: Koinónia (forthcoming)) (hereafter Lőwy, *Kálvária*).

5. In other sources he is referred to as *Lieutenant* Colonel Mihai *Gurguş*.

6. Francisc Păcurariu, *Românii şi maghiarii de-a lungul veacurilor* (Romanians and Hungarians through the centuries) (Bucharest: Editura Minerva, 1988), 507; Moshe Carmilly-Weinberger, *A zsidóság története Erdélyben (1623–1944)* (The history of Jewry in Transylvania, 1623–1944) (Budapest: MTA Judaisztikai Kutatócsoport, 1995), 302–303.

7. Szabolcs Szita, "Az 1944–1945: Évi polgári, diplomáciai és katonai embermentés történetéhez" (The history of civil, diplomatic, and military rescue of people in 1944–1945), in *Magyarország 1944: Üldöztetés—embermentés* (Hungary 1944: Persecution–rescue), ed. Szabolcs Szita (Budapest: Nemzeti Tankönyvkiadó—Pro Homine—1944 Emlékbizottság, 1994) (hereafter Szita, *Persecution–Rescue*). See also his article in *Holocaust Füzetek* (Holocaust papers), Budapest, no. 7 (1997), 105–15. Examples from Transylvania include the following locations: Arad, Dés, Kápolnomonostor, Kolozsvár, Marosvásárhely, Nagyvárad, Sepsiszentgyörgy, Szatmárnémeti, and Szászrégen.

8. Szita, *Persecution–Rescue*. According to Mrs. Stefánia Pálné Zeőke, who was a family friend of the writer, Mrs. Tamási was from the Lipótváros section of Budapest. (Personal communication dated March 8, 2004, to Daniel Lőwy.)

9. Randolph L. Braham, *A népirtás politikája: A Holocaust Magyarországon* (The politics of genocide: The Holocaust in Hungary) (Budapest: Belvárosi Könyvkiadó, 1997), I, 344–63; II, 1012–122 and 1075–77 (hereafter, Braham, *Népirtás*).

10. László Karsai, "Tropfen im Meer: Solidarität und Menschenrettung in Ungarn," in *Solidarität und Hilfe für Juden wahrend der NS-Zeit*. Regionalstudien 3., eds. Wolfgang Benz and Juliane Wetzel (Berlin: Metropol Verlag, 1999), 207–46 (hereafter Karsai, "Tropfen").

11. The cases from Northern Transylvania include the rescue of one labor serviceman, Szatmárnémeti Christians' requests to the city's orphanage to be allowed to adopt Jewish children, and ninety people in Nagyvárad having charges filed against them for safeguarding Jewish property.

12. Gábor Kádár and Zoltán Vági, "Zsidók és nem zsidók—Szolidaritás és embermentés a Vészkorszakban" (Jews and non-Jews—Solidarity and human rescue during the Holocaust), in *Holocaust Füzetek* (Holocaust papers), Budapest, no. 10 (1998), Magyar Auschwitz Alapítvány—Holocaust Dokumentációs Központ (hereafter, Kádár-Vági).

13. Deportáltakat Gondozó Országos Bizottsága (National Welfare Committee of the Deportees), an Hungarian-Jewish organization founded in March 1945 in Budapest.

14. Kádár-Vági, 73 and 76 (Szatmárnémeti), 64 and 84 (Nagyvárad), and 64 (Bárdfalava).

15. Ibid., 33, 36–37, 64, and 78.

16. For bibliographical references to the rescue activities of these church leaders, see the bibliographies cited in footnote 1.

17. Gabór Jakab, "A meggyilkolt bíboros kései utóda: Márton Áron" (The late successor of the murdered cardinal: Áron Márton), in *Korunk* (Our era), Kolozsvár, no. 10 (1990), 1278–86; János P. Szőke, *Márton Áron* (Nyíregyháza: Görög Katolikus Püspöki Hivatal, 1990); Salamon Márton-László, "Márton Áron, A népek igaza" (Áron Márton: The righteous gentile), in *Szabadság* (Liberty), Kolozsvár (June 22, 2000), 8; and Daniel Lőwy, "Fehérek közt egy európai" (A European among white people), in Lőwy, *A téglagyártól a tehervonatig: Kolozsvár zsidó lakosságának története* (From the brickyard to the cattle wagons: The Jewish history of Kolozsvár) (Kolozsvár: Erdélyi Szépmíves Céh, 1998), 123–26 (hereafter Lőwy, *Téglagyár*).

18. Gyula Groó, "Járosi Andor prófétai szolgálata" (The prophetical service of Andor Járosi), in *Lelkipásztor,* Győr, (December 1949); Imre Kádár, "Veszélyes percek embere: Járosi Andor útja" (The man of dangerous times: The path of Andor Járosi), in *Lelkipásztor,* Győr (December 1949), 469–71; Daniel Lőwy, "A Szamos-parti város Wallenbergje" (Kolozsvár's Wallenberg), in *Menora—Egyenlőség*, Toronto, (October 31, 1997), 10–12; Lőwy, "A Szamos-parti város Wallenbergje: Járosi Andor" (Kolozsvár's Wallenberg: Andor Járosi), in *Credo Evangélikus Műhely*, Budapest, no. 1–2 (1998), 51–55; and Lőwy, *Kálvária*.

19. Mózes Teréz, 203.

20. Ibid., 221.

21. Moshe Carmilly-Weinberger, *Istoria evreilor din Transilvania (1623–1944)* (The history of Jewry in Transylvania) (Bucharest: Editura Enciclopedică, 1994), 167, 175; Carmilly-Weinberger, *A zsidóság története Erdélyben,* op. cit., 302–303; and Carmilly-Weinberger, "Ajutorul României în acțiunea de salvare a evreilor în timpul nazismului" (The help extended by Romania for the rescue of Jews during the Nazi regime), in *Curentul* (The stream), Bucharest (November–December 1988).

22. "'Inter arma caritas': Embermentő tevékenység a Vöröskereszt Nemzetközi Bizottságának közreműködésével (1944 nyara–1945 eleje)" ("Inter arma caritas": Rescue activities with the participation of the International Committee of the Red Cross), in Szita, *Persecution–Rescue*, 185–211.

23. Mónika Miklya Luzsányi, ed., *...hogy véget érjen a sötétség* (...so that the darkness should come to an end) (Budapest–Kolozsvár: Koinónia, 2003); Charles Fenyvesi, "Man of Action, Man of God: Gabor Sztehlo," in Charles Fenyvesi, *When Angels Fooled the World: Rescuers of Jews in Wartime Hungary* (Madison: University of Wisconsin Press, 2003), 163–214.

24. Tamás Majsai, "The Deportation of Jews from Csíkszereda and Margit Slachta's Intervention on Their Behalf," in *Studies on the Holocaust in Hungary*, ed. Randolph L. Braham (New York: Columbia University Press, 1990), 113–63; Ilona Mona, *Slachta Margit* (Corvinus Kiadó, 1997); and Tibori Szabó, "Csík County," in *The Geographic Encyclopedia of the Holocaust in Hungary*, ed. Randolph L. Braham (forthcoming) (hereafter, GEHH). Margit Slachta (1884–1974) was posthumously recognized by Yad Vashem as a Righteous Among the Nations (1985), and in 1995 she was also honored by the Hungarian government.

25. Ibid.

26. Jenő Lévai, *Szürke könyv: Magyar zsidók megmentéséről* (Grey book: On the rescue of Hungarian Jews) (Budapest: Officina, 1946).

27. Uri Asaf, "Christian Support for Jews During the Holocaust in Hungary," in *Hungarian-Jewish Studies*, ed. Randolph L. Braham (New York: World Federation of Hungarian Jews, 1966), 65–112.

28. Ibid., 66–67.

29. Included in these cases are actions taken in Budapest by politicians Margit Slachta, Miklós Mester, Sándor Vita (see below), and Defense Minister Nagybaconi Nagy Vilmos, who improved the living conditions of Jewish men drafted for labor service. In addition, Austrian artist Hella De Pinedo hid two children from Szatmárnémeti in her home in Budapest, while two labor servicemen were saved in Biharnagybajom. Cases no. 341 and 342, on help provided to a couple to escape to Romania, have undisclosed locations. This reduces the total number of cases on Northern Transylvania to about seventeen (approximately 3 percent of the overall number of cases noted).

30. Lőwy, *Téglagyár*, 134–74. My main sources were: *Egység* (Unity), the Hungarian-language Jewish weekly published in Kolozsvár from 1946 to 1949; my "Aradról indult Igaz ember" (A righteous born in Arad), in *Szövétnek* (The lamp), Arad (April 1998), 23–27; and personal communications, parts of which were also used in *Téglagyár* and my *A sárgacsillagos kor tanúságtevői* (Eyewitnesses of the yellow-star era) (Kolozsvár: Koinónia, in press).

31. See, for example, the entries on Csík, Kolozs, Háromszék, and Udvarhely counties by Zoltán Tibori Szabó, and those on Beszterce-Naszód, Bihar, Szilágy, and Szatmár counties by this author.

32. György Rózsa, poet, journalist, translator, and editor. After World War II he worked at the State Council for Minorities. See Dávid Gyula, ed., *Romániai Magyar Irodalmi Lexikon* (Encyclopedia of Hungarian literature in Romania), vol. IV (N-R) (Bucharest-Kolozsvár: Erdélyi Múzeum-Egyesület—Kriterion Könyvkiadó, 2002), 772. Other staff were Editorial Director Ignác Stern, Editorial Secretary László Erős (from 1948), and co-workers Béla Benczel, Dr. Miklós Elekes, László Erős, Ernő Fischer, Sámuel Kahána, Miklós Kallós, Hillel Kohn, Ottó Kornis, György Neumann, Ottó Rappaport, and György Rózsa. Ádám Anavi, Károly Balla, Artúr B. Bárdos, Imre Farkas, Aliz W. Rózsa, László Salamon, György Szántó, and Erzsébet Vajda signed frequent literary contributions. The successor of *Egység*, entitled *Új Út* (New route), was published from March 1949 through March 1953. In 1952/1953 Miklós Kallós acted as the editor-in-chief, while László Erős maintained his position of editorial secretary. As *Új Út* continued the numbering of *Egység*, the number of issues printed in eight years totaled 354. For details, consult Edgár Balogh, ed., *Romániai Magyar Irodalmi Lexikon*, vol. I (A-F) (Bucharest: Kriterion Könyvkiadó, 1981), 439; and Péter Kuszálik, *Erdélyi hírlapok és folyóiratok 1940–1989* (Newspapers and magazines in Transylvania, 1940–1989) (Budapest: Teleki László Alapítvány Közép-Európa Intézet, 1996).

33. Ernő Fischer was an editor and columnist of *Egység*.

34. At the time of the roundup of the Jews in Kolozsvár, Ilona Jagamos took the little girl from the arms of her parents in the street. The child's name was Anna Blumenfeld; Mrs. Jagamos raised her for a while, then an aunt from Debrecen assumed care of her. After the war the girl changed her name to Gaál and became an educator in Debrecen. Personal communication by Zsuzsanna Ferencz, Bucharest, September 7, 9, 15, and 18, 2002. See Lőwy, *Kálvária*.

35. f. e. *Egység*, vol. I, no. 6 (June 13, 1946), 5.

36. The "mother and child" cited in *Egység* were Margit Bányai, wife of Professor László Bányai, and their son, Lacika. They were sent to the village of Kendilóna (Luna de Jos in Romanian). After the war László Bányai, Jr., immigrated to Germany and became a nuclear physicist living near Frankfurt-am-Main. Information from Zsuzsanna Ferencz in Lőwy, *Kálvária.*

37. Margit Bányai's elder brother. Information from Zsuzsanna Ferencz, ibid.

38. f. *Egység*, vol. I, no. 33 (December 20, 1946), 2.

39. Starting in 1939 Ilona Jagamos (in other sources: Jagamas, 1919–1983) published articles in *Keleti Újság* (Eastern newspaper), *Ellenzék* (Opposition), *Hölgyfutár* (Woman courier), and *Pásztortűz* (Herdsman's campfire). After the war she wrote for *Világosság* (Lightness), *Utunk* (Our road), *Igazság* (Truth), and *Dolgozó Nő* (Working woman), all published in Kolozsvár. She also contributed to *Művelődés* (Culture) in Marosvásárhely, and to *Ifjúmunkás* (The young worker) and *Tanügyi Újság* (Education journal) in Bucharest. After she was banned from publication she wrote under pen names. Information from Zsuzsanna Ferencz in Lőwy, *Kálvária;* see also Edgár Balogh, ed., *Romániai Magyar Irodalmi Lexikon*, vol. II (G-K (Bucharest: Kriterion Könyvkiadó, 1991), 458.

40. *Egység,* vol. I, no. 14 (August 10, 1946), 3.

41. Bokor Elemérné in *Egység*, vol. II, no. 43 (February 28, 1947), 4. Elsie Németi's name is misspelled in the article as "Némethy."

42. Lőwy, *Kálvária.*

43. f. e., *Egység*, vol. I, no. 6 (June 13, 1946), 5.

44. *Egység*, vol. I, no. 15 (August 16, 1946), 2.

45. Lőwy, *Kálvária.*

46. *Egység*, vol. I, no. 9 (July 4, 1946), 5.

47. German and Hungarian forces occupied Arad on September 13, 1944, ten days after the anti-Nazi *coup d'état* in Bucharest. The occupation lasted until September 22, 1944. Over these nine days approximately 70 percent of Arad's Jewish population of 10,000 was obliged to wear the yellow star, and preparations were made for their deportation after Nazi officers Adolf Eichmann, Dieter Wisliceny, and other deportation "specialists" arrived in the region. Braham, *Népirtás*, 898.

48. *Egység*, vol. I, no. 9 (July 4, 1946), 5.

49. f. e. *Egység*, vol. I, no. 5 (June 6, 1946), 4.

50. Ibid.

51. The German and Hungarian troops withdrew from the city on October 10, 1944, and the 2nd Ukrainian Army arrived the next day. For a detailed account see Daniel Lőwy, János Demeter, and Lajos Asztalos, *Kőbe írt Kolozsvár* (Kolozsvár engraved in stone) (Kolozsvár: NIS Kiadó, 1996).

52. f. e. *Egység*, vol. I, no. 6 (June 13, 1946), 5. These people are difficult to identify solely based upon their last names only. Those accused at the People's Court included *Károly Balogh*, a former official of the Phönix factory in Nagybánya, who volunteered to participate in the searching of Jews for hidden valuables; *István Bede*, a sergeant in the Hungarian army, who after drinking in a tavern in Máramarossziget, shot a Jewish boy on the street (see also footnote no. 62 on Gusztáv Sarkady); and *József Lázár*, a member of the Arrow Cross Party in Szilágysomlyó, commander of premilitary units, who participated in the roundup of Jews, and personally searched Jews to confiscate their goods. In Randolph L. Braham, *Genocide and Retribution: The Holocaust in Hungarian-Ruled Northern Transylvania* (Boston: Kluwer-Nijhoff Publishing, 1984), 116, 161–62, and 169–70 (hereafter Braham, *Genocide*).

53. Ibid., vol. I, no. 15 (August 16, 1946), 2.

54. Löwy, *Téglagyár*, 158–59.

55. For some biographical details, see Dávid Gyula, ed., *Romániai Magyar Irodalmi Lexikon* (Bucharest: Kriterion Könyvkiadó, 1992), III, 63 (hereafter, *RMIL-III*).

56. A native of Baja, Dezső Miskolczy (1894–1978), a professor of psychiatry, moved to Kolozsvár in fall 1940. For some biographical details, see *RMIL-III*, 601–602.

57. *Egység*, vol. I, no. 15 (August 16, 1946), 2; Dr. Wilhelm Prach was a Saxon from Transylvania, his name is misspelled in the article as "Vilmos Prack."

58. Olga Moskovits, "Az olvasó írja" (Correspondence from the reader), in *Egység*, vol. I, no. 20 (September 20, 1946), 2.

59. The individual referred to as "Vadas" may be József Vadász, an electrician who denounced two Jewish men hiding in a bombed house in Nagyvárad. Lajos Ormos was a driver in Nagyvárad, while István Kerényi, residing in Szatmárnémeti, denounced a Christian female hiding a two-year-old Jewish girl. All four were sentenced by the People's Tribunal in Kolozsvár. Braham, *Genocide*, 98, 111, 205, and 211.

60. *Egység*, vol. I, no. 5 (June 6, 1946), 4.

61. Löwy, *Téglagyár*, 232.

62. Randolph L. Braham, *Genocide and Retribution: The Holocaust in Hungarian-Ruled Northern Transylvania* (Boston: Kluwer-Nijhoff Publishing, 1984), 134–35 and 221 (hereafter Braham, *Genocide*).

63. *Egység*, vol. I, no. 6 (June 13, 1946), 5. First names of the three denouncers were identified based on the records of the People's Tribunal in Kolozsvár. Sándor Oláh, a twenty-one-year-old tailor in Retteg, Szolnok-Doboka County, beat Jews during searches aiming especially at violating women. Zoltán Osváth was a mason in Nagybánya. Gusztáv Sarkady was a barber from Máramarossziget, who while dazed by drink urged Sergeant István Bede to shoot a Jewish child (see also footnote no. 51 on István Bede). Braham, *Genocide*, 161–62, 185, 210, and 211.

64. Löwy, *Téglagyár*, 143.

65. *Egység*, vol. II, no. 54 (May 16, 1947), 5.

66. Löwy, *Téglagyár*, 160.

67. The fate of the Kertész couple was dramatic. In the Kolozsvár ghetto they joined the privileged Kasztner group, and traveled via Budapest to Bergen-Belsen, where they learned that Uli, their daughter, was also in a different section of the same camp. In an attempt to join her parents, Uli requested a hearing before an SS-officer. Rather than Uli being allowed to join the Kasztner group, the Kertészs were removed from it and they both died before the camp was liberated. Löwy, *Kálvária*.

68. *Egység*, vol. I, no. 16 (August 23, 1946), 7.

69. Ibid., vol. I, no. 6 (June 13, 1946).

70. f. e. *Egység*, vol. I, no. 5 (June 6, 1946), 4. The listed officers committed the following anti-Jewish actions: Major General Kozma, commander of the Székler frontier units, and Colonel Körmendy, commander of the Honvéd battalions in Maros County, both participated at the roundup of the Jews in Marosvásárhely (Braham, *Népirtás*, II, 615–16). Kugler-Füleki, a private functionary from Maros County and a leading member of the Arrow Cross Party, appointed himself as the leader of the ghetto in Szászrégen, initiating searches for hidden Jewish valuables. József Gecse, a potter and member of the Arrow Cross Party, searched and tortured people in the ghetto of Dés. Although not a public official, shoemaker Péter Czeisberger participated in the roundup of Jews in the ghetto of Nagybánya, beat them cruelly, and searched for hidden valuables. Starting in 1942, József Haracsek, president of

the Baross Association in Nagybánya, forwarded lists of Jews to the recruiting centers calling for the concentration of Jews into labor center units (Braham, *Genocide*, 116, 120–21, 153, 180–81, 208, and 211).

71. Rajnay was appointed prefect of Bihar County on May 17, 1944. Daniel Lőwy, "Bihar County," in GEHH.

72. *Egység*, vol. II, no. 42 (February 21, 1947), 3.

73. Ibid., vol. I, no. 15 (August 16, 1946), 2.

74. Ibid., vol. I, no. 10 (July 11, 1946), 5.

75. Ibid., vol. I, no. 17 (August 30, 1946), 2.

76. Ibid.

77. Ibid., vol. I, no. 14 (August 10, 1946), 3.

78. Ibid., vol. I, no. 11 (July 18, 1946), 3.

79. Ibid., vol. I, no. 20 (September 20, 1946), 2.

80. Ibid., vol. II, no. 42 (February 21, 1947), 3.

81. Ibid., vol. I, no. 20 (September 20, 1946), 2.

82. Ibid., vol. I, no. 11 (July 18, 1946), 3.

83. Ibid., vol. I, no. 17 (August 30, 1946), 2.

84. According to official sources, by July 21, 1944, there were a significant number of new county officials in Hungary due to the resignation of the previous incumbents or their dismissal by the new government. The new executive staff included thirty-three new prefects, seven new deputy prefects, twenty-seven new mayors, and fifty-eight chief magistrates (*főszolgabíró*). *Tiszti Címtár* 1944: július 21 lezárt *Pótfüzete* (Addendum to the officers' directory as of July 21, 1944). Cited by Karsai, "Tropfen," 207–46.

85. For details on the trial and conviction of these and other county officials in Northern Transylvania, see Braham, *Genocide*, passim.

86. *Egység*, vol. I, no. 8 (June 27, 1946), 5. For some details on these individuals, see Braham, *Genocide*.

87. Ibid., vol. I, no. 10 (July 11, 1946), 5.

88. Ibid., vol. I, no. 23 (October 11, 1946), 5. After his liberation, Oliver Lustig authored a number of Holocaust-related works, including his autobiographical *Blood-bespotted Diary*.

89. *Egység*, vol. I, no. 14 (August 10, 1946), 3.

90. Ibid., vol. I, no. 33 (December 20, 1946), 2.

91. Kádár-Vági, 34 and 104. Gyula Csomor's humane attitude is also mentioned by Karsai, "Tropfen," 207–46.

92. Though the location is not specified in the article, such a large concentration of Jewish survivors at the time of and subsequent to "the bombings" (that is, in July 1944 or thereafter) could be located only in Budapest.

93. *Egység*, vol. I, no. 23 (October 11, 1946), 5.

94. Kádár-Vági, 37 and 104.

95. *Egység*, vol. I, no. 10 (July 11, 1946), 5.

96. *Ibid.*, vol. I, no. 30 (November 29, 1946), 3.

97. In addition, after the August 23, 1944, *coup d'état* in Bucharest, Reviczky extended help to Romanian intellectuals relocated to Nagybánya. For details, see Silvestru Augustin Prunduş and Clemente Plăianu, *Cei 12 Episcopi Martiri* (The twelve martyred bishops) (Cluj-Napoca: Casa de Editură "Viaţa Creştină," 1998). Web-version at: <http://www.bru.ro/maramures/alexandru_cei12.asp> See also: <http://www.catholic-forum.com/ saints/candidates/prota004.htm>

98. *Egység,* vol. I, no. 10 (July 11, 1946), 4.
99. Szabolcs Szita, *Persecution–Rescue,* 19.
100. *Egység,* vol. I, no. 9 (July 4, 1946), 5.
101. Ibid., vol. I, no. 24 (October 18, 1946), 5.
102. U. Z. "Lehetett így is..." *Egység,* vol. I, no. 12 (July 25, 1946), 5.
103. Ibid., vol. II, no. 35 (January 3, 1947), 9.
104. *Új Út,* vol. IV, no. 153 (May 6, 1949), 6.
105. Eusebiu Camilar, *Negura* (Bucharest: Editura de Stat, 1949).
106. Daniel Lőwy, "A kolozsvári Concordia zsidó színház története" (The history of the Concordia Jewish theatre in Kolozsvár), in *Múlt és Jövő,* no. 1 (2000), 75–79.
107. Béla Vágó, "The Destruction of the Jews of Transylvania," in *Hungarian–Jewish Studies,* ed. Randolph L. Braham (New York: World Federation of Hungarian Jews, 1966), 218.
108. Ernő Gáll, "Kettős kisebbségben" (In double minority status), in *Korunk,* series III, vol. II, no. 8 (August 1991), 957–69.
109. Miklós Domahidy, ed., *Ilyen volt Haynal Imre* (Portrait of Haynal Imre) (Unterhaching: Az Európai Protestáns Magyar Szabadegyetem (Bern) kiadása, 1989).
110. Professor Lajos Csőgör's testimony regarding Professor János V. Demeter, Budapest, February 15, 1997. Lőwy, *Téglagyár,* 274.
111. Imre Haynal's award was given to his son, Professor András Haynal, who lives in Geneva. See Ernő Lazarovits, "Igaz emberek kitüntetése" (Awarding righteous people), on the web at http://www.interdnet.hu/zsido/UJELET/archiv/u990412.html (accessed on December 16, 2004).

Gendarmes before the People's Court

Judit Molnár

The history of the Royal Hungarian Gendarmerie, especially the role it played in the Holocaust, and the later verdicts in the postwar trials of gendarmes are issues much debated by historians (in Hungary and abroad), by survivors, by former gendarmes, and even more widely by politicians. Discovery of the truth is rendered even more difficult by the scarcity of contemporary documents concerning the gendarmerie. We still do not know whether the papers of gendarmerie districts have been destroyed or simply not been found. Here are a few examples to illustrate the point.

Gendarme Captain Károly Kövendy says that while people were at first wary of gendarmes, later "they came to like them because gendarmes shared their joys, and if they were in trouble, they could turn to the gendarmes for information and help."[1] According to him, the Jews in Hungary "lived unmolested until May 1944,"[2] and the government justified charging the 22,000-strong gendarmerie with ghettoization and deportations[3] by saying that "if the gendarmerie were to carry out that cruel order, not an hair of the Jews shall fall to the ground!"[4] Kövendy claims that during the postwar retribution period, between 1945 and 1949, 5,000 gendarmes were executed for war crimes and crimes against humanity.[5]

Béla Rektor, also a gendarme writing after leaving Hungary, puts it more delicately saying some plainclothes police and gendarme detectives "often resorted to unlawful methods" to find out "where wealthy Jews had hidden their possessions." At the same time he claims that "gendarmes never once used their firearms" during the round ups of Jews.[6] He estimates that the wartime losses of the gendarmerie were over 50 percent.[7]

The literature on the subject before 1989, that is, before the change of the political system, usually emphasized the gendarmes brutality against Communists and members of other left-wing movements.[8] Apart from that, the activities of gendarmes in 1944 and the methods they used while rounding up and deporting Jews were discussed by the literature on the Holocaust in Hungary, in particular in the books written by Jenő

Lévai immediately after the war,[9] and the document volumes edited by Elek Karsai.[10]

Although the judgment of the gendarmerie occasionally falls into the crossfire of politics,[11] there has also been an effort in post-1989 works to describe the activities of the gendarmerie from its establishment in 1881 until its dissolution in 1945.[12] However, the role the gendarmerie played in the Holocaust has not yet been thoroughly treated. Only a few studies have examined the reason why Eichmann's "specialists" could chiefly rely on the gendarmerie when the Jews were to be gathered in ghettos and holding camps, and deported in the spring and summer of 1944.[13]

Because the documentation relating to the gendarmerie is incomplete, it is impossible to know exactly how many gendarmes served in 1944, and how many actually took part in the deportation of Jews. In the cabinet meeting of June 21, 1944, where it was first mentioned in reference to an article in a foreign newspaper stating that the Jews deported from Hungary were "gassed and then incinerated in Poland," the superintendent of the gendarmerie, Lieutenant General Gábor Faragho, said about the conduct of his gendarmes carrying out the deportation: "If we consider that we have deported more than 400 thousand Jews with the purpose of labor service and resettlement, then we must dismiss as irrelevant that complaints have been filed against some of the 20,000 Hungarian gendarmes."[14]

The superintendent of the gendarmerie confirmed in all his depositions in the People's Court trials after the war that the Royal Hungarian Gendarmerie played the primary role in the deportation of Hungarian Jews. At that time, however, he said that their number had been 16,000.[15] Other high-ranking gendarmerie officers also had differing memories with regard to the number of the gendarmerie in 1944. The figures were between 16,000 and 32,000.[16] It is known for a fact that the full force of the gendarmerie was set at 12,300 within the borders of the Treaty of Trianon.[17] After the territorial re-annexations between 1938 and 1941, however, the number of gendarmerie districts as well as the number of persons serving in the organization significantly increased. The question is whether the official numbers were adhered to within the borders defined by the Treaty of Trianon in the first place. One should also ask how many men increased the force during the war years? High-ranking gendarme officers said in People's Courts trials that the size of the force was nearly twice as large in the latter period.[18] However, József Parádi, in his textbook on the history of Hungarian law enforcement, puts the strength of the gendarmerie at 14,000 in 1944.[19] He adds that in the spring-summer of 1944, 1,400 gendarmes, that is 10 percent of the total force, "had a sad task to perform: They rounded up and escorted to trains the Jewish population following the plans drawn up by the Germans." This passage, barely seven and a half pages in length, reveals that most of the Jews "escorted" to the trains, that is over 400,000 people, were being deported to Auschwitz. The number usually accepted in the literature on the subject for the strength of the gendarmerie is 20,000, which is the number provided by Gábor Faragho, the head of the gendarmerie, in 1944. Further research will have to unearth more precise figures.

In the following I am going to describe first the structure of the gendarmerie between the two world wars, then the connection between organs of public administration and public safety in Hungary, and conclude with an analysis of the role of the gendarmerie in the Holocaust in Hungary on the basis of the People's Court trials.

The Royal Hungarian Gendarmerie was one of the most important Hungarian state organizations between 1881 and 1945. Its task was first and foremost to enforce laws and decrees in the provinces, as well as to curb the unrest of the peasant rural population and to keep at bay the very weak left-wing socialist and, from the late 1930s, the increasingly powerful extreme rightist Arrow Cross agitation, demonstrations, and strikes. In the spring-summer of 1944, its most important task was to concentrate, plunder, and deport the Jews in Hungary.

On the basis of contemporary documents as well as of what little scholarly analysis has been produced on the subject since 1989, it can be firmly established why Adolf Eichmann and his experts on the "resettlement" of Jews counted first and foremost on the gendarmerie when it came to deporting the Jews.

From its beginnings in 1881, the gendarmerie was a strictly organized, military-type organization of public security.[20] Both the rank-and-file and officers received intense military training, which after World War I emphasized unconditional loyalty to Regent Miklós Horthy. In the Gendarmerie Oath, loyalty to the regent preceded loyalty to the constitution and to the laws of the country.[21] It is also important to note that the gendarmerie was a strictly *law-enforcement* organ; its members were recruited mainly from among young people in peasant families, for whom belonging to the gendarmerie meant social advancement to a secure livelihood, and state employment with a pension.[22]

The heads of the provincial administrations relied on the police in the cities, and on the gendarmerie in other areas of the counties, such as in subordinate districts, and villages. The internal divisions of the gendarmerie did not follow county boundaries, but rather the internal divisions of the Hungarian army and the boundaries of national military districts. As the maps show, interwar Hungary was divided into seven military and/or gendarmerie districts; between 1940 and 1944, however, the number of gendarmerie districts increased to ten. (See Table 1 below for maps outlining these districts in 1926 and 1944.) This came because of the re-annexation of territories in the north, the northeast, and the south, leading to the creation of Gendarmerie Districts Eight, Nine, and Ten in Carpatho-Ruthenia and in Northern Transylvania. Unlike the police organs, which were under the supervision of the Ministry of the Interior, the gendarmerie functioned under the dual control of the Ministry of the Interior and the Ministry of Defense. (See the organization chart in Table 2 below.) What differentiated the two public security organs was that, unlike the gendarmerie, the city police had both executive and limited legislative authority, meaning that the police chief of a city could issue a decree or a resolution within his independent jurisdiction. The gendarmerie, on the other hand, operated exclusively as an executive organ, receiving orders from the magistracy of subordinate districts and counties on the lowest level, or from the minister of the interior or the secretary of state of the interior at the highest level. A gendarmerie district covered three or four full counties and parts of two or three other counties.

Table 2, displaying the structure of the Hungarian administration and the gendarmerie in 1944, clearly shows the dual control over the gendarmerie. The ten gendarmerie districts were under the supervision of the secretary of state of the interior from the public security viewpoint, while, with regard to discipline and training, gendarmerie officers and non-commissioned officers were under the command of the superintendent of the gendarmerie.

Table 1

Gendarmerie Districts in Hungary (1926)

Gendarmerie Districts in Hungary (1944)

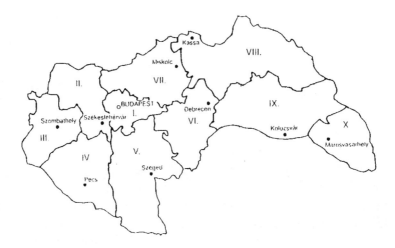

Table 2

Hungarian Administration and Gendarmerie in 1944

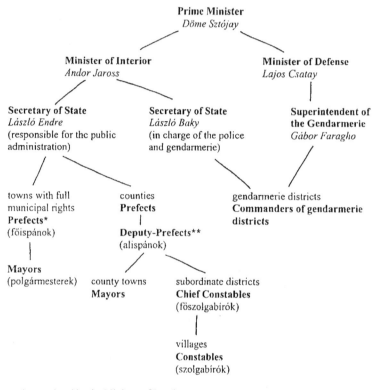

Prime Minister
Döme Sztójay

Minister of Interior
Andor Jaross

Minister of Defense
Lajos Csatay

Secretary of State
László Endre
(responsible for the public
administration)

Secretary of State
László Baky
(in charge of the police
and gendarmerie)

Superintendent of
the Gendarmerie
Gábor Faragho

towns with full
municipal rights
Prefects*
(föispánok)

counties
Prefects
|
Deputy-Prefects**
(alispánok)

gendarmerie districts
Commanders of gendarmerie
districts

Mayors
(polgármesterek)

county towns
Mayors

subordinate districts
Chief Constables
(föszolgabírók)
|
villages
Constables
(szolgabírók)

*   appointed by the Minister of Interior
** elected by the municipal assemblies

The ten gendarmerie districts were comprised of three to four gendarmerie battalions (*osztály*), consisting of three to four gendarmerie companies (*szárny*), in turn consisting of two to four platoons (*szakasz*). Gendarmerie platoons were divided into three to six gendarmerie patrols (*örs*).[24] One gendarmerie patrol was usually responsible for maintaining law and order in two or three villages. This network basically carried out the round up and deportation of Jews in 1944. After 1930, every gendarmerie district had a detective subdivision as well, charged mainly with the investigation of political cases and common criminal cases. Right-wing organizations, such as the Arrow Cross Party led by Ferenc Szálasi, as well as left-wing organizations, and ethnic minority movements were investigated separately, as were Jewish, especially Zionist, organizations.[24] In 1944, the main task of the detective subdivisions was to search for the hidden Jewish possessions.

Gendarmerie schools under the authority of the central gendarmerie command also played an important role in 1944. The cadets were deployed to whichever gendarmerie districts needed extra help. In brief, the administration relied on the police in the country's capital, in cities with full municipal rights, and in other county towns, while in the rest of the country, that is more than three quarters of Hungary, the administration relied on the gendarmerie. As it was said in those days, the gendarmerie was "the rear-guard of the police."[25]

It is safe to say that, on the whole, rigor, discipline, and, with a few exceptions, one hundred percent follow-through, blind obedience, and a tendency to brutality characterized the gendarmerie both before and after the German occupation of Hungary. Thus, it was not a coincidence that the Eichmann-Sondereinsatzkommando, arriving in Hungary on March 19, 1944, could expect the assistance of the gendarmerie in the execution of the Final Solution program.[26]

Historians, however, find themselves in a difficult position when analyzing the actual activities of the gendarmerie and the role the organization played in the Hungarian Holocaust, as I have already indicated. No doubt the first step toward uncovering the history of the Holocaust in Hungary should be studying the documents of the individual gendarmerie districts.[27] The lack of contemporary gendarmerie documents, however, compels historians to use indirect sources, including the postwar People's Court trials, which in several instances have original documents to support the charges in the files.[28]

Probably the most important of those are the daily reports by Gendarme Lieutenant Colonel László Ferenczy, liaison officer with the German Security Police.[29] Our research has shown that contemporary documents from the papers of Gendarmerie Districts Four, Five, and Six were also appended to the court files.[30] In most of the cases, however, the indictments and the sentences were based on evidence in the statements of the defendants and the witnesses. There is no trace of the defendants themselves requesting that their reports be dug out from among the papers, and if the court attempted to examine these documents, it often discovered they could not be located.[31] Therefore, the great gaps in contemporary documents lend special significance to the People's Court files. Of course, these documents should be used with appropriate caution in an analysis of the period because during the trials some gendarme officers consistently stood by their claims while others contradicted themselves.

On the Hungarian side, after the two secretaries of state of the interior, László Endre and László Baky, Lieutenant Colonel Ferenczy perhaps played the most important role in directly controlling the round up and deportation of the Jews, especially after Farahgo appointed him liaison officer at the end of March.[32] The issue of Faragho's responsibility can be raised with good reason since in addition to the appointment, he also instructed Ferenczy to personally and verbally report to him all gendarmerie actions.[33] In November 1945, Ferenczy claimed that, "With respect to the deportations in the country, I presented myself to Lieutenant General Faragho every week and gave him detailed reports, which he listened to without a word."[34] Faragho received all Ferenczy's written reports as well. In April 1946, when he had to confront Ferenczy in court, Faragho admitted that the latter had also verbally reported to him on the course of the deportations every two or three weeks. At the same time he declined responsibility by saying, "I had no choice" but to acknowledge these reports without a word.[35] Ferenczy claimed much more as far as Faragho was concerned, saying that it was the superintendent of the gendarmerie together with Endre who had drawn up the plan for the deportation of the Jews from Budapest and its environs. The confrontation in court between the two gendarmerie officers was inconclusive.[36]

We do know that the three Lászlós (Endre, Baky, and Ferenczy) cooperated perfectly with Eichmann and his men. Following preliminary talks, a meeting was called on April 7in the Ministry of the Interior, where those present were informed "in strict confidentiality" that Hungary would be soon cleansed of Jews.[37] Rounding up the Jews was the responsibility of the police and the gendarmerie with jurisdiction in their respective territories. If necessary, the gendarmerie was to provide armed assistance to the police in the towns. The order of the round-ups was determined according to gendarmerie districts. First the eastern part of the country, Gendarmerie Districts Eight, Nine, and Ten were to be "cleansed." (About two weeks later it was decided that simultaneously the southern border zone would also have to be "cleansed" of Jews.)[38] This would be followed by the Gendarmerie Districts Two and Seven (northern Hungary), and then Five and Six. After that the Jews in Western Hungary were to be rounded up in Gendarmerie Districts Three and Four, and finally Gendarmerie District One around Pest would follow. According to the plans and in accordance with the confidential decree, Budapest would have been completely "cleansed" of its Jews, but that never happened because Regent Horthy ordered the deportations stopped on July 6, 1944. Each operation was preceded by a briefing like the one held on April 7 at the Ministry of the Interior for local police and gendarmerie commanders and heads of the administration. Most of these briefings were chaired by László Endre and László Ferenczy. László Baky also appeared occasionally instructing those present in detail about the procedure. The text of the above confidential decree is included in the files of a number of People's Court trials,[39] and as far as the confidential briefings are concerned, we also have one of the memoranda written about the Munkács meeting.[40]

Following the German occupation of Hungary none of the top leaders of the ten gendarmerie districts was removed. Yet not all the commanders of the gendarmerie districts executed the anti-Jewish orders with the same zeal. Of the ten commanders of the gendarmerie districts, six are known to have been prosecuted after the war. In one case (János Papp) out of the six, there was no indictment and the person in question was regarded as politically vindicated. In the case of another commander (Győző Tölgyessy), the People's Prosecution requested the American authorities to extradite him, but there is no indication in the file that this occurred. Two commanders (Tibor Paksy-Kiss, László Liptay) were sentenced to years of penal servitude, and two (László Hajnácskőy, József Szilády) were executed.

The commander of Gendarmerie District Ten (Marosvásárhely) was "fortunate" enough not to be forced to execute the ghettoization.[41] This was because masses of Ukrainian refugees were wandering across his territory at that time and he did not have the manpower to implement the measures against Jews. (He was the one cleared by the screening committee after the war.) Consequently, the commander of Gendarmerie District Nine (Kolozsvár) was put in charge of organizing the round-up of Jews throughout Northern Transylvania.[42] The latter, a gendarmerie colonel, asked to be retired for health reasons, but when refused, he performed his job thoroughly, often inspecting on the spot whether his gendarmes were carrying out the "cleansing."[43] His reports to Ferenczy indicate that there were no problems in areas under the direct control of the gendarmerie; difficulties arose only in towns that called for the assistance of the gendarmerie. The most flagrant case took place at Nagyvárad, where the training battalion of the local gendarmerie school extended help to the "impotent" police. The gendarmerie district commander found it especially useful that students "had the opportunity to practice the mastery" of body searches and guard-duty.[44] The members of the battalion performed their tasks rather too zealously. Informed of their brutality, the superintendent of the gendarmerie himself initiated proceedings against them.[45] The case was not prosecuted and in early July the student battalion was among the units transferred to Budapest to assist in the round-up and deportation of the capital's Jews.[46] It would become standard practice in the other areas to have training battalions assist the local gendarmerie in the holding camps. In the end, the People's Court sentenced Tibor Paksy-Kiss, the commander of Gendarmerie District Nine, to ten years of penal servitude; the National Council of People's Courts increased the sentence to fifteen years.

The commander of Gendarmerie District Six (Debrecen) pleaded not guilty before the People's Court after the war, adding, "I issued the orders and instructions according to orders from above."[47] He claimed that he had selected the best possible locations for housing the Jews, putting them in drying sheds and furnaces of a brick factory. The People's Court in Debrecen sentenced this gendarme colonel to death at the end of April 1945 because it was found that the gendarmes under his command had abused the Jews both in the holding camp and during the deportation. The sentence was carried out a week later.[48]

Nor was the situation any better in Gendarmerie District Five (Szeged). Although having been heard to criticize the Germans, and having shown "sympathy for the fate of the persecuted Jews," as a number of witnesses testified at a People's Court trial, the commander of Gendarmerie District Five remained at his post.[49] The gendarmerie colonel claimed before the Court that he had not gone to the brick factory in Szeged because he "did not want to see the languishing and the destitute...when he could not help them in any way."[50] The same gendarmerie colonel "forgot" to mention, however, that he had personally instructed the gendarme patrols under his command to deal with nothing else besides ghettoizing, body searches, and transporting the Jews to the holding camps.[51] They were to perform no other "official functions" unless it was vitally urgent. The original text of his order is attached to the papers of the People's Court trial of the deputy mayor of Szeged. The commander of Gendarmerie District Five was acquitted, but the National Council of the People's Courts sentenced him to seven years of penal servitude.

On the other hand, the commander of Gendarmerie District Four (Pécs) personally proposed to the minister of the interior that "the zone along the southern border be cleansed of Jews with special dispatch."[52] In his People's Court trial, the same commander did not deny having given several orders in connection with the ghettoization in his district, and that he demanded "the strictest discipline" of his subordinates. On May 1, 1944, he suggested that the superintendent of the gendarmerie should relieve or transfer three gendarme officers because "one cannot expect that they will execute the measures against the Jews with the loyalty and enthusiastic initiative expected of gendarme officers."[53] The colonel claimed that originally it had not been his task to organize holding camps in his district. However, "on the day of the transportation the gendarme companies [that is, the companies ordered there to round up and deport the Jews] were unexpectedly instructed to leave for Budapest immediately." On hearing this, he provided his own gendarmes to carry out the deportation. The colonel was partly truthful inasmuch as immediately before the deportation, students from gendarme schools were ordered to the camps. But this did not mean that the gendarmes on duty at a given place did not take part in the roundup and deportation of the Jews. The commander of Gendarmerie District Four was sentenced to death by the People's Court and was executed in February 1947.[54] It should be added that the sentence in the case of this gendarme colonel was so severe because, in addition to taking the initiative in the deportation, he had also tried to accommodate the Arrow Cross and had accepted the position as head of the Department of Public Security in the Ministry of the Interior.

In summary, Eichmann and his colleagues needed the cooperation of the local administration and the police in addition to that of the gendarmerie. The documents researched thus far, however, make it clear that they needed the gendarmerie above all: exactly that militarily organized, disciplined executive organization, whose members never asked questions but carried out their orders, whether these actions consisted of confiscating possessions, body-searches, moving Jews into ghettoes or brick-factories, or crowding them into freight cars.

The People's Court trials make it quite clear that most of the gendarmes, from the district commanders down to the smallest local station, carried out these orders. Secretaries of state Endre and Baky, and Gendarme Lieutenant Colonel Ferenczy identified with the idea of "dejewification," issued the appropriate instructions and supervised their execution in harmonious cooperation with Eichmann and his *Kommando*.

There were very few gendarme officers like László Endre, Commander of the Gendarme Station at Csillaghegy (and namesake of the Interior Ministry's state secretary), who saved the lives of nearly 400 people, including Jews, Polish refugees, and Social Democratic politicians. In November 1945, he said that he had disobeyed the law and his superiors because as a father of three children he had tried to imagine how the persecuted felt, and how he would feel if his children were treated so cruelly.[55]

On the other hand, Ferenczy, also a father of three children, whose youngest child was a few-weeks-old baby at the time of the German occupation, did not try to imagine what it was like to be persecuted.[56] Only when hundreds of thousands of people had been deported from Hungary, and when he received the so-called Auschwitz protocols in the middle of June, did it occur to him that he should look into what was going on in Auschwitz.[57] However, it was only after weeks of pondering that he presented himself to Premier Döme Sztójay, and then to the Regent at the beginning of July.[58] By that time only the Jews in Budapest and those in the military forced labor units remained in Hungary.

The documents of the provincial administrations indicate that during the first months following the arrival of the Red Army in Hungary the suppression of the gendarmerie as an organization was not yet considered. Indeed, the administration leaders in the provinces started to take measures for its reorganization during the early months of 1945.[59] Gendarmerie officers and non-commissioned officers proudly returned to Hungary after they had fled to the West. Ferenczy himself said at the People's Court that he had asked the American authorities in July 1945 to return him to Hungary.[60] The government's decree on the dissolution of the gendarmerie was issued on May 10, 1945.[61] The outcome of the debates in the cabinet meetings was that the gendarmerie should not be re-established, but its experiences in terms of equipment and training might be put to use.[62] It would definitely seem that Gábor Faragho, a member of the new cabinet, was instrumental here in that eventually the gendarmerie was not declared collectively responsible, and that a "special screening committee" was set up.[63] Contrary to the original plan, gendarmes were not obliged to appear before the screening committee, but their cases were investigated at their own request. The screening committee had investigated the cases of 2,252 gendarmes by the end of October 1948, clearing 271 of them.[64] However, notwithstanding the claims of the emigrant Kövendy, 5,000 gendarmes were not executed in Hungary after the war. According to the present state of research, by 1951 the People's Courts had found 2473 gendarmes guilty in one way or another, which accounts for 9 percent of all people's court decisions.[65] According to the records of the ÁVH (State Security Authority) there were nearly 16,000 former gendarmes in Hungary in 1950.[66] By February 24, 1951, 227 persons had been executed in Hungary, and this number includes fewer than ten gendarmes.[67]

Notes

1. Károly Kövendy, *Magyar királyi csendőrség: A csendőr békében, háborúban és emigrációban, 1881–1945* (Royal Hungarian Gendarmerie: Gendarme in peace, in war, and in emigration, 1881–1945) (Toronto: The Author, 1973), 46.

2. Ibid., 125.

3. Ibid., 417.

4. Ibid., 125.

5. Ibid., 417.

6. Béla Rektor, *A magyar királyi csendőrség oknyomozó története* (A pragmatic history of the Royal Hungarian Gendarmerie) (Cleveland: Árpád Könyvkiadó Vállalat, 1980), 256–57. The memoires of gendarmes either do not mention the deportations in the provinces or emphasize only rescuing activities. See, for example, József Szendi, *Csendőrsors: Hernádnémetitől Floridáig* (Gendarme fate: From Hernádnémeti to Florida) (Miskolc: Magyar Demokrata Fórum Miskolci Szervezete, 1990); and Imre Finta, *Koldus és király* (Beggar and king) (Toronto: Magyar Írók Világklubja, 1994).

7. Ibid., 290.

8. Ervin Hollós, *Rendőrség, csendőrség, VKF 2* (Police, gendarmerie, VKF 2) (Budapest: Kossuth, 1971).

9. Jenő Lévai, *Fekete könyv a magyar zsidóság szenvedéseiről* (Black book on the sufferings of Hungarian Jews) (Budapest: Officina, 1946); and Jenő Lévai, *Szürke könyv magyar zsidóük megmentéséről* (Gray book on the rescue of Hungarian Jews) (Budapest: Officina, 1946).

10. Ilona Benoschofsky and Elek Karsai, eds., *Vádirat a nácizmus ellen: Dokumentumok a magyarországi zsidóüldözés történetéhez* (Indictment of Nazism: Documents of the history of the persecution of Jews in Hungary), vol. 1 (Budapest: MIOK, 1958) (hereafter, *Vádirat 1*); vol. 2 (Budapest: MIOK, 1960); and Elek Karsai, ed., *Vádirat a nácizmus ellen: Dokumentumok a magyarországi zsidóüldözés történetéhez* (Indictmant of Nazism: Documents of the history of the persecution of Jews in Hungary), vol. 3 (Budapest: MIOK, 1967).

11. See, for example, "Emléktáblát avattak tegnap Budapesten a két világháborúban elesett csendőrök tiszteletére" (Memorial tablet unveiled yesterday in Budapest to honour gendarmes fallen in two world wars), *Népszabadság* (October 20, 1999), 9; and Sándor Szakály, "Nem szerecsenmosdatás" (Not whitewashing sinners), ibid.

12. Csaba Csapó, *A magyar királyi csendőrség története 1881–1914* (The history of the Royal Hungarian Gendarmerie 1881–1914) (Pécs: Pannónia, 1999); Sándor Szakály, *A magyar tábori csendőrség története 1938–1945* (The history of the Hungarian military police 1938–1945) (Budapest: Ister, 2000); Ferenc Kaiser, *A magyar királyi csendőrség története a két világháború között* (The history of the Royal Hungarian Gendarmerie between the two world wars) (Pécs: Pannónia, 2002).

13. For details, see Randolph L. Braham, *The Politics of Genocide: The Holocaust in Hungary* (New York: Columbia University Press, 1994), chapter 13.

14. Magyar Országos Levéltár (Hungarian National Archives – OL), K 27, Minutes of the Council of Ministers, June 21, 1944.

15. Budapest Főváros Levéltára (Municipal Archives of Budapest; hereafter, BFL), People's Court trial of József Czigány, B 18.167/1949, 96.

16. In one of his statements, József Czigány remembered 16,000, then in another statement later he added that during the war that number grew to 32,000. Ibid., 83, 157. According to the statement of Gyula Balázs-Piri, the total strength of the gendarmerie was probably 30,000. Ibid., 98.

17. See Act VII/1922. For the strength and structure of the gendarmerie between the wars, see also "Előterjesztés a magyar államrendőrség létszámára és fegyverzetére" (Proposal for the strength and armament of the Hungarian State police), *Belügyi Szemle* (Review of internal affairs) 4 (1982): 55–61.

18. See note 16.

19. József Parádi, ed., *A magyar rendvédelem története* (The history of Hungarian law enforcement) (Budapest, 1996), 118.

20. For the text of Acts II/1881 and III/1881, see *Magyar Törvénytár* (Hungarian corpus juris) (Budapest, 1896), 4–5. For the Decree No. 1690/1945, ME of the Provisional National Government on the dissolution of the gendarmerie, see *Magyar Közlöny* (Hungarian gazette) 26 (May 10, 1945), 3–4.

21. For the text of the Gendarmerie Oath, see Kaiser, 168.

22. For details, see Csapó, 66–83, 97–105; and Kaiser, 110–14.

23. For details, see Kaiser, 55–64.

24. See, for example, Veszprém Megyei Levéltár (Archives of Veszprém County), Papers of the chief constable of the District of Pápa, 2270/1944. Several documents of similar nature have been discovered in the Archives of Baranya County (BML).

25. Zoltán Pinczés, *Csendőrség és közigazgatás* (Gendarmerie and public administration) (Budapest, 1936), 409.

26. Ernst Kaltenbrunner, chief of the Reichssicherheitshauptamt (the State Security Main Office), said in the first days of the occupation that "he would find it difficult to operate in his own field of work without the cooperation of the Hungarian police and gen-

darmerie." György Ránki, Ervin Pamlényi, Loránt Tilkovszky, and Gyula Juhász, eds., *A Wilhelmstrasse és Magyarország: Német diplomáciai iratok Magyarországról 1933–1944* (Wilhelmstrasse and Hungary: German diplomatic papers on Hungary 1933–1944) (Budapest: Kossuth K., 1968), 795.

27. For the history of Gendarmerie District Five in 1944, see Judit Molnár, *Zsidósors 1944-ben az V. (szegedi) csendőrkerületben* (Jewish fate in 1944 in the fifth gendarmerie district) (Budapest: Cserépfalvi, 1995).

28. To this day none of the gendarmerie districts' files have been found. The Hungarian National Archives and the Archives of the Institute of Military History have only very incomplete files on personnel matters and the gendarme detective departments.

29. Ferenczy's reports were attached to the files of a number of People's Court trials either in the original or in certified copies. Original copies are attached to the files of the Endre-Baky-Jaross and the Ferenczy trials and copies in the files of other trials such as that of Leó László Lulay. For the text of the reports, see László Karsai and Judit Molnár, eds., *Az Endre-Baky-Jaross per* (The Endre-Baky-Jaross trial) (Budapest: Cserépfalvi, 1994), 497–522.

30. See, for example, Állambiztonsági Szolgálatok Történeti Levéltára (Historical Archives of State Security Services – ÁSZTL), People's Court trials of László Hajnácskőy V-146.147; Csongrád Megyei Levéltár (Archives of Csongrád County – CSML), People's Court trial of Béla Tóth Nb. 35/1945; and BFL, People's Court trial of Tibor Paksy-Kiss, Nb. 5045/1945.

31. BFL, B 18.167/1949, Czigány's plea for annullment, 158; and B 17.258/1949, Lulay's sentence.

32. In his pre-trial testimony to the People's Prosecutor, Ferenczy claimed that he was appointed on March 28, in his trial he named March 25. ÁSZTL, People's Court trial of László Ferenczy V-79.348, 54, 84. Faragho claimed firmly and repeatedly that he had appointed Várbíró, who spoke German well. According to him, Ferenczy, who did not speak German, had been appointed by Baky. Karsai and Molnár, 368. In Ferenczy's trial Faragho named Captain Borbíró the liaison officer he had appointed. ÁSZTL, V-79.348, 155. (In Ferenczy's trial Faragho mistakenly mentioned a certain Captain Borbíró. In 1944 no captain existed with such name. Obviously he was thinking of Captain György Várbíró.) Faragho's statement is contradicted by Gendarme Colonel Barnabás Endrődi, who testified that he had learned from Faragho in early April 1944 that "László Ferenczy has been posted as liaison officer with the German security service because the Germans explicitly insisted on him." Ibid., 125.

33. Ibid., 56.

34. Ibid., 76.

35. Ibid., 160. At that time Ferenczy changed his statement, allowing that it was indeed once every two or three weeks that he made personal reports. It took repeated summons to have Faragho actually appear at Ferenczy's trial as a witness. Both the People's Prosecutor and the counsel for the defence insisted on questioning him. At one point, the court was forced to adjourn because Faragho could not be located. Ibid., 153.

36. Ibid., 157–60. Gábor Faragho was never prosecuted after the war, but he testified as a witness in the People's Court trials of several gendarme officers. The reason for this omission probably was because as military attaché in Moscow, he was the leader of the peace delegation that went there on September 28, 1944. In the Provisional National Government he was minister of public supply from December 22, 1944, to July 21, 1945. In

1951 he was resettled at Újfehértó, but upon the request of the Soviets he was allowed to retire to his farm near Kecskemét, which he was not to leave until September 1953.

37. For the notes taken at the meeting of April 7, as well as the text of the decree on the holding camps, see *Vádirat 1*, 123–27.

38. For details, see Molnár, 60–72.

39. See, for example CSML, Nb. 35/1945.

40. Karsai and Molnár, 526–27.

41. ÁSZTL, V-140.906/2, People's Court trial of János Papp V-142.803/1.

42. Ibid., V-140.906/1.

43. BFL, Nb. 5045/1945. 23.

44. Karsai and Molnár, 505.

45. BFL, B. 18.167/1949.22, 63.

46. ÁSZTL, V-79.348; and BFL, Nb. 5054/1945.

47. ÁSZTL, People's Court trial of Károly Jánosi and accomplices, V-78.644.

48. ÁSZTL, People's Court trial of Gyula Nagy and accomplice, V-98.767.

49. BFL, People's Court trial of László Liptay, Nb. 725/1946.

50. Ibid.

51. CSML, Nb. 35/1945.

52. ÁSZTL, V-146.147.

53. Ibid.

54. Ibid.

55. Magyar Zsidó Múzeum és Levéltár (Hungarian Jewish Museum and Archives - MZSML), Deportáltakat Gondozó Országos Bizottság (DEGOB) (National committee for the care of deportees), Protocol 3642.

56. ÁSZTL, V-79.348.71.

57. Ibid., 75., 85., 140.

58. Ibid., 75.

59. BML, Pécsváradi járás főszolgabírájának iratai (Papers of the chief constable of the district of Pécsvárad), 30/1945.

60. ÁSZTL, V-79.348.72.

61. *Magyar Közlöny*, May 10, 1945. 26. szám 3–4.

62. Minutes of the cabinet meeting, January 12, 1945, in László Szűcs, ed., *Dálnoki Miklós Béla kormányának (Ideiglenes Nemzeti Kormány) minisztertanácsi jegyzőkönyvei 1944. december 23.–1945. november 15.* (Meetings of the cabinet of Miklós Béla Dálnoki [provisional national government] December 23, 1944–November 15, 1945) (Budapest: Magyar Országos Levéltár, 1997), 120.

63. Ibid., 304, 332, 336, 359, 365–67; *Magyar Közlöny*, May 10, 1945. 26. szám 3.

64. Zoltán András Kovács, "Csendőrsors Magyarországon 1945 után" (The fate of gendarmes in Hungary after 1945), in *Katonai perek a kommunista diktatúra időszakában 1945–1958* (Military trials under the communist dictatorship, 1945–1958), ed. Imre Okhváth (Budapest: Történeti Hivatal, 2001), 124.

65. Ibid., 119. The number of persons indicted and arraigned in the people's courts in Hungary is 59,429, of which 26,997 were found guilty. See Tibor Zinner, *XX. századi politikai perek: A magyarországi eljárások vázlata 1944/1945–1992* (20th-century political trials: The scheme of the procedures in Hungary 1944/1945–1992) (Budapest: Rejtjel, 1999), 32.

66. Okhváth, 125.

67. Zinner, 32.

Postwar
Historical/Sociological

The She'erit ha-Pletah:
Holocaust Survivors in Northern Transylvania

Jean Ancel

At the beginning of June 1944, the Nazis and the proto-Fascist Hungarian government completed the deportation campaign in Northern Transylvania. Out of a total of 150,000 Jews, they deported over 130,000 to the Auschwitz extermination camp.[1] On October 25, 1944, the liberation of Northern Transylvania from the Nazi and Hungarian forces was completed. On January 27, 1945, the Soviet Army liberated the Auschwitz extermination camp. Only on March 9, 1945, was Northern Transylvania returned to Romanian sovereignty. By early May 1945, all the extermination and labor camps, including those in Germany, had been liberated. These parameters frame the tragedy of Northern Transylvanian Jews and the development of a phenomenon familiar in the history of the Jewish people, namely, *She'erit ha-Pletah* ("the surviving remnant").

The first Jews liberated were several thousand men from labor battalions deployed in central Transylvania. In the second half of October 1944, hundreds of Jews who had been in hiding and others who had escaped from the battalions, or who had been part of the battalions freed by the Romanian or Soviet forces, returned to central Transylvania and the northwestern districts. In Cluj (Kolozsvár in Hungarian) some 120 Jews were liberated in mid-October. Owing to the stream of survivors from all regions, the number of Jews in Cluj grew during November, that is, before the arrival of the deportees from the liberated Polish and Austrian camps in February 1945, to some 600 people. The number of Jews in the other large cities also grew at the same rate.

By the close of 1944, many survivors of the labor battalions, including young people, and Holocaust survivors from near-by regions and countries had reached Northern Transylvania. At the beginning of February 1945, the first survivors of the death camps in Poland reached Cluj. Solitary girls came from Auschwitz, labor servicemen without families from the Ukraine and from Bor, Yugoslavia—all of whom were without family or home, alone, desolate, ill, spiritually debilitated, and

155

desperate. During the period February–March, hundreds of Jews who had been hiding in Budapest returned to the region. In May–June the first survivors arrived from Western Europe. By autumn 1945, their number had swelled to a few tens of thousands—not all of them originally from the area. They came from the camps in Germany to which Jews had been transferred from Northern Transylvania. By October 1945, almost everyone who had wanted to return had done so.[2]

In the first months after their return, deportees sought relatives who had survived the camps or labor battalions. It was terrifying to see hundreds of survivors finally comprehend that their hopes, unrealistic from the outset, had proven false. At the end of 1945, hundreds left the region, most at their own volition and some in an organized way, heading west in the direction of Vienna and from there to Italy with the help of the Zionist movement and the Mossad. These young people did not want to be rehabilitated in their native land, and they realized that their relatives would not return.

Estimates of the number of survivors from Northern Transylvania vary. Holocaust survivors who returned from the death camps in Poland via Germany (about 20,000), and those from Hungarian labor battalions (15,000), numbered between 30,000 and 35,000. The survival rate was approximately 20 percent. On September 1, 1945, Romanian authorities determined that an estimated 29,405 Jews had survived, based on a count of those entering the country.[3] One may safely say that some 85 to 90 percent of the deportees to the concentration camps did not return to the region, while some 65 percent of the members of the labor battalions survived and returned to Transylvania. If we take into consideration those who returned from Soviet captivity after 1948, that is, Jews from the Hungarian labor battalions taken prisoner by the Soviet army even though they were Jews, we can estimate the number of survivors at 20 percent, some 30,000–32,000 of all the Jews who lived in Northern Transylvania in May 1944.

Some deportees returning to Romania were in fact Jewish refugees from regions near and far. They arrived in increasing numbers to Romania, which at the time was the only country with American Jewish Joint Distribution Committee (commonly known as "the Joint") depots.[4] The refugees believed that from Romania they could continue to Palestine or to other countries. We must not forget that the war continued to rage in central Europe until May 1945, and even after that date it was no simple matter to reach western or southern Europe. These refugees included Jews from Hungary, Slovakia, Poland, and other countries, as well as from territories annexed by the Soviet Union, such as Carpatho-Rus. While helping these refugees was important, doing so made it much more difficult to help Romanian Jews, especially the thousands of survivors from Transnistria's camps, dislocated Jews from the villages and boroughs in Moldova, men freed from the forced-labor detachments, and so on. Refugees and Holocaust survivors took advantage of the opportunity provided by the opening of the Romanian border, declaring themselves Romanian citizens or relatives of citizens and mingling with the Transnistria deportees and refugees from the Soviet Union who did have Romanian nationality. It is impossible to determine the number of refugees in Romania during this period (1944–47), since many found ways to leave the country for other destinations. The Red Cross estimated that in 1945 about six thousand refugees reached Romania from Hungary. The World Jewish Congress and Romanian Jewish organizations put the number of refugees who arrived during 1945–47 at between 20,000 and 28,000.[5]

Immediately after the liberation of Cluj, the Jews organized the Democratic Jewish Association (*Gruparea Democrată Evreiască* in Romanian; *Népközösség* in Hungarian). Similar organizations were also set up through the end of 1944 in other large cities. Towards the end of the year a framework was established that included all the local organizations, with its center in Cluj under the leadership of László Ardás. The Association aimed to provide food and clothing for the survivors, to restore Jewish property to its rightful owners, and to represent the Jews before the authorities. The Association enjoyed the support of international Jewish organizations, as well as that of the local government. At the end of 1944, preparations were made for a reorganization of the communities, and by the end of 1945 fifty-six Jewish communities were functioning in the cities of Northern Transylvania, mostly outside the Szekler Land.[6]

Beginning in April 1945, the Association in cooperation with the Zionist organizations, which had also renewed their activities, sent special trains to the extermination camps to gather survivors, to offer them aid, and to return them to Romania. The Association set up canteens and clubhouses, and in many places opened shelters for youth and even for adults until they were rehabilitated. The Joint and other

Jewish organizations outside of Romania sent money and made it available for the rehabilitation of survivors who had returned from the camps. Yet the rehabilitation encountered many obstacles, both from the local population and, at times, from the new village and town administrations established by supporters of King Michael and of Iuliu Maniu's National Peasant Party, which gained the backing of most of the Romanian population. The difficulties and enmity did not fade even when the leadership passed into the hands of the Left, led by the Communists, who in most places removed Romanian national and nationalist authorities. The disposition towards the Jews remained hostile and the new Romanian leadership opposed rehabilitation of the Jews that would include the return of all their property, arguing that such action would foster anti-Semitism.

Another claim was that the renewal of capitalism should not be encouraged by the restoration of factories and business, which would distance those benefiting from the distribution of the deportees' property from the new government controlled by the Communist Party. Consequently, most survivors who returned to villages and towns soon left and moved into ten cities that then held 90 percent of the Jewish population.[7]

In Romania itself, a hostile mood developed toward the repatriated deportees. The anti-Jewish campaign was waged during the fierce political struggle between the Romanian Communist Party on one side and traditional forces and the King on the other. The Communist Party, supported by the Soviet army of occupation, had gradually seized control of all state institutions. Yet, the traditional forces and the King, although denounced as "reactionaries," in fact represented the Romanian people and the weak Romanian democracy. Rumors circulated about the entry of two million Jews from the Soviet empire who would support the Communist Party and tilt the results of the general elections scheduled for November 19, 1946. Antonescu-government propaganda, about what the Romanian people could expect if the Red Army occupied the country and the role that Jews would play in the new regime, seemed about to become reality. In August 1946, the Special Intelligence Service (*Serviciul Special de Informatii* - SSI) reported, "Hatred of the Jewish element is on the rise. Among the things contributing to this are rumors that Jews have come to Romania from various areas in Poland, Czechoslovakia, and Russia, and will remain here as settlers."[8]

In different parts of Romania, especially Southern Bukovina and Northern Transylvania, in villages and towns from which the Jews had been evicted in June 1941, as well as in Moldova, Jews who tried to return to their homes were attacked and dozens were murdered. At the time the censor prevented publication of reports about these events, but the facts are now available. According to a previously unknown report by the SSI, "In various parts of the country, Jews have been and continue to be murdered, and their murderers have not been identified or have not been punished.... Zionist circles, in particular, exploit these anti-Semitic eruptions to increase the psychosis of immigration to Palestine."9 Jews who had settled in villages in Southern Transylvania, replacing Germans who had fled, were attacked. In Timiş-Torontal County, "the local [Romanian] population greeted them with great hostility and even physically attacked them and refused to accept them in the villages."10 The authorities attributed these outbursts to the propaganda campaign against the Jews conducted by "reactionary circles."

The exact number of Jews murdered throughout Romania under these circumstances is not known, but according to the documents available they numbered just under one hundred. The authorities, whose political complexion changed rapidly as the Communists tightened their control over the country, could not ignore the problem. As far as they were concerned, the more Jews who left the country, the closer the problem of the deportees and refugees came to a "solution."

Two contradictory phenomena altered the composition of the Jewish population in Northern Transylvania in 1945–48. On the one hand, thousands of Jews came to the region from other parts of Romania, especially hundreds of refugee families from Bukovina, themselves survivors of the ghettos in Transnistria. In addition, thousands of Jews from Moldova fled that region owing to famine and shortages. Yet, on the other hand, a wave of emigration and *aliyah* began that reduced the number of Jews by one-quarter until the stabilization of Communist rule in 1948.

The process of assimilation, including intermarriage, among a part of the surviving remnants played a major role at the time, and in the second half of 1945 a change took place in the way the Jews organized themselves. Under pressure from Jewish Communists, whose number continuously increased, the Jewish Association was disbanded, and in Romania and Transylvania a Jewish Democratic Committee (*Comitetul*

Democratic Evreiesc) was established that operated under the directive of the Romanian Communist Party. The Committee's aim was to draw the Jews closer to the Communist Party and to distance them from the Zionist movement. Among the young people, in the competition between the two organizations, the Zionists won. The Zionist youth movements encompassed approximately 80 percent of all Jewish youth.[11] But Jewish youth who participated in meetings initiated by the Communist Party and its front organizations, together with Hungarians and the few Romanians who had initially supported the Party, stood out by their presence and their vociferousness in their confrontations with supporters of the King and the Romanian historical parties, increasing the hatred towards the Jews, the Communists, and the Russians. Seething with rage at the Hungarian Fascists for murdering members of their families and for robbing them of their property, embittered Jewish youth seeking revenge joined the left-wing organizations and the Communist Party. This trend, however, did not last very long.

The Communists, who seized power after publication of the forged results of elections at the end of November 1946, recognized the problem but did not believe that the predicament of the survivors and refugees needed rapid resolution. For them, the Jews had to participate in the "struggle" for democracy, that is, to support the Communist Party in its struggle against the traditional forces, rather than continuing to demand the restoration of their property and their rights and asking for special consideration and allowances and the like. "The Jewish masses cannot conduct a private struggle separate from the struggle of the Romanian people to strengthen democracy and develop the country," read an internal report.[12]

During this period a hidden, though sometimes visible, rift developed between two factions: the many Jews who wanted to rehabilitate themselves—they stormed the schools and universities, found jobs in the government bureaucracy, and opened businesses and workshops—and the thousands of Holocaust survivors, displaced persons, and refugees who did not wish to or could not be rehabilitated in Romania. For them, the only solution was illegal emigration by means of the *Bricha* (Flight) network. The Zionist youth movements did what they could to help young people leave Romania by every possible route, but they were not equipped to offer legal or illegal immigration to the tens of thousands of survivors and displaced persons who desired to go to Palestine.

* * *

Orthodox Jews of Southern Transylvania tried to revive the destroyed communities in Northern Transylvania. The Central Orthodox Bureau (*Biroul central ortodox*) held consultations at the beginning of May in Alba Iulia in Southern Transylvania and decided to send a delegation of six rabbis to visit 106 Orthodox communities, the number they thought remained in Northern Transylvania, to conduct a survey and investigate ways for "reviving the desolated communities."

The Orthodox rabbis who visited the region "came to realize that the spiritual destruction was even greater than the victims of the sword and famine," even though some 80 percent of the Jews had been annihilated in the Holocaust.[13] The synagogues and study halls had been turned into workshops or places of entertainment by the Hungarian authorities; *mikva'ot* (ritual baths) and Talmud Torahs had been destroyed. Religious life did not exist and kosher food was not available. Many of the returnees from the death camps distanced themselves on their own volition from any traditional way of life in an expression of revolt against the tragedy of the Holocaust and in protest against the policy of the Satmar rebbe. The "rebellion" against Judaism also continued via intermarriage as an expression of frustration and revenge. Missionaries, who also offered material support, tried to go after willing souls among the survivors. Orthodoxy's conclusion was to carry on as if nothing had happened, to rebuild Diasporic life, to rehabilitate Jewish life on the ruins of the destroyed communities.[14]

This decision ignored not only the survivors' changed worldview, which stemmed from the spiritual upheaval they had undergone, from the self-examination they had made regarding everything connected to the meaning of observing the commandments, and even from the desire to continue to be believing Jews, but also from the political situation in Romania where the Communist Party, which negated any form of religion, was about to take over the country. The Satmar followers (Hasidim)—the few survivors who had returned and the rabbi who had been spared deportation—continued the debate and their hatred of Zionism as if it had been halted for a few months owing to a mere administrative issue. Redemption, they said, cannot come from the Zionist idea, and the Land of Israel cannot provide "material" redemption before the coming of our righteous Messiah. The opponents of Zionism immediately supplied an explanation for the tragedy that had befallen: The horrendous Holocaust had come as Divine punishment for having transgressed the three negative commandments described in the Talmudic tractate *Ketubbot*. The Germans and the Hungarians were absolved of any guilt; they were mere instruments in the hand of God. According to this kind of logic, the sacrifice of the six million had occurred because of the "Hiding of the Face of God" the Creator, who did not want to see his beloved, chosen people led to slaughter, as the phenomenon of punishment is described in the Bible.[15] In the years preceding the Holocaust and even in the freight cars transporting believing, innocent Jews to the gas chambers, Rabbi Shlomo Zalman Ehrenreich, the rabbi of Şimleul Silvaniei, continued to blame Zionism and the Zionists for what was happening to the Jews and not the Germans or the Hungarians.

On October 14, 1941, Simhat Torah, Rabbi Ehrenreich said that over the course of its history, had the people of Israel kept the Torah, God would never have allowed the enemy to tyrannize them; instead, they would have evoked respect. But the people did at times neglect the Torah and chose to emulate the non-Jewish nations (*goim*)—and in consequence they suffered. Ehrenreich accused the Zionists of polluting the Land of Israel; they abrogated commandments and neglected Torah study. Giving them money to build the future Jewish State was similar to giving money to Haman to destroy Judaism. The Zionists were raising their children as heretics—thereby slaughtering them and provoking divine anger (Isaiah 1:4). Ehernreich's anti-Zionism, like that of Rabbi Joel Teitelbaum of Satu Mare (Szatmárnémeti in Hungarian), Rabbi Avraham Yehoshua Freund of Năsăud (Naszód in Hungarian), and Rabbi Shaul Brach of Carei (Nagykároly in Hungarian), continued through the ghetto and in Auschwitz: "*Nur die Reshoim, di Tzionim, hoben uns hier gebracht*" (The evil ones, the Zionists, brought us to this point). On the train to Auschwitz he repeated the accusation that the Zionists were responsible, but added that the Orthodox had to share the blame for not protesting enough: "*Rak hatzionim garmu zot vehagzeirah haiita yaan shelo machine dai negdam*" (Only the Zionists caused this and the decree came because we did not protest enough against them).[16]

The Central Orthodox Bureau in Transylvania began a struggle to maintain the autonomy of the Orthodox communities in order to obtain money from the Joint for the restoration of the communities and religious life—actually for the continuation of the past with the current

Holocaust survivors. Even the leaders of Orthodoxy in Transylvania were aware of the upheaval that the remnants of the Transylvanian Jews who had returned from Auschwitz or from the labor camps had undergone. They wanted to act swiftly.

> Serious danger was hovering, for on the one hand, this mass plucked from the fire, which had fallen into apathy, might come to despair and even, heaven forbid, commit suicide, while on the other hand, the one who hurled harsh words towards the Heavens over what the Lord had wrought, Heaven forfend, might turn their backs to religion. In these days of chaos difficult, grave issues faced the bureau.[17]

Orthodoxy's new enemy was the Federation of Jewish Communities in Romania, dubbed "reform" even though their rabbis were Orthodox in every way. (Judaism in Reform format was unknown in Old Romania.) The second enemy was the chairman of the Federation and the Romanian branch of the Joint, Wilhelm Filderman, who refused to put at the disposal of the Orthodox Bureau the entire sum of aid needed for building Jewish communities along strictly Orthodox lines. Who should be taken care of first? The 60,000 Jews displaced from villages and towns; the 40,000 deportees from Transnistria who intermittently returned depending upon the occasional good will of the Soviet authorities; the 28,000 refugees from neighboring countries, most of whom were also Holocaust survivors who streamed into Bucharest; or to those who wanted to revive Jewish life in the Orthodox way from the point it had ceased in April 1944 when the ghettos had been established? Rabbi Tzvi Jacob Abraham went to the United States at the end of November 1945 and was joined by Rabbi Joel Teitelbaum of Satu Mare, Rabbi Jekuthiel Judah Halberstam of Cluj, Rabbi Moses Teitelbaum of Sighetu Marmatiei (Máramarossziget in Hungarian), and other rabbis to enlist the support of Orthodox Judaism and to serve as "proponents" for Orthodoxy in Transylvania.

On March 4, 1946, the "Federation of Transylvania Jews in America" was founded in New York. Proponents, who also met with the directors of the Joint and with the Romanian ambassador, obtained from the Joint and other sources large sums of money for the rehabilitation of the Orthodox way of life in Transylvania, "to revive the desolated communities and so on" and "to restore the members of the community to the rightful path," as the Orthodox leaders put it.[18]

Within less than two years all this work proved to be for naught. The Communist regime confiscated most of the buildings and houses, the *mikva'ot*, the Talmud Torahs, and even the synagogues in which money that could have helped make life better for the Holocaust survivors had been invested. And then the Jews who had faithfully hated the Zionist idea itself did everything they could to reach the Zionist state.

* * *

Most young Jewish survivors from Northern Transylvania succeeded in building new lives, they married and raised children, and appeared to lead normal lives. But they did not cope with the consequences of their tragedy, and nightmares are still part of their life. Even after thirty or forty years they do not fully understand the readiness of the Hungarian authorities and, in most cases, also of their Hungarian neighbors to rid themselves so quickly of their Hungarian-speaking Jews: the Hungarians acquiesced in the morbid desire of the Germans to kill and destroy the Jewish masses, even when the outcome of the war was clear. The surviving remnants in Northern Transylvania are unable to accept this reality and continue to bear deep within their souls the images of their loved ones as they remember them on the railroad platform at Auschwitz.

A young Jewish girl who survived Auschwitz alone and married another survivor and "gained," as she said, "34 years together," asked herself twenty years ago: "We the Jews, what lesson should we learn from all this? How should we treat these events without transferring to the next generations the cry: People, what have you done? What have you done to us and what have you done to yourselves?"[19]

Notes

1. Randolph L. Braham, *Genocide and Retribution: The Hungarian-Ruled Northern Transylvania* (Boston: Kluwer-Nijhoff, 1983), 17; Bela Vago, "The Destruction of the Jews in Transylvania," *Hungarian Jewish Studies* 1 (1966): 194; Moshe Carmilly-Weinberger, *The Tragedy of Transylvanian Jewry* (Jerusalem: Yad Vashem, 1964), 298, n. 30.

2. Bela Vago, "Introduction" to Northern Transylvania section, in *Pinkas Hakehilot: Romania* (Encyclopedia of Jewish communities, Romania), eds. J. Ancel and T. Lavi (Jerusalem: Yad Vashem, 1980), 17.

3. M. Carp, *Cartea Neagră* (The black book) (Bucharest: Atelierele Grafice Scocec, 1947), 18.

4. Wilhelm Filderman, head of both the Federation of Jewish Communities in Romania and the Joint director for that country, noted this in his records (Yad Vashem, Filderman Archives, P-6/29, 282). We must remember that in all of Romania the Joint was able to operate an office only in Bucharest.

5. Memorandum from the Federation of Jewish Communities in Romania sent to the United Nations inquiry commission, February 19, 1946, in ibid., P-6/31, 80–7; interview with Filderman in the Romanian press after the anti-Semitic ferment caused by the spread of rumors about the admission to Romania of two million Jews from the Soviet Union and other countries in *Jurnalul de Dimineaţă,* August 10, 1946; and various reports by the Joint and other relief organizations operating under its auspices in the Filderman Archives, P-6/27, 104–11 and 137–41; P–6/29, 281–92; P-6/31, 1–5, 29–35, and 46–7; P-6/32, 39–45, 77–97, and 181–88. See also the figures in the pamphlet issued by the World Jewish Congress, *Romanian Jewry in the Postwar Period* (in Hebrew) (Tel Aviv, no date).

6. The area of the three counties in Transylvania (Csík, Háromszék and Udvarhely – in Romanian Ciuc, Trei Scaune, and Odorhei) that are inhabited primarily by Hungarians identified as Szeklers.

7. Vago, "Introduction," 18.

8. United States Holocaust Memorial Museum Archives (USHMM), RG-25.004M, reel 10/Romanian Information Service Archives Bucharest (SRI), File 2699, Report by the SSI office in southern Transylvania, August 12, 1946, 331.

9. Ibid., SSI report, No. 42, January 29, 1946, 308.

10. Ibid., SSI report, May 7, 1946.

11. Yitzhak Perri-Friedman, *Toldot hayehudim be'Transylvania ba'meah ha'esrim* (The history of the Jews in Transylvania in the twentieth century) (Tel Aviv: Hotsa'at Tarbut, 1995), II, 928.

12. USHMM, RG-25.004M, Reel 10/SRI, File 2699, "The Condition of the Jews in Romania during the Second World War," Siguranţa (Security Police) Memorandum, January 11, 1947, 426.

13. Anonymous, *Le Koroth Hayahdut be Translyvania* (History of the Jews of Transylvania), vol. I (New York: A. Lamberger, 1951), 192.

14. Perri-Friedman, 188.

15. Ibid., 183.

16. Gershon Greenberg, "Shlomo Zalman Ehrenreich's (1863–1944) Religious Response to the Holocaust: February 1939–October 1943. Şimleul-Silvaniei (Szilagagysomlyo), Transilvania," *Studia Judaica* 9 (2000): 75, 77.

17. *Le Koroth Hayahdut be Translyvania*, 237.

18. Perri-Friedman, 192–93.

19. Itzhak-Zvi Unechama and Ana Gonen, *Yavueni rachameicha veechie Darkeinu Bachaim* (Let thy tender mercies come unto me, that I may live our way in life) (Tel Aviv, 1999), 201.

The Revival of Anti-Semitism in Post-Communist Hungary: The Early 1990s[1]

Ivan T. Berend

The Holocaust eliminated half of the Jewish population of Trianon Hungary; as a result of postwar emigration, by 1956 even fewer Jews remained in the country. The majority of the survivors left Hungary, either immediately after the war and the Kúnmadaras and Miskolc pogroms in 1946, or between 1945 and 1948 when all private businesses were eliminated. After the Revolution of 1956, a major new wave of emigration followed. Jewish communities virtually disappeared from the Hungarian countryside and the remaining 80,000 or so resided mainly in Budapest. A group that once had comprised 5 percent of the country's population had shrunk to roughly 0.8 percent. Most of its members were intellectuals, business managers, and clerks in partially state-owned businesses concerned with foreign and domestic trade. Unlike the 1950s, when a rather visible "over-representation" of Jews characterized the Stalinist regime, including the quintet of Mátyás Rákosi, Ernö Gerö, Mihály Farkas, József Révai, and Gábor Péter, Jewish political overrepresentation practically disappeared during the three-decades-long János Kádár era. Throughout this period, and especially during the 1960s, the reform-Communist opposition within the party, together with a nonparty dissident opposition to the regime, contained a large proportion of Jews. These groups played a historic role in reforming the regime, making it more social democratic. After 1988 this reform wing gradually took over the party and pushed toward peaceful revolution.

Thus, after the collapse of state socialism in 1989, the sudden and strong revival of anti-Semitism came as a surprise. Yet this phenomenon was not at all unique. The same thing happened in Poland and Romania although Jews represented only 0.01 percent and 0.1 percent of the population respectively. "Anti-Semitism without Jews," as Paul Lendvai coined the term in the title of one of his books,[2] albeit odd, was quite common in post-Communist Central and Eastern Europe.

Is there a rational explanation for this irrational trend? Certainly there is, but it is necessary to take note of the historical context. The phenomenon would be incomprehensible without considering the historical lack of undisturbed nation-building and the resulting exaltation of nationalism in the area. Anti-Semitism was an organic part of the "tribal nationalism," to use Hannah Arendt's term,[3] that emerged during the nineteenth century in Central and Eastern Europe. This trend was a consequence of the lack of an organic homogenization of various ethnic, linguistic, and religious groupings within the borders of the absolutist state in the early modern period, and the absence of an early capitalist transformation—historical developments that might have constructed nations and reinforced the will to form nation-states. All of the countries of the region lost their independence between the fifteenth and nine-teenth centuries and were absorbed into huge multi-ethnic empires. The nation-building and nation-state formation that characterized the West did not happen in "the belt of mixed population," as C. A. Macartney called Central and Eastern Europe.[4] Unlike the West, people, nation, and territory did not clearly overlap in this part of the continent.

When the romantic national idea arrived in the region via Germany, nationalism had a strongly ethno-cultural character, and the will to create nation-states automatically became xenophobic. The nation was consid-ered to be a tribal unit, an ethno-cultural-blood relationship. He who did not belong to the "tribe" was an alien, and, in most cases, considered an enemy. These nationalities viewed neighboring peoples as rivals against whom they were forced to struggle because, for one thing, the rivals of-ten coveted the same territory. Furthermore, in regions of mixed popula-tions, nearly all of the countries had minorities living in neighboring lands and desired to include them in their own nations. Tribal national-ism, in other words, sought to expand the state to absorb its minorities living beyond its borders. These population elements constituted what the Pan-German movement termed *staatsfremde* minorities: they were aliens in the state in which they lived. The obverse of this notion was the determination that other nations' minorities within one's own borders, the *volksfremde* minorities, were also alien bodies and therefore enemies of that nation's destiny.[5] "National hysteria," as István Bibó called this sentiment, became an integral part of Central and Eastern European nationalism.[6]

As a consequence, from the beginning, German, Polish, and Roma-nian nationalism organically merged with anti-Semitism. The Jewish minorities, 10 percent of the population in Poland and 5 percent in Romania, were not considered part of the nation, but alien, dangerous, and hostile elements. In Romania, Jews were not eligible for citizenship; in Poland, the Roman Dmowski-led nationalists suggested mass Jewish emigration as the mechanism to defend the purity of the Polish race.[7]

Nineteenth-century Hungary did not follow this pattern. As a multinational entity with only half of its population ethnic Hungarian, nationalism was strongly assimilationist during the time of the Austro-Hungarian Empire (1867–1918). The Hungarian nation was considered indivisible, with all its minorities a part of it. Schools and other institutions made a crucial effort to Magyarize the population. Slovaks and Romanians within Hungary's borders were considered as belonging to the Hungarian nation; as were Jews who were "Hungarians of Mosaic religion" and, in fact, who were often ardent Hungarian nationalists.

After World War I, with the introduction of the concept of *România Mare* (Greater Romania) and the establishment of Yugoslavia and Czechoslovakia, this situation changed dramatically. Romanians and South Slavs now had their own nation-states, but these also contained non-Romanian and non-South Slav minorities. These new multiethnic countries became assimilationist: officially pursuing the "nationalization" of the Germans, Hungarians, and Ukrainians in Romania, and the creation of a Yugoslav nationality to include Croats, Serbs, Bosnian Muslims, and Kosovar Albanians.

In Hungary, forced to concede two-thirds of its prewar territory and 60 percent of its former population, the situation was reversed. Great Hungarian territorial revisionism and xenophobia dominated the ideology, which aimed to reestablish *Nagy-Magyarország* (Greater Hungary). A quarter of a century of virulent and violent anti-Semitism became an integral part of post-1918 Hungarian nationalism.

Moreover, anti-Semitism came to be associated with anti-Communism. After the Bolshevik Revolution, the concept of "Jewish Communism" emerged and grew to dominate Central and Eastern European anti-Semitic movements. In Hungary, it became the cornerstone of political ideology after the formation of the Hungarian Soviet Republic of 1919. Bloody pogroms and anti-Jewish legislation played a prominent role in the Horthy regime.

"Jewish Communism," of course, was merely another form of the well-known concept of eternal Jewish conspiracy—a new narrative for the old medieval myth of well-poisoning, disease-spreading, and Christian-girl-murdering Jews. In modern times, when political anti-

Semitism gained ground, these medieval ideas were replaced by the idea of an international conspiracy of Jewish bankers, stock traders, and media magnates. In one way or another, an imagined Jewish conspiracy to gain world dominance formed the essence of political anti-Semitism (clearly expressed by the "Protocols of the Elders of Zion" fabrication). Late-nineteenth-century German, Polish, and Romanian anti-Semites spoke about a secret Jewish plan to conquer their countries in order to establish a "new Palestine."[8] Anti-Semitism was part of the Hungarian nationalist idea throughout the Horthy regime.

After the shock of losing World War II, followed by a radical regime change, the permanent Soviet army presence, and the formation of the Soviet Bloc, Hungarian nationalism was suppressed under state socialism. Furthermore, the Holocaust led to a strange psychological reaction among the Jews who remained in Hungary: nobody discussed it; they sought to forget their Jewishness, and in many cases did not even tell their children about it. Even the word "Jew" was taboo: if somebody said the word, it was spoken in hushed tones. Anti-Semitism nonetheless did not disappear. It was, in fact, official policy under the codename of 'anti-Zionism' in the final years of high Stalinism, when the Soviet "Doctors' Plot," the Czechoslovak Slansky Trial, and the preparation of the Hungarian Doctors' Plot sought to channel dissatisfaction into the reservoir of traditional anti-Semitism.[9] In some countries of the region, anti-Semitism returned from time to time, for instance in Poland in 1968 when many of the few remaining Jews in the country were dismissed from their jobs and encouraged to emigrate, or in Romania where the Jews were literally "sold" to Israel. In Hungary, however, nothing similar happened during the Kádár era. The problem was not even discussed openly; it was swept under the rug.

How, then, did anti-Semitism re-emerge after the collapse of Communism in Hungary? One factor was the ideological and value vacuum that characterized the former state socialist countries after 1989. Hungary's political and economic institutions, its value system, its official ideology, and even its artistic style collapsed in 1989. This vacuum was filled partly by borrowing free market ideology, but mostly by traditional, reemerging religious fervor and nationalism all over Central and Eastern Europe. This change was clearly signaled by a religious renaissance in many of these countries, and the spectacular collapse of all of the multinational states: Yugoslavia, the Soviet Union, and Czechoslovakia. Instead of the eight countries that had existed previously, there were now twenty-six independent states. Unfinished nation-building put nationalism back into the driver's seat in the region.

The floodgates opened, and a nationalistic xenophobic flood engulfed Central and Eastern Europe. Swiftly, the typical features of tribal nationalism surfaced again and led, in the most extreme cases, to bloody ethnic cleansing. The Muslim-Christian conflict engulfed the Balkans, anti-Roma (Gypsy) atrocities spread like wildfire from Transylvania to Prague, and anti-Semitism reemerged in Russia, Poland, Romania, and Hungary. In some cases, anti-Semitism was again dressed in the cloth of anti-Communism, according to the post-1917 traditional pattern of equating Jewry with Communism. It did not matter that, in reality, the fall of Stalinism in Hungary in 1956 had eliminated Jewish "over-representation" in both the party and the government.[10]

Some of the post-1989 Hungarian governments, particularly the József Antall- and Viktor Orbán-led governments in the early and late 1990s respectively, played the nationalist card. They wanted to represent fifteen million Hungarians, as Antall explicitly stated in one of his speeches, defending ethnic Hungarians at home and those who were citizens of neighboring countries. Lajos Für, minister of defense in the Antall government, stated in February 1992: "The concept of the Hungarian nation in the Carpathian Basin is not limited to the citizens of the Hungarian Republic. The notion of the Hungarian nation in Europe means a Hungarian-speaking united nation."[11]

A quasi-rehabilitation of the Horthy regime stressed the heroic anti-Soviet struggle to halt communism during World War II, as well as Horthy's so-called efforts to save the Hungarian Jews. The Hungarian Holocaust, if mentioned, was interpreted strictly as a German action. One populist writer-editor, Sándor Püski, went so far as to suggest that the Horthy regime entered World War II to save Hungarian Jews! The regent, argued Püski, elected not to break with the Germans, maintaining that alliance to protect some few hundreds of thousands of Jews, and that Horthy "did not care about the interests of 14 million Hungarians," as he wrote in *Magyar Nemzet* (Hungarian nation) in 1988.[12] The propaganda about the so-called Jewish-AVO (secret political police) and equating the Rákosi era with the entire forty years of state socialism in Hungary, became part of this political interpretation. The early 1990s television

series by Mária Schmidt, a chief counselor of Prime Minister Viktor
Orbán, clearly represented this trend.

Openly anti-Semitic attacks engulfed the media. István Benedek, in
Hitel (Credit), a right-populist periodical, reintroduced the idea of
communism as Jewish revenge. This concept, oddly enough, was first
formulated in 1943 by the populist writer László Németh in his famous
Szárszó speech, before the Hungarian Holocaust, when he stated that the
deaf are those who do not hear Shylock already sharpening his knife.[13]
"Hungarian-Jewish relations," stated Benedek,

> were poisoned not by Nazism, but by Bolshevism. I understand the angry
> revenge of the first years [after the war]. There were grave reprisals for
> grave personal injuries, unjust and inhuman in the same way.... The
> Jews...are proud of having been able to be just as vile as the fascists, and
> then became so accustomed to depredation that they could not stop. Now
> they silently strive after judeocracy and loudly cry anti-Semitism against
> everyone who tries to turn against their tyranny.[14]

The same argument was presented in 1990 by György V. Domokos:
"Regarding Jewish ambitions in post-World War II Hungary," he maintained,

> I would have done everything to rise above others, in order to avoid being
> humiliated again.... I would not allow people to seek an explanation for
> the high number of Jews in Hungarian...Communism.... The non-Jews
> have limited tolerance.... This is why the Jews should be understanding
> and limit their ambitions to acquire power.... Anti-Semitism is a reaction
> to something. The dictatorship of the minority can exist.[15]

Radical right-wing journals such as *Szent Korona* (Holy crown) and
Hunnia Füzetek (Hunnia notebooks) wrote about a Hungary that will be
"free from aliens," and also about Jews who are "preparing to take
over."

Anti-Semitic trends in the early 1990s were not only spontaneous
outbursts by marginal figures and second-rate pundits, but also a reaction
to the decades-long suppression of anti-Semitism. The victors of the first
free elections in March 1990, the Hungarian Democratic Forum (*Magyar
Demokrata Fórum* - MDF) and its coalition allies were a conglomerate
of various right-of-center parties and political groupings. Within the
MDF itself, a radical right wing, led by István Csurka, one of the vice
presidents of the party, published the most open and vicious attacks. In

an interview in the *The New Yorker*, Csurka stated in 1989: "It cannot be denied that there was a special group of Communist party leaders, represented by György Aczél. As a Jew, he collected around himself Jewish people in the leadership in the Kádár era.... They are still in power in the press, television, radio...."[16] In January 1990, he added on his radio program that a minority "makes life for Hungarians of völkisch-national character impossible in Hungary...the large völkisch masses of Hungarians cannot feel at home in their own country. Wake up Hungarians!" In March 1991, he praised the MDF government: "If this government remains in place...the game is up, forever, for Bolshevism, cosmopolitanism, foreigners dressed in liberal clothing [all well-known code names for Jews], and the humiliation of the nation. Then, it will finally be a Christian middle stratum who creates European Hungary...the property of the Hungarians."[17]

Another founder of the MDF, the populist writer and then president of the World Association of Hungarians, Sándor Csoóri, explained the alien character of Jewry in 1990: "The last time the Jews could identify themselves with the national problems of Hungary," he stated, "was the pre-World War I period; but today reversed tendencies of assimilation are appearing in the country. Liberal Hungarian Jewry is trying to 'assimilate' the Hungarians into their style and thinking. For this they have even fabricated a parliamentary springboard for themselves."[18]

In 1992, MDF presidium member Gyula Zacsek published an article titled "Termites Are Devouring the Nation," which stands as one of the clearest expressions of the right-wing idea of a Jewish-American conspiracy against Hungary. He attacked George Soros, the Jewish, Hungarian-born American multi-millionaire philanthropist, who financed dissidents against the Communist regimes throughout Central and Eastern Europe during the 1980s via his Open Society Fund. According to Zacsek's argument, Soros' actions planned to help the cosmopolitan (i.e. Jewish) Communists to preserve their power by giving it over to the similarly "cosmopolitan" dissidents. "The Soros Foundation was the vital tool and resource in laying the groundwork for this transition."[19]

István Csurka repeated this conspiracy theory in his 1992 study, this time attacking the president of the Hungarian Republic, Árpád Göncz, who resisted certain demands by the MDF. Göncz—who received a life sentence after the 1956 Revolution—resisted the government party, argued Csurka, "because he was ordered to do so by the Communist, reform-Communist, liberal, and radical nomenklatura and the middle men of Paris, New York, and Tel-Aviv."[20]

The Hungarian extreme right returned to the Nazi argument, so well-known from Hitler's *Mein Kampf*: the caricature eternal Jew, part of an international Jewish conspiracy, appears as Communist, anti-Communist liberal, American multi-millionaire, and so on, all, despite their fundamental differences, with the same goal: world conquest.[21]

Clearly, open anti-Semitism is an important trend in post-Communist Hungary, especially since it is so strongly present in the governing party. Prime Minister József Antall, a moderate conservative, attempting to keep his party and coalition together, did not distance himself and his government from his own right-wing extremists for years. After an early 1993 debate in the United States Congress, which sent a strong message to Hungary, Antall, at last, distanced his government from the Csurka wing, which had left the party and founded its own right-extremist party.

This radical nationalist and anti-Semitic *Magyar Élet Pártja* (Hungarian Life Party) was unable to muster the 5 percent threshold of votes to become a parliamentary party. At the 1998 elections, however, they gained seats in local electoral districts and entered the parliament as a kind of informal, outside member of the coalition that supported the Alliance of Young Democrats Party (*Fiatal Demokraták Szövetsége -* FIDESz), the government party, and the Orbán government (1998–2002), and contributed to its sharp shift toward the right, and ultimately to its defeat in the 2002 elections.

The revival of anti-Semitism in post-state socialist Hungary is a strange political phenomenon. One might believe that anti-Jewish sentiments without direct political action belong to the category of so-called "intellectual anti-Semitism." This latter term, however, had already been discredited by its advocates, including Houston Stewart Chamberlain, Eugen Diederichs, and the "innocent" anti-Semitism of László Németh and the Hungarian populists in the late 1930s and early 1940s.

Leszek Kolakowski speaks about different categories of anti-Semites: those who demand the extermination of Jews; others who only consider them to belong to an inferior race, or maintain that Jews merely represent a culturally alien people; and those who only feel antipathy against them. Nevertheless, the different types of anti-Semitism, warns Kolakowski, differ only quantitatively and represent different stages of the same danger. This warning strongly echoes Max Horkheimer's earlier message: if you want to explain anti-Semitism, you have to remember National Socialism. Without considering what happened in Germany, it is senseless to speak of anti-Semitism elsewhere.

Revitalized anti-Semitism in the early 1990s, noisy and vitriolic and frightening to many as it was, has proven, nevertheless, incapable of influencing or hindering either political transformation or the rise of a democratic system in Hungary.[22] The right wing was small, and a few years after its reappearance it remained on the whole isolated from the mainstream. Furthermore, the right-of-center parties that collaborated with the radical right twice lost elections after serving only a single term and were replaced by a left-of-center socialist-liberal coalition that has blocked the right-wing's advance. Fighting for popularity and electoral victory, however, certain political forces and parties play from time to time the nationalist card. Xenophobia and anti-Semitism, often dressed in anti-communism or anti-Jewish-communism, may for a brief period mobilize a fraction of the population. Thus, the anti-Semitic tradition may occasionally resurface, although after the virtual disappearance of Jewry it may slowly disappear from Hungarian political life. Joining the European Union makes support for a xenophobic policy, especially when it is launched by the government or a government party, more difficult, more outdated and baseless, but not yet impossible. Ethno-cultural conflicts, after all, have reappeared within the European Union and need to be addressed and handled.

Notes

1. Some of the sources for this study were used in my "Jobbra át! (Right face!): Right-Wing Trends in Post-Communist Hungary," in *Democracy and Right-Wing Politics in Eastern Europe in the 1990s*, ed. Joseph Held (Boulder, CO: East European Monographs, 1993), 105–34.

2. Paul Lendvai, *Anti-Semitism without Jews* (Garden City, NY: Doubleday, 1971).

3. Hannah Arendt, *The Origins of Totalitarianism* (Cleveland: Meridian, 1958).

4. C. A. Macartney, *The Habsburg Empire, 1790–1918* (London: Weidenfeld & Nicholson, 1968).

5. R. D'O. Butler, *The Roots of National Socialism, 1873–1933* (London: Faber and Faber, 1941).

6. István Bibó, *Válogatott tanulmányok* (Selected studies), vol. 2. 1945–49 (Budapest: Magvető, 1986).

7. Ivan T. Berend, *History Derailed: Central and Eastern Europe in the Long Nineteenth Century* (Berkeley: University of California Press, 2003).

8. Ibid.

9. George H. Hodos, *Show Trials: Stalinist Purges in Eastern Europe, 1948–1954* (New York: Praeger,
1987.

10. Ivan T. Berend, *Central and Eastern Europe, 1944–1993: Detour from the Periphery to the Periphery* (Cambridge: Cambridge University Press, 1996), 363–71.

11. See note 1, above.

12. *Magyar Nemzet* (Hungarian nation), (Budapest), December 14, 1988.

13. Gyula Juhász, *Uralkodó eszmék Magyarországon, 1939–1944* (Dominant ideas in Hungary, 1939–1944) (Budapest: Kossuth Kiadó, 1983).

14. István Benedek, *Hitel* (Credit), (Budapest), September 1990.

15. György V. Domokos, *Népszabadság* (People's freedom), (Budapest), April 1990.

16. David K. Shipler, "Letter from Budapest," *The New Yorker* (November 20, 1989): 99.

17. *Magyar Fórum* (Hungarian forum), (Budapest), March 1991.

18. *Hitel*, September 1990.

19. *Magyar Fórum*, September 3, 1992.

20. Ibid., August 20, 1992.

21. Adolf Hitler, *Mein Kampf* (Boston: Houghton Mifflin, 1971), 312–26.

22. Leszek Kolakowski, "Die Antisemiten" in *Der Mensch ohne Alternative*, ed. Leszek Kolakowski (Munich: Piper, 1967); and Max Horkheimer, "Die Juden und Europa," *Zeitschrift für Sozialforschung* VII (1939). Both reprinted in *Zsidókérdés Kelet- és Közép-Európában* (The Jewish question in east central Europe), ed. Róbert Simon. (Budapest: ELTE Jogi Kar, 1985).

Identity on the Move: Hungarian Jewry between Budapest and the DP Camps, 1945-1948*

Alice Freifeld

The dominant narrative of the Holocaust concludes with the departure of the Jewish remnant from Central Europe. In the first issue of *Commentary* (November 1945), readers were informed of the plight of surviving Jews state by state. The remnant of Polish Jewry returned to an empty community in an inhospitable society and pogroms. Departure from Poland and return to displaced persons (DP) camps in Austria and western Germany seemed to be the inevitable outcome. The magazine noted that, "Budapest, with 120,000 Jews, was probably the largest Jewish city in Europe." Nevertheless, the lengthy article included only one additional sentence on Hungary.[1] Hungarian Jews also faced a sea of betrayal at home and were frightened by pogroms similar in kind if not in number of victims to those in Poland. During the years of flux, 1945–47, Budapest was a way station to the DP camps, and Hungarian Jews would become the second largest Jewish population in the DP camps. However, Hungary never became as close to being *Judenfrei* as Poland. With about 80,000 Jews remaining during the Communist era, anti-Semitism and Jewish reintegration in Hungary would face real opposition rather than ghosts from the past. The *Commentary* article is noteworthy not because Hungarian Jewry gained little attention, but because Hungarian Jewry did not easily fit into the general discourse. Hungarian Jews continue to be understood as an anomaly in the scholarship of the immediate postwar years. It is, however, Hungarian Jewry's unique situation, straddled between emigration and Budapest, that permits us to reexamine suppositions about Jewish postwar options and adaptations.

---

* Research for this project was partially funded by a Life Reborn Fellowship to the United States Holocaust Memorial Museum in Washington, D.C. The Museum is not responsible for any errors or judgments expressed in this essay.

A version of this paper was delivered at the Imperial War Museum, January 2002, and published as "Displaced Hungarian Jewish Identity, 1945–1947" in *Beyond Camps and Forced Labour: Current International Research on Survivors of Nazi Persecution* (Osnabrück, Germany: Secolo Verlag, 2004).

The Hungarian Holocaust experience came late in the war, but then with lightening speed in the spring and summer of 1944 two-thirds of the Jews perished, first in the outlying districts, then in concentric circles around Budapest.[2] Liberation proceeded more slowly. As the Red Army advanced, small, woeful Jewish communities collected themselves in the cities of Miskolc and Debrecen, Pécs and Szeged as they waited while the armies engaged in a bitter battle for Budapest in January and February 1945. The Hungarian majority had experienced the German occupation lightly, as a European event, quick, bureaucratic, targeting strategic sites and defenseless minorities. Christians shamefacedly turned aside during the deportations in the spring and summer of 1944. However, with the advance of the Red Army and the siege of Budapest, personal security and desecration of property by a vengeful, hostile occupier fell directly on the majority for the first time. The Soviet conquest of Hungary, Hitler's last ally, was brutal with as many as a million Hungarian POWs and civilians transported to the Soviet Union. The waves of Red Army troops advanced in chaotic, irregular patterns. With the carnage of the Battle of Budapest over, second-line Red Army troops were unleashed on the public in the capital. Soviet soldiers resented the wealth they encountered in Hungary and took revenge for the intensity with which the Hungarians had fought for a lost cause. Virtually every Hungarian knew someone who had been raped, robbed, or was languishing in a Soviet labor camp.

The Jews still in Hungary were saved from certain death by Soviet soldiers, and no one else. While there are numerous instances wherein Jews experienced the wrath of the occupiers, in the end they felt an overriding sense of relief. While most Magyars muttered about a "so-called liberation" for Hungary's last Jews, this was "the Time of Liberation," not simply a Soviet construction by "librettists of official Communist propaganda."[3] Jewish Hungarians have mentioned in their memoirs kindnesses by Soviet soldiers. Oftentimes it was a chance exchange in Yiddish with a Jewish Russian officer or soldier that marked the moment of re-inclusion in humankind. The differences between cultured and barbaric nations were lost in the rubble of lives and human suffering.

The two experiences of 1944–45, defeat and liberation, would divide memory and the nation. Relief and joy in liberation seemed to call the Hungarian identity of Jews into question, juxtaposing them as the liberated from those Hungarians who lost the war.[4] "Before and After the Siege" demarcated a fatal and final juncture, what was called the "Zero Hour" in West Germany. In the interwar period, Hungary had defined the boundary between itself and the Soviet Union as a divide between the Christian West and the Communist East. The Horthy regime's legitimacy was constructed as a reaction to the Béla Kun regime of 1919 and the defeat in World War I. To be Hungarian in 1945 was to encounter yet another defeat, after which fear exacerbated a real vulnerability and a perceived sense of victimization. Furthermore, this was magnified by the cultural chasm between the Hungarians and the Russians, over which the former viewed the latter as a collection of Eastern peoples, "perplexing, unknown and inexplicable," who had descended upon them.[5] The identification of Jews with Communism became as reflexive as the previous identification with liberalism, and both stereotypes would coexist. With the Soviet occupation in 1945, it was not just Béla Kun and his 1919 cadre from the Russian prison camps that constituted the threat to Hungarian nationalism, but the Red Army itself. The post-1945 talk about Jewish revenge served as a surrogate for the fear of Russian revenge.

The Hungarian experience of occupation preceded the liberation of the concentration camps and the international humanitarian outcry that deafened ears to Hungarian pleas. Feeling isolated, the Hungarian public focused on the rubble in their cities and countryside, and on what had happened to them after the siege of Budapest. Although a great many were relieved that the war had ended, there is no doubt that the majority of Hungarians experienced 1945 as a defeat: siege, collapse, and occupation. The victims, the imprisoned, the deported, and the resisters viewed the end of the war as liberation, but they were a minority. For the majority the end was greeted with a sullen silence. The Hungarians were stunned by the disaster that had overwhelmed them: total defeat, tens of thousands of missing; assertiveness was futile. Defeat also hollowed out the national political consensus, and vanquished the old irredentist debate. The return to restricted Trianon-like borders was now inevitable and indeed further losses of and restrictions on Hungarian sovereignty were possible. Hungarian nationalism had played out its cards in a fatal way. Defeat was not only a diminution of physical space, but also a dangerous encounter with the unknown. Hungarian nationalism found what strength it could in arguments of vulnerability, not in its achievements, as it faced the possibility of even further deterioration of Hungary as a nation.

The current effort in Hungary to construct a post-Communist identity has fostered a renewed interest in the brutality of 1945 and the immediate postwar experience. In the controversial "House of Terror" in Budapest, Fascist and Communist oppressions have been conflated into an era of occupation. In the service of rehabilitation politics, historical causation has been obscured. This newly constructed martyrology has allowed the repressive aftermaths of World War II and the revolution of 1956 to speak for the Communist era. In the process, distinctions between victims and perpetrators have become fluid. This continues an anti-Communist Cold War tendency to divide recent history into idyll and horror, severing the connection between the suffering the Hungarians imposed and the suffering imposed on them. In the histories of Central Europe, but also in Holocaust testimonials, the DP experience has been squeezed into a corner and forgotten. The years of the provisional government and the Jewish DP problem has been conceptualized as an interlude, in which DPs were suspended between the Holocaust and new lives elsewhere. At the time, however, the immediate past lay heavily on the present. Hungarians were compromised by their ex-enemy status, and recriminations by their victimized Jewish minority only made their situation worse.

In France, the returned Jews would be included in the "absents."[6] The forced laborers, POWs, political prisoners, and French Jews all could be welcomed back into the bosom of the grateful *patrie*, and they would also be complicit in fostering a closed system of amnesia concerning Vichy. In defeated Hungary the nation was not in the mood to celebrate the Jews' return, nor could the return of the deported be integrated into a wider celebration of a postwar normality. Hungary had been a collaborationist state without a successful resistance movement and had no easy way to move from the camp of the losers to the camp of the victors. The Hungarians were largely euphoric over the quick and easy territorial acquisitions during the 1938–1944 period. Once the irredentist yearning to reconnect the Magyar-speaking populations of Greater Hungary had been accomplished, Hungarian Jews were left without standing. The alliance with Germany remained as a rebuke to the misery that accompanied it, such as the bloodletting and loss on the River Don, and the anxiety of a population awaiting certain defeat and occupation. A resistance legend would later be developed, but it rang as hollow as the Soviet-inspired collaborationist myth. Hungarian nationalists (save the fanatics) had been opposed to genocide, but the general public had difficulty making sense out of these conflicting notions and emotions. In a negative sense the Horthy regime continued to play a stabilizing role in the postwar system by encouraging a "path into silence" regarding the deportations. The past remained restricted to the private sphere and the present was given over to public proclamations about rebuilding.

The first war crimes trials were held in Pest while fighting was still going on in Buda. These early trials at the Academy of Music were packed because they served as a source of information about what had happened to missing relatives. As the full extent of the catastrophe became evident during the following months, the Hungarian majority felt exposed to international blame, while its own grievances were overshadowed. "Discovery" of the concentration camps in Germany in March and April 1945 marked a second beginning to the liberation story. Certainly this framed the DP problem. The timing for the Hungarians, as for the Germans, could not have been worse. At the very moment when dependence on foreign succor was greatest, the full extent of the crimes became evident. The accused majority felt threatened by the Jewish victims' claims on the international conscience, while individually and collectively Hungarian Christians felt like martyrs suffering defeat, rape, and pillage.

The Hungarian Jewish "DP problem" can be divided into three phases: an initial military and medical emergency, which involved the massive and largely voluntary repatriation of incarcerated Hungarian Jews; followed by an extended humanitarian project of administered peoples, in which Hungarian Jews became the leading returnees in the half-illicit traffic to the DP camps in Austria and West Germany; and finally, a hurried resolution of a political liability, in which West German reconstruction and the establishment of Israel emptied the DP camps. A final wave of Hungarian-Jewish emigration from Hungary in 1947 was driven by apprehension that Sovietization would soon preclude all options for leaving. The three phases paralleled the general Hungarian pattern of occupation trauma, stabilization, and the imposition of Stalinist isolation.

I.

In the spring and summer of 1945, armed with soap and DDT spray guns, the Allied armies and United Nations Relief and Rehabilitation Association (UNRRA) succeeded in delousing camp survivors and others, building makeshift showers, and providing sanitation, food, and medicine that averted the real danger of epidemic. A dose of good luck even spared Europe from widespread influenza.[7] The Jewish DP situation was first tackled as a medical emergency and then a psychic pathology. Survivors were generally young, single, and eager to seek partners. Helen Bamber, a twenty-year-old British Jewish Relief Unit worker who would become a central force in Amnesty International and founder of the Medical Foundation for the Care of Victims of Torture, worked in these initial months in a camp in Kaunitz inhabited almost entirely by young Hungarian Jewish women. She recalled that, "with food, their bodies had begun to discover the energy and fertility that many of them had never experienced. They were suddenly awash with sexuality," and surrounded by soldiers.[8] Bamber was aware of the loss of moorings for these young women who moved into adulthood or back into life without the traditional guiding institutions, such as parents, schools, synagogues, law, and order. She lectured the girls on sexuality and relationships built out of self-respect—something that was exceedingly tenuous but not completely lacking in the camp.[9]

With a twenty-three-year-old former architecture student at its helm, this small camp of 586 inhabitants was a model of self-administration, as Earl Harrison, President Truman's personal emissary on the conditions of DP camps, noted in his handwritten records.[10] His report, published in September 1945, was a blistering call for reform of the DP camps. Harrison described DPs housed together with their former captors, still in concentration-camp uniforms, and consuming three-quarters of their calories in wet, black bread.[11] Since Anglo-Americans understood the Jewish catastrophe as religious persecution, they insisted on rules of administration that made no religious distinctions. Refugees were categorized by "nationality" or "place of origin." Hungarian Jews, as "citizens" of an ex-enemy nation, found themselves ineligible for direct United Nations or Allied military relief.

After Harrison issued his report, efforts were made to accommodate Jews as a special case, more food and medical care were forthcoming, and separate DP camps were created. Grudgingly, the concept of "stateless" was introduced into the organizational vocabulary.[12] The Allied DP program had been conceived under the rubric, "Everyone must go home!" By the end of the summer, West Europeans had been repatriated, leaving the DP camps to the East Europeans. Hungarian Jews complied more willingly than others who were returning to countries under Red Army authority; for example, the Hungarian women at the Kaunitz camp did not stay over the winter. Angry mobs protesting forced repatriations to Poland and the Soviet Union brought the issue to a boil. Jews declared themselves "stateless" and avoided the transports east.

One orphanage reported the arrival of Gyula, "a boy of fifteen who stated that he was born in Hungary and was of Hungarian nationality. He had been moved, as a worker, from camp to camp, first to Czechoslovakia and later to Germany." The social worker directed him to the German welfare authorities. "A couple of days later he reappears crying, pleading that he is really Czech," and was given "temporary" shelter. While nationality was flexible, age was even more fluid. Older children learned to adjust their birth dates—to be older in the camps, and to be younger after the war, since it was "common knowledge that movement out of Germany would be more likely for younger children rather than for older ones." "Frequently it has been impossible to establish clearly the identification of each child. Small children sometimes don't know their names, or anything about their personal histories. Even some older children have blotted it out, or become confused."[13]

The Hungarian camp survivors began arriving back in Hungary in the fall of 1945. One female survivor brought back to health in the American zone and returned to Hungary on October 16, 1945, wrote, "Now that I've arrived, I feel like I was completely reborn, I'm beginning to learn about the world, everything seems nice, because I can see, hear and feel. I am happy that I'm alive and this also seems fantastic after so much suffering."[14] The deportees and the denizens of Budapest, including Jews, had experienced two very different traumas. The citizens of Budapest looked "with shudders at the bald, dirty, unkempt returnees. The returnees don't speak much.... They lie on the straw bedding in transient homes and in...emergency hospitals, and except for the daily reading of the list of the returnees and looking for their lost relatives and fighting for a little food, nothing interests them. They are totally paralyzed," a Hungarian psychologist reported.[15] While depressed and lethargic, the returnees did emerge from the "chrysalis of ugliness." "Ugliness is easier to deal with—it separates you," Bamber observed.[16]

According to Hungarian welfare statistics, 82,144 Hungarian Jews returned in 1945 and an additional 1,187 in 1946. The surviving Hungarian Jewish population was demographically distorted. In Budapest the working-aged men had been taken to forced labor, so the surviving families lacked providers. In the countryside the women, children, and elderly were most likely to die in the concentration camps leaving a disproportionate number of single men. The proportion of children, ages 0–15, in the Jewish population had dropped to one-third of prewar levels. Sixty percent of the returnees were women, 35 percent were men, and five percent were children.[17] The need for a companion was overwhelming. The average family size was only 1.7 persons. Returning Jews were lonely, and survivors were generally young, single, and eager to seek partners. The year 1945 was a catch-up year in Hungary, with prewar alliances renewed, but with prewar boundaries defining social intercourse removed. Intermarriage rates soared, as did connections across class and strata. Similarly in the DP camps, the injunction— everyone must go home—seemed to have become translated as everyone must get married. To like or to love someone was often a whim apart, with the result that among the legal immigrants to Israel between 1948 and the close of the DP camps 10 percent were infants or children born since the war.[18]

II.

Many Hungarians, anxious about loved ones still imprisoned in the Soviet Union, looked at the returning deportees with hostility. György Parragi, a Hungarian Smallholder Party columnist, evoked the old hatred: "That damned race never suffered. They came home fatter than they left.... Now there are more Jews in the country than before they were taken away for a holiday."[19]

In Hungary, food distribution was uneven. The worst off were the urban population and the industrial workers. On the fixed-price ration cards, Budapest residents could only obtain 556 calories daily (vs. 1470 in Denmark, 1840 in Luxemburg, and 1850 in France). Hungarians could buy food on the more-or-less permitted free market to supplement rations, but according to the American Legation in Hungary, this amounted to only 1,766 calories daily; 1,478 for non-agrarian classes. "The prices are so high that many can't afford them."[20]

Hungarian Jews, concentrated in Budapest and lacking direct food sources, relied upon foreign relief services. The American Jewish Joint Distribution Committee (known as "the Joint") directed 9,000,000 Swiss Francs to Hungarian Jewry in 1945, providing food, medicines, clothes, and some cash.[21] The Joint distributed approximately 1,360,000 meals and 503,000 food packages to Hungarian Jewry by the end of December 1945; 41.5 percent of Hungarian Jews used Joint public kitchens, a third received monetary subsidies, and between 10 and 15 percent received clothing and medical aid.[22] The Joint insisted this was not enough. In December 1945, Arthur Schoenfeld, the American minister in Budapest, sent an alarmed telegram, reporting that in Budapest daily rations had fallen to an average of only 858 calories per person. An unstable currency and massive inflation exacerbated food scarcity in the city.

A U.S. legation report warned of "the result of hunger, e.g. decline in output, will to work; danger of epidemics and mortality rates rising."[23] The U.S. Legation received plaintive and irate letters, including several from teenagers who complained that the food packages were going to the Jews rather than the needy, working poor people who were more hungry and in greater need.[24] Catholic humanitarian aid did exist, but it increasingly had to be funneled through UNRRA. In May 1946, the Soviets refused to grant clearance for direct distribution of 250 tons of foodstuff from a Hungarian-American Catholic aid society.[25]

Jews were also caught in a half-submerged discourse with a despondent, deprived, and resentful Hungarian nationalism. Gyula Illyés, populist poet-laureate, complained in his diary that "about half a million Budapest Gentiles, that would be every second citizen, had been instrumental in sheltering persecuted Jews, but the press and the Jewish community showed no gratitude for such rescue action, which in the minds of those sheltered was apparently a matter of simple moral duty requiring no special acknowledgment."[26] On the other hand, Ferenc Hevesi, chief rabbi at the Dohány Street Synagogue, noted, "We have the feeling of living among murderers, and I never know whether the man opposite me in the tram is not my father's or my brother's murderer."[27] István Bibó, the Peasant Party theorist, sought to reframe the discussion of national responsibility by arguing that even if Hungarians had made efforts to save or protect Jews, it was clearly not adequate. The question was how to repair society after the catastrophe. He argued against the Jewish hope that communism with its internationalist ideology would eliminate the underlying ethnic animosities. Bibó warned of the potential vulnerability of a Jewish population with weakened confessional affiliations. As Bibó suspected, the task of forging a post-Fascist identity for Hungarians would prove daunting.[28]

Hungarian society as a whole had a dislocated identity: the Arrow Cross went underground; religion moved into the private sphere; the Communist Party aggressively sought converts; and the compulsion to Magyarize was strong. Invisibility and suspicion were key responses to the immediate postwar chaos. For many Budapest Jews being inconspicuous had become a life-saving reflex. After the Holocaust the former expectations of Hungarian Jews were dashed and their identity called into question under the new circumstances. Imre Kertész, the 2003 Nobel Literature Prize winner, locates his identity not in being a Jew, but in being tortured as a Jew. Hungarian Jews had been stripped of their Hungarian identity and then were obliged to reclaim or repudiate it.

Jews could credibly rationalize making a new beginning in Hungary. Bibó initiated an open ethical debate in pursuit of an equitable society and an alternative to communism. But the Communists promised security against a Fascist resurgence and an internationalist ideology to offset Hungary's increased homogeneity. Hungary had in fact served Jews well as long as the state was a part of a large multi-ethnic kingdom, but after the borders were redrawn in 1918–19, Hungarian Jews in these new states were resented as Magyar stand-ins. In pluralistic societies loyalty can be demonstrated by one's conduct in acts of "good citizenship." Loyalty is needed and appreciated to offset centrifugal tendencies. After the demise of Austro-Hungarian Empire in 1918, the Magyar political class no longer needed to cobble together an ethnic Hungarian majority.

In the interwar period there was an imbalance between Budapest, the metropolis, and the dwarf state it inhabited. This resulted in an economic stagnation that aroused nostalgia for the bucolic world of a lost Hungary. Hungary, it was said, had allowed its ethnic identity to be diluted, washed too thin by the pull to the west, by urbanization, and by the heavy influence of urban Hungarian Jews. Hungarian non-Jewish intellectuals presumed that the power and the beauty of their culture had been sullied and weakened by inauthentic representatives. The bearers of

Magyar culture in the lost borderlands had all too often been bilingual, cosmopolitan, and Jewish. By rejecting the liberal claim of inclusion, Hungarians had abandoned the converts to Hungarian culture and the hyphenated Hungarians. In the early 1920s Hungary was the first European country to subject Jews to formal quotas. Legislation after 1939 and the murderous months of 1944 completed the process of the criminalization of the Jews.

Within its truncated borders, after World War II as it had been in the interwar period, Hungary was one of the most ethnically homogenous states in Europe. There were only three remaining minorities: Jews, Germans, and Roma. Communism permitted the onus of Hungarian weakness to remain squarely on liberalism/capitalism and by extension on the Jewish and German entrepreneurial classes that had dominated Budapest and Hungarian commerce. The nation was wrapped into a new Soviet imperium that limited national aspirations with its own demands for uniformity. Prewar nationalist intellectuals, such as Gyula Szekfü, would transition directly from interwar historical analysis to that of national statesman in the Communist regime.

The traumatized Hungarian Jewish community that remained was also tattered, compromised, and divided. Blame was directed at Budapest from the provinces. The official Jewish leadership claimed unity, but after the "collective tragedy," the collectivity was torn asunder. Accusations of complicity and murder were hurled at the Budapest Jewish leadership. Orthodox and Hassidic provincial Jews suspected that assimilationist, urban society had knowingly abandoned them. The wounds gaped wide open. Ill-will and blame burdened the community, while a myriad of wrong choices and personal weaknesses overwhelmed individuals. A sense of betrayal adhered to the essence of the individual as a Hungarian, a Jew, and a person.[29] Personal identities became disengaged from other associations.

The formation of post-Fascist, post-Holocaust identities and the identification of Jews as Hungarians, as Jews, or neither has to be placed within the context of a general Hungarian identity crisis in the wake of total defeat. While Hungarians may have taunted Jews for their suspect patriotism, Hungarian identity was clearly at a nadir. A crisis of identity among Magyars paralleled the displaced identity of Hungarian Jews. Both agreed that to begin anew was essential, but how to proceed was an open question. "The country lay in total ruin, so people said, but that was merely a flowery expression. In reality the country had not perished; to the contrary it began to live vigorously," commented writer Sándor Márai.[30] Those who could imagine themselves in the new society stayed.

The years between 1946 and 1948 could be prosperous years for Jewish survivors in Hungary. Currency stabilization, the issue of the new currency (the forint), the winding down of the black market, and the repair of the transportation infrastructure made normal commerce possible. Pent-up demand for goods allowed businessmen with nothing to lose a chance for prosperity.[31] But there was a fragile underside to this revitalization. One vegetable and wine merchant, a Jew, discovered that the driver of his truck had been a member of the Arrow Cross. When asked whether he had believed in Nazi ideology, the employee said, "I believe in it same way I believe what the Communists are teaching now. I believe in what I must in order to earn a living for myself and my family. I believe in what I am ordered to believe." The merchant decided he would continue to employ his driver, since another driver would also have something to hide; "I knew his secret." The driver, for his part, cautioned the merchant, "The Communists will put you behind bars.... You're a gentleman who is thankful to the Russians for saving your life. You have to acknowledge, though, that you have a capitalist soul. Do not make the mistake of believing that the Communists don't know every step you take." With this the driver "indicated that he had to report everything" about the merchant to the "authorities."[32]

Americans sought to induce regret amongst Fascist perpetrators, while Communists were content that the Hungarian population steal away from its past and be strong-armed onto a new path. Since a significant portion of the Hungarian public had taken part in Fascist activities, "prosecuting reactionary tendencies" would have excluded large numbers from public life. The war crimes trials in the American zone were based on the assumption that the guilty could be determined and separated from the public. Hungarian war crimes trials spread out into the provinces, focusing on the *kisnyilasok*, lower-level Arrow Cross members. Provincial People's Courts passed over 16,000 sentences.[33] These trials spread the power of a new judicial order into the provinces; trials against local personages resonated as verdicts of collective responsibility. Authorities proceeded as if the public was quite capable of repeating their behaviors.[34]

The public tended to interpret the arrests and trials as a form of Jewish revenge. Jews were conspicuous in the immediate postwar police force. Sándor Márai offers a portrait of a Jewish policeman, a former bank officer, dining at an elegant restaurant. He was feared, greeted, seated, and served as an eminent figure in his impeccable all-new uniform, and the Gypsy band played, at his request, "You are lovely, most beautiful, Hungary." The Jewish police officer commanded the right to be a patriot, despite the fact that or precisely because he "had every reason to hate...the Hungary that was possibly 'more lovely than the whole world,' but whose officialdom had murdered his mother and siblings, humiliated him and wounded his human dignity, a Hungarian citizen born in Hungary."[35] One notorious round-up by the police, mainly Jews, left sixteen detainees drowned in the Danube.[36] Within the first year, Rabbi Hevesi preached two sermons at the Dohány Street Synagogue urging Jews not to join the police.[37]

Police indifference, however, allowed the situation in the rural town of Kunmadaras, population 12,000, to turn into an anti-Semitic outbreak. The community faced the reintegration of 102 Jews—an unusually high survival rate for rural Hungary—with expectations that their belongings would be returned. Indictments by the People's Courts of local worthies, a priest and a schoolteacher, triggered a panic among "respectable" elements. Rather than the typical Arrow Cross men recruited from bars or the unemployed, six of the seven arrested were women of standing. Elsewhere it was the Communists traditional base that showed the same anti-social tendencies. Even ironworkers were implicated when a political rally flamed into an anti-Semitic demonstration in the town of Ózd.

While these provincial Hungarian incidents were less deadly than those that took place in Poland, they did send a shock wave of fear through the Hungarian Jewish population. This was not exactly anti-Semitism without Jews, but an indication that the decimated provincial Jewry found little welcome on their return. Authorities claimed this to be a "new anti-Semitism," since the activists of the anti-Semitic agitation had not been connected to the Arrow Cross. It was understood as anti-Semitism without ideology, that is, it was no longer fueled by Nazi ideology, which had been discredited, but rather by economic exigencies of the moment: hard times, simple greed, and material opportunism. While the official Jewish response wholeheartedly agreed that "the population is strongly infected with post-liberation neo-anti-Semitism," they dismissed the notion that this "new anti-Semitism" was anything but the old prejudice with a new economic spin. Economic restitution would, by the government's assessment, enflame society anew, while for the Jews restitution would become the litmus test of social justice restored.[38]

Neo-anti-Semitism, essentially a continuation of the old refrain, was not unexpected, and not the Jews' chief complaint. What was startling and disconcerting was the "cool indifference of the new anti-Fascist regime."[39] In 1945 Jewish hopes had revolved around a Government Commission on Abandoned Wealth. When subsequent decrees did not differentiate between property confiscated from the Jews during the war and property abandoned by those fleeing the Russian army, the Jews felt doubly despoiled, because they had expected special consideration. Initially, both in the DP camps and in Hungary, administrative policy turned a blind eye to racial, religious distinctions in the distribution of aid or restitution. While the U.S. occupying forces in Germany were quickly called to task by public opinion and the Harrison report, in the Soviet zone demands for restitution were dismissed as "bourgeois logic." The Russian liberators abhorred the outmoded notion of minorities or special groups within a nation, leaving the Jews of Hungary "to solve for themselves problems which the government said no longer existed."[40] American diplomats reported that,

> Those few Jews who succeeded in coming back from German deportation are hurriedly leaving their homes in the provinces and trying to find asylum in the capital. The situation is aggravated by the fact that the press never mentions the anti-Semitic excesses, because it is forbidden to do so. The Government is partly unable to do anything in this matter, partly is unwilling to make itself unpopular by protecting the Jews.[41]

Pogroms, a denial of restitution, and the Stalinist presence further decimated provincial communities, but Budapest served as an anchor for Hungarian Jews. It was large enough to provide a sense of security and a community of the almost like-minded. At the very least, it provided the comfort of the familiar and a community of others having shed the same identities in similar ways. As Viktor Karády has shown, emigration, Zionism, total assimilation, and communism could all be understood as options or antidotes. Each required abandoning some essential aspect of individual past identities, such as language, religion, home environment, or occupation. Individuals sometimes attempted to embrace seemingly contradictory options simultaneously, such as joining the Communist Party and a Zionist youth group.[42]

III.

Wedged between the Holocaust and Cold War, Europe underwent the largest migration of peoples in fifteen-hundred years. Between 1945 and 1948, expulsions (the involuntary transfer of ethnic groups from one country to another) were pursued by victors and losers alike. The evictions and expropriations of ethnic groups implicated all occupying Allied powers in Europe in a continued policy of ethnic cleansing after the war. The forced repatriation of ethnic groups ranged from deadly to non-violent. This shuffling of peoples was rationalized by western and eastern regimes as the only way to create stability in the region. The emigration of Jewry was part of a mass movement out of Hungary and the East generally. Less than 20 percent of the prewar minority populations remained in Hungary at the time the borders closed in 1948.[43]

In Hungary the exchange of Slovaks was a concession to Czechoslovakia and proceeded more in the nature of a quid pro quo, but the expulsion of the Swabians (Hungarian Germans) and the rapid Magyarization of the remaining German-Hungarians was an explicit, forceful, state-driven act of ethnic cleansing bolstered by public support. The evictions and expropriations became integral to the Sovietization of Hungary.[44] The expulsion of the Swabians began by eliminating German-language islands and purging the countryside often in the name of agrarian reform. The contradiction between condemning the despoliation of the Jews in 1944 and pursuing the despoliation of Hungarian Germans under the guise of agrarian reform left the whole notion of restitution in deep confusion and stasis. Jewish demands for the return of apartments, tools, and so forth were turned aside as bourgeois acquisitiveness. "Democracy" was equated with the principle of "no special consideration." The futility of fighting anti-Semitism and asserting a Jewish identity amidst an official policy of ethnic cleansing aimed at other minorities was all too apparent. A soothing official rhetoric of inclusion spoke of the equality of all citizens, amnesty and rehabilitation, and the punishment of war criminals, but these sentiments lacked the force of consensus.

The American Legation in Budapest reported that, "The Hungarian Government declared more than once that it will now prevent emigration from Hungary. In fact, the government facilitated the emigration to Palestine while issuing group passports for immigrants to Palestine. These group passports must bear the clearance by the Russians." The Hungarian government did not usually grant individual passports. "The Hungarian Government is not responsible for the strengthening of the frontier control."[45]

The decision of Hungarian Jews to stay or leave would take on an irreversible character, but the choice at the time was not simply between staying and leaving. False papers procured in Budapest were not a direct ticket to Palestine or even to emigration out of Europe. Hungarian Jews who left became DPs and entered camps in Austria and western Germany where life was on hold—for many it seemed to be a limbo that would never end. To survive at all, to reconstruct one's identity, or to leave were all age-bound categories. The children who had survived in the ghetto or had made it back home stayed in Hungary; the old who had not left were also inclined to stay put. Some stayed because they found connections back in Hungary and determined that Budapest could be home again; others were too debilitated to start off anew. Identity was in flux, whether to stay or leave was an open question. The official Jewish report on potential emigration in March 1946 claimed that "almost the entire middle class would like to emigrate." Certainly the situation within the Jewish community was "uncertain, chaotic." Almost half (45 percent) of Hungarian Jews claimed they wanted to join the 12,000 Hungarians who had already emigrated to Palestine; a third had their sights on emigration elsewhere, this left about a quarter of Hungarian Jewry wanting to stay in Hungary.[46] During the interval, Zionist communal living arrangements were popular among the young adults. Budapest was a major transit point to Austria and beyond. More than 50,000 Polish, Sub-Carpathian, and Romanian Jews passed through Hungary. But only 5,000 to 6,000 Hungarian Jews had joined them, primarily children and young people.[47] In part this was because the Zionist leadership requested its Hungarian following not to emigrate, at least not yet. However, before the borders were sealed Hungarians of all stripes would join the flood of DPs.[48]

While Hungarian Jewish DPs were distinguished in 1945 by their willingness to go home, by 1947 they had become the most prominent infiltrees, illegally making their way to the West. The estimates of those who wished to stay or emigrate fluctuated wildly depending on who was making the estimate. In March 1946, the U.S. Department of State reported that between 23 and 25 percent, around 35,000, of Hungary's Jews, wished to remain, according to Jewish religious and Zionist estimates.[49] Zionists claimed that 30,000 to 40,000 were ready to emigrate to Palestine immediately and 100,000 more would go as soon as they could. The Association of Hungarian Zionists was teaching young people the Hebrew language, agricultural skills, and practical trades needed in Palestine, while the Jewish Agency for Palestine provided for orphaned Jewish children.[50]

"For the average Jew, Palestine (or any other likely territory) is chiefly attractive because it offers the possibility of emigration. He feels he has no future in Hungary. He wants to get out as soon as he can."[51] This is reiterated in the U.S. Legation report:

> Our own investigation shows the first choice of the Hungarian Jews would be either the United States or Australia; but knowing that immigration to Palestine will be easier to realize, they report at the Zionists for immigration to Palestine hoping that from here they might be able to make their way somewhere else.[52]

"Mass movement started about March/April 1947, reaching its peak about July/August 1947 when about 1,500 Jews were arriving weekly in Vienna."[53] Movement from both Czechoslovakia and Hungary to Vienna took place through well-organized routes. From Vienna the Jews moved on to DP Camps in the U.S. zone of Austria. Some movement from Germany into the U.S. and French zones took place en route for Italy. This was estimated at 300 to 500 weekly.[54] One assumes that a substantial number of Hungarian Christians also entertained the idea of leaving. A network through Italy seemed to work indiscriminately with Hungarians seeking transport to South America and Hungarian Jews moving toward the boat docks to Palestine. Border guards—Hungarian, Czech, and Austrian—looked the other way as Jewish relief organizations moved people using vehicles with U.S. Army markings.

The DP camps were likened to Chicago or New York, where "people can become lost in them from the camp authorities."[55] Unfortunately they have become more lost to us as historians as well. Identities were not only in flux, but bought and sold for rations, which in turn supported the black market. This explains the remarkable invisibility of the Hungarians in camp records. There were also comparatively few Hungarian-language newspapers in the camps, even though the Hungarians were the second largest group in the Jewish DP camps. In the voluminous records of Bad Reichenhall, one camp with a large Hungarian presence, the only obvious indication of any Hungarian presence in the official memoranda was a request, quickly acted upon by camp authorities, to secure a Magyar-speaking soccer coach. There remained no compulsion, advantage, or purpose to sustaining a public Hungarian presence, save for a chance to relax into one's native speech. Budapest Jewry was not Yiddish-speaking, and unlike the Poles had not found solidarity in a Jewish language.

To infiltrate the DP camps required temporarily stepping out of categories of group identity altogether. Arrivees were not only stateless but usually without papers. The "nub of trouble is that Jews have no papers—no status—have nothing," wrote Harrison in a note to himself.[56] The Allies would subsequently scramble to document the administered peoples in hopes also of stemming the movement. In a decade when one's fate could be decided by one's identity papers, issues of identity were not trivial or merely psychological. Hungarian Jewish survivors had been moved through Auschwitz so late and quickly that few were tattooed with German identity numbers. New documents, particularly those obtained from the Americans, were coveted. One man wedged his precious GI-issued Dachau ID into a hidden compartment in his shoe rather than risk its confiscation at an eastern border; one woman proudly coaxed a U.S. military officer to provide a meaningless letter, which she carried across Europe as a talisman.

The DP camps were hardly inviting. Large Jewish DP camps like Feldafing were worlds set apart. DPs were "other"; children were warned not to play too close to the fences. Other camps were former resorts or hotels in the city center—the once idyllic turned into transient homes. But often camps included requisitioned houses throughout a community where DPs interacted with locals, trading their extra rations of cigarettes for foodstuffs. Farmers even preferred doing black-market trade with DPs, since this would be lower profile and less likely to tarnish their reputations in the community. For the most part, legal or black-market work did not consume a great deal of the refugees' time.

Boredom ruled. These remained cut-off communities where the principal occupation was waiting around and killing time.

DP camp administrators were frustrated by the amount of lawlessness and disobedience, the unwillingness to work, and the slovenliness with which public spaces were maintained in DP camps. As explanation, Allied psychiatrists diagnosed former concentration camp and forced labor camp inmates as sick. World War II had seen a vast expansion in the field of psychology. There were only thirty-five U.S. Army psychiatrists at the time of Pearl Harbor; by war's end there were over a thousand.[57] They were prone to rank DPs by nationality with Hungarians deemed more re-educable than those groups such as the Poles who had suffered a more prolonged trauma. The focus was on extreme insecurity as the central trait of the DP, Jewish and non-Jewish alike. Insecurity was used to explain the intense search for relatives and friends, the demand for rosters of the missing, the banding together, the restoration of religious practices, and the like. It was also insecurity that was said to foster black-market activity and generate selfishness, rivalry, and suspicion of those in authority. Having had for years no chance to vent their rage, one November 1945 report declared, they do so now in "relatively benign atmosphere of their present settlements, with friendly American authorities, and no fear of punishment, they lash out at their friends and their benefactors, and seem to be ungrateful."[58] Psychology was intended to rehabilitate, but implicit in its medical bias is the notion of illness. Camp life had made its victims ill. A cure required a personal exploration of the wells of blackness in order to expunge its darkness. But if one spoke too much about one's experiences one was not yet cured.

For the Jewish DPs, the loss of national identity was but one of the problems. It was clearly not the only aspect of their identity that was in flux during this period—religious identity, professional identity, family identity were all tenuous. Americans provided reeducation and rehabilitation projects, presumably to turn DPs into productive future citizens as hairdressers, seamstresses, shoemakers, and carpenters. These were the occupations that were more likely to open the door to emigration to the United States. Zionists also privileged physical labor. Camp administrators stressed the rehabilitative function of work. They fumed about DP laziness, but the Jews projected work to a life in the future.

IV.

In Hungary, many Jews who had survived by submerging themselves in the wider Gentile population completed their assimilation. In 1949, the first full year of Communist rule, intermarriage reached 37 percent. Large numbers of Jews chose to have their names formally stricken from the Jewish rolls. This "laying down the burden of Judaism" was an updated version of assimilationism. By the end of the 1950s, 50 percent of Jews had Magyar-sounding names. German Hungarians similarly adopted Magyar names.[59] The disproportionate number of Jews who left Hungary in 1956 suggest that the debate within Budapest Jewry about whether to stay or not continued in a subterranean fashion during the Stalinist era in Hungary.

The patchwork and fluidity of Hungarian Jewish identity suggests that identity may be quite opportunistic. Certainly, more caution is needed in the general trend to attach agency and motivational drive to proclamations of identity, however heartfelt. A "hard" concept of identity that suggests a core to one's personality, nationality, or ethnicity fails the postmodern test for fluidity and multiplicity, while a "soft" concept trails off in a miasma of overlapping and contradictory identifications. Identity is a term that has overreached itself.

Yet for the historian, the concept of identity is tethered to this period of the aftermath. It was precisely the confusion of displaced identities that prompted Erik Erikson in the 1940s to universalize the "identity crisis" as a central contemporary problem. Erikson's own identity crisis revolved around the contrast between his Scandinavian features and those of his stepfather and Jewish mother. The disjuncture between his social background and his Danish Nordic appearance was accentuated in significance by the eugenic politics of his time. His work, of course, focused on adolescents, a life-stage denied by the war and concentration camp experience; society had been disassembled into adults that could work or make war, and children or the old who could not. The central tension of Imre Kertész's novel *Fateless* is that its adolescent protagonist chooses to move step by step through the conditions demanded by his identity as defined by others.

In the aftermath of World War II, Hungarians, Hungarian Jews, German Hungarians, and other subjects of Trianon Hungary hurried to shed inconvenient associations and scrambled to assume new identities. These new identities shared an iconic quality with pronounced normative characteristics: the Soviet Man, Zionist *Kibbutznik*, or Americanized consumer. The political move to solidify West Germany as an U.S. ally impelled the final dispersion of the DPs out of Europe. The Cold War defined a West German identity and interrupted the sorting out process of postwar Hungarian culture and politics. After the Stalinist takeover in Hungary, the border was no longer porous, the journalistic debate and healing discourse ended, and options for the remaining Hungarian Jews became severely limited. With the founding of Israel and a new U.S. immigration law, the DP camps emptied and closed by 1950. For those who remained in Hungary—Jew and non-Jew—this meant being stuck with the last of the many identities they had assumed, that of Communist subject.

The search for a post-Fascist Hungarian identity settled into a seemingly slavish imitation of Moscow and, among Budapest Jewry, a flight from bourgeois norms. The years of transience, flux, and identity shifts faded into the past, because these three years of extraordinary movement of peoples was followed by forty-three years of immobility, with a brief hiatus in the fall of 1956. Yet, identity was less resolved than stylized, frozen in place. The Communist spiritual prison, Imre Kertész noted, demanded a certain pantomime from its occupants and dispensed with the obligation to define any "authentic" national persona. Once Hungary's connection to the West began to be restored after 1989, the scramble for identities became active and public once again. With the collapse of Eastern European communism, the real anomaly seems to have been the era of forced identity choices of either/or, either here or there.

Notes

1. "The Month in History," *Commentary* 1:1 (November 1945): 33.

2. Randolph L. Braham, "The Holocaust in Hungary: Some Issues and Problems," in *The Holocaust in Hungary: Fifty Years Later*, eds. Randolph L. Braham and Attila Pók (New York: Columbia University Press, 1997), 43–44.

3. Sándor Márai, *Memoir of Hungary, 1944–48* (Föld, föld!), trans. Albert Tezla (Budapest: Corvina/Oxford University Press, 2000), 128.

4. Paul Hollander, "Growing Up in Communist Hungary," in *Red Star, Blue Star: The Lives and Times of Jewish Students in Communist Hungary (1948–1956)*, eds. Andrew Handler and Susan V. Meschel (New York: Columbia University Press, 1997), 102–103; András Kovács, "The Jewish Question in Contemporary Hungary," in *The Holocaust in Hungary: Forty Years Later*, eds. Randolph L. Braham and Bela Vago (New York: Colum-

bia University Press, 1985), 209; Raphael Patai, *Jews of Hungary: History, Culture, Psychology* (Detroit: Wayne State University Press, 1996), 597; Vera Ranki, *The Politics of Inclusion and Exclusion: Jews and Nationalism in Hungary* (New York: Holmes and Meier Publishers, 1999), 189.

5. Márai, 46.

6. Megan Koreman, *The Expectation of Justice: France, 1944–1946* (Durham, NC: Duke University Press, 1999), 73–81.

7. Office of Public Information, *The Story of U.N.R.R.A* (Washington, D.C., February 15, 1948), 23–24.

8. Neil Belton, *The Good Listener: Helen Bamber, A Life Against Cruelty* (New York: Pantheon, 1999), 106–107.

9. Ibid., 107.

10. United States Holocaust Memorial Museum Archives (USHMM), RG-10.088, Earl G. Harrison Papers, 1945–46.

11. "The Harrison Report," *The Department of State Bulletin* 13 (September 30, 1945): 455–63. See also, Gemma Mae Newman, "Earl G. Harrison and the Displaced Persons Controversy: A Case Study in Social Action" (Ph.D. Diss., Temple University, 1972), I, 202.

12. Zorach Warhaftig, *Relief and Rehabilitation: Implications of the UNRRA Program for Jewish Needs* (New York: Institute of Jewish Affairs, 1944), 17; See also, Hannah Arendt, "The Stateless People," *Contemporary Jewish Record* 8:2 (April 1945): 137–53.

13. USHMM, RG-19.034.06, Gerta Fischer Papers, "Report on the D.P. Children's Team 182 Center, Indersdorf Children's Home" (January 1946).

14. Országos Levéltár (OL) (Hungarian national archives), Jewish Archive, Budapest, XXXIII-5-c 3.d box 2.

15. István Kulcsár, "A maradék zsidóság lelki keresztmetszete 1946-ban: Tanulmány" (The psychological picture of the remnant Jewry in 1946: A study), in *Maradék zsidóság* (Remnant Jewry) (Budapest: Officina, 1947). See also, Ilona Benoschofsky, "The Position of Hungarian Jewry after the Liberation," in *Hungarian-Jewish Studies*, vol. 1, ed. Randolph L. Braham (New York: World Federation of Hungarian Jews, 1966), 240.

16. Belton, 106–107.

17. Rita Horváth, *A Magyarországi Zsidó Deortáltakat Gondozó Országos Bizottsága (DEGOB) története* (History of the national committee for the care of the Jews of Hungary), vol. 1, *MAKOR* (Budapest: Hungarian Jewish Museum and Archives, 1997), 25–26.

Prior to April 30, 1945—9,000; May 1945—12,758; June—25,678; July—14, 759; August—9,909 ; September—5,550; October—2,859; November—1,131 ; December—500. *1945 Total:* 82,144. *1946:* January—166 ; February—108; March—102; April—84 ; May—116 ; June—161; July—201; August—93; September—156. *1946 Total:* 1187. DEGOB December 1945 statistics: 63,000 people from Trianon Hungary returned in 1945 of which 51,000 were Jews.

18. Robert S. Wistrich, ed., *Terms of Survival: The Jewish World since 1945* (London: Routledge, 1995), 46.

19. László Karsai, ed., *Befogadók* (Integrators) (Budapest: Aura, 1993), 179, as cited in Miklós Hernádi, "Unlearning the Holocaust: Recollections and Reactions," in Braham and Pók, 665.

20. National Archives and Records Administration (NARA), College Park, MD, RG-84, U.S. Legation Budapest Correspondence, Box 66, Folder 850, Report for January–October 1945.

21. Ibid., Box 103, Folder 840.1, "Memorandum on the Position of Jews in Hungary and their Endeavours to Emigrate," 8.

22. See for example, ibid., Box 100, File 711.9, László Pál, Keszthely to the U.S. Legation, Budapest, received May 8, 1946.

23. Ibid., Box 66, folder 850, Report for January–October 1945.

24. Ibid., Report dated December 14, 1945.

25. Ibid., Box 103, Folder 840.1, Report dated May 20, 1946.

26. Gyula Illyés, *Naplójegyzetek 1929–1945* (Diary notes) (Budapest: Szépirodalmi Könyvkiadó, 1986), 379, cited in Miklós Hernádi, "Unlearning the Holocaust," 669.

27. OL, Jewish Archive, Budapest, XXXIII, Dec. 31, 1945.

28. István Bibó, "Zsidókérdés Magyarországon 1944 után" (The Jewish question in Hungary after 1944), *Válasz* (Response) 8 (October–November 1948): 778–877, reprinted in Zoltán Szabó, ed., *Harmadik út* (The third road) (London: Magyar Könyves Céh, 1960), 227–354.

29. OL, Jewish Archive, Budapest, Ernő Munkácsi's response to accusations, ML, XXXIII-8-a #14/1947-18 (1-d), Budapest, Fisch circular, December 23, 1947.

30. Márai, 122.

31. Ibid., 222.

32. Edmund Mandel, *The Right Path: The Autobiography of a Survivor* (Hoboken, NJ: KTAV Publications, 1994), 218.

33. László Karsai, "The People's Courts and Revolutionary Justice in Hungary, 1945–46," in *The Politics of Retribution in Europe*, eds. István Deák, Jan T. Gross, and Tony Judt (Princeton, NJ: Princeton University Press, 2000), 233.

34. See Jeffrey Herf, *Divided Memory: The Nazi Past and the Two Germanys* (Cambridge MA: Harvard University Press, 1997); and Miklós Hernádi, "Unlearning the Holocaust."

35. Márai, 203.

36. Handler and Meschel, 22–23; Ranki, 192.

37. Hal Lehrman, "Hungary: Liberation's Bitter Fruit," *Commentary* 1:3 (January 1946): 29.

38. OL, Jewish Archive, XXXIII-8-A-16. (The OL# at bottom of the document is different record number: XXXIII-5-1, 2.d. László Kender).

39. Lehrman, 31.

40. Ibid., 32.

41. NARA, RG-84, Box 103, Folder 840.1, "Report on the Situation of the Jews in Hungary; Trend to Mass Emigration and its Practical Possibilities," March 21, 1946.

42. Victor Karády, "Identity Strategies Under Duress Before and After the Shoah," in Braham and Pók, 170; András Kovács, "The Jewish Question in Contemporary Hungary," in Braham and Vago, 215.

43. Mark Kramer, "Introduction," in *Redrawing Nations, Ethnic Cleansing in East-Central Europe, 1944–1948*, eds. Philipp Ther and Ana Siljak (Oxford: Rowman and Littlefield, 2001), 57.

44. Ibid.

45. NARA, RG-84, Box 103, Folder 840.1.

46. Ibid.

47. Patai, 614.

48. Ranki, 193–95.

49. NARA, RG-84, Box 103, Folder 840.1

50. Ibid.

51. Lehrman, 33.

52. NARA, RG-84, Box 103, Folder 840.1, "Report on the Situation of the Jews in Hungary: Trend to Mass Emigration and its Practical Possibilities," March 21, 1946

53. NARA, RG-260, Records of U.S. Occupation Headquarters, World War II, U.S. Forces Austria, U.S. Allied Command Austria (USACA), Internal Affairs Section, Box 16.

54. Ibid.

55. USHMM, RG-19.009, William Ramkey Papers.

56. USHMM, RG-10.088, Harrison Papers.

57. Nathan G. Hale, Jr., *The Rise and Crisis of Psychoanalysis in the United States: Freud and the Americans*, 1917–1985 (New York: Oxford University Press, 1995).

58. USHMM, RG-19.009, William Ramkey Papers, "The Jewish Displaced Persons and Their Rehabilitation: A Psychologist's Report," November 19, 1945.

59. Karády, "Identity Strategies," 169.

The Christian Churches and Memory of the Holocaust in Hungary, 1945–1948

Paul Hanebrink

In 1947, a Hungarian rabbi named Henrik Fisch published a small pamphlet of speeches that Hungary's Catholic and Protestant church leaders had made in 1938 and 1939 in favor of anti-Semitic laws. In his preface, Fisch, whose immediate and extended family had been murdered at Auschwitz, argued that "there was a causal connection between Auschwitz" and the anti-Semitic speeches made by Hungary's most prominent bishops.[1] By preaching anti-Semitism, and by supporting anti-Jewish laws, Hungary's Christian churches had, he claimed, helped to shape the political "atmosphere" in Hungary, a "climate" in which political leaders could feel encouraged to look for radical solutions to the country's so-called "Jewish question." Because they had condoned persecution, Hungary's Christian church leaders thus bore a measure of responsibility for the mass murder of Hungarian Jews. But Hungary's Catholic and Protestant church leaders rejected these arguments. Instead, they argued that, when evil in the form of Nazi occupation had descended on Hungary, their churches had, in fact, opposed totalitarian terror and Nazi racism. Those who agreed with Rabbi Fisch were simply wrong. Instead of helping to create an atmosphere of terror, the churches had been outspoken in fighting it.

Historians have good reason to be skeptical of the arguments that Hungary's religious leaders made after World War II. As Randolph Braham and others have shown, the Protestant and Catholic churches' unwillingness to clearly and publicly denounce the segregation and deportation of Hungary's Jews in 1944 undoubtedly contributed "to the climate that made the unhindered implementation of the 'final solution' possible."[2] We should also remember that after the First World War both the Hungarian Catholic and Protestant churches fully embraced the idea that Hungary was a "Christian nation" and that they had supported policy-makers who wanted to reduce "Jewish influence" in their nation's society and culture. However, I would argue that historians should also study this debate about the churches' responsibility for genocide as a historical problem of its own. At the center of this debate is an argument

201

about how to place 1944 in Hungarian history. Survivors, such as Rabbi Fisch, found precedents and pre-conditions for the mass murder of 1944 already present in Hungarian society on the eve of World War II and they blamed Hungarian social institutions like the Christian churches for their existence. But others, including the Hungarian Communist Party, were also critical of the churches, accusing them of having supported a repressive, antiquated, and militaristic regime. Faced with this challenge to their social power, Hungary's Catholic and most of its Protestant church leaders found meaning in the Holocaust by linking it to their current situation. They denied any connection between their efforts to address Hungary's "Jewish question" before the war and the murderous events of 1944. Instead, they argued that Nazi occupation and Arrow Cross terror should be seen as one chapter in a struggle against totalitarianism that was still going on. This paper will examine more closely how Hungary's Christian religious leaders shaped their initial memory of the Holocaust in the face of the growing Communist threat.

Between 1945 and 1948, a coalition government dominated by the Communist Party ruled in Hungary. For many inside and close to the coalition, religion was a central question in any discussion of the future of the new Hungarian republic.[3] The Communist Party saw Hungary's institutional Christian churches, and especially the Catholic Church, as significant obstacles to their long-term goal of creating a Soviet-style one-party state in Hungary. However, non-Communist socialists and progressive democrats, still independent in these years, were also hostile to organized religion, seeing it as a force for reaction and a brake on the democratic aspirations of the Hungarian people. In the liberal, socialist, and Communist media, journalists accused Catholic and Protestant religious leaders of teaching Hungarians anti-democratic values. The churches, they argued, had helped Hungary's political leaders to demolish the nation's liberal and progressive traditions after World War I by demonizing them as "Jewish" and foreign. By preaching "proto-fascist" demagoguery, and by diverting public attention away from real social injustice, the churches had helped to make possible the legal, and then physical, exclusion of Jews from Hungarian society.[4] Across the left, public intellectuals concluded that the "Christian Hungary" championed by the churches between the two world wars had been a society hostile in every way to modern and progressive ideas of justice and equality.[5] The fact that pogroms occurred again in several places in 1946 only confirmed that "reactionary clericalism" was not dead in Hungary, even after the mass murder of 1944. Hungary's Communist Party also joined non-Communist progressives in attacking "clericalism" as the spirit of counter-revolution and in calling the Catholic Church a pillar of "Horthy-fascism." Across the spectrum of the left, however, religious institutions, and the Catholic Church in particular, stood out as the quin-tessential "enemies of the people," contributing causes of the war's atrocities and implacable foes of freedom and progress.

The Catholic Church
      The Hungarian Catholic Church rejected this criticism outright. Before the war, prominent Catholics argued, the Church had opposed political extremism from both the far-left and the far-right.[6] Now, after the war, the Church remained even more committed to defending the values of Christian civilization against radical extremists. To Catholic leaders throughout Europe, the horrible dislocation and slaughter of war only proved that the Church had been right all along about the threats that modern political and social trends posed to traditional moral order.[7] Nazism and communism threatened Christian civilization equally, they argued, because both movements aimed at setting up an all-powerful state ruled according to a secular and materialist ideology. Against this grave threat, the Catholic Church in Hungary and elsewhere in Europe, had pronounced itself ready to defend Christian Europe.[8] Hungary's Catholic leaders thus found particular meaning in the events of 1944. They interpreted the German occupation of Hungary in that year as a reign of terror over the country unconnected to anything that had come before it. This terror aimed at destroying all independent organizations and beliefs—what we today might call civil society. Faced with radical evil, Catholic churchmen maintained that they had stood against terror.[9] They had defended freedom of conscience and the right to worship and they had continued to deny that racial laws had the power to negate sincere conversion. Catholic spokesmen also recalled the many men and women of the church—figures like Sister Margit Slachta—who had also tried to the best of their abilities to assist persecuted Jews. Moreover, a number of Church figures, including József Mindszenty himself, still the Bishop of Veszprém in those days, had been imprisoned by the Arrow Cross. Now, after 1945, in a Hungary occupied by the Soviet army, the Church stood ready to oppose new violations of "human rights" and

"Christian morality," such as unfair trials before the people's courts and, above all, Communist harassment of Hungarian Catholics in the public practice of their religious faith.[10] All of these, Cardinal Mindszenty and the Hungarian Catholic Church maintained, were equally grave attacks against the norms of Christian civilization. Because of this, Catholic leaders resented what they considered to be the excessive attention paid to the persecution of Jews during World War II. Jewish suffering might be undeniable, but, the Church's defenders argued, it was far from being the whole story of Hungary's battle against totalitarian terror.

Hungary's Catholic leaders also rejected any association with Nazi anti-Semitism. The German occupation of Hungary had, they argued, brought to power a radical approach to Hungary's "Jewish question," so far removed in principle and practice from the Church's own views about Jews as to be something entirely different. In the years after World War I, Catholic leaders, including Cardinal Mindszenty, who was a well-known parish priest in Zalaegerszeg until 1944, had argued that carefully constructed social, economic, and legal discrimination could address Hungary's so-called "Jewish problem" in a balanced and rational manner. The hatred that had inspired genocide and mass murder was, however, entirely irrational, steeped in myths of blood and race that the Church had long opposed. There was no similarity or continuity between the two and the fact that Hungary's Catholic bishops had voted for some anti-Jewish laws and against another proved that they had known the difference.

However, these strong distinctions—between rational anti-Judaism and irrational Nazi racism and between anti-totalitarianism and Nazi terror—did not settle the question of anti-Semitism in postwar Hungary. By dividing the country so starkly into defenders and enemies of Christian European civilization, Catholic leaders breathed new life into certain elements of the "Jewish question" in Hungary. In part, this was a response to the prominent members of the Communist Party who were themselves of Jewish origin. In part, this was also a response to the zeal with which survivors turned to the People's Courts and to the non-Catholic media for justice against those who had murdered their families and friends. However, it had been well established in Catholic circles for decades that secularism, socialism, and revolution—ideologies embraced by those who opposed the Church's vision of the world—were all peculiarly Jewish evils. This "Jewish spirit" had brought disaster to Hungary in 1919 in the form of the Bolshevik revolution; it would undoubtedly do so again if Christian Hungarians were not vigilant. Of course, no Catholic bishop called for any explicitly anti-Jewish legislation or policy after 1945; this aspect of inter-war Christian nationalism was gone for good. But asserting from the pulpit that the Jews had killed Christ, or that, as Bishop Gyula Czapik wrote in a pastoral letter in 1948, the Jews had been responsible for the "terror" that murdered Christ,[11] could only inflame anti-Jewish prejudice among those used since 1919 to think of the nation's enemy as Judeo-Bolshevism. Such statements reinforced the notion among believers that Hungarian society was locked in a Manichaean struggle between Christian civilization and its anti-Christian enemies. In this tense ideological climate, traditional religious anti-Semitism could resonate with much broader meaning far outside the walls of the church. Thus, opposition to communism led many Catholic leaders in post-1945 Hungary to marginalize the Holocaust in the memory of World War II and to place old forms of anti-Semitic rhetoric into new contexts.

Hungarian Protestantism: The Case of the Reformed Church

As institutions, Hungary's Protestant churches had been no less enmeshed in the socio-political structure of inter-war "Christian" Hungary than the Catholic Church had been. But unlike Cardinal Mindszenty's Catholic Church, Hungarian Calvinists argued much more frequently that a society trying to rebuild from a devastating war had to acknowledge and repent its sins. Only days after the Soviet army had finally driven the Germans from Budapest, László Ravasz, Calvinist bishop of the Danubian Synod and the leading figure in Hungary's Reformed Church, preached his first sermon of the postwar era on the subject of sin and repentance. Speaking in the famous church on Calvin Square in Pest, Ravasz found meaning in the devastation and suffering by seeing it as a sign of divine anger at the worldly obsessions of men. Violence had been repaid with more violence. Only by profound reflection on one's sins—a duty incumbent on everyone, individually—could men hope to knit together the bonds of civility and reconstruct their society.

However, this call for penitence was not as clear as it might seem at first glance. The sins of men had led to the horrible devastation of war, and leaders like Bishop Ravasz did discuss the particular suffering that Jews had endured during that war. Protestant leaders were also more willing than Catholic bishops were to concede that they might have done or said more on behalf of Jews, even if they also maintained that they had clearly spoken out against persecution.[12] But Hungary's Protestant bishops typically marginalized the mass murder of Jews in their nation's collective memory by finding similarities or even equivalences between the persecution of Jews and the suffering to which (Christian) Hungarians had been subjected during the war. For example, Bishop Ravasz remembered the last year of the war in Budapest thusly:

> While we were still our own masters, whole groups of people were slaughtered in Budapest like harmful beasts of prey and were closed inside a ghetto like some kind of infectious herd, and it only took a few months before every human life in Budapest became absolutely uncertain, and everyone lived for weeks like the most oppressed victims of the ghetto.[13]

In one breath, Bishop Ravasz recognized that the violence of war had had "multiple faces,"[14] and that Budapest's Jews had endured a particular fate. In the next, the bishop erased this distinction, arguing that everyone in the city had suffered like Jews. A specific memory of genocide was clouded still further by the broad list of sins for which the nation had to repent, according to Calvinist and Lutheran church leaders. In his February 1945 sermon, Reform Bishop Ravasz offered a long litany of transgressions, reminiscent of the Catholic Church's invective against modernity: Hungarians had been too individualistic, had embraced rampant capitalism, had indulged in vain pleasures and superficial pursuits, such as playing bridge.[15] It was generally left to the listener to imagine how these things differed—as sins—from murder. In most cases, Protestant calls for self-examination and penitence remained what historian Tamás Majsai has called "a confused jumble of flowery words," so general as to be meaningless.[16]

However, some members of the Calvinist Church wanted public penitence to cut more deeply and to contribute to the transformation of Hungarian society. Writing in leftist journals like Béla Zsolt's *Haladás* (Progress) as well as in their own Church journals, they described how right-wing attitudes had dominated Church debate in the late 1930s and early 1940s.[17] They also remembered that their Church had consistently tried to make it harder for Jews to convert to Christianity, even as the anti-Jewish decrees became harsher and more numerous. These reformers believed that Calvinism could only reclaim its moral authority in the new Hungary if it broke completely with its past, and if they, as Calvinists and as Christians, examined the part they had played in the ruin of their country. A group of these reform-minded Calvinists met in August 1946 in the northeastern city of Nyíregyháza to imagine how their Church, under new leadership, might lead the way in Hungary's moral rebirth.[18] Calling themselves the Free Council (*Szabad Tanács*), the assembled churchmen argued that the Hungarian nation, led by the Reformed Church, had to act on its own without reference to others when it begged forgiveness for all its sins. National renewal could only come from this kind of profound and sincere repentance. Of the murder of Hungarian Jews, they said:

> Under the burden of the responsibility that falls on us, and suffering together with our people because of the sins and omissions we committed against the Jews—conscious of the horrible pain which the surviving Jews bear on account of the inhumane carrying off and horrible extermination of their loved ones—and though it comes late, we ask Hungary's Jews before God for forgiveness.[19]

By accepting collective responsibility, the Council declared, Hungarians could find sense in their own suffering and could thus renew themselves, finding their way amidst the wreckage to the new and just society so many hoped for in those days.

The Free Council's declaration was not well received. Almost immediately, it touched off a storm of outrage among Hungarian Protestants, Calvinists, and Lutherans alike.[20] In direct response to the Council's declaration, Calvinist Bishop László Ravasz stated emphatically that the Reformed Church had no need to ask Jews for forgiveness.[21] He publicly chastised the Council for presuming to do penance for the collective sins of a whole people. He asserted, as he had done many times, that totalitarian terror and racial violence, unconnected to anything before and which Ravasz called "Hitlerism," had descended on Hungary in 1944–45.[22] In the face of this challenge, Ravasz insisted, no less forcefully than did Hungary's Catholic Episcopate, that his Church had spoken out against evil when so many good people had been terrorized into silence. He also reminded critics that many men and women in the Protestant churches had risked their lives to help Jews in those months. The Church, he said, had always sought only rational ways to

solve Hungary's undeniable "Jewish question."[23] It had always repudi-
ated the "soul-destroying danger of anti-Semitism" and "every kind of
blood libel or mad legend which evil men invent and stupid men
believe."[24] Ravasz also accused the men of the Free Council of political
irresponsibility. True democracy, he argued, required self-discipline,
restraint, and moral character only to be found in the Gospels. Without
these checks, reconstruction would be in vain and democracy would become "dictatorship."[25] At a time when the Communist Party was trying
to establish itself as the chief political and moral arbiter in Hungary, the
meaning of these remarks, however generally phrased, was clear. It was
counter-productive and even dangerous, Ravasz seemed to suggest, to
undermine the position of the Church with ill-considered blanket statements about collective responsibility. Such criticism only gave ammuni-
tion to the Churches' enemies. In the weeks and months that followed,
conservative allies of Ravasz expanded on this response with rebuttals of
their own by addressing the charges that leftist churchmen made in
progressive newspapers.[26] Through their articles, it was clear that the
Free Council's approach to mastering the past remained marginal within
Hungary's Reformed Church.

   In this way, the most ambitious attempt to acknowledge the responsibility of Hungary's Christian churches for the "climate"—to use Rabbi
Fisch's word—in which the segregation, deportation, and murder of
Jewish Hungarians had been possible came to nothing. In the years that
followed some of the men who participated in the 1946 Free Council
continued to write about the role that inter-war Protestant Church leaders
like László Ravasz had played in the anti-Semitic politics of inter-war
and wartime Hungary. Their work, however, supported, and sometimes
was explicitly intended to legitimize, Communist rule after 1948 and
after 1956.[27] As I have tried to show, Catholic and conservative Protestant leaders found a different meaning in the history of 1944 and the
Holocaust in Hungary, in large part because of their anti-Communist
convictions. In the face of grave political challenges, they represented
1944–45 as a period unconnected to prior Hungarian history. They
denied any link between the murderous violence then and their own role
in the anti-Semitic politics in Hungary that had preceded it. Instead, they
focused on those religious Christians who had helped persecuted Jews,
holding them up in contrast to the Nazi occupiers and their Hungarian
henchmen. The result was a view of the past in which the churches—

Catholic and Protestant—had opposed terror and racism and defended Christian morality and culture as best they could. This very insistence on the defense of Western Christian civilization, I have argued, only placed old accusations of "anti-Christian" behavior in a new context, allowing religious leaders to justify past anti-Jewish rhetoric by focusing on the present anti-Christian threat. Of course, the Communist Party ultimately ended any possibility of open self-criticism, crushing the independence of the Christian churches in Hungary, through blandishments in the case of the Protestants, by force in the case of the Catholic Church. These complexities reveal the political perils of coming to terms with Hungary's anti-Semitic past in the immediate postwar years.

Notes

1. Henrik Fisch, ed., *Keresztény egyházfők felsőházi beszédei a zsidókérdésben* (Speeches in the upper house by Christian church leaders on the Jewish question) (Budapest: The Author, 1947), 16–18.

2. Randolph L. Braham, "The Christian Churches of Hungary and the Holocaust," *Yad Vashem Studies* 29 (2001): 266.

3. Peter Kenez, "The Hungarian Communist Party and the Catholic Church, 1945–1948," *Journal of Modern History* 75 (December 2003): 864–89.

4. See, e.g., the many articles by Béla Zsolt in his newspaper, *Haladás* (Progress). Among others: "Emberi és politikai hála" (Human and political gratitude) (October 27, 1945).

5. Again, this is the tone in newspapers like *Haladás*. See, e.g. Béla Zsolt, "Lipótváros" (September 11, 1947).

6. See, e.g., the 1938 article by the Archbishop of Kalocsa, Count Gyula Zichy, "Küzdelem a szélsőségek ellen" (Struggle against the extremists), *Politika* 7:1 (January 2, 1938): 3–4.

7. Damian van Melis, "'Strengthened and Purified through Ordeal by Fire': Ecclesiastical Triumphalism in the Ruins of Europe," in *Life After Death: Approaches to a Cultural and Social History of Europe During the 1940s and 1950s*, eds. Richard Bessel and Dirk Schumann (Washington, D.C., and Cambridge, U.K.: German Historical Institute and Cambridge University Press, 2003), 231–42.

8. This was the general tenor of the 1938 Eucharistic Congress, held that year in Budapest.

9. See, e.g., the various essays in Antal Meszlényi, ed., *A magyar katolikus egyház és az emberi jogok védelme* (The Hungarian Catholic Church and the protection of human rights) (Budapest: St. István Társulat, 1947).

10. Margit Balogh, *Mindszenty József* (Budapest: Elektra Kiadóház, 2002), 111–17.

11. Cited in Kenez, 868.

12. Albert Bereczky, *Hungarian Protestantism and the Persecution of Jews* (Budapest: Sylvester, 1945).

13. Sermon of 11 February 1945. ("Amit vet az ember, azt aratja"; Man harvests what he sows) Gyula Bárczay, ed., *Ravasz László: Válogatott írások, 1945–1968* (Selected writings, 1945–1968) (Bern: Európai Protestáns Magyar Szabadegyetem, 1988), 24.

14. Pieter Lagrou, "The Nationalization of Victimhood: Selective Violence and National Grief in Western Europe, 1945–1960," in Bessel and Schumann, 245.

15. Bárcsay, Sermon of February 11, 1945, 24.

16. Tamás Majsai, "Szempontok a Soá 1945 utáni (Magyarországi) evangélikus és református egyházi recepciójához" (Points of view on the evangelical and reformed church reception in the post-1945 Holocaust era Hungary) in *Magyar megfontolások a Soáról* (Hungarian considerations about the Holocaust), eds. Gábor Hamp, Özséb Horányi, and László Rábai (Budapest: Balassi, 1999), 184–85.

17. See, e.g., Károly Rátkai, "A kálvinizmus örök. Református presbiter és Mauthauseni gályarab levele a 'Haladás' szerkesztőjéhez" (Calvinism is eternal. Letter of the permanent Reformed elder of Calvinism and of of the galley slave to the editor of "Haladás"), *Haladás* (January 12, 1946).

18. The most important speeches and declarations were reprinted. See Benő Békefi, ed., *Országos Református Szabad Tanács. Nyiregyháza, 1946. Augusztus 14.–17. Határozatai, deklarácioi, kérelmei és az ott elhangzott közérdekű beszédek* (National Reformed Free Council, Nyíregyháza, August 14–17, 1946. Decisions, declarations, demands, and public speeches) (Budapest: Sylvester, 1946).

19. Ibid., 73.

20. Majsai, "Szempontok" (Viewpoints), 190–91.

21. See his opening presidential address to the National Association of Reformed Clergymen of September 25, 1946, "ORLE elnöki megnyitó beszéd" (ORLE presidential opening speech), in Bárczay, 69–86, esp. 76–77.

22. Ravasz explained these views to the progressive media in "Védőbeszéd és vádirat. Interju Ravasz László ref. Püspökkel" (Defense speech and indictment. Interview with László Ravasz, bishop of the Reformed church), *Haladás* (December 22, 1945).

23. Ibid.

24. Bárczay, 77

25. Ibid., 69–70

26. See, e.g., "Muraközy Gyula válasza Rátkai Károlynak a 'Haladás' c. lapban megjelent cikkére" (Gyula Muraközy's response to Károly Rátkai concerning his article in "Haladás"), *Élet és Jövő* (January 19, 1946).

27. See, e.g., Imre Kádár, *The Church in the Storm of Time: The History of the Hungarian Reformed Church during the Two World Wars, Revolutions, and Counter-Revolutions* (Budapest: Biblioteca, 1958). For a critical appraisal of the post-1948 church and men like Imre Kádár, see Gyula Gombos, *The Lean Years: A Study of Hungarian Calvinism in Crisis* (New York: Kossuth Foundation, 1960).

United States Holocaust Memorial Museum Archival Collections Relating to the Holocaust in Hungary

Radu Ioanid and Ferenc Katona

The United States Holocaust Memorial Museum (USHMM) has signed and implemented archival agreements in almost every European country, in addition to several countries in Asia and Latin America. The Museum signed these agreements with various government agencies, including national archives; intelligence agencies; ministries of interior, foreign affairs, and defense; and many private archives affiliated with Jewish and non-Jewish organizations. It is fair to state that none of the countries with which our Museum has worked has had such stringent privacy laws as Hungary. These privacy laws have constituted the main obstacles that made access to Holocaust-related records in the Hungarian government archives very difficult, and precluded their export. To solve this problem, the Museum in 2003 signed with Hungary a government-to-government agreement, which now allows the export of microfilmed records that USHMM has been filming for many years. These privacy laws explain in part why the Hungarian collections from the Museum's archives, in terms of quantity and quality, are not yet at the level they should be compared to our collections from other East and Central European countries. Even if we take into consideration the Randolph Braham Collection, described below, and the 1.5 million pages of trial records from the Budapest Municipal Archives (*Budapest Főváros Levéltára*), the Hungarian USHMM collections are still less complete compared to our Belgian, German, Austrian, Bulgarian, Romanian, or French collections.

It is important to note that the Hungarian archivists were always friendly and forthcoming when the Museum's negotiators worked there, and the survey and reproduction work has continued with measurable results. However, we have encountered very serious problems in obtaining reliable information about and retrieving significant collections of Holocaust-related archival records in most Hungarian archives.

The Museum had and continues to enjoy extraordinarily positive cooperation with the Budapest Municipal Archives, which holds the vast majority of the most important records of Hungarian war crimes trials.

Although our access to the National Archives of Hungary (*Magyar Országos Levéltár*) has been relatively good, it is clear that many of the archival collections of potential interest to our Museum are not kept in this archive. Moreover, there are some questions about the full extent of what records are held at the National Archives. For example, massive amounts of Aryanization records were not brought to our attention until recently. In order to clarify what additional collections of potential interest exist or may have recently been deposited at the National Archives of Hungary, the best approach would be to review the institution's full list of archival fonds, including those that may for the moment have certain restrictions applied to them.

In the Archives of Military History (*Hadtörténelmi Levéltár*) the records to which we have been allowed access up to now are very limited and not of the quality and quantity that has been found in other East and Central European countries. Systems of forced labor administered by the military generated massive amounts of paperwork and reports. But in Hungary's Military Archives, we have seen just a few references to Hungary's carefully organized wartime military-related forced labor service system. It is possible that these records are in the separate archive of the Hungarian military's counter-intelligence agency, or that parts of the material may be in the Military Archives, but still be classified. It is simply not credible, however, that no records exist. We recently heard informally that that Jewish forced labor records exist within an extensive card file in the Military Archives. The only way to clarify the situation is to undertake a careful review of the full list of archival fonds of these institutions, making it clear that the list must include all collections, regardless of whether they are open for research, somehow administratively restricted, or classified at the present time.

Most of the archival records of the former Communist Ministry of Internal Affairs are currently held by the Historical Archives of the State Security Agencies (ÁBTL, *Állambiztonsági Szolgálatok Történeti Levéltára*, formerly known as *Történeti Hivatal*, the "Office of History"). Again, our experience with this institution has been very mixed and clouded by a lack of clear information about what collections are actually in their control. Thus, at one point we were told that the forced labor system records had been moved to ÁBTL, but it has been impossible to either confirm this or see these records. One could rightfully suspect that records relating to the Hungarian gendarmerie that carried out the deportations, deportation lists, and records of the Jewish Council might be at the ÁBTL. But again, no definitive information has been offered by ÁBTL or anyone else. ÁBTL has not been willing to share reliable information regarding the full extent of its archival holdings. This is totally out of keeping with our experience in other ex-Communist countries, where the records of the former Ministries of Interior have been made massively available and have provided us with a wealth of information on the Holocaust. It is difficult to understand or contemplate that a governmental organization of democratic Hungary might believe it to be in the country's interest to hide the history of a long-discredited Fascist regime that disappeared over six decades ago!

We have learned that ÁBTL holds some Gestapo files and also records relating to the immediate post-World War II activities of the American Joint Distribution Committee. We have also learned that ÁBTL has developed a sophisticated computer database regarding its holdings. A thorough review of the full list of holdings will be required to determine what collections at ÁBTL might relate to the Holocaust.

Finally, despite repeated requests, we have been denied information regarding Holocaust-related records in the archives of the Hungarian intelligence agencies. Agency leaderships told us that all Holocaust-era records had been transferred to ÁBTL. ÁBTL, meanwhile, told us that not everything had been transferred. No one would share with us the list of collections actually transferred, while everyone told us that exactly what we were interested in was in the hands of another institution. A review of the transmittal lists created when archival collections were turned over would clarify what has been transferred to ÁBTL. In addition, it will require a thorough review of a list of the complete current archival holdings of the Hungarian intelligence agencies to identify Holocaust-related records that they may still have under their control. For example, during the Communist regime, especially during the Stalinist period, the intelligence agencies closely surveilled and kept files on Zionist organizations both in Hungary and abroad. Surveillance records relating to Zionist and other Jewish organizations still exist in every ex-Communist country. Only Hungary has failed to identify them.

These are important categories of records/collections/archival fonds that are being made inaccessible in the Hungarian government archives. Not only are the materials themselves inaccessible, but information regarding where they are being kept is unavailable. These records include:

records related to the forced labor of Jews; records related to the deportation of Jews; actual deportation records from 1944; records of the Hungarian gendarmerie; records of the investigation of the Kamenets-Podolsk massacre; and various categories of records that would have been kept by the country's intelligence agencies. Chances are that records relating to wartime Jewish councils exist, but no definitive information has been provided. Furthermore, records of post-war Jewish organizations that involved Holocaust survivors are also unavailable.

These sets of records relate to the most sensitive part of the history of the Holocaust in Hungary. While it is possible that some of these records, at a certain point during or after the war may have been destroyed, it is more than highly unlikely that all of precisely these collections vanished in bombardments, evacuations, etc. Nor is it credible that the wartime Hungarian bureaucracy or the postwar Communist bureaucracy systematically destroyed all records of this type. Those bureaucracies often relied on such records for both political and economic purposes.

Despite these problems, many records pertaining to the Holocaust in Hungary have already arrived. The following survey identifies several archival references illustrating the richness and breadth of the Museum's collections relating to Hungary.[1]

The Randolph Braham Collection (RG-52)

Professor Braham donated to the Archives the result of his many decades of tireless document collecting. At this moment the Randolph Braham Collection occupies more than fifty archival boxes containing original material and reproductions, including research material collected in archives of Hungary, Romania, Germany, Great Britain, the Netherlands, Israel, and the United States. The records include, among other things,

- an extended manuscript version of his 1962 two-volume document selections,[2]
- documents relating to his service as an expert witness at legal procedures against Gendarmerie Captain Imre Finta and journalist Ferenc Koréh, and the proceedings relating to a libel suit involving Bruce Belton (a.k.a. Béla Berend), and
- folders containing Professor Braham's extensive correspondence with the "dramatis personae," as he calls witnesses to and participants in the events.

The Braham collection also contains audio and video interviews and presentations made at various events. Part of the Braham collection is the 180-reel series of documents, known by researchers as the I-series (*I-sorozat*), collected in the 1960s by Elek Karsai, obtained from Budapest in the mid-1980s by Professor Braham, and donated by him to the Archives in the mid-1990s.[3] RG-52 at this point comprises twelve series, of which number three is a collection of documents pertaining to the Holocaust in Northern Transylvania. It includes records of the 1946 Cluj/Kolozsvár trial.[4]

The USHMM's Archives also contain a large number of records related to war crimes trials and investigations of crimes committed during the Hungarian administration of Northern Transylvania (1940–1944). The original records are held in two Romanian government archives, namely the Archives of the Romanian Information Service (SRI, *Serviciul roman de Informatii*, Romania's counter-intelligence agency) and from the Romanian State Archives (*Arhivele de Stat*). Record Group 25.004M contains over 160 (16 mm) microfilm reels that comprise over 320,000 pages of records covering the trials and court investigations related to crimes committed in Northern Transylvania under Hungarian administration. While a few of these trials concern the mistreatment and killing of ethnic Romanians and Roma, most address the ghettoization, deportation, and killing of Jews in Northern Transylvania, particularly the events on counties, such as Bihor/Bihar, Bistrița-Năsăud/Beszterce-Naszód, Ciuc/Csík, Cluj/Kolozs, Trei Scaune/Háromszék, Maramureş/Máramaros, Mureş/Maros-Torda, Odorhei/Udvarhely, Satu Mare/Szatmár, Sălaj/Szilágy, and Someş/Szolnok-Doboka. The files describe in detail cases of atrocities against the Jews committed by Hungarian civil service, police, and gendarmerie; the ghettoization and forced labor of Jews in Northern Transylvania; and, finally, their deportation to the extermination camps under German jurisdiction. Similar materials relating to court trials and investigations consist of over 2,000 pages from the Regional Archive of Cluj, a branch of the Romanian State Archives. Another 6,000 pages from the same source contain Romanian police investigations relating to the persecution, arrest, internment, and deportation of Jews in Northern Transylvania and the investigation of war criminals.

The Aladár Szegedy-Maszák Papers (Accessioning in Process)

Returning to the field of systematic, but relatively small scale collecting, one of the latest major Hungarian acquisitions by the USHMM Archives is the Aladár Szegedy-Maszák Collection, occupying approximately twenty archival boxes, donated by the family of the late Ambassador Szegedy-Maszák.

Aladár Szegedy-Maszák (1903–1988) was a Hungarian diplomat stationed in Berlin between 1932 and 1937, when Kálmán Kánya and Döme Sztójay served as legation heads. After 1937 he served in the Hungarian Ministry of Foreign Affairs until the German occupation. The Gestapo arrested him on April 14, 1944, and deported him to Dachau, where he was liberated in 1945. One year later he became the Hungarian Ambassador to Washington, but in 1947 he resigned and did not return to Hungary. He held important U.S. Government positions until his 1969 retirement.

We would like to direct the attention of experts on the Holocaust in Hungary to the full manuscript of Mr. Szegedy-Maszák's multi-thousand-page memoirs.[5] The collection, consisting of his research notes, drafts, journals, pro memoria, and correspondence, will be soon available for research.

* * *

In addition to the Braham and Szegedy-Maszák collections, the United States Holocaust Memorial Museum also has three relatively small collections relating to the Holocaust in Hungary.

The Patai Diaries (Accession No. 2000.155)

A Baltimore psychiatrist and amateur harpsichord player donated the Patai diaries to the Archives. The entries cover the years from 1934 until 1949, and fill twenty-eight notebooks (approximately 3,000 pages).

Imre Patai (as far as we know not related to József and Raphael Patai) was an electrical engineer, student of physics, inventor, and industrialist. Researchers can find records of his company—Vacuum-technikai és Villamossági Rt. (Vacuum Technology and Electronics, Co.)—in the holdings of the National Archives of Hungary.[6] He took copious notes about his everyday life during those most extraordinary years. Reading the notes one becomes acquainted with a highly cultivated and quite well-connected man. After the war he immigrated to America, and passed away in 1949. His wife, Ágnes Jámbor, was a concert pianist, a pupil of Edwin Fischer, and a finalist in the 1937 Chopin Piano Competition. She passed away in 1997 and left Patai's diaries to her chamber music partner, the Baltimore psychiatrist.

The collection is a treasure for those looking for original and authentic first-hand accounts about daily life in Budapest during the years of the Holocaust. (Notes about the year 1944 alone occupy five volumes at approximately 500 pages.) Events of daily political life, soon to become history, receive characteristic treatment by Patai, a quintessential representative of the Budapest Jewish bourgeoisie.

The Patai diaries contain many significant details for analyzing such intriguing questions as what did the Budapest Jews know and when did they know it? It is quite late, on May 15, 1944, that he makes an entry about the ghettoization, which started a month before.[7] Less than a week after the first deportations, on May 21, he wrote that "allegedly groups are being transported from the countryside towards Germany, or maybe towards death. No confirmed news arrived however about killings or mass murders."[8] On May 29, Patai mentioned cattle cars and "mass-annihilations," and the news that someone has received a postcard from Wiesbaden about the arrival of loved ones.[9] No doubt Patai heard something about a Waldsee card, but substituted a well-known German geographical name starting with a W: Wiesbaden.[10] In the June 7 entry one can read that a certain Dr. Szőnyi, an employee of the Jewish Community, "knows the newest rumors about ghettos, the dragging away and slaughtering of countryside Jews."[11]

The Gyula Nádor Journals (Accession No. 2000.13.1)

Deported Szolnok businessman Gyula Nádor kept journals in Strasshof and Bergen-Belsen. Nádor passed away a few days after his liberation, but his handwritten notebooks were found and brought to Budapest by his son-in-law and camp mate, Gyula Vermes.[12] Nádor's older daughter, who survived the Holocaust in Budapest, preserved the journals. She donated the original documents to the USHMM Archives in 2000.

Nádor wrote his first Holocaust-related notes when he was taken from his Szolnok home to Szentgyörgypuszta, near Debrecen, on May 5, 1944. He started writing his thoughts in a notebook on July 31, when he described his way back to Szolnok and his deportation to Strasshof. On January 1, 1945, already in Bergen-Belsen, he began to write in another blank booklet with the words, "In the holy name of God." He noted that he had to keep track somehow of the passing days—his diary allowed him to do so.

This highly organized fifty-two-year-old man, a shipping and transportation expert by trade, could never comprehend that if two trains pulled out at about the same time from the same Szolnok railway station carrying the same cargo (deportees), why did those trains not arrive in Strasshof at about the same time. There was no way for him to know that two transports left Szolnok carrying deportees. One took him to Strasshof, the other train took his wife, younger daughter, and infant grandson to Auschwitz: a geographical name Gyula Nádor never learned, although we know from his journal that he had heard the name at least once, but he did not understand what it meant. His March 14, 1945, entry reads: "Lajos Gere met his two […] sisters-in-law, who arrived here a week ago […] from Poland, from a place called Auspitz."[13] Auspitz, with a "p," was a common family name in Hungarian Jewish circles; it had real meaning. The word "Auschwitz," the name of the death camp on the East already liberated by the Soviets, had no meaning on March 14, 1945, for a Hungarian Jew in Bergen-Belsen.

Shortly before his death Gyula Nádor was liberated at Zielitz, north of Magdeburg, on April 13, 1945. His last diary entry describes the hours when the train carrying him from Bergen-Belsen towards Magdeburg stood idle on the tracks, abandoned by most of its German guards. He captures the moment when the first American tank appeared not far from the train. Following his last words a different handwriting appears on the page, the neat American handwriting of the GI who liberated Gyula Nádor, Corporal Frank Gartner.

The April 13, 1945, Zielitz events, the liberation of former Bergen-Belsen inmates by the Americans, were also recorded by another man liberated at the same moment, graphic artist and writer Ervin Abádi. Among other things he drew a picture about the American tank Nádor mentioned, and the picture was donated in 1992 to the USHMM's Arts and Artifacts Branch of the Collections Division by Hungarian survivors now living in New Jersey.[14]

* * *

It is remarkable how individuals saved precious papers that initially seemed to be only family memorabilia, but turned out to have archival and historical value. Our donors, who now reside in America, Canada, Australia, and elsewhere, left or were forced to leave their native country as refugees, and they could take with them very little. Many, however, made sure that they brought postcards received from loved ones in labor service, notes hastily scribbled in a camp or in the air raid shelter, or testimonies written under the most unusual circumstances.

The USHMM Collections Division and its Archives welcomes donations of personal papers pertaining to the Holocaust, and provides information about our permanent collections to researchers and the interested public.

Notes

1. Several papers published in this volume attest to the frequent use of these collections by scholars and researchers. Regularly up-dated inventories of the collections are available through the Museum's web site (www.ushmm.org), and in paper format in Brewster Chamberlin and Carl Modig, *Archival Guide to the Collections of the United States Holocaust Memorial Museum,* 2nd ed. (Washington, DC: USHMM Center for Advanced Holocaust Studies, 2003).

2. *The Destruction of Hungarian Jewry: A Documentary Account,* 2 vols. (New York: World Federation of Hungarian Jews, 1963).

3. Accession number: 1997.A.0294

4. For details consult Chamberlin and Modig, 376–84.

5. The manuscript is also available in the National Library of Hungary (*Országos Széchényi Könyvtár*) and has been partially published as *Az ember ősszel visszanéz...: Egy volt magyar diplomata emlékirataiból* (In autumn one remembers: Excerpts from the memoirs of a former Hungarian diplomat), 2 vols. (Budapest: Európa Könyvkiadó, 1996).

6. Fond number Z 1330. The finding aid is published in Ákos Koroknai, ed., *Villamosipari és finommechanikai repertórium* (Repertory of electric industry and precision mechanics) (Budapest: National Archives of Hungary, Budapest, n.d.).

7. Ibid., 42–44.

8. Ibid., 50.

9. Ibid., 53–54

10. For details about the subject, see Gábor Andor Tooth, "A művészet erejével válaszolva: Waldsee, 1944" (Responding by the power of art: Waldsee, 1944), in *Múlt és Jövő* 3 (2004): 96–99.

11. Accession number: 2000.155, vol. 16, 68–69.

12. Many of the names mentrioned in the diary are listed in one of the latest volumes of the Names series edited by Gavriel Bar-Shaked (*Names: Jász-Nagykun-Szolnok County, Names of the Jews Deported from Szolnok County* (Jerusalem The Beate Klarsfeld Foundtion/Yad Vashem, 2004)). The names of the Nádors are on page 96, the names of the Vermes family are on page 141. Gyula Vermes survived the Holocaust. Other names mentioned in

the diaries, for example Aladár Ungár, Ferenc Szabados, Jenő Friedmann, Mrs. Imre Balázs, et al., are also listed in the book.

13. In the original Hungarian: "Gere Lajos találkozott két [...] sógornőjével, akik egy héttel ezelőtt kerültek ide [...] Lengyelországból, Auspitzból."

14. Object number: 1992.193.40. The Ervin Abádi pictures were also published in Erwin Abádi, *Elmondom – My Story, 1942–1945* (Budapest: n. p., 1947). The book is available in the Rare Books collection of the USHMM Library. Similarly, Canadian donors deposited in the USHMM Archives a Hungarian-language New Testament that was in the pocket of their relative, Mr. Pál Szegő, a devoted Christian of Jewish birth, when in late 1944 he was rounded up and taken first to Bruck an der Leithe and later to Mauthausen. He used all of the blank surfaces in the book to keep a journal, and when he immigrated to Canada, he had the fragile little book in his luggage. The journal is a stunning testimony about human suffering and courage, humbleness and devotion (Paul Szego diary – Accession number: 2004.375).

Hungarian Jews' Perceptions of Anti-Semitism

András Kovács

Between March and November 1999, under the auspices of the Minority Research Institute of the Department of Sociology, at Eötvös Loránd University in Budapest, I conducted a sociological survey of the current situation of the Jewish community in Hungary. In the course of the survey, the team interviewed 2015 respondents.[1] The most important demographic and social data were collected for four generations—from respondents' grandparents to their children. Participants in the survey responded to questions concerning their relationship towards Jewish traditions and their acceptance or rejection of various forms of Jewish identity. They were also asked their opinions on assimilation, integration, and dissimilation; on Israel; and on the contemporary significance of the Holocaust. Finally, we attempted to gauge the opinions of Hungarian Jews on the state of their own community, on their relationships with non-Jews, and on anti-Semitism in post-Communist Hungary.[2]

In this article I shall analyze the data that we collected on the latter subject. First, I shall reveal how Jews living in Hungary define anti-Semitism, and whether—when it comes to classifying particular statements as anti-Semitic—any significant differences exist between younger and older groups of Jews, between better- and less-educated Jews, and between those with a stronger and those with a weaker sense of Jewish identity.

I shall then explore how the various respondent groups judge the extent, intensity, and gravity of anti-Jewish sentiment in the country, examining in particular whether respondents themselves have experienced such sentiment or have been subjected to discrimination. I shall reveal whether respondents think that anti-Semitism will increase or decrease in the coming years. Finally, I shall touch upon the policies that respondents consider desirable for tackling anti-Semitic phenomena.

Evidently the images formed by Jews and non-Jews determine in large part the nature of the relationship between the two groups. In his well-known article on anti-Semitism, István Bibó identified as a cause of modern anti-Semitism the development of situations in which Jews and non-Jews form negative images of each other in the course of regular and repeated social interactions.[3] In Bibó's view, such situations arise from "disturbances in societal development." Obviously, Jews will relate differently to their non-Jewish environment when they perceive strong anti-Semitism around them, rather than a friendly and accepting environment. The data compiled during our survey allowed us to examine whether or not perceptions of anti-Semitism influence interactions between Jews and non-Jews in ordinary everyday life. I shall deal with this particular issue in the final part of the study.

Perceptions of Anti-Semitism:
What Is Anti-Semitism and Who Are the Anti-Semites?

If, within a given society, agreement exists between Jews and non-Jews about what constitutes anti-Semitism, then anti-Semitism will probably be negligible. Usually, however, the situation is not so harmonious. As recent acrimonious political and cultural debates demonstrate—two typical examples are the Walser debate in Germany and the debate following the publication of the Sebastian diary in Romania[4]—even today great divisions of opinion occur among non-Jews with regard to the statements, attitudes, and phenomena that society should regard as anti-Semitic. But Jewish groups also lack agreement on this issue. While they have different social status and levels of integration, and represent various versions of Jewish identity, they also define anti-Semitism in different ways. Indeed often such differences of view, as well as the associated disputes, formulate the various options connected with Jewish identity and the relationships with non-Jewish society. Therefore, when examining perceptions of anti-Semitism, we should pay particular attention to the ways in which Hungarian Jews define anti-Semitism and to whether or not any differences arise among the various groups of Jews in their perceptions of anti-Semitism. We should also examine whether these opinions differ from the typical opinions of non-Jewish groups in society.

In the course of our survey, we asked respondents to tell us whether, in their view, seven statements repeated regularly in the course of debates on anti-Semitism were anti-Semitic or not. Several years earlier, we had posed this same question about identical statements to a representative sample of the Hungarian adult population.[5] The division of responses appears in Table 1.[6]

Table 1
How Should Anti-Semitism Be Defined in Hungary Today?
(I—total adult population; II—residents of Budapest with high school education or more) (Percentage, excluding "don't know")

In your opinion, is a person an anti-Semite if he or she...

	Not an anti-Semite			An anti-Semite		
	Jews	I	II	Jews	I	II
...always registers who is Jewish among his/her acquaintances	65	66	74	30	23	21
...would not marry a Jew	29	36	42	66	52	52
...thinks that Jews have recognizable features	61	70	84	33	19	12
...thinks that the interests of Jews in Hungary are very different from the interests of non-Jews	24	50	58	67	35	35
...thinks that Jews are no longer capable of integrating into Hungarian society	17	38	43	76	48	49
...thinks that the crimes committed against the Jews were no greater than those committed against the victims of Communism	12	51	62	80	30	33
...thinks that Jews are hostile to the Christian faith	14	39	47	77	42	43

The results demonstrate an interesting pattern. Both a majority of Jews and a majority of non-Jews agree that a person is not an anti-Semite merely because he/she "always registers who is Jewish among his/her acquaintances" or "thinks that Jews have recognizable features." The two groups also agree that a person who "would not marry a Jew" may be considered an anti-Semite. Nevertheless, even with these three statements, we may already identify differences that become obvious when we look at judgments about other statements. In general Jews are more likely to consider these statements anti-Semitic than are non-Jews.

The discrepancies are greatest between the Jewish sample group and the group comprising educated Budapest residents. For instance, while just 61–65 percent of the Jewish group consider these statements—which express an awareness of difference—non-anti-Semitic, 74–84 percent of the educated Budapest residents' group have the same opinion.

Whereas a majority of respondents do not consider statements that register Jews as an external social group to be anti-Semitic, the responses do indicate stark differences of opinion in connection with two other statements. While the great majority of Jews (80%) consider people who equate the abuses of Communism with the persecution of the Jews to be anti-Semitic, the majority of non-Jews (51%)—and above all a considerable majority of the educated Budapest residents group (62%)—do not consider such a view to be anti-Semitic. Similarly, the two groups fall into opposite camps regarding whether or not someone is anti-Semitic if he/she thinks that Jews constitute a separate interest group within modern Hungarian society.

One of the great anti-Semitism debates in the early 1990s arose after the well-known Hungarian poet Sándor Csoóri stated that, after their experiences of persecution, the Jews of Hungary were no longer capable of integrating into postwar Hungarian society.[7] Today, some years after Csoóri made these remarks, both a majority of Jews and a majority of non-Jews consider them to be anti-Semitic—although in the latter group the majority is relative (48%) because large numbers expressed no response to this question. The relative majorities of the two groups appear, however, on opposite sides in their judgment of people who state that Jews are hostile towards the Christian faith: according to a majority of the educated Budapest residents group, this is not an anti-Semitic statement.

Generally speaking, the breakdown of opinions indicates a latent tension. Whereas at least two-thirds of the Jews consider five of the seven statements to be anti-Semitic, the absolute majority of non-Jews consider merely the rejection of marriage to be an anti-Semitic attitude. The differences arising in connection with statements comparing the Holocaust with the abuses of Communism or expressing Jewish hostility towards Christianity demonstrate that tensions are greatest in areas linked to the ideological conflicts of the past ten years, and that tensions are particularly great between the Jewish group and the group having the most similar social status, that is, the educated Budapest residents group.

If we examine the breakdown of opinions among the Jewish group, we see that—although the great majority of Jews consider five of the seven statements to be anti-Semitic—there are characteristic differences between those who consider fewer of the statements to be anti-Semitic in their content and those who consider more of them to be anti-Semitic. Overall, 25 percent of the full Jewish sample defined six or seven of the statements as anti-Semitic, while 14 percent of the respondents considered two or fewer of the statements to be anti-Semitic. As we examined the differences, it became obvious that sensitivity towards anti-Semitism hinges on the relationship of respondents with Jewish identity. In the course of an analysis of typical Jewish identity strategies, we found among the respondents a group whose members had become detached from Jewish tradition during the last two generations: the parents of these respondents still preserved some elements of Jewish tradition, but the respondents themselves did not. Two-thirds of this group belong to the older generation—having been born prior to 1945. In the postwar years, this group experienced rapid social mobility and attempted to make up for the obstacles to mobility imposed upon them during years of persecution. The characteristics of this group strongly resemble the attributes of the group most sensitive to anti-Semitism: its members are over-represented in the older age group (over 55 years old), among college (but not university) graduates, the well-off, and former Hungarian Socialist Workers Party (the ruling party before 1990 - HSWP) members. (Within this group, the university graduates differ from those with lower educational qualifications in that they more likely regard statements expressing an awareness of difference as anti-Semitic.) Scholars have well established that anti-Semitism plays an important role in the formation and construction of certain Jewish identities. It seems that it is this group in which this role is greatest. On the other hand, respondents who became detached from Jewish religious or cultural traditions generations ago, or who still preserve and maintain (or have recently returned to) such traditions, exhibit less sensitivity towards anti-Semitism: these respondents consider merely an average (or below average) number of the statements to be anti-Semitic.

As the next step in our survey, we examined whom the respondents consider to be anti-Semitic in Hungarian society today. Respondents indicated which of the groups listed below are characterized to a greater or lesser degree by anti-Semitism, and to identify "manifestly anti-Semitic" groups. The results are shown in Table 2.

Table 2
Who Are Anti-Semites in Hungary Today? (Percentage)

	Strong anti-Semitism	A greater or lesser degree of anti-Semitism	No choice made
MIÉP[8] supporters	90	5	2
conservative politicians	14	51	29
former Communist functionaries	2	23	66
the conservative media	20	46	28
priests	8	34	49
descendants of the old ruling classes	14	35	42
practicing Christians	5	26	62
intellectuals	2	22	69
the poor	7	30	55
young people	2	27	62
old people	4	28	60
uneducated people	27	43	24
residents of Budapest	3	28	52
rural inhabitants	5	27	57

Summarizing the responses, we see that almost one-quarter of respondents (23%) consider merely a few (0–3) groups to be anti-Semitic, whereas almost one-third (32%) identify 10–15 groups as anti-Semitic. Males, Budapest residents, members of the 35–54 age group, and the well-off are particularly likely to suspect anti-Semitism among the various groups. It seems that social status and the strength of Jewish identity together determine the apperception of anti-Semitic groups: in groups detached from Jewish traditions and who have a weak sense of Jewish identity, those of a higher social status identify a greater than average number of anti-Semitic groups and those of a lower status identify a lower than average number of anti-Semitic groups. This difference may also indicate that anti-Semitism is a stronger identity-forming factor in assimilated groups of a higher social status than among assimilated Jews of a lower social status. On the other hand, among Jews who maintain Jewish traditions in some manner or another, those of a lower social status perceive a greater than average number of anti-Semitic groupings within society.

A majority of respondents make no link between anti-Semitism and age or place of residence. Nor do they link anti-Semitism to poverty, religious beliefs, or Communist convictions. The majority tends to search for the social core of anti-Semitism on the right wing of current Hungarian politics, among the descendants of groups influential in interwar society, and in poorly educated sections of modern society. Respondents who preserve Jewish traditions and possess relatively low social status evaluate the categories relating to this issue in a remarkably undifferentiated manner. On the other hand, those with left-wing social and political attitudes, as well as former Communist Party members, identify social groups connected with the prewar regime as the main bastion of anti-Semitism, while middle-aged Budapest residents (35–54 age group) with a higher education perceive greater than average anti-Semitism among the current representatives of the right wing, that is, among conservative politicians and the conservative press. Older members of this group are particularly wary of the traditional spectre of fascism: according to them, MIÉP supporters and "people with no edu-cation" constitute the core of anti-Semitism.

Based on responses to the two previous series of questions, we may isolate a group whose members regard at least six of the listed state-ments and at least ten of the listed groups as anti-Semitic—that is to say, in whose eyes anti-Semitism is rife throughout non-Jewish Hungarian society. This group, which constitutes 10 percent of the total sample and whose members typically live in Budapest, contains a lower than aver-age number of young people and a higher than average number of people aged fifty-five to sixty-nine. The poorly educated are under-represented in this group, while college graduates are over-represented. Former membership in the HSWP is a characteristic feature of members of this group. As we have already noted, the core of this group, which is highly sensitive to anti-Semitism, is comprised of individuals who reached adulthood during the first decade and a half after the Second World War and who probably took advantage of the opportunities for social mobility available during that period, but failed to attain a high social status. This group's members, whilst becoming very much secularized during their rise in society, are still not detached from Jewish traditions by more than one generation. An indication of the acute identity problems faced by members of this group is their high level of support for assimilation: below average numbers of people in this group are in favor of avoiding the complete assimilation of the Jews. On the other hand, however, the number of people in the group who agree that Jews have been incapable of integrating fully into society ever since their wartime persecution is greater than average. This difference means that although many in the group would like to get rid of their Jewishness—which they perceive as a stigma—they nevertheless consider such a move impossible. Perceptions of anti-Semitism obviously play a great role in the construction of this stigmatized identity.

Estimates of the Intensity of Anti-Jewish Sentiment

Concerning their judgment of anti-Jewish sentiment, the respondents divide into three groups of equal size: one-third consider anti-Semitism in Hungary today a minor problem, just over one-third (37%) regard it as a widespread phenomenon, and about one-third consider it a definite problem. Five percent of respondents believed that anti-Semitism is "very widespread" in the country. The proportion of people who think anti-Semitism a minor problem is slightly higher than average among young people.

Table 3

Perceptions of the Extent of Anti-Semitism in the Country
According to the Age of Respondents (Percentage)

Age groups	under 34	35-54	55-69	over 70	Total
A minor problem	39	33	32	27	32
Quite a problem	28	31	29	35	31
A widespread problem	33	36	39	38	37
Total	100	100	100	100	100

We asked respondents to indicate on a scale of one to five their perceptions of anti-Semitism (5 = a very major problem, 1 = a negligible problem). The sample average on the scale was 3.06. Compare this figure with the results of a survey conducted with a sample of the full adult Hungarian population in June 2002, according to which the average of the respondents' answers to the same question on a scale of one to four was 2.00, while the average of the respondents' answers who were Budapest residents with a high school education (who most closely resemble the social and demographic composition of the Jewish population) was 2.18—that is, considerably lower than the value measured among the Jewish sample.[9]

In the course of the survey, we also asked respondents to estimate the size of groups harboring anti-Jewish sentiments. Based on responses to this question, we arrived at a set of data that may be evaluated somewhat differently.

Table 4
How Many People in Hungary
(as a Percentage of the Country's Total Population)
Are Currently Hostile Towards Jews? (Percentage)

In your opinion, what percentage of people are hostile towards Jews?	Share of responses (percentage)
0	11
1-10	27
11-20	16
21-30	18
31-50	17
51+	11
Total	*100*

If—somewhat arbitrarily, of course—we say that an estimate of 0–10 percent corresponds to a non-existent or "negligible" level of anti-Semitism, then we may say that according to 38 percent of respondents hostility towards Jews is absent or hardly present in Hungarian society today. The group that estimates that 11–30 percent of people are hostile towards Jews corresponds roughly with those who perceive anti-

Semitism to be "quite a problem." On the other hand, 28 percent of respondents think that, currently, at least one in three people in Hungary view Jews with hostility.[10]

According to almost two-thirds of respondents (63%), anti-Semitism has increased in Hungary in recent years.

Table 5
Has Anti-Jewish Sentiment Increased or Decreased in Recent Years?
(Percentage)

Anti-Jewish sentiment has...	Under 34	35-54	55-69	Over 70	Total
Decreased	10	5	4	6	6
Remained the same	32	28	30	33	31
Increased	58	67	66	61	63
Total	*100*	*100*	*100*	*100*	*100*

There are great differences among respondents in their judgment of recent changes in the level of anti-Jewish sentiment: the share of respondents who think that anti-Semitism has increased in Hungary in recent years is more than ten times as large as the proportion of those who think that it has decreased. In each of the age groups, the share of those who think that anti-Semitism has strengthened is larger than the share who think that it has weakened. The difference is the greatest in the 55–69 age group (in this age group, the former group is almost seventeen times larger than the latter). On a scale of five (5 = anti-Semitism has very much increased, 4 = has somewhat increased, 3 = has stayed the same, 2 = has somewhat decreased, 1 = has very much decreased) the average response was 3.39. Once again this result may be compared with the results for samples of the full adult population and of educated Budapest residents: the average on a scale of five for the full adult population was 3.11 and for educated Budapest residents 3.29. That is, Hungarian public opinion has also perceived an increase in hostility towards Jews in recent years—even if the perceived increase is less than that perceived by those directly affected by such hostility.[11]

If we examine opinions relating to the strength and dynamism of anti-Semitism together, we find a correlation between evaluations of the strength and dynamics of hostility towards Jews. The stronger a person perceives anti-Semitism to be, the more he or she will be inclined to regard it as dynamic—more than three-quarters of those who perceive anti-Semitism to be widespread consider levels of anti-Semitism to have increased in recent years, yet this view is shared by only 40 percent of those who perceive anti-Semitism to be merely a minor problem. (By way of comparison, just one-fifth of those who consider anti-Semitism to be widespread see no change in the intensity of anti-Semitism in the recent past.) Nevertheless, the fact that most members of the group perceiving low levels of anti-Semitism still consider anti-Semitism to have increased also demonstrates that this is the dominant perception among the Jewish population.

Respondents based their opinions concerning the intensity and extent of anti-Semitism primarily on information acquired through mass communication, signs in the streets (graffiti), and the comments of strangers on the streets. Between two-thirds and three-quarters of the interviewees stated that they had encountered manifestations of anti-Semitism during the last decade. Twenty to twenty-five percent of respondents stated that they had witnessed displays of anti-Semitism in their own house, in their neighborhood, or at their place of work. Sixteen percent stated that they had perceived anti-Semitism at state institutions or among government authorities. Nevertheless, the majority of perceived anti-Semitic phenomena had not been directed at the respondents themselves: when we asked respondents whether they personally had "experienced some kind of grievance or disadvantage that was linked to their being Jewish," 82 percent said that they had not. A majority of those reporting personal encounters with anti-Semitism identified the public expression of anti-Semitic remarks as the source of their personal grievances.

Expectations with regard to the future are somewhat brighter than evaluations of the past. Half of respondents think that the degree of anti-Jewish sentiment is unlikely to change in the coming decade. Meanwhile the other half believe that there will be a change: although the number of people who think that anti-Semitism will increase is twice as high as the number of people who expect a decrease, this ratio is still just half of the proportion of people who perceive that anti-Semitism has grown in the recent past (33% as against 63%). Age has a limited influence on respondents' expectations for the future. At best, we may merely state that the ratio of those who think that anti-Semitism will increase is somewhat lower among members of the oldest group.

Table 6
Will Anti-Semitism Increase or Decrease in the Next Ten Years?
Breakdown by Age of Respondents (Percentage)

Anti-Semitism will...	Under 34	35-54	55-69	Over 70	Total
Decrease	18	14	16	15	16
Stay the same	47	51	51	58	51
Increase	35	35	33	27	33
Total	100	100	100	100	100

A majority of respondents consider it unlikely that anti-Semitic discrimination will exist in the future. Just 4 percent think that there is "a serious likelihood of Jews being persecuted" in Hungary in the next ten years. One-third of respondents consider this possibility out of the question, while more than 60 percent think that there might be some anti-Semitic discrimination, but that such measures are rather improbable. The age of respondents did not influence expectations.

Table 7
Breakdown of the Various Age Groups According to
Whether or Not They Fear that Jews Will Be Persecuted
During the Next Ten Years in Hungary (Percentage)

	Under 34	35-54	55-69	Over 70	Total
No	32	29	32	32	31
Possibly	65	66	65	65	65
Yes	3	5	3	3	4
Total	100	100	100	100	100

As the answers to the four questions (evaluation of the intensity of anti-Semitism, forecasts for previous and future trends, and evaluation of the likelihood of discrimination) indicate, Jews in Hungary have divided opinions in their judgment of the extent of anti-Semitism and the threat it poses. If we combine the answers to the questions, we see that 28 percent of respondents providing valid responses consider anti-Semitism to be insignificant in the country and do not expect it to strengthen in the near future, 59 percent of respondents perceive some anti-Semitism and are somewhat afraid that it might increase, while 12 percent of the sample consider anti-Semitism to be widespread in the country and to pose a real threat.

Next, we examined the factors that led respondents to achieve high scores on the indicator formed on the basis of respondents' answers to the four questions. We may call this indicator "the fear of anti-Semitism indicator."[12] The analysis produced the interesting result that social and demographic variables (with the exception of gender) had no great influence on opinions: age, level of education, family income, and household equipment did not significantly influence the development of opinions. On the other hand, women are far more likely than men to fear anti-Semitism, and such fears are, on average, stronger among Budapest residents than among residents of other towns and villages. The groups that have great fears of anti-Semitism are found among the lower levels of the Jewish social hierarchy (typically minor bureaucrats and "other white-collar" workers); they adhere strongly to Jewish traditions and are somewhat more religious than average.

Certain attitudes of respondents far better explain the fear of anti-Semitism than do the above social and demographic variables. The data show that respondents who on the one hand have a strong Jewish identity and on the other hand felt more at home under the pre-1990 system have greater fears of anti-Semitism than do others. The feeling of "being at home" under the old system does not amount to a political opinion or position: former Communist Party members are no more afraid of anti-Semitism than are people who were never party members. The fear of anti-Semitism primarily characterizes those people who consider the old system more transparent, simple, and caring, and who fear the effects of a market economy, crime, and violence. This group comprises people for whom the change of political system has brought the loss of routine rules and norms of behavior, as well as the creation of new and challenging life situations.[13] Among such groups, the fear of an uncontrolled eruption of anti-Semitism clearly gives rise to a law-and-order mentality and provides a motive for supporting stricter policies in this area. Indicatively, the group with the greatest fears of anti-Semitism considers anti-Semitism to have been far stronger during the 1956 Revolution than do other Jewish groups, and at the same time this group's appraisal of the Kádár era is the most favorable and its evaluation of the decade after the

change of political system the least favorable—in both cases its evaluation is significantly different from that of the other groups of the
sample.[14]

Thus, we measured perceptions of anti-Semitism using two different but interrelated indicators. We designed the indicators to demonstrate
the estimated strength of anti-Semitism and the degree of fear of anti-
Semitism. Summarizing our findings, we may state that two groups of
Jews perceive anti-Semitism and fears of anti-Semitism as greater than
average. The two groups share many social and demographic characteristics: their members are primarily Budapest residents; they are less
educated than the sample average (they are typically people with college
or high school qualifications); and they are situated rather low on the
employment hierarchy. The difference between the two groups pertains
to their relationship towards Jewish tradition. One of the groups forms
part of a relatively closed cluster of the Jewish population that maintains
tradition and fosters religious belief. Among the members of the other
group, there are greater than average numbers of people who broke away
from Jewish traditions during the first decade after the Second World
War, following changes in social status and the associated process of
secularization.

Policies for Tackling Anti-Semitism

During the past decade, public debate has on several occasions
examined the policies that should be employed under the new democratic system in the struggle against political and ideological extremism.
Supporters of permissive liberal solutions have been against any legal
restriction or sanctioning of the public expression of extremist views—
including anti-Semitism and denial of the Holocaust—unless such views
include an incitement to violence. The opposing side—with reference to
the example of the legal provisions in force in most European countries—has considered certain restrictions on the freedom of speech to be
admissible in extremist cases. The findings of our survey, which have
been analyzed elsewhere, demonstrate that the great majority of Hungarian Jews have liberal social and economic attitudes and express
opinions reflecting such liberal convictions.[15] In the following, I shall
examine whether or not respondents support the liberal position in the
debate on the freedom of expression of extremist opinions.

According to our findings, with regard to this particular issue, a majority of respondents reject liberal views. Even though, as already noted, only a small proportion of respondents fear anti-Semitic discrimination in the next ten years, a great majority of them (85%) nevertheless believe that people should not be allowed to disseminate anti-Jewish views. This proportion hardly differs from the figure for the full adult population, even though with regard to other issues—for example, abortion, homosexuality, and so forth—Jews express opinions more liberal than those of non-Jews.[16]

With respect to this issue, a notable difference exists between younger and older age groups—in the case of people over 55 and particularly those over 70 (see Table 8). The number of people in the oldest age group who consider the dissemination of anti-Semitic views to be unacceptable is 10 percent higher than in the youngest age group. And while just 8 percent of the older group would tolerate the dissemination of anti-Semitic views, one-fifth of the younger group consider the public expression of anti-Semitic views to be admissible (or admissible subject to certain restrictions).

Table 8
Should People Who Regularly Make Anti-Jewish Statements
Be Allowed to Disseminate Their Views Freely? (Percentage)

	Under 34	35-54	55-69	Over 70	Total
They should not be allowed.	81	80	88	92	85
They should be allowed.	17	18	10	8	13
They should be allowed, subject to certain restrictions and regulations.	2	2	2	0	2
Total	100	100	100	100	100

Opinions are somewhat more divided with respect to a question that has split Hungarian public opinion in recent years: should the publication and sale of *Mein Kampf* be permitted in the country? While more than two-thirds (70%) of respondents think that the distribution of *Mein Kampf* should be banned, 17 percent of them were against any restrictions and 9 percent thought that the sale of the book should be permitted subject to certain regulations.

Respondents voiced liberal opinions most often with regard to the third delicate issue, the criminal prosecution of people who deny the Holocaust. While a majority of respondents fully agreed (47%) or essentially agreed (12%) that "persons who cast doubt on the Holocaust should be brought to justice," 11 percent only partly agreed and 26 percent disagreed with the legal sanctioning of the denial of the Holocaust. Thus, in all three subject-areas, the majority of Jews are clearly inclined to accept restrictions on the public expression of anti-Semitic views. University or college-educated men aged less than forty-five who reside in Budapest and enjoy a high social status most often expressed the permissive liberal position.

Summary

Our survey does not, of course, serve as a basis for drawing conclusions on the strength of anti-Semitism in present-day Hungarian society. It does, however, provide an impression of how Hungarian Jews perceive anti-Semitism in their society. Their judgments may be correct, but perhaps respondents under/overestimate the intensity and dynamics of anti-Jewish sentiment. Based on our survey, it is impossible to say whether the responses distort the real situation, and if so, in which direction.

Considerable differences of opinion exist between Jews and non-Jews concerning the definition of particular statements and views as anti-Semitic. Such differences are the greatest between the Jewish population and the educated Budapest residents group, whose members are of similar social status. This difference indicates a considerable tension, because this social milieu is the one in which most Hungarian Jews live and communicate daily.

About one-third of Hungarian Jews think that anti-Semitism is insignificant in the country. Nevertheless, one-third of them consider anti-Semitism widespread. Indeed 5–10 percent of Jews feel that they live in a particularly hostile environment. As we have noted, non-Jews have a quite different opinion on this matter: they consider the intensity of anti-Semitism to be far less. This discrepancy may stem from the fact that certain views regarded by Jews as anti-Semitic are not considered so by non-Jews. But it is also possible that non-Jews pay little attention to statements that Jews regard as anti-Semitic. Such statements, however, greatly influence Jews as they attempt to appraise the situation: many reports of encounters with anti-Semitism refer to phenomena observed in the symbolic and political sphere—in the media, at public meetings of extremist political organizations, or in street graffiti. Only a minority of respondents had perceived anti-Semitism in everyday life, and almost none reported personal experiences of discrimination or of anti-Semitism coupled with violence.

The great majority of Jews expect the State to offer protection against manifestations of anti-Semitism, even where these amount to no more than expressions of hatred. A majority of non-Jews also condone action by the State against anti-Semitism. The question is, however, whether the two groups have in mind the same statements of abuse when giving their approval to restrictions on free speech.

The images of the external social world of group members greatly influence the social behavior of the various societal groups and their interactions with adjacent groups. And this is so regardless of whether such images are distorted or accurate. Our research findings indicate that great differences exist between Jewish and non-Jewish groups in Hungarian society in respect to their judgments of issues connected with anti-Semitism. This difference doubtless contributes to the creation of group boundaries, as well as the development of mutual expectations that serve to determine interactions between members of the two groups.

Notes

1. The costs of the project were paid by the American Jewish Committee, the American Jewish Joint Distribution Committee, the Conference on Material Claims Against Germany (the Claims Conference), the Jewish Agency, the Magyar Zsidó Hitközségek Szövetsége (Association of Hungarian Jewish Communities), the Magyar Zsidó Örökség Közalapítvány (Hungarian Jewish Heritage Foundation), and the Ronald S. Lauder Foundation. The data analysis was supported by the Vidal Sasson International Center for the Study of Antisemitism at the Hebrew University of Jerusalem.

2. For the main results of the survey, see András Kovács, ed., *Jews and Jewry in Contemporary Hungary: Results of a Sociological Survey* (London: JPR, 2004).

3. István Bibó, *Válogatott tanulmányok* (Selected studies), vol. 2. 1945–49 (Budapest: Magvető, 1986), 685–704.

4. For the Walser debate, see, for example, *Die Zeit* (June 6, 2002). For the article on Mihail Sebastian's *Journal* that provoked the Romanian debate, see Gabriel Liiceanu, "Sebastian, mon frere" *22* (April 29–May 5, 1997). For subsequent reactions, see George

Voicu, "L'honneur national roumain en question," in *Les Temps Modernes* 606 (November/ December 1999), 143–52.

5. We conducted this survey in 1995 with a sample of 1500 people. For the research findings, see *Anti-Semitic Prejudices in Contemporary Hungary: Analysis of Current Trends in Anti-Semitism, Acta* 16 (Jerusalem: The Vidal Sassoon International Center for the Study of Anti-Semitism, The Hebrew University, 1999).

6. We compared the responses of the Jewish sample with the responses of the sample of the full Hungarian population and the responses of the sample of Budapest residents with high school education—this group being the closest to the Jewish population in terms of social status.

7. See Sándor Csoóri, "Nappali Hold I–IV" (Daytime moon I–IV), *Hitel*, vol. III no. 17, 2. and 4-6.l. (August 22, 1990); vol. III, no. 18, 4-7.l (September 5, 1990; vol. III, no. 19, 4-6.l. (September 10, 1990); and vol. III, no. 20, 4-7.l. (October 3, 1990). For an analysis of the debate, see Monika Kovács, "Kategorizáció és diszkrimináció: Az antiszemitizmus, mint csoportnyelv" (Categorization and discrimination: Anti-Semitism as group language) *Világosság* (May 1993): 52–9.

8. MIÉP (*Magyar Igazság és Élet Pártja;* Hungarian Truth and Life Party) was the extreme right party of the Hungarian parliament between the years 1998–2002. The party received around 250,000 votes in the elections in 2002, an amount that did not exceed the 5% threshold for re-entering the parliament.

9. The size of the national sample was 1000 people, and the survey was performed by TÁRKI. Due to the two types of scale, any comparison of the averages should be treated with caution. The following basic divisions arose on a scale of four: anti-Semitism in the country is very widespread—4%, widespread—16%, a minor problem—44%, a very minor problem—24%, don't know—12%. Compared with the results for the Jewish sample, many more respondents in the full sample thought that anti-Semitism in Hungary is a "very minor problem" (24% as against 2%), while the share of those who thought that anti-Semitism is "very widespread" was about the same (4% as against 5%). It is worthwhile comparing the results of the research on the national sample with the results of the research carried out in 1995—also on a national and representative sample. At that time 2% of participants in the survey stated that anti-Semitism is "very widespread" and 21% that it is "widespread." Meanwhile 49% thought that it was "a minor problem" and 17% that it was a "a very minor problem." Thus, the ratio of those who have chosen an extreme position on the scale has risen.

10. According to sociological surveys carried out during the past decade, about 25% of the Hungarian adult population have anti-Semitic prejudices, and 8–10% are extreme anti-Semites. Therefore, 18% of respondents correctly estimated the proportion of people hostile towards Jews.

11. In the full Hungarian population, 23% of respondents believed that anti-Semitism had increased, while 49% thought that it had stayed the same, and 15% that it had declined. In the 1995 research, 33% of respondents thought that anti-Semitism had increased, 32% that it had stayed the same, and 22% that it had declined. Thus, during the past decade, 23–33% of the adult population essentially perceived a constant increase in the intensity of anti-Semitism.

12. We established the indicator in the form of a principal component (PC). The four statements constituted one PC, whose eigenvalue was 2.037, explained variance 50.9%, and the loading of the various components: [1] .728; [2] .761; [3] .712; [4] .649.

13. In order to explain the intensity of fear of anti-Semitism we used regression analysis. We defined as the dependent variable the principal component described in note 7. We included as an independent variable in the analysis basic social and demographic variables as well as several attitude variables. As a result of step-by-step analysis, seven independent variables were left among the series of independent variables: strength of Jewish identity (beta = .171), the feeling of "being at home" under the old system (beta = .164), gender (beta = .124), doubts in the justice system (beta = .107), opposition to economic liberalism (beta = .075), place of residence, towards Budapest (beta = .057), and support for conservative norms (beta = .054). These variables explain 11% of the variance of the dependent variable ($R^2 = 11\%$).

14. We also used a scale of five for the evaluation of the historical-political periods. The respondents had to evaluate on the scale which of the listed historical periods had been "positive or negative for Jews living in Hungary" (5 = clearly positive, 1 = clearly negative). Amongst those groups in the Jewish sample who greatly fear anti-Semitism, the average evaluation of the Kádár era was 3.40, whilst among other groups it was 3.17. The average evaluation of the decade after the change of political system was 2.37 in the first group and 3.06 in the second.

15. See Kovács, ed., *Jews and Jewry in Contemporary Hungary*, 39–41.

16. The 1995 survey of a national sample found that 83% of the adult population were against the free dissemination of views by people who regularly make anti-Semitic statements, and that just 9% support their being allowed to do so.

Why Was There No *Historikerstreit* in Hungary after 1989–1990?

Attila Pók

To some the question in the title of this paper might seem odd in relation to a country where so many public debates have addressed historical issues during the last fifteen years. This was especially the case during the immediate post-Communist years that will be the focus here, specifically the prime ministership of historian József Antall (1990–1993). A "Historikerstreit" is, however, very different from a series of debates on historical issues. As it emerged in 1986 in its powerful form in the Federal Republic of Germany, it consisted of a political-historical discourse on two most crucial questions about mid-century German history: the uniqueness of National Socialist persecution and destruction of the Jews in Europe, and the responsibility of German society as a whole for this tragedy.[1]

The Holocaust and Trianon

The question I would like to concentrate on is why Hungarian "political-historical" discourses during these years did not focus on the specifically Hungarian aspects of these issues: the connections between "traditional" anti-Semitism and the Holocaust on the one hand, and Hungarian society's responsibility for the Holocaust on the other. How can one explain the phenomenon that, in the frequently quite fervent historical-political public discourses, relatively little attention was paid to a key problem of twentieth-century Hungarian history: is the Holocaust in Hungary the ultimate stage in the long-term evolution of Hungarian anti-Semitism, rooted in early-modern and modern Hungarian economic, social, and cultural history, or does the behavior of Hungarian society during the Holocaust have more recent antecedents and can be traced from what we might call the "Trianon-syndrome," that is, the social trauma caused by the tremendous territorial losses following World War I? In other words, the purpose of this paper is to situate these problems among the historical issues that arose during the debates inside and outside the parliament during the years of the first post-1989–90 government. I would like to pose the following question: why in such a past-oriented society, where historical analogies are frequently more instrumental in defining political platforms and programs than economic and social political issues, the attempts to formulate a sincere and courageous confrontation with this problem did not develop into a nation-wide debate? Why, in short, was the responsibility of Hungarian society and its political elite for the destruction of two thirds of Hungarian Jewry not part of the period's self-examination?

Levels of "Undertaking History"

An examination of the historical issues discussed by politicians, as well as the general public discourses, offer us at least three levels of "undertaking history." In addition to the scholarly research and publication with their accepted methods of scrutiny, history as a collective memory has an important cohesive force, which is frequently used and abused by politicians to achieve political mobilization and legitimization. Both are different from history education on the primary and secondary levels where the presentation of historical complexity is limited by the capabilities of students.[2]

In this paper my focus is on the second level as reflected in acts of parliament, statements of politicians, and historically motivated rituals and exchanges in the media.

History and Historians in the Transition Process

In the political program of the "democratic opposition" published in June 1987, the last section was dedicated to "1956 in contemporary Hungarian politics." It argued that a reevaluation of 1956 was a basic precondition of a new "social contract" as a way out of the crisis. Simultaneously, the Communist Party leadership also realized the significance of the reevaluation of the recent past. The Party Conference of May 1989 appointed a small team of experts to evaluate the last four decades of Hungarian history. The relevant chapter of the team's report blamed the Party leadership (and not internal and external hostile forces) for creating a crisis situation in October 1956 and used the term "popular uprising" (instead of the common official usage, "counterrevolution") to describe the events from October 23 to November 4. This terminology was cited in a broadcast interview with a member of the Politburo, Imre

Pozsgay, on January 28, 1989, and had an enormous political impact. The February 11–12 Central Committee session that adopted this document also decided to allow the introduction of a multi-party system in the country. The reevaluation of 1956 thus served as a "historical basis" of the ensuing talks between various groups of the opposition and the Party.[3]

1956 in the New Parliament

The next major steps with significant historical implications along the road of the political transition included the reburial of the leader of the 1956 revolution, Imre Nagy, on June 16, 1989, and the proclamation of the republic on October 23. The statement of the interim head of state, Mátyás Szűrös, on this latter festive occasion referred to the liberal national revolution of 1848, the proclamation of the republic in November 1918, the years of pluralistic democracy between 1945 and 1948, and the 1956 revolution as the antecedents of the new republic. Following the successful "round-table" negotiations, in the first freely elected parliament in forty years. 386 members of parliament (MPs) represented six parties with the center-right wing Hungarian Democratic Forum (*Magyar Demokrata Fórum* - MDF) as the strongest force. Twenty-seven of them were historians, including the prime minister, the speaker of the house, two ministers, and several secretaries of state. The average age of the MPs of the parties in the governing coalition (MDF, with the Smallholders and the Christian Democrats) was well beyond fifty, so most of them experienced 1956 as adults.

In the opposition, the majority of the liberals (representatives of the Alliance of Free Democrats (*Szabad Demokraták Szövetsége* - SZDSZ)), were generally younger (born in the late 1940s and early 1950s), most members of the Alliance of Young Democrats (*Fiatal Demokraták Szövetsége* – FIDESZ) were born in the first half of the 1960s, and the Socialists included all generations who unreservedly cherished the memory of the 1956 revolution. Thus at its opening ceremony, the new parliament, in the presence of the head of the Habsburg family, a descendant of the last king of Hungary, and Béla Varga, the speaker of the last democratic parliament after World War II, enacted the memory of the 1956 revolution into law.

Professor György Szabad, an expert in nineteenth-century Hungarian history and the speaker of the new parliament, defined 1956 as the new democracy's most important connection to the Hungarian past. The parliament also successfully requested that the Soviet leadership condemn the 1956 intervention: this indeed happened a few days before the dissolution of the Soviet Union when Prime Minister Antall visited Moscow in early December 1991.

Debates on the Coat of Arms and the National Holidays

Although the acceptance of the 1956 revolution as the immediate historical antecedent of the new republic was unanimous, diverging views surfaced when it came to two other historical issues on the new parliament's agenda: the choice of a new coat of arms and new national holidays. Although the overwhelming majority of MPs voted for the old coat of arms with the royal crown, used before the last proclamation of the republic in 1946, a group of liberals argued in favor of the coat of arms without a crown as initiated by the leader of the 1848 revolution, Lajos Kossuth, in 1849. Their point was that the crown stood for continuity with the pre-1945 regime and symbolized the territorial integrity of pre-World War I Hungary that might offend the sensitivities of the neighboring countries.

Society in general seemed to be more divided about this issue than the MPs. According to a public opinion poll of November 1989,[4] 49 percent preferred the "crown" and 34 percent the "Kossuth version." Among young citizens, more educated people, residents of Budapest, and Protestants and atheists, the "Kossuth version" was more popular; while older people, Catholics, less-educated people, and residents outside Budapest preferred the "crown." Comparable differences in interpreting Hungary's historical heritage also surfaced in the parliamentary debates on the choice of the primary national holiday. The fact that August 20, the day dedicated to the founder of the first Hungarian Kingdom, Szent István (Saint Stephen), was selected could be and was interpreted by parliamentary and non-parliamentary critics of the government as a return to pre-1945 conservative traditions. As early as September 1990, the largest oppositional party, the liberal SZDSZ, published an evaluation of the first 100 days of the government that, among other things, argued,

> Fears rise about the undisguised nostalgia, which the parties of the governing coalition feel for the pre-1945 Hungary. The spirit of the coalition

recalls the Hungary between the two World Wars. The governing parties decreasingly admit the continuity between 1956 and 1945–47, and increasingly refer to our historical deadlock of Horthyte[5] Hungary. This was alarming to everyone who wished that the transformation of the form of government not bring back the vanished world of the former upper classes, but show the way towards a democratic Europe at the turn of the millennium.[6]

Horthy and Hungary's Role in World War II

Hungary's role in the Second World War entered the agenda of fierce political debates when on July 30, 1990, a former high-ranking officer of the Horthy army and a member of the MDF faction appeared in parliament wearing the old uniform and declared that Hungary's "crusade" against the Soviet Union was legitimate because World War II was fought against the threat of Communism. Then, following a family request, on September 3, 1993, Miklós Horthy, Hungary's head of state between 1920 and 1944, was reburied in his home village, Kenderes. The event was officially a "private affair" in the presence of six members of the government and about 50,000 people. The reevaluation of Horthy and his regime became an important issue because, according to some politicians close to Christian-Democratic government circles, the Horthy regime was more legitimate than the Communist regime imposed on Hungary by the Soviet Union. The day before Horthy's reburial, liberal intellectuals set up a "counter-event" under the title "Final Good-Bye to the Horthy Regime."

Restitution and Retribution

These historical controversies were far from being academic and symbolic political exchanges, especially with regard to compensation for nationalized and otherwise confiscated (or stolen) properties; these were historically determined practical matters. In the first relevant 1991 laws,[7] compensation was restricted to property "lost" after June 8, 1949; this left most Jews and/or their descendants uncompensated. Additional 1992 laws,[8] however, broadened the basis for compensation back to 1939. It was in the course of public discourse related to these laws that the place of Jews in Hungarian society was seriously debated. Other than in this context, the subject did not frequently arise in the early 1990s.

The Antecedents of the 1989–1990 Transition Process

The "practicality" of these debates also surfaced in the evaluation of the decades of Communist rule. Many pseudo- or semi-scholarly books were published about Communist crimes with the single purpose of proving the brutality of the Communist elite without differentiating among periods of open terror (1949–1962), of relative consolidation (during the 1960s and 1970s), and of the beginning of the decline (starting in the mid-1980s). The parliamentary "reflection" of these publications was the "Justitia" plan dealing with the possibilities of "making justice" for the crimes committed during the Communist era. Was there any way to ensure that, after the fall of Communism, the "perpetrators" would not be better off than the "victims"? What about the statute of limitation? These questions in turn led to an expansion of the scope of the debates. Questions about the social basis of the Hungarian Communist Party arose: were 20 percent of the active population forced into the Party? Was the number of "true" Communists just around 30,000, and was this figure relevant for 1945, late 1956, or late 1989? Did the majority of the Hungarian population (at least between 1962 and the early 1980s) accept the aims and the methods of the Party leadership?

Another set of questions examined the cause of the decline and collapse of the Kádár regime and dealt with the "hierarchy" of four major factors:

- The fundamental transformation of the international political and economic environment;
- the structural deficiencies of the economic and political pillars of the socialist-Communist system;
- the activities of the two main groups of dissidents (national-populist and democratic opposition); and
- the divisions in the Party leadership as a result of the work of the reform Communists.

The respective debates were largely shaped by the political issues of the day. The Christian-Nationalist side presented the socialists as direct successors of the former Communist elite, whereas the liberal and socialist politicians frequently referred to their conservative rivals as representatives of the worst destructive conservative-nationalist traditions of the interwar and Second World War period.

I hope this short survey shows that the two issues (the relationship between "traditional" anti-Semitism and the Holocaust, and Hungarian society's responsibility for the latter) that, in my opinion, should have been in the center of the "mainstream" historical debates were marginalized. Furthermore, they seemed to have been "expropriated" by the radical right together with the evaluation of the post-World War I revolutions and the Trianon peace treaty.[9] Why did this happen?

In order to attempt an answer to this question, respective developments from May 1990 to May 1994 have to be organized into five major groups.

Official Symbolic Commemorations,
Paying Tribute to the Victims of the Holocaust

Continuing the policy of the Németh government, just a few weeks after the new government entered office (July 8, 1990), the president of the republic and the prime minister attended the unveiling of a monument dedicated to the victims of the Holocaust on the territory of the former Budapest ghetto; the minister of the interior spoke at the unveiling by the Danube of the monument dedicated to Jewish Hungarian martyrs (October 14); and the president of Israel was most cordially received in Budapest (June 1991). However, occasionally the intention to hold a dignified, festive commemoration yielded to political practicalities. For example, in József Antall's March 19, 1991, commemoration in the form of a "pre-agenda statement" in parliament, he said:

> [In 1944] Hungary had already waged war for years, serious tribulations, violations of law occurred, or rather laws contrary the concepts of human rights and humanism were effective. But nobody should forget that until March 19, 1944, Europe's largest Jewish community was still alive...tens of thousands of foreign refugees and homeless people lived in relative security...the political parties that are here today are heirs to the political ideas that opposed Hitler's Germany and believed in parliamentary democracy.[10]

The facts referred to here are, of course, true, but no word was spoken about those who carried the responsibility for the ensuing horror. Three years later at a similar commemoration, the speaker of the house tried to be more balanced when he said, "...the foreign occupation committed the worst crimes against the nation and unfortunately there were accomplices to these anti-human and antinational crimes."[11]

Nothing was said, however, about the responsibility of the Hungarian state apparatus that was active during the deportations.

Legal Measures

In 1991 and 1992, the Hungarian Parliament passed several laws on compensation and restitution regarding "unfairly" committed damages to Hungarian citizens between 1939 and 1949. After an extensive debate in 1992, a most promising law (May 12, Law XXXII) was passed in Parliament relating to compensation for individuals unlawfully deprived of their freedom and their lives for political reasons. This meant a straightforward recognition of the Hungarian state's responsibility. As significant as this law might have been (and the leaders of the Hungarian Jewish community recognized it as such), its great symbolic and practical value was substantially reduced by two factors.

First, it did not offer compensation to the Jewish inmates of forced labor camps, to the members of labor battalions, and to those who were murdered in the course of deportation.

Second, the originally suggested sum of one million HUF (Hungarian Forint) to be paid for the loss of one life was, after six years of debate, finally reduced to a ridiculous 30,000 HUF, the equivalent of about $100. The huge moral advantage of initiating this compensation process at a time "when the issue had not been put in the glare of the spotlight even in the advanced democracies,"[12] thus became insignificant.

Another legal matter showed a similar picture. The Paris Peace Treaty (Act XVIII of 1947, Article 27, Clause 2) obliged Hungary to return the assets of Hungarian Jews who perished without known heirs "to Hungarian organizations of those affected by the discriminative laws" within twelve months. The March 11, 1993, Hungarian Constitutional Court Resolution pointed out that this obligation had not been met and this unconstitutional situation was to be remedied by the Hungarian Parliament by the end of 1993. This did not happen.

The debates frequently brought, and continue to bring up, the comparison of Auschwitz and the Gulag and their respective victims. Instead of a sincere, collective acknowledgement of this terrible chapter of Hungarian history, the noble intention of taking the unavoidable legal measures for symbolic compensation thus led to confrontations and the opening of old wounds. This was not a favorable political and social environment for a "Historikerstreit."

Moral and Financial Support to Jewish Cultural and Social Institutions

Following the dynamic events in 1989 and early 1990 (among other things, reopening the Budapest office of the American Jewish Joint Distribution Committee on June 15, 1989; Edgar Bronfman, president of the World Jewish Congress, opening his organization's first office in a Communist country on July 10; the creation of the Hungarian-Israeli Friendship Association on December 19; and the launching of cultural periodicals), the revitalization of Jewish cultural and social life in Hungary continued at full speed. In September 1990, two new schools (the American Foundation School and Lauder Javne) were opened, a Jewish Community Center was built, the National Rabbinical Seminary started a teacher training section, and the state contributed to the reconstruction of numerous synagogues. An unfortunate statement by György Landeszmann,[13] the chief rabbi of Budapest, about the lack of values in the Hungarian national cultural heritage and the ensuing debates, however, revealed a great social sensitivity over definitions of Jewish contributions to Hungarian culture.

Latent Anti-Semitism

Fortunately we can rely on the results of excellent sociologists, such as András Kovács,[14] when we attempt to uncover the dominant attitudes toward the Jews in post-1989–90 Hungarian society. Keeping in mind the methodological difficulty caused by the fact that most people are unwilling to tell the truth about their prejudices and hatreds, on the basis of extended empirical investigations the number of anti-Semites in Hungarian society during the 1990s can be estimated at 25 to 33 percent. This attitude is, of course, far from a belief in the necessity of the destruction of Jews, but it indicates the support of views such as: Jews can not find their places in present day Hungarian society, the interests of non-Jews are different from those of Jews, Jews were responsible for Communist rule in Hungary, and the emigration of Jews should be encouraged. These notions are part of a larger trend of rising xenophobia and violence directed against foreigners.[15] These general tendencies certainly show huge regional, social and age stratification, but from our present perspective they can be defined as an additional obstacle to an open and sincere "Historikerstreit."

Openly Anti-Semitic Publications and Statements

Unlimited freedom of speech, the proliferation of poor quality publications (frequently by non-professional publishers) allowed for numerous openly anti-Semitic statements in the early 1990s. István Csurka, one of the most successful writers of the Kádár period, in his January 14, 1990, radio broadcast identified the representatives of the Communist dictatorship as Jews. The ensuing clamor was more a spectacular scandal than a serious debate over the social basis of Communism in Hungary, in the same way as Csurka's numerous other public statements stirred up passionate hatred. Csurka and the followers of his "national radicalism" raised important, critical issues (such as who supported Communism in Hungary; who controls economic, cultural, and political power in post-Communist Hungary; what will be the future of the national cultural heritage in the globalization of the world; and so on), but because they approached everything with disgusting anti-Semitic fury, they pushed the issues beyond the scope of honest, respectable, and serious debate.

Csurka's views fed what is sometimes described as the anti-Semitism of the mob.[16] These anti-Jewish stereotypes, deeply embedded in popular culture, were suppressed in socialist Hungary. The fact that they could be openly aired after the collapse of Communism does not necessarily mean that they had become more powerful. A prime example of another type of more sophisticated, intellectual anti-Semitism is the views of a populist poet, Sándor Csoóri, who, in a fall 1990 article, argued that Jewish attempts to assimilate pose a major threat to Hungarian national culture.[17] The ensuing debate reproduced more stereotypes of the confrontations between "populist nationalists" and "urbanist cosmopolitans" between the two world wars than it did the real social, cultural, and political problems of the day.

What did not happen was a continuation of a debate connected to György Száraz, a non-Jewish writer and journalist, who in 1975–76, a time when the pro-Arab official Hungarian position caused some second thoughts for numerous Jewish Hungarian Communist officials, published an essay and a book under the title "In the Footsteps of a Prejudice."[18] The lack of an open and sincere re-examination of the

Hungarian society's attitude towards the Holocaust, the shocking ignorance of numerous young people concerning the facts of this most tragic chapter of Hungarian history, together with the emerging strong collective identity among young Jewish intellectuals pushed Száraz's work into the foreground of public interest. Száraz pointed out how at the turn of the nineteenth and twentieth centuries Hungarian religious anti-Semitism was transformed into socially motivated anti-Semitism. He also described the emergence of legends about the conspiracy of cosmopolitan Jews against the territorial integrity of post-World War I Hungary. The impressive scholarly output from the second half of the 1970s addressing the cultural, social, and economic history of Hungarian Jews and Hungarian anti-Semitism was hardly reflected in the post 1989–90 political and everyday discourse.[19] Ancient stereotypes resurfaced as if no substantial research had ever been undertaken. One might also argue that because Hungary's literary, artistic, and scholarly output on the Holocaust was unrivaled in the Soviet Bloc, there seemed to be no need to discuss this issue because other historical-political questions were more essential for the new, open, democratic public opinion.[20]

I cannot share this view and argue that in spite of serious political and even financial efforts to address the past and present of the Hungarian Jewry the situation was unfavorable for a serious, sincere debate for other reasons.

Looking for a Counterpoint and Continuity

The attitude of the Christian upper-middle class in the process of being resurrected could have been negatively balanced by the former hypercritical dogmatic Marxist evaluation of the "reactionary" Horthy regime.

The task of the moderately conservative nationalist elite, who carry an exclusive responsibility for the nation, was the search for its historical roots. József Antall, Jr., the new prime minister, could proudly refer to his father's merits. As a high official of the Horthy regime, József Antall, Sr., saved many Jews and had been recognized as a "Righteous among the Nations" by Yad Vashem. The new establishment looked both for a counterpoint, a "cursed" "anti-period," and "blessed" continuities, and this political aim could hardly be implemented by presenting complexities and fine shades of motivations. This was, of course, not peculiar to the regime. If we look at Hungarian history—how leading politicians of the early Horthy regime related to the liberalism of Dualist Hungary, or how official Communist rhetoric evaluated the Horthy regime—we repeatedly see black and white simplifications. To make things even more complicated, a call for a balanced evaluation of the Horthy regime, arguing that it was not Fascist or semi-Fascist, but noting that from a conservative authoritarian platform it tried to curb the radical right, was part of the liberal criticism of dogmatic Marxist historiography. In a post-Communist political-ideological environment the same view could have a politically strong apologetic message.

Lack of Adaptive Mourning

Due to the clashes between the decades of official representation of "fraternal unity" with the peoples of the Soviet Bloc and the sorrowful semi-official and private collective memories of the Trianon trauma (in addition to the lack of collective mourning), Trianon with its revolutionary antecedents and aftermath was (and still is) an unhealed wound in the national body. The dimensions of national disaster were far beyond imagination. Who or what could bring such a fundamental change in the life of a nation, taking one thousand-year-old Hungary to the brink of complete destruction? That phenomenon must be of some extreme, hardly rationally conceivable force. Resurrection is rarely possible without self-examination and atonement, as some kind of guilt must be lurking in the air. If an individual or a small group is struck to a comparable extent, the first step towards recovery is the ritual of mourning. Mourning and its rituals, funerals expressing sadness but at the same time acceptance and acknowledgement of the tragic loss, are the necessary prerequisites for healthy life. This "adaptive mourning" frees the individual or the community from the obsession with the past and opens the possibility of contemplating a vision of the future. This adaptive mourning was not a feasible alternative for Hungarian society after World War I—no nation in the world would have acknowledged the acceptance of the loss of two thirds of its homeland and more than one third of its national community. Nonetheless, despite the lack of "adaptive mourning," the causes of the tragedy and the culprits had to be determined. To blame the victorious Entente powers or the new neighbors, exclusively external factors (as was the case with the Bulgarians), was not a realistic alternative because they were still in a position to impose further losses on the country. There remained one serious option: the national community could find some part of itself that it could cut off or remove and then project the guilt onto the amputated part.[21] The part of the Hungarian self that became that object was the "familiar foreigner," the Hungarian Jew. Hungarian Jewry was sufficiently familiar to be seen as part of the self, and yet sufficiently foreign for exclusion from the new conception of what it meant to be Hungarian. This amputation, unfortunately, turned out to be very concrete: not very long after the Red Terror of the Hungarian Soviet Republic (which also had Jewish victims) hundreds of Jews were killed by the White Terror. This was a completely new phenomenon in Hungary: politically motivated pogroms demanding a high death toll of Jews were not part of former Jewish-Gentile relations in Hungary.

Let me make the point more emphatically: it is not the frequently referred to numerus clausus law of 1920 (in which the remnants of Hungarian liberalism did not use the word Jew or Israelite when limiting the number of Jewish students in Hungarian higher education),[22] but the anti-Jewish brutality of the White Terror that introduced a qualitative turn in the history of anti-Semitism in Hungary, which can be defined as a major step on the road to the Holocaust. The Holocaust in Hungary is thus more closely connected to nationalism than to traditions of anti-Judaism and modern anti-Semitism. If we study the anti-Jewish arguments of the period of the Second World War, we see that they are rooted much more in the social, political, and economic realities of World War I and postwar Hungary than in the anti-Judaic intellectual heritage of the nation. In the aftermath of another differently traumatic transformation, similar mechanisms of scapegoating surfaced to infiltrate the political discourse. This was yet another factor contributing to the creation of an unfavorable environment for sober, sincere debate.

The Logic of Party Politics

The logic of party politics in the newly rediscovered pluralism was also conducive to divisions, to allocating responsibility rather than trying to face national tragedies without constantly looking for the current political message of any action. No doubt, Jews were quite visible in the leadership of the two main opposition parties, the Alliance of Free Democrats and the Young Democrats, and were also connected to the Socialists whereas the ruling coalition practically lacked a Jewish presence. The political confrontations between government and opposition (quite natural in every functioning democracy) were thus occasionally interpreted as a Jewish-Christian conflict. This was further complicated by the practical debates about the definitions of "Hungarian" in connection with the preparation of a new bill on the rights of national and ethnic minorities, which was passed in 1993.[23] Under certain conditions this law gave special privileges to the registered minority groups that were demanding them, but the leaders of the Jewish community refused the national or ethnic minority status and only a very small splinter group created the National Alliance of Jews in Hungary. The old debate on ethnic-national or religious definition of "Jewishness" did not reemerge. Hungarian society, however, did not recognize the great significance of this gesture showing the completion of the assimilation process.

Let me conclude by referring to a historical issue that was in the foreground of Hungarian political life on the eve of the sixtieth anniversary of the beginning of the Hungarian Holocaust. Following the recommendations of the Pál Teleki Memorial Commission, the Cultural Commission of the Budapest municipal government decided to erect a monument to Pál Teleki, an internationally widely acknowledged geographer, who was Hungary's prime minister in 1920–21 and 1939–41. A man of great contradictions, he made tremendous efforts to keep Hungary out of World War II, and opened up Hungary's borders for Polish refugees. But as a professed anti-Semite he also proudly carried responsibility for passing the first major piece of anti-Semitic legislation in Europe, the numerus clausus law of 1920. It was also during his tenure as prime minister that the Hungarian Parliament passed the second racially based anti-Jewish law in 1939. All political parties represented in the Hungarian capital's Cultural Commission agreed that the Teleki statue be unveiled on April 3, 2004, the anniversary of Teleki's tragic suicide in 1941. That happened to be very close to the day the mandatory use of the yellow star by Jews was introduced sixty years earlier. A strong civic protest movement initiated by a few intellectuals thus made the politicians stop the process and "temporarily suspend" the implementation of the decision to honor Teleki. Perhaps for the first time after 1989–90, the "frontlines" of a public discourse on a crucial historical issue were not defined by party affiliation, and a wide-ranging debate about the complexity of Teleki's personality and politics began.

Are we witnessing the beginning of the Hungarian "Historiker-streit"?

Notes

1. For a summary of the German case, see *"Historikerstreit": Die Dokumentation der Kontroverse um die Einzigartigkeit der nationalsozisalistischen Judenvernichtung* (Munich-Zürich: Piper-Verlag, 1987), especially the contributions by Christian Meier and Jürgen Kocka.

2. On this subject, see my article, "Undertaking History—Shaping the New Europe," in *Approaches to European Historical Consciousness: Reflections and Provocations*, ed. Sharon Macdonald (Hamburg: Körber Stiftung, 2000), 163–67.

3. For the most recent summary of this process, see Ignác Romsics, *Volt egyszer egy rendszerváltozás* (Once upon a time there was a change of systems) (Budapest: Rubicon, 2003).

4. Quoted by Heino Nyyssönen, "Historical Debates in the First Free Elected Parliament in Hungary 1990–1994" (Manuscript, 1997), 7.

5. The reference is to Miklós Horthy, head of state between 1920 and 1944.

6. Nyyssönen, 14.

7. Hungarian Parliamentary Law 1991:XXV (A tulajdonviszonyok rendezése érdekében, az állam által az állampolgárok tulajdonában igazságtalanul okozott károk részleges kárpótlásáról [On the partial recompensation of the damage unjustly caused by the state to the properties of the citizens, aiming at the regulation of property relations]); Hungarian Parliamentary Law 1991: XXXII (A volt egyházi ingatlanok tulajdoni helyzetének rendezéserol [On the regulation of the proprietory rights of real estate formerly owned by the churches]).

8. Hungarian Parliamentary Law 1992:XXIV (A tulajdonviszonyok rendezése érdekében, az állam által az állampolgárok tulajdonában az 1939.május 1.–étol 1949. június 8.–ig terjedo idoben alkotott jogszabályok alkalmazásával okozott károk részleges kárpótlásáról [On the partial recompensation of the damage caused to the properties of the citizens as a result of the application of legal acts passed beween May 1, 1939, and June 8, 1949, aiming at the regulation of property relations]); Hungarian Parliamentary Law 1992:XXXII (Az életüktol és szabadságuktól politikai okokból jogtalanul megfosztottak kápótlásáról [On the compensation to people who were divested of their lives and liberty for political reasons]).

9. For the emergence of the radical right in Hungary, see Ferenc Fehér and Ágnes Heller, *Magyar-Szomália felé?* (Heading towards Hungarian-Somalia?), *Népszabadság* (January 9, 1993); also published in István Feitl, ed., *Jobboldali radikalizmusok tegnap és ma* (Right-wing radicalism yesterday and today) (Budapest: Napvilág, 1998), 221–26. For a comprehensive survey, see László Bartus, *Jobb magyarok: A szélsőjobb útja a hatalomhoz* (Better Hungarians: The extreme right on the road to power) (Budapest: L. Bartus, 2001).

10. *Országgyűlési Értesítő 1990–1994* (Parliamentary reporter), 6759.

11. Idem., 34087.

12. See the article by Péter Feldmayer in *Magyar Hírlap* (January 5, 1992).

13. *Heti Magyarország* (February 26, 1993).

14. András Kovács, *A latens antiszemitizmus mérése* (Checking latent anti-Semitism), www.mtapti.hu/mszt/1994/kovacs.htm

15. Charles Hoffmann, *Gray Dawn: The Jews of Eastern Europe in the Post-Communist Era* (New York: HarperCollins Publishers, 1992), 104–109; and György Csepeli and Antal Örkény, eds., *Gyűlölet és politika* (Hatred and politics) (Budapest: Minoritas, 2002).

16. For an analysis of Csurka's views, see Zsófia Mihancsik, "A Vasárnapi Újság antiszemitizmusa és populizmusa" (Anti-Semitism and populism of the radio program Sunday News), in Cepeli and Örkény, 364–99.

17. "Nappali hold" (Daylight moon), *Hitel* 18 (1990).

18. György Száraz, "Egy előítélet nyomában," *Valóság* 8 (1975). An enlarged version was published as a book under the same title (Budapest: Magvető, 1976).

19. For example, works by György Borsányi, Mária Ember, Tibor Erényi, Ferenc Glatz, Péter Hanák, Gyula Juhász, Elek Karsai, Miklós Lackó, György Ránki, Szabolcs Szita, Károly Vörös, and Miklós Szinai.

20. Randolph L. Braham, "Anti-Semitism and the Holocaust in the Politics of East Central Europe," in *Anti-Semitism and the Treatment of the Holocaust in Postcommunist Eastern Europe*, ed. Randolph L. Braham (New York: Columbia University Press, 1994), 8.

21. Jeffrey S. Murer, "Pursuing the Familiar Foreigner: The Resurgence of Anti-Semitism and Nationalism in Hungary since 1989," (Ph.D. diss., University of Illinois, Chicago, 1999).

22. Law XXV/1920 declared that the ethnic, racial affiliation of students in higher education should reflect the respective composition of the country's population.

23. Georg Brunner, *Nationality Problems and Minority Conflicts in Eastern Europe* (Gütersloh: Bertelsmann Foundation Publishers, 1996), 132–34.

Hungarian Politics and the Post-1989 Legacy of the Holocaust

Michael Shafir

A short fourteen years have passed since what has justifiably been called the *annus mirabilis* 1989,[1] which counted among its wonders Hungary's "negotiated revolution."[2] Miklós Haraszti, one of those who contributed to the erosion of the former regime's power, called this event "the hand shake tradition,"[3] a result of the June 13–September 18, 1989, National Roundtable.[4] Ten years on, Haraszti described the phenomenon as the first "consensus-seeking democracy...in Hungarian history," but wondered how long it would last, apparently concerned that this "tradition" might lack the first requisite of traditions: longevity. Four more years have passed and Hungary might today successfully compete for the title of European "Miss Political Polarization." A "dialogue of the deaf," occasionally accompanied by street-scuffling and mutual incrimination, threatens to plunge the country back into what increasingly resembles the cleavages of the last century.

Nothing illustrates better the current deep divisions than the politics of "public space." Public space is a meaningful mirror of political competition. It is, as Romanian historian Andrei Pippidi writes, "symbolic history"[5] at work. As such, symbolic history is always entangled in the separate, but nonetheless, associate process of a "clash of memories." Budapest has been recently the scene of three significant such clashes.

On February 13, 2004, at the Buda Castle, politicians representing the ruling coalition of the Socialist Party (*Magyar Szocialista Párt* – MSzP) and the Alliance of Free Democrats (*Szabad Demokraták Szövetsége* – SzDSz) marked the 59th anniversary of the liberation from Nazi rule in a ceremony boycotted by the main opposition party, Alliance of Young Democrats-Hungarian Civic Party (*Fiatal Demokraták Szövetsége* – *Magyar Polgári Párt* – FIDESZ-MPP). On the previous day, FIDESZ had boycotted a ceremony at which high-level Hungarian officials and the Israeli Ambassador to Hungary laid a wreath at the 13th district memorial to the victims of World War II and the martyrs of the Arrow Cross and the Nazi occupation. FIDESZ Representative on the

Budapest Municipal Council András Kupper said his party was "outraged that this terrible event...should be remembered as [the capital's] liberation," adding that "during the Soviet occupation, tens of thousands of innocent Hungarians were robbed, raped, executed and deported." Deputy Budapest Mayor Janós Schiffer, however, countered that "February 13, 1945, was a day of liberation for all those who were not shot dead, who were not deported to Auschwitz, who...came out from the basements of their destroyed buildings." He added that Kupper apparently sided "with those who should have been brought to justice for their war crimes." Following this, Foreign Minister and MSzP Chairman László Kovács said that divisions in Hungarian politics between a democratic right and a communism-tainted left were no longer relevant, and that the real division separated the political forces committed to democracy and those who threatened it. He was apparently responding to a FIDESZ-initiated move in the European People's Party (EPP) to politically isolate former Communists such as himself. Finally, the SzDSz representative at the Buda Castle ceremony, Imre Mécs, called on Hungary to face its own past. Germany, he went on to explain, has not been afraid to do so, and though the experience had been painful, that country is nowadays a model democracy.[6]

On February 14, 2004, about 800 members and sympathizers of the neo-Nazi Blood and Honor Association (*Vér és Becsület Egyesület*) organized a "counter-commemoration" in Budapest's main Hero Square intended as a memorial ceremony to honor those who lost their lives in the failed attempt by German and Hungarian soldiers to break out of the Buda Castle under Soviet assault. At a makeshift monument formed by a cross with a military helmet placed on it, the speakers attacked both the governing party and FIDESZ. The demonstrators pledged to be "soldiers of honor" worthy of the tradition of the Hungarian Royal Armed Forces, the German Wehrmacht, and the Waffen-SS, and they placed flowers on the site where Arrow Cross leader Ferenc Szálasi is believed to be buried.[7]

Finally, a third symbolic history clash over public space focused on the controversial figure of former Prime Minister Pál Teleki. Pro-FIDESZ associations and civic groups commissioned and the Budapest Municipal Council approved the erection of a statue to be unveiled on April 3, 2004. Following protests by the Federation of Hungarian Jewish Communities (*Magyarországi Zsidó Hitközségek Szövetsége –*

MAZSIHISZ), which considered the Teleki statue a symbol of "institutional, nationalistic anti-Semitism," and by the Simon Wiesenthal Center, the Council first suspended and later rescinded its authorization.[8] Hungarian Jews felt that a statue honoring the man who, in his first term as prime minister (1920–1921), introduced the 1920 *numerus clausus* law in universities—the first such law to be introduced in post–World War I Europe[9]—was a slap in their face. Teleki was apparently also involved in the drafting of the "First Jewish Law" under the 1938–1939 conservative government of Kálmán Darányi—this time establishing quotas for Jews allowed to practice business and the liberal professions. During his second term as prime minister (1939–1941) the law defining "a Jew" was considerably tightened.[10] For most Hungarians, however, Teleki's second term is associated with the short-lived recuperation of Northern Transylvania under the 1940 Second Vienna Award, with the attempt to steer a middle course between conservatives and radical-right politicians at home, and to balance a pro-German with a pro-British orientation in foreign affairs. Indeed, Teleki committed suicide rather than make a decision to either attack neighboring Yugoslavia as a German ally or face a German invasion.[11] While still the country's prime minister, Viktor Orbán said on December 27, 2000, that he considered Teleki to be his model politician. His visions, the former premier said, are far more helpful for contemporary Hungary than "other fashionable ideas." Like Teleki, who had pursued a policy of revision of the Trianon-imposed borders, "our starting point must be our own national self-interest" and that concept "is not an abstract category, but the common interests of the entire Hungarian nation," Orbán said.[12] In the eyes of incumbent Socialist Culture Minister István Hiller, however, Teleki's responsibility for the discriminatory laws overrode any consideration for the late premier's anti-war stances. "We do not want to have a [Teleki] statue in Buda Castle, especially not on the 60th anniversary of the Holocaust," Hiller said in parliament.

I believe the three incidents encapsulate much—alas, too much—of what constitutes contemporary Hungarian politics. They speak volumes about the abundance of what Timothy Garton Ash describes as "residual" mutual perceptions in post-Communist Gentile-Jewish relations;[13] they illustrate the mutual anathematizing of political rivals; they show that words are used to preempt perceived threats and demonize adversaries; and they constitute one more proof that pessimists (among whom

I count myself) are right when they believe that there is always room for worse. All three incidents are also illustrative of the political instrumentalization of the Holocaust. Indeed, a closer look at the pronouncements cited above demonstrates that none of the three groups (the Socialist-Liberals, the conservatives, and the far right) is really innocent of this attempt.

Nowhere in the world—not even in Israel—does the Holocaust and its treatment stand at the center of current political debates, and within the general political disputation the Holocaust is instrumentalized everywhere. Naturally, there is no reason why Hungary should be any different. The attempt to analyze the political discourse on the Holocaust runs the danger of either missing the point or of over-focusing and losing one's balance. In my attempt to avoid the former danger, I shall take it for granted that the reader is acquainted with the major developments in Hungary since 1989. Avoiding the latter danger is far more difficult. As a political scientist, I have of course my biases. I do my utmost to remember Philip E. Converse's urging never to forget the first commandment of our "trade": ask oneself time and time again "whose political scientist are you?"[14] But I would also like to remind the reader of the nineteenth-century German historian Johann G. Droysen's remark that "only a mindless person is objective."[15] Should I pretend that as a Jew I equally abhor the manipulation of *any* symbols? Or that I find such manipulation *equally* amusing or *equally* revolting?

Symbols are about the past but are for the present. And I have yet to run into any book or article that is written with a readership of the past in mind. Viewed from this perspective, the "public space" and the "public discourse" form a single, albeit entangled, dimension. In analyzing the anti-Semitic aspects in Hungary's post-Communist political discourse, András Kovács perceives that discourse as being largely a reflection of attempts by different political parties and currents to create "an identity on a symbolic level."[16] The process of forging political identities encompasses both disputes *about* symbolic public space and disputes over the implications of overt or encoded public discourse. Are we to treat those symbols in a post-modernist manner where "anything goes"?

Let me illustrate this dilemma with but one example. One can, as George Schöpflin does when he analyzes "commemoration," see in it a "ritualized" recalling of a society's fundamental tenets. "A society without memory is blind to its own present and future, because it lacks a moral framework into which to place its experiences," he writes.[17] There is at first glance little to argue against that perception. No polity can function without—to use Benedict Anderson's terminology—a positive "imagined community" to which reference can be made.[18] The symbolic aspect of memorials and commemorations is even more pronounced in societies whose national identity is fragile and whose future is uncertain. The distortion (but not obliteration!) of national symbols in East Central Europe under the Communist regimes and the search for either new or renewed "symbols" in the wake of the regime-change motivated Jacques Rupnik to note that the "demolition of [Communist] statues, restoration of former denominations to streets, are but the exterior aspects of the search for a 'usable past,' whose force is proportional to the fragility of national identity and uncertainty in face of the future."[19] Viewed from this angle, the intent to erect a statue to Teleki is perfectly comprehensible.

But one cannot ignore the other side of the coin, and that side is particularly strong in societies that left behind one past but are uncertain of what should replace it and who should be chosen to symbolize it. Which past is deemed as worthy to be "used" or "re-used"? Schöpflin notes that "It is very difficult for one community to look with nothing worse than indifference at the commemoration pursued by another. Yet if we are all to survive in the European tradition that I believe is our heritage, living in diversity is a *sine qua non*." This, he adds, is difficult at moments, but "If we have the confidence in ourselves, in our values, then the commemorations of the others need not be seen as offensive." His advice is particularly directed at national minorities, which are told that "Majorities have the same rights to cultural reproduction as minorities and those rights should be respected."[20] The question arises, however, whether cultural reproduction commemorating those who contributed to the *biological* destruction of others is not outside the "European tradition."

This study is divided into three chronological parts. The first part deals with the "hows" and the "whys" of handling the legacy of the interwar era and the Holocaust under Hungary's first post-Communist government of József Antall.[21] The second part attempts to understand the reason for the transformation of Viktor Orbán from a grassroots liberal anti-Communist rebel into a conservative politician. The third and last part considers the policies of right-wing "inclusion" pursued by Orbán and its impact on the responses to the Holocaust.[22]

First Circle: Identity Creation on a
Symbolic Level in the József Antall Era

Next after a government by generals, there may be no group of people less fit to govern than historians. The cabinet led by József Antall between May 1990 and his death in office on December 12, 1993, had three historians in key positions: the premier himself, Foreign Minister Géza Jeszenszky, and Defense Minister Lajos Für. Their repeated pronouncements demonstrate that their main frame of reference was the past, rather than the future. And when in Hungary one says "past," one says "Trianon"—the national trauma of several generations of Hungarian politicians and intellectuals.

Catapulted to the head of the Hungarian Democratic Forum (*Magyar Demokrata Fórum* – MDF) rather unexpectedly after the resignation of Zoltán Biró in October 1989, Antall's background should have predicted his performance in office. Never a dissident under the Communist regime, he came from a traditional Hungarian family and in numerous interviews after becoming premier he emphasized his commitment to public service, Christian values, moral rectitude, and democracy.[23] His father served as a civil servant in Hungary's wartime government and was commissioner for refugees from 1939 to April 1944, when he was arrested by the Gestapo for having rendered assistance to Hungarian and Polish Jews.[24] József Antall, Sr., who died in 1970, would eventually be recognized as a "Righteous Among the Nations" by Yad Vashem.[25] To assume that Premier Antall was an anti-Semite, or oblivious to the suffering of the Jews during the Holocaust, is therefore a far-fetched proposition, although theoretically possible.

Antall's education and his family background had made him into an (albeit closet) anti-Communist and, above all, into a nationalist. His famous August 13, 1990, statement that he perceived himself as being the premier of not only ten million Hungarians, but also "in spirit" of fifteen million Magyars—that is to say the leader of ethnic Hungarians beyond the Trianon borders—speaks for itself.[26] To the extent that the Holocaust was to play any part in the post-Communist task of nation rebuilding, Antall would emphasize the roles played by people like his father, rather than those played by Holocaust perpetrators and by the Nazis' collaborators.[27] In other words, "symbolic history" was to play the "socialist realism" role—only in reverse. If for Stalin and Andrei Zhdanov the "typical hero in typical circumstances" existed in a fictitious present, Antall and his supporters placed him in an almost-fictitious past.

Much of the same applies to Jeszenszky and Für. Addressing a largely Jewish audience on Holocaust Remembrance Day 1994, Jeszenszky remarked that apart from having over half-a-million Holocaust victims, Hungary had also given refuge to Jews. Furthermore, the 1920 Trianon Treaty, which had torn large segments of the Hungarian nation from the motherland, had a traumatic Holocaust-like affect on the country.[28] The statement is emblematic of what may be termed "comparative trivialization," though when making it Jeszenszky was obviously not intentionally trivializing.[29]

Für acquired a rather unenviable reputation for saying the wrong thing at the wrong time when it came to Hungary's neighbors. At times, it seemed as if most of his ideas were drawn straight from Johann Gottfried Herder. He told an audience in Miskolc in February 1992 that "the concept of the Hungarian nation in the Carpathian Basin is not limited to the citizens of the Hungarian Republic." A "Hungarian nation in Europe," he said, must mean "a Hungarian-speaking united nation." Consequently, "To defend national security in the Carpathian Basin is inseparable from the defense of the whole Hungarian nation." Hungarian state institutions, he said, were duty-bound "to do their best to stop the endangering of the Hungarian minorities outside the Hungarian borders."[30] His deputy, Ernö Raffay, headed an MDF committee tasked with restoring the so-called "Irredenta statue," erected under the Horthy regime and symbolizing the territories torn from "mother country" by the Trianon Treaty.[31] In fact, not one, but three Trianon statues would eventually be restored during Orbán's term in office.[32]

With this background, one can begin to comprehend that the legacies of the Holocaust and communism in post-Communist Hungary are in part a function of a "clash of memories." This involves a certain manipulation, to be sure, but it also involves self-manipulation: one chooses to "remember" one's own heroes and one's own traumas (that is to say, to represent history for one's own community) not for the sake of deliberately dismissing the traumas suffered by the *other*, but for enhancing the cohesiveness of one's own kin.

Now, "kin" can mean many different things. It can mean relatives and it can mean folk; it can mean the nation-state within its current borders or the nation including diasporas for whom Hungary is the kin-state; and it can also mean *Volk* in its Germanic sense of an organic community of past, present, and future generations based on *Blut und Boden*. No evidence I am aware of places Antall in the last category.

There is plenty of evidence, on the other hand, to place him and his government in the category of "kin-statesmanship." I believe that this was the main, though not necessarily the only, motivation that determined Antall to allow Admiral Horthy's reburial in September 1993 and to refer to him shortly before as a "Hungarian patriot," who "should be placed in the community of the nation and the awareness of the people."[33] Ministers in Antall's government attended the funeral and Antall himself visited the grave shortly before his death. Horthy's re-interment was modeled on the 1906 reburial of Ferencz Rákóczi, and would later serve as model for Antall's own funeral.[34] Whether István Rév is right or not in interpreting the similarity of the Horthy and Antall corteges as implying the elimination of the epoch that separated Horthy from Antall I would not venture to guess.[35]

Intentions aside, this was bound to lead to the "clash of memories" mentioned above. Let me emphasize that I do not deal here with Horthy's complex relationship and attitudes towards the Jews, but with "who remembers whom and why" and with "who remembers what and why." István Deák, who has written extensively on him, calls Horthy "neither a fascist nor a liberal." The regent, he writes, "was not a monster, but he was not a humanitarian either. He was no democrat, but never tried to be a dictator. He claimed to have been a lifelong anti-Semite; still, under his reign and despite the deportations, more Jews survived the Nazi terror, in sheer numbers, than in any other country within Hitler's Europe, except perhaps Romania."[36]

Yet for many Jews Horthy remains the head of a state that was responsible for the death of at least 550,000 of its citizens,[37] most of whom perished before the Nazis deposed him on October 15, 1944. Of those, some 375,000 were exterminated at Auschwitz after the mass deportations carried out between May 15 and July 9, 1944. The deportations took place under the Nazi occupation, following the dismissal of the Miklós Kállay government and its replacement by the cabinet headed by pro-Nazi General Döme Sztójay. At that time, Horthy was still head of state (he was deposed, arrested, and sent into exile in October), and hence cannot be fully exonerated. Yet most Budapest Jewish survivors owe their lives to Horthy who stopped the deportations in early July 1944.[38]

Neither the anti-Jewish legislation passed during Horthy's long regency, nor the fact that approximately 64,000 Jews had lost their lives in Greater Hungary before the Germans invaded the country in March 1944 is, or can be, ignored by "Jewish memory."[39] The deaths of between 40,000 and 45,000 labor servicemen drafted into the military and sent to the eastern front, the murder of "alien" Jews deported to Kamenets-Podolsk in Galicia in the summer of 1941, and the massacres in and around Ujvidék (Novi Sad) in January–February 1942 cannot be laid at the door of the Germans.[40]

These developments triggered among some segments of post-Communist Hungarian Jewry what might be termed as a "Sartrerian reaction," for it was Jean-Paul Sartre's famous—if often contested—thesis that Jewish identity-consciousness owes its existence to anti-Semites.

This reaction was not merely a matter of some mistaken de-codification of the real significance of Antall's message. There are good reasons for the message to be perceived as it was, for it took Antall far too long to disassociate himself from the Populists in the MDF. The official split was repeatedly postponed and finalized only in June 1993, when the MDF's National Steering Committee voted to expel the Populists' leader, István Csurka, from the party. Antall had opted to close both eyes and ears to Csurka and his associates' mounting attacks on what they considered his far too moderate policies towards national minorities at home and in support of Hungarian ethnic minorities abroad. Only after the U.S. Congress began to debate the situation in Hungary did the premier decide to act.[41]

Unlike the Antall wing of the MDF, the Csurka-led Hungarian Justice and Life Party (*Magyar Igazság és Élet Pártja* – MIÉP) was glued into the organic community type of kinship. From the start it obviously sought historical association with the radical-right Party of Hungarian Renewal (*Magyar Megújulás Pártja* – MMP) led by Béla Imrédy, and its successor party, the Hungarian Life Party (*Magyar Élet Pártja* – MÉP), headed by Pál Teleki.[42] But these two figures do not exhaust Csurka's "models" from interwar Hungarian politics. The playwright-turned-politician became notorious in the West for an article entitled "Setting the Record Straight," published in August 1992 in the MDF weekly *Magyar Fórum*. Csurka's terminology in that tract was, "if not vintage

Ferenc Szálasi...at least vintage Gyula Gömbös."[43] Gömbös had once been a member of the Party for the Protection of the Race (*Fajvédö Párt*), established in 1923 by Tibor Eckhardt and Endre Zsilinszky, and later headed a secret group called the Hungarian Scientific Race Protection Society.[44] "Setting the Record Straight" combined anti-Semitic paranoia and conspiracy theories with the usage of the Hungarian equivalent of *Lebensraum* (*Élettér*) and racist jargon aimed at the Roma.[45] About the latter, Csurka wrote in a Social Darwinist mode that they had been living among Hungarians "for far too long" and that in the future society should support "the strong, fit-for-life families who are prepared for work and achievement" and not populations whose "deterioration...has genetic causes."[46]

A fortnight later, *Magyar Fórum* published an article authored by MDF presidium member Gyula Zacsek under the telling title "Termites are Devouring the Nation." The article was "a Nazi-type attack against the Jewish-cosmopolitan conspiracy led by George Soros, the Jewish Hungarian-born American multi-millionaire and philanthropist who helped the 'cosmopolitan' (meaning Jewish) Communists to preserve their power by giving it over to the 'cosmopolitan' dissidents."[47]

The target was not diffuse in the least. As early as 1990, Sándor Csoóri, a poet and essayist belonging to the Populist stream, sounded the trumpet of what would eventually become a rather commonplace reference among the adversaries of the SzDSz. The clash was a classic revival of the Populist-Urbanist ideological division that cuts through modernizing Hungary's history. The SzDSz would eventually be referred to as the "ZsDSz (*Zsidó Demokraták Szövetsége)*," meaning "Association of Jewish Democrats," and indeed many of these former dissidents were scions of families of disillusioned Jewish Communists who now held prominent positions in the party's leadership. Writing in the MDF biweekly *Hitel* in September 1990, Csoóri said that contemporary Hungary was witnessing a "reverse assimilation trend" in that it is "no longer the Hungarian nation that wishes to assimilate Jews, but liberal Jewry that wishes to assimilate the Hungarian nation," a purpose for which it employs "a more powerful weapon than it has ever possessed, namely, the parliamentary system."[48]

Csoóri, Csurka, and Zacsek were not the only members of the Antall-led governing coalition to indulge in this form of public discourse. Long after Antall's death, József Torgyán, chairman of the

Independent Smallholder and Bourgeois Party (*Független Kisgazda és Polgári Párt* – FKGP), addressed a March 1996 electoral rally warning against the "liberal-Bolshevik" danger that is "paralyzing" the "powers of the Hungarian nation.... We, however, cannot be paralyzed. We are Hungarian. In the spring, the Hungarian manually clears away the vermin. Let us also clear away the vermin."[49]

The question remains: why did Antall agree for so long to march alongside the Csurkas and the Torgyáns in post-Communist Hungarian politics. For brevity's sake, I propose to ignore the "politicking" aspects of the answer and to concentrate instead on its generic aspects.

In an important article on the transformation of former Communist parties in East Central Europe, Michael Waller pointed out that right after the system's collapse such political organizations benefited from an advantage that they might not always have come to use in the first (naturally anti-Communist) free ballot, but which they later were amply capable of taking advantage of, namely "organizational continuity," which included access to assets.[50] Other parts of the political spectrum, ranging from the liberals to conservatives, "historical parties" and populist-nationalists, do not benefit from such access at the start of their political road. Rejecting continuity with communism, they must replace it with other resources, among which "historic continuity" figures more prominently than it does in the case of the "successor parties." At first sight, this has little to do with the treatment of the Holocaust. On closer scrutiny, however, it turns out that many—which is not to say *all*—"historic" conservatives and, it goes without saying, populist-ultra-nationalists, as well as those intellectuals associated with them, are often found to be part of the Holocaust-denying or Holocaust-trivializing landscape.

In an article analyzing what is termed as the "assault on historical memory" in post-Communist Hungary, Randolph L. Braham, the world's most important historian of the Holocaust in that country, describes the spectrum of Holocaust denial as follows:

> While the number of xenophobic champions of anti-Semitism—like that of the Hungarian neo-Nazis actually denying the Holocaust—is relatively small, the camp of those distorting and denigrating the catastrophe of the Jews is fairly large and—judging by recent developments—growing. With their political power and influence, members of this camp represent a potentially greater danger not only to the integrity of the historical record of the Holocaust but also and above all to the newly established

democratic system. Unlike the Holocaust deniers, who are a fringe group of "historical charlatans,"...the history cleansers who denigrate and distort the Holocaust are often "respectable" public figures (e.g., intellectuals, members of parliament, influential governmental and party figures, and high-ranking army officers).[51]

In this regard, Hungary is hardly unique. The diagnosis applies across the board in East Central Europe, though local variations play a role. One of the main reasons for the widespread presence of the "respectable public figures" casting doubt on the singularity of Holocaust rests precisely on the absence of "organizational continuity" and the resulting over-pronounced necessity of compensating for that absence with appeals to the legitimizing "historic continuity." Paradoxically, these politicians are the legatees of communism to a far larger extent than they would ever become aware. For in Hungary and elsewhere in the former Communist world, the legacy of the Holocaust was distorted to serve political purposes and to present the saga of the Second World War as that "era when 'Communists and other progressive elements' had struggled against, or became the victims of, 'Hitlerite and Horthyite Fascism.' Somehow there seemed to have been no Jews among these heroes and victims; instead, all were 'anti-Fascist Hungarians'."[52]

But as Tony Judt noted, the "mismemory of Communism is... contributing in its turn to a mismemory of anti-Communism."[53] Judt made the comment in connection with Romania's Marshal Ion Antonescu being turned into a national hero, but the observation is equally valid for Hungary, Slovakia, Croatia, and other former Nazi-allied states. What is more, with Antonescu, Szálasi, László Bárdossy, and Jozef Tiso having been executed as war criminals, or Corneliu Zelea Codreanu having been assassinated at the orders of King Carol II in 1938, they may fit very well into the natural post-Communist search for replacing manipulated "state-organized" martyrdom on the altar of proletarian internationalism, with martyrdom on the altar of national, anti-Communist values. As many have observed, political transformation often requires a revision of history and Communist parties had long experience in this exercise.

And so we come to András Kovács's concept of "creating an identity on a symbolic level." "Mainstream," and allegedly democratic, party leaders in search for alternatives to organizational resources face a double dilemma when coming to forge that identity. These parties, Kovács writes, can either opt for placing themselves somewhere in the Western political spectrum or to "express a relationship with certain emblematic periods, events or individuals in the country's own history."[54] In actual fact, however, one option does not necessarily rule out the other. For example, a political organization may associate itself with the European People's Party, and still proceed to identity-forging on mainly autochthonous values. Among the parties that gained access to parliament in the first free post-Communist elections (March–April 1990), the MSzP was the only one that did not face that choice, since it had access to resources. The SzDSz and (originally) FIDESZ opted for a Western-type of liberalism. On the other hand, the MDF, the FKGP, and the Christian Democratic People's Party (*Kereszténydemokrata Néppárt* – KDNP)—which would practically vanish from the political scene during the May 1994–May 1998 parliamentary term[55]—all made what can be called the "introvert option."

Organizations for which this is the main option fight among themselves "for the appropriation of history" in which they attempt to "demonstrate historical tradition and continuity."[56] But a second dilemma emerges once the introvert option has been made, namely whether or not to distance themselves from the less seemly aspects of remote or immediate history—and to what extent to do so. Opting for distancing themselves from figures such as those mentioned above is in many cases tantamount to renouncing historic legitimacy as well. For what historic legitimacy can one claim if, as a Slovak or a Croat politician, one casts aside any continuity with the only time an independent Slovak or Croat state existed?

I believe we can now close the circle. We have thus far demonstrated that "symbolic history" is closely interconnected with the search for a form of political legitimacy and that both are part and parcel of the post-Communist party-forging of political identities. The time has also come to address the question raised above: why did it take Antall so long to distance himself from the more extremist shades of the coalition he headed? By now it should be clear that given Antall's value-system, he had little choice. This was the only coalition in which all parliament-represented introvert forces would gather under a common umbrella. He was well aware of Csurka's machinations against his leadership of the MDF, and there was no love lost between him and Torgyán, who in 1992 departed from the ruling coalition. Furthermore, Antall (the only person who at the time had access to Communist secret police files) was also aware that both had a shady past of collaboration with the State Security Division (*Államvédelmi Osztály* – AVO) (later called State Security Office; *Államvédelmi Hivatal* – AVH)—the dreaded Hungarian secret police.[57]

Holocaust denial, minimization, or trivialization by comparison may be common to all politicians. Still, their motivations may be different, as might the goals pursued. It would be just as unwise to overlook these differences as it would be to assume that they are reason enough for protesting here but deferring there. It is comforting to learn that Antall's political models as national leaders were Ferenc Deák, Baron József Eötvös, and, above all, Count István Bethlen,[58] at least preferable to Orbán's latter-date model of Teleki, and certainly less threatening than Csurka's hero-models. But at the end of the day, what counts are not models, but policies.

Viktor Orbán's 'Transfiguration' or the Making of a Radical Conservative

There is surprising consensus among analysts of Hungary's contemporary scene on the self-defeating impact that the over-emphasis on "symbolic history" had for the defeat of the MDF at the May 8 and 29, 1994, polls. The agreement cuts across those never-openly-acknowledged, yet all-the-more-real divisions.[59]

Why would, then, Viktor Orbán repeat—and outdo—his predecessor's mistakes? As always, simple questions invite complex answers. This is partly due to the fact that, as one scholar put it, "FIDESZ's history...offers an intriguing puzzle: it has been one of the most unusual political parties, starting out as a youth organization in 1988 and by 1998 emerging into governmental position. Its road to power, however, was neither smooth nor straightforward, but riddled with contradictions, inconsistencies, and 180-degree turns that require explanation."[60] Several points seem to be of cardinal (if not really equal) importance in providing that elucidation insofar as the handling of the memory of the Holocaust is concerned.

First and foremost among these is anti-communism, which at the same time is perhaps the only trait that did not undergo change in the evolution of FIDESZ since its founding on March 30, 1988, in the midst of political turmoil. Its charismatic leader became known in Hungary and abroad due to the fiery speech he delivered on June 16, 1989, at the Heroes' Square ceremony that preceded the reburial of the earthly remains of Imre Nagy and his associates. That speech, in which he called on the Soviet Union to remove its occupation troops, was televised live and not only put his previously "invisible party on the political map,"[61] but also established Orbán's reputation as one who would never trust a Communist. Not even a former one, as it later turned out.

Closely linked to anti-communism, yet distinct from it, is the generation gap. The SzDSz's early leadership came from the ranks of intellectual dissidents with ideological links to the "New Left"-oriented "Budapest School."[62] While the contribution of these intellectuals to the demise of the former regime had been essential, they were just as adverse to the revival of old-type nationalism and to the Populists within the MDF. The abundance of "symbolic history" in the MDF's record was for them repulsive; furthermore, it seemed to entail personal dangers, as the Populists were portraying the SzDSz as the "party of Jews" and seeking (with Antall's blessing) to eliminate from the media Jews who do not "defend the national interests" and who are the harbingers of "destructive modernism" engaged in a dangerous global plot to destroy the "essence" of Hungary and the "Hungarian nation."[63] The former "revisionist" Marxists had evolved towards a sort of "Social Liberalism."[64] When, after their victory at the polls in 1994, the former Communists, though capable of forming a cabinet by themselves, extended an invitation to the SzDSz to join the ruling coalition, the SzDSz did so. It was a self-defensive reaction, prompted by the fact that the "majority of Hungarian Jews seem to follow the century-old political strategy of supporting political forces that they believe to be heirs to the universalistic ideas of Enlightenment and as such able to protect them from the real and imagined threats of anti-Semitism." It was for this reason, as András Kovács writes, that "a section of the Jewish intelligentsia strongly supported the creation of the 'unnatural' government coalition of the former Communists and their former liberal opposition in 1994."[65]

At its start, FIDESZ was also on the barricades of the struggle against nationalist revival. In 1990, the party's parliamentary group walked out of a session called to mark the Trianon Treaty's unjustness.[66] As late as 1992, in a speech delivered at the FIDESZ congress, Orbán told his colleagues that the MDF "by and large represented a rotten, decaying old world that would never again return to Hungary."[67] It seems that at that time Orbán never contemplated the possibility of becoming one of the main promoters of that return. His FIDESZ had joined the Liberal International, just as the SzDSz did.

Still, there were obvious differences between the two liberal formations and FIDESZ could by no means be regarded as a sort of SzDSz "youth wing." As Michael Waller put it, at that point in time the party's "requirement that members be under the age of 35 was in itself sufficient to give the party a particular identity, involving a rejection of the Communist past, carried further to an independence also of earlier Hungarian traditions."[68] The "liberalism" displayed by FIDESZ was substantially different from the SzDSz's "Social Liberalism." It inclined towards a "Liberal Conservatism" with no, or only slight, sensibility towards social problems. In short, the early FIDESZ looked like a Thacherite party, and "lacking any roots in Marxism was clear-cut anti-Communist, more radical, in some issues, than SzDSz."[69] This orientation was not shared by all FIDESZ leaders, and was to cause a split in the party in 1993, when founding member Gábor Fodor left it, disagreeing with Orbán's orthodox "free-marketeering." Eventually, Fodor joined the SzDSz.[70]

The age limit was abolished at the 1993 congress, which also did away with the last elements of the party's "grassroots movement" features, introducing hierarchical discipline and redefining FIDESZ as a "liberal-center" group with a *national* commitment.[71] Relatively little attention was paid at that time to this—as it turned out—major signaling of FIDESZ's change of course. In part, this was due to the fact that in the 1994 elections FIDESZ remained in an alliance with the SzDSz. But the alliance—involving stepping down in favor of the best-placed candidate in runoffs for single-member constituencies—as well as a pre-electoral agreement providing for obligatory consultations ahead of signing any agreement with a third party, was (insofar as FIDESZ was concerned) primarily aimed at pre-empting precisely what emerged in the wake of the elections: a MSzP-SzDSz coalition. Orbán hoped that the elections would engineer an MDF-FIDESZ-SzDSz government.[72] The election results were a debacle for FIDESZ, which made it into the legislature with great difficulty and found itself sharing the opposition benches with a greatly enfeebled MDF and other parties of the right.[73]

During this 1994–1998 opposition period FIDESZ underwent its "transfiguration" from a liberal into a radical-conservative formation. The evolution was crowned in the year 2000, when the party left the

Liberal International and joined the conservative EPP. An important milestone on this road was the party's 1995 congress, at which its name was changed by adding to FIDESZ the additional denomination of Hungarian Civic Party (*Magyar Polgári Párt*). Once more, not enough attention was then paid to this idiomatic transformation. As it would eventually turn out, for Orbán and his friends "civic" had an inclusive connotation, aimed at the gradual absorption, and eventual monopolization, of the right-wing side of Hungary's political spectrum. That process is still underway in contemporary Hungary.

FIDESZ's populist economic policies "were accompanied by support for a strong state and a conservative Catholic line on social issues." Furthermore, in its electoral propaganda before the 1998 elections and in pronouncements during its 1998–2002 rule of the country, there was an obvious siding with provincial Hungary against the Budapest capital,[74] perceived as being dominated by foreign capital and non-Hungarian values—which often meant Jewish influence—even if it was left to MIÉP and other extremists to call the spade a Jew.

But what Orbán did was not merely to assimilate his party into the traditions of the Populists, but to literally turn "inclusion" into the key of his party's tactics. Two paradoxes emerge from this. First, the anti-Communist Orbán resorted to Communist tactics. As designed by Ken Jowitt, the concept of "inclusion" refers to a third stage in the development of ruling Leninist parties, in which the Communist Party perceives "that the major condition for its continued development as an institutionalized charismatic organization is to integrate itself with, rather than insulate itself from, its host society."[75] In Hungary itself, the famous September 1987 Lakitelek conference was a good illustration of "inclusive" tactics operated by the regime and laid the basis for a long and fruitful collaboration between the Populists and the party reformists headed by Imre Pozsgay.[76]

Second, the new anti-Communist premier would turn to those who *collaborated* with the Communist regime against the Urbanites (now the SzDSz) who by-and-large were *targeted* by that regime and viewed as its most dangerous challenge.

The evolution would also be reflected in the Populists *cum* MDF shift of vocal support of Hungarian ethnic minorities abroad, resulting in the famous and controversial "Act on Hungarians Living in Neighboring Countries" ("Status Law") passed by the Hungarian parliament on June

19, 2001.[77] Inaugurating a new building of the Office for Hungarians Beyond Borders (*Túli Magyarok Hivatala*) on August 19, 1999, Prime Minister Orbán said that "all citizens of Hungary and Hungarians beyond borders are members of a single and indivisible nation,"[78] which sounded quite close to Antall's "spiritual" premiership of fifteen million Magyars. At the opposite end of the political spectrum, Socialist Premier Gyula Horn had explicitly called himself the prime minister of 10.4 million Hungarians.[79]

This brings us back to András Kovács's concept of "creating an identity on a symbolic level." It should have become quite clear by now that this is precisely what Orbán set out to do when he engaged in transforming FIDESZ from a liberal into a neo-conservative party. As I have noted elsewhere, FIDESZ's "transfiguration" can be explained in terms of sheer political opportunism, but also in terms of "awareness of the opportunity to fill in the niche left open by the practical political demise of the MDF after Antall's death in December 1993 and the disastrous MDF electoral performance in 1994."[80] As Csilla Kiss would eventually formulate it, FIDESZ moved "into the conservative space vacated by the fragmented" MDF—a "move that was made possible by the coincidence of FIDESZ's need to change and the vacuum on the right."[81] But as George Schöpflin had once asked, what could "conservative" mean in the post-Communist context, since the recent past in Hungary was a Communist one?[82] Questions might invite radically different answers and mine are miles apart from Schöpflin's.[83] In a nutshell, while the British-Hungarian political scientist believes that much of FIDESZ's and Orbán's negative image is maliciously invented by Westerners who themselves are subjected to the powerful influence of the "pro-left" Budapest Jews, I regard that image as having been generated by Orbán and company's toying time and time again with "symbolic history." The treatment of the Holocaust on one hand, and the related "Jews equal communism" institutionalized insinuation embodied in the House of Terror museum are part and parcel of that game.

A Self-Defeating 'Inclusion'

Quite soon upon taking over as premier in 1998, Orbán visited the Hungarian pavilion at the Auschwitz exhibit and immediately decided to reconstruct the display, originally built by the Communist regime. The plans for redesigning the exhibit, as Randolph L. Braham described them, were little else than a pro-Horthy apologia designed to sanitize the Nazi era in general and the Hungarian involvement in the "Final Solution" in particular. The plans called for portraying a "virtual symbiosis of Hungarian and Jewish life since the emancipation of Jews in 1867, downplaying the many anti-Jewish manifestations as mere aberrations in the otherwise enlightened history of Hungary." Attention was obviously focused on "the positive aspects of Jewish life in the country, emphasizing the flourishing of the Jewish community between 1867 and 1944, the rescue activities of those identified as Righteous Among the Nations, and Horthy's saving of the Jews of Budapest."[84] More importantly, the same plans blamed the Germans almost exclusively for the destruction of the Jews. The exhibition was canceled after protests from MAZSIHISZ, whose spokesman said the country's Jewish communities did not wish to see the project halted, but "to see it is done right."[85] "Symbolic history" was part of the game from the start of the Orbán reign.

A plaque commemorating Horthy's notorious gendarmes was unveiled in 1999 at Budapest's War History Museum (*Hadtörténeti Múzeum*) in the presence of junior coalition FKGP member Zsolt Lányi, chairman of the parliament's Defense Committee, triggering strong protests from the Jewish community.[86] Shortly thereafter, a high official of the same coalition, Orbán advisor Mária Schmidt, again triggered the Jewish community's protests by stating—in French radical-right Jean-Marie Le Pen-like manner—that the Holocaust had been but a "marginal issue" of the history of World War II. No less emblematic for the "trivializing" way in which the Holocaust would soon be presented as relatively benign when juxtaposed with the Communist atrocities, was the manner in which Schmidt developed her argument. The word "Holocaust," she said, should not be applied only to the extermination of the Jews during World War II, since the Communists had also committed genocide. Viewed from this perspective, she said, "the Holocaust, the extermination or rescue of the Jews, represented but a secondary, marginal point of view [as it was not an objective] among the war aims of either belligerent." Yet the West, which was Stalin's ally during the war, refuses to be confronted with its own responsibility because this would "endanger the legitimacy of the Western democracies."[87] In face of protests, Orbán issued a statement largely exonerating Schmidt and expressing his "full confidence" in her.[88]

It was Schmidt, again, who in 2002 became director of the House of Terror (*Terror Háza*) museum, located in central Budapest, in the building that served as the headquarters of Ferenc Szálasi's Arrow Cross in 1944–1945 (when it was called "House of Loyalty"; *Hüség Háza*) and later became the headquarters of the Communist secret police. It was not by chance that the museum was inaugurated on the eve of the 2002 elections, with Orbán giving an address at the opening ceremony. The attempt was obviously being made to link the rival MSzP with the age of terror on which the museum concentrated—the Communist one. Although allegedly dedicated to both Nazi and Communist terror, only two out of the some two-dozen rooms of the museum are dedicated to the former. The museum suggests that, on balance, Communist terror had been by far worse than the Jewish Holocaust. More important, perhaps, was the implication in the exhibit: against a background in which both FIDESZ and MIÉP commentators routinely mentioned the Jewish origins of some of Hungary's most notorious Communists (Gábor Péter, the first AVO chief was Jewish), the implicit message received by the museum's visitors was that the Jews were responsible for the country's postwar ordeal.[89]

While I do not rule out comparison between the Holocaust and the Gulag, neither do I believe that the uniqueness of either can be rendered by playing the numerology game of "which produced more victims" or of "who is guiltier." To play that game is to engage in what Alan S. Rosenbaum and later Vladimir Tismaneanu properly termed as "competitive martyrdom."[90] I believe that it is legitimate to ask questions about why Communist ideology fascinated so many Jews and about the roles played by Jews in Communist systems.[91] There is, however, a huge gap between asking those legitimate questions and comparing what is comparable in the two genocides on one hand, and denying, belittling, or obliterating that which is inherently unique to each of them, on the other. And the latter is precisely what House of Terror is doing, thus fully fitting into an East Central European pattern that has been dubbed the "symmetric" or the "double-genocide" approach to the Holocaust—one of the several forms of the "comparative trivialization" of the Shoah.[92]

Furthermore, the museum obviously reflects the attempt—to which Braham drew attention long before the site's inauguration—to turn Germany's last ally into its last victim.[93] For nowhere can the visitor learn anything about the Hungarian state's own responsibility for either the

Nazi or the Communist terror. On the contrary, the first leaflet one picks up in the museum speaks of Horthy's Hungary as having been involved in "desperate attempts" to maintain "its fragile democracy." Until the Nazi occupation of 1944, one is told, Hungary "had a legitimately elected government and parliament, where opposition parties functioned normally." No word of the anti-Jewish legislation, no word of the 64,000 Jews who perished under Horthy rule before the Nazis occupied the country.

The "Auschwitz exhibition cleansing attempt" now accomplished, the visitor is eventually shown a room where photographs of prisoners incarcerated in the Communist secret police dungeons are displayed. That they look desperate is no wonder. But among those figuring as victims of the Communist atrocities—though never identified—one can recognize Arrow Cross leader Ferenc Szálasi and his deputy, Mihály Kolosváry-Borcsa, as well as two other officials (László Endre and László Baky) convicted and executed in 1946 for the deportations and death of Jews at Auschwitz—that is, *before* the Communist takeover. The museum's message regarding who is to be considered a "victim" and who a perpetrator of totalitarianism is thus conveyed without a need for further captions and comments. Leon Volovici once noted that "the real target of the Jew = Bolshevik propaganda" is "not the number of Jews in the Communist elites, but the alleged Jewish collective culpability for the misdoing and disasters of the Communist regimes." That alleged collective guilt is aimed at balancing and neutralizing "the real culpability and real responsibility for crimes committed against the Jewish population."[94]

As a matter of fact, the museum has nothing more suitable to offer for its second room (dedicated to the Szálasi period) than a videotape showing the pro-Nazi dictator delivering a speech in which he calls for the patriotic defense of Budapest against the Soviet forces. Why, then, should the Blood and Honor neo-Nazi organization not feel legitimized in organizing an annual ceremony in the memory of those heroic fighters? And why should not MIÉP feel legitimized in its attempts to bring about the judicial rehabilitation of Hungary's 1941–1942 premier László Bárdossy, executed for war-crimes in 1945, as indeed Csurka tried to do in 1999 and again in 2001?[95]

Faced with the center-left opposition, Orbán often leaned in parliament on the support of Csurka's MIÉP, which had for the first time made it into the legislature, gaining fourteen seats in the 1998 elections. Between the runoffs, when it became apparent that MIÉP had made it into parliament, Csurka gave the Fascist salute during a televised interview.[96] Rather than becoming more restrained, the electoral success radicalized MIÉP—the more so as the government became dependent on MIÉP votes after losing its majority in parliament in September 2001 due to a split within the FKGP.[97] FIDESZ did nothing to distance itself from MIÉP Deputy Chairman Lóránt Hegedüs, who on August 16, 2001, published in MIÉP's Budapest 16th-district local newspaper *Ébresztö* (Reveille) an article using crude anti-Semitic language. In that tract, Hegedüs wrote:

> The Christian Hungarian state would have warded off the [ill effects] of the Compromise of 1867, had not an army of Galician vagabonds arrived, who had been gnawing away at the country which, despite everything, again and again, had always been able to resurrect from its ruins the bones of its heroes. If their Zion of the Old Testament was lost due to their sins and rebellions against God, let the most promising height of the new Testament's way of life, the Hungarian Zion, be lost as well.... Since it is impossible to smoke out every Palestinian from the banks of the Jordan using Fascist methods that often imitate the Nazis themselves, they are returning to the banks of the Danube, now in the shape of internationalists, now in jingoistic form, now as cosmopolitans, in order to give the Hungarians another kick just because they feel like doing so....
>
> So hear, Hungarians, the message of the 1000th year of the Christian Hungarian state, based on 1000 ancient rights and legal continuity, the only one leading you to life: *Exclude them! Because if you don't, they will do it to* you.[98]

Some time earlier, Hegedüs had delivered a Nazi-like speech in parliament, with neither FIDESZ Parliamentary Speaker János Áder nor FIDESZ Parliamentary Group Leader József Szájer uttering a word of protest.[99] As Hegedüs is an ordained pastor of the Calvinist Church, the National Synod of that Church condemned his having expressed views "contrary to the Christian gospel, inconsistent with the Calvinist faith, and unworthy of the Church" and decided to ban pastors from active membership in political parties.[100]

Not only did FIDESZ refrain from criticizing its de-facto political ally, but it exerted its influence and succeeded for some time to have the Council of Europe take MIÉP off its list of extremist parties.[101] It was also due to this collaboration that MIÉP was allotted its own radio station, Pannon Radio, which broadcast from a building in Budapest's *Szabadság tér* (Liberty Square) in which Pastor Hegedüs and his father (also a Calvinist pastor with the same name) reside. Hegedüs's controversial article was repeatedly aired by Pannon Radio[102] and the station was several times warned and three times fined by the National Radio and Television Board for broadcasting MIÉP party propaganda in general (which is forbidden under current legislation) and transgressing legislation regulating radio and television broadcasts prohibiting "inciting to hatred against persons, sexes, peoples, nations, national, ethnic, linguistic or other minorities, or any church or religious group."[103] In July 2002, the *Neue Zürcher Zeitung* described Pannon Radio as "the most evil forum in Eastern Europe today."[104] The station was finally closed down by the new Péter Medgyessy government in December 2002, after Csurka had tried to circumvent the law by buying a dominant stake in it through a foundation. As the news came in the same week in which Hegedüs was handed his suspended sentence, Csurka told a rally of his supporters, "This is no longer Hungary, but Palestine!"[105]

Views similar to those of Pannon Radio were beamed on the state Kossuth Radio's Sunday talks show *Vasárnapi òjság* (Sunday news), which Orbán described as his favorite program.[106] When Jewish organizations protested against the broadcasts, one of the participants, István Lovás,[107] called the protest an attempt at "intimidation," adding that "a command to halt must be given to those in Hungary...who wish to provoke an intellectual intifada." It goes without saying that for the participants in this Sunday-morning talk show, the Holocaust was just "Shoah-business." Tibor Franka, a reputed extreme-right *Magyar Forum* journalist, told listeners on March 12, 2000, that anti-Semitism is just an invention that "serves the interests of those who benefit from the Holocaust, who pocket the abandoned wealth of the victims of the Holocaust in one way or another." A few months earlier, it was explained on *Vasárnapi òjság* that these profiteers "want to do away with everybody who dares to express an opinion that is different from the views of MAZsIHISz." Prominent among such people, according to the same radio station, were members of the SzDSz who "keep mentioning Auschwitz and label people anti-Semites" whereas in fact "99 percent of them had been members of the Hungarian Socialist Workers Party." It was such people that "defame Hungary's current civic government...by causing tensions. But the government cannot post guards beside every [Jewish] grave." Journalist Zsolt Bayer, an ultranationalist working for the pro-FIDESZ *Magyar Nemzet*, told listeners on July 23, 2000, "I abhor the fact that many people...dare say explicitly that of all the things that ever happened here, only the Holocaust was a crime, or that everything the Communists did in the world and in Hungary was nothing compared to the Holocaust."[108] The same person, incidentally, would write after the 2002 elections that they had been won by the MSzP with the "votes of white trash in Pest."[109] Orbán apparently had nothing against this "competitive martyrdom" game, for he was a frequent guest on *Vasárnapi òjság*, leading SzDSz Chairman Gábor Kuncze to remark in January 2002 that the premier was courting the votes of the extreme right, since *Vasárnapi òjság* was considered to be a "mouthpiece for MIÉP and...a stain on the public service media."[110]

And so he was. At the end of the day, this proved to be his greatest miscalculation. He repeatedly refused to rule out the possibility of a post-electoral coalition with MIÉP, noting as early as April 2001 that it "would be unfortunate...if Hungarians were to decide about their fate according to what people abroad would say."[111] By November that year, in an interview with the German daily *Süddeutsche Zeitung*, Orbán said in reference to a possible FIDESZ-MIÉP partnership that "in principle" he does not rule out anything. Orbán told his German interviewer that he believed FIDESZ would garner the absolute majority in the 2002 elections and be able to form a government without right-wing extremists or former Communists. Asked why he refused to distance himself more clearly from MIÉP, Orbán replied that French President Jacques Chirac does not begin his daily activity by distancing himself from National Front leader Le Pen either. It was, he added, in any case just part of the "Hungarian political folklore" for the left wing to describe anyone who does not belong to its own political spectrum as an anti-Semite. The interviewer nonetheless insisted: if this is the case, why are Orbán's pronouncements becoming more and more nationalistic? These, came the reply, are his tactics for preventing the radical right from gaining ground ahead of Hungary's accession of the European Union, for membership in that organization stirs anxiety among the country's population.[112] Indeed, on the eve of the 2002 ballot Orbán had made MIÉP jargon into his own to such extent that he was warning that a Socialist victory would bring Hungary under the yoke of international finance capital.[113] He thus managed to scare off parts of the moderate right that would have made his "natural" electorate. For example, the Christian Democratic Party leadership recommended its supporters back the MSzP in the second round.

Orbán would have every reason to regret his choice of tactics after the 2002 ballot results. For by having "out-Csurkaed Csurka" and thereby preventing MIÉP's accession to parliament (the party garnered 4.36 percent, just under the 5 percent threshold), he was left with no one with whom to form a coalition. Furthermore, MIÉP's failure to pass the threshold was in good part due to the much higher turnout (over 70 percent) than in previous elections, particularly in the (for Csurka) deciding first round (56.26 on May 10, 1998, vs. 70.3 percent on April 7, 2002).[114] The high participation in voting was, in turn, much of Orbán's own making, having been prompted by his polarization of Hungarian society.[115] "Inclusion" had worked—but to its promoter's detriment.

What Next? In Lieu of Conclusions

On election night of April 21, 2002, as defeat could no longer be doubted, Orbán told a forum of party faithful that "a slight majority of Hungarians decided to tilt the balance toward a Socialist world," but added, in a defiant tone, that the future of Hungary would be a nation of fifteen, not ten million Magyars.[116] Antall was vindicated. On June 7, 2003, in a ceremony in Transylvania where he was awarded a prize by a Hungarian government-financed private university, Orbán told the audience that the Magyars would never give up the hope to regain "our home, *Hungaria Magna*—our lost paradise."[117] It is true that the statement was qualified; it was included in a remark on European unification, which, Orbán said, would enable the old dream to be fulfilled.

FIDESZ does not seem to have drawn any significant lesson from its electoral defeat. Officially, its doctrine is now entrenched in what Orbán describes as the *polgári* (middle-class) values of "family, country, nation, work, security and unity."[118] Those are reasonable conservative values, fitting into FIDESZ's self-definition as of the year 2000. Yet if everyone knows what a family and job security mean, words such as "country," "nation," and "unity" are ambiguous enough to leave room for more than one interpretation. And here we return to subjectivity. If for latter-day FIDESZ supporter and European Parliament member George Schöpflin, the MSzP-SzDSz alliance is the captive of an internationalist tradition in which "the West" and "Europe" have replaced the former socialist internationalism,[119] in my eyes FIDESZ is, to paraphrase an earlier Schöpflin, a political formation whose ideology is "democratic in form and nationalist in content."[120]

Thus far the Orbán-led drive to unify (read *include*) the right under FIDESZ's banner has met with relatively little success. Only some insignificant parties—the Hungarian Christian-Democratic Alliance, the pro-FIDESZ Romany Lungo Drom organization, and the party's own youth organization, Fidelitas—have responded to his appeal and ran jointly in the June 2004 European Parliament elections.[121] In fact, his attempt to have the cake and eat it too has had the opposite effect than expected: parliamentary party allies such as the MDF are beginning to be wary of Orbán and to occasionally distance themselves from his positions. On the other hand, on the overtly extreme right end of the political spectrum, the effort has prompted the establishment of at least one new political party that perceives Orbán as a Janus-faced politician. This is the *Jobbik Magyarországért Mozgalom* (Movement for Hungarian right—a name construction rendering both senses of the word "right" in the Hungarian language). Its chairman, Dávid (sic!) Kovács, said that the party shares with FIDESZ the goal of unseating the current government, but the nationalist rhetoric of Viktor Orbán is not sufficiently accompanied by deeds. Furthermore, according to Kovács, the movement's ideology calls for the unification of all nationalist Christian forces rather than being *polgári,* as FIDESZ's is.[122]

The new movement immediately acted to capture attention. In November 2003 it staged a demonstration outside the Hungarian Television (MTV) protesting against a recent cancellation of the *Éjjeli menedék* (Night shelter) program. That program had been pulled off the air after airing British Holocaust-denier David Irving's long-known version of the 1956 Revolution: the revolution had started off as an anti-Jewish uprising. *Éjjeli menedék,* known for its editors' rightist sympathies, also broadcast the speech on this theme, which Irving had earlier delivered at a MIÉP rally in Budapest.[123] At that rally, Tamás Molnár, deputy chairman of *Jobbik Magyarországért Mozgalom,* called on participants to oust the media liberals, who "represent foreign interests, lisp, and are alien-hearted people." Addressing the same crowd, the movement's deputy chairman Ervin Nagy lamented that nationalists in Hungary had only one TV program—the *Éjjeli menedék.*[124]

The Movement for Hungarian Right was not alone in protesting the elimination of *Éjjeli menedék*. Upon learning about the move, FIDESZ issued a statement saying that the MSzP-SzDSz coalition was ruthlessly attempting to stifle any opinion that differs from its own.[125] The next day Orbán called on *polgári* groups to come to the defense of the program's editor, and on November 2 he stated that it was worrisome that programs representing *polgári* or Christian values are under repeated harassment.[126] Irving, for one, remained unimpressed, declaring that he was by now accustomed to being attacked for his ideas, particularly by Jewish intellectuals, such as Hungarian-born Arthur Koestler. His statement (of course) was made on *Vasárnapi òjság* (Sunday news).[127]

The new Hungarian government had shown determination to end such manifestations as early as April 2003. An exhibition titled "Soldiers of Miklós Horthy—Arrow Cross People of Ferenc Szálasi" was opened at the Jurisich chateau in the western Hungarian town of Kőszeg on March 19. Glorifying the deeds of the two regimes, the exhibition made no mention of their crimes or victims. Its director, Kornél Bakay, had been a MIÉP candidate in the last elections. It was closed down in April, following MAZSIHISZ protests and considerable pressure applied from Budapest on the local authorities.[128] A text among the exhibits had explained to visitors that "The Hungaranist Movement is not identical with Italian Fascism or with the German National Socialism. The Hungarian Arrow Cross supported neither a totalitarian state, nor racial superiority. On the contrary, they were the determined enemies of Bolshevism and international capitalists."[129] This quote brings us right back where we started—namely at "symbolic history" and the "clash of memories." There is no reason to believe that people like Bakay can ever be convinced they are wrong and wrong-doing. There is no way a dialogue can be established with the likes of Csurka. That would be a waste of time and energy. Mutual anathematizing is likely to go on between "them" and "us."

But there is also no reason for a war to be endlessly waged between "memories" when it comes to the clash between Jewish and Hungarian memory writ large. Residual mutual perceptions are not necessarily *eternal* mutual perceptions. In the likely scenario of a return to power of the FIDESZ conservatives, it might take a serious effort at both ends to mend the damage. On FIDESZ's side, this would entail ridding the party of its deeply-rooted belief in an international Jewish conspiracy directed against the Hungarian nation. It would also entail a considerably larger dose of sensitivity towards handling the affairs of public space. But above all, it would entail renouncing inclusionist policies, which also means renouncing the neo-Zhdanovist division of the world into two irreconcilable camps. In domestic politics, FIDESZ must somehow be able to return to the politics of compromise, and this has little to do with handling the Holocaust. In foreign policy, it might have to be less supportive of Hungarian extremists in neighboring countries. And that has even less in common with handling the memory of the Holocaust.

But some of this applies to Hungarian Jews as well. They must understand that the other side also has a right to memory and that the two memories cannot always coincide. They must, above all, understand that the Gulag has a right to its own, separate memory. And it might be wise to publicly acknowledge that right and partake in its observation. Somehow, Hungary's Jewish community must also understand that its association with, or support of the MSzP, will be resented by many among Hungarian society for as long as people like Gyula Horn, a former member of the post-1956 Communist *pufajkás* vigilante squads are in power.[130] Horn's sidelining has helped, as has the recent decision of the cabinet headed by the young (and therefore—unlike his predecessor—untainted by a Communist past or suspicion of having been an informer) Premier Ferenc Gyurcsány to finally open the files of the Hungarian secret police.[131] The reconciliation process might take no more than one generation, perhaps even less. "Symbolic history" is not necessarily an either-or option, as the compromise reached at the end over the Teleki monument shows.[132]

Reconciliation will not be easy. There is nothing new about that on the Jewish side. But let us face it: it's not easy to be Hungarian either!

Notes

1. See Timothy Garton Ash, *The Magic Lantern: The Revolution of '89 Witnessed in Warsaw, Budapest, Berlin and Prague* (New York: Vintage Books, 1999), 156

2. Rudolf Tőkés, *Hungary's Negotiated Revolution: Economic Reform, Social Change and Political Succession* (Cambridge: Cambridge University Press, 1996).

3. See Miklós Haraszti, "The Handshake Tradition: A Decade of Consensus Politics Bears Liberal Fruit in Hungary—But What Next?" in *Between Past and Future: The Revolutions of 1989 and Their Aftermath*, eds. Sorin Antohi and Vladimir Tismaneanu (Budapest: Central European University Press, 2000), 272–79.

4. See Tőkés, 304–60.

5. Andrei Pippidi, *Despre statui și morminte: Pentru o teorie a istoriei simbolice* (On statues and tombs: Towards a theory of historic symbols) (Iasi: Polirom, 2000).

6. *Magyar Hírlap, Népszabadság, Magyar Nemzet,* February 13, 14, and 24, 2004; *Népszava,* February 13 and 14; and Agence France Presse (AFP), February 14, 2004.

7. *Magyar Hírlap, Népszabadság, Magyar Nemzet, Népszava,* and Associated Press (AP), February 14, 2004.

8. AP, February 16, 2004; Reuters, February 26, 2004.

9. See Paul Lendvai, *Ungurii* (The Hungarians) (Bucharest: Humanitas, 1999), 395. The English version is *The Hungarians: A Thousand Years of Victory in Defeat* (London: Hurst & Co., 2003).

10. Anyone with one parent born into the Jewish faith was to be considered a Jew. Andrew G. Janos, *The Politics of Backwardness in Hungary 1825–1945* (Princeton, NJ: Princeton University Press, 1982), 302

11. Ibid., xxxv, 300, 307.

12. *RFE/RL* (Radio Free Europe/Radio Liberty) *Newsline,* December 29, 2000.

13. Timothy Garton Ash, *History of the Present: Essays, Sketches and Despatches from Europe in the 1990s* (New York: Random House, 2000), 41.

14. Philip E. Converse, "The Nature of Belief Systems in Mass Publics," in *Ideology and Discontent,* ed. David E. Apter (New York: Free Press, 1964), 206–61.

15. Cited in Yehuda Bauer, *Rethinking the Holocaust* (New Haven: Yale University Press, 2001), 2.

16. András Kovács, "Antisemitic Discourse in Post-Communist Hungary, 1990–1994," in *Jews and Antisemitism in the Public Discourse of the Post-Communist European Countries,* ed. Leon Volovici (Lincoln, NE, and Jerusalem: University of Nebraska Press, and The Vidal Sassoon International Center for the Study of Anti-Semitism, forthcoming).

17. George Schöpflin, *Nations, Identity, Power* (London: Hurst and Company, 2000), 74.

18. Benedict Anderson, *Imagined Communities: Reflections on the Origins and Spread of Nationalism* (London: Verso, 1991).

19. Jacques Rupnik, "Revoluflie—restauraflie" (Revolution—restoration), in *Lettre internationale* (Romanian edition) 4 (Winter 1992/1993): 4.

20. Schöpflin, *Nations, Identity, Power,* 77–78.

21. Since there is no significant discontinuity between the cabinet headed by Antall and the short-lived cabinet lead by his successor Péter Boross, I choose to discuss policies towards the legacy of the Holocaust as being part of a single unity

22. For various reasons I am leaving out of consideration the first MSzP-SzDSz 1994–1998 coalition, but will refer to its impact whenever relevant.

23. Tőkés, 365–66.

24. Ibid., 365.

25. István Deák, "Anti-Semitism and the Treatment of the Holocaust in Hungary," in *Anti-Semitism and the Treatment of the Holocaust in Postcommunist Eastern Europe,* ed. Randolph L. Braham (New York: Columbia University Press, 1994), 99–124.

26. *Magyar Távirati Iroda* (Hungarian press agency), August 13, 1990. As George Schöpflin observes, the figure of fifteen million is, in fact, a Hungarian national myth. The country's population is 10.4 million, but over 500,000 are not ethnic Magyars, but members of national minorities. "Even if one includes Hungarian in the diaspora, in North America

and Western Europe, it is difficult to arrive at a figure of 15 million." Schöpflin, *Nations, Identity, Power*, 371n.

27. László Karsai, "The Radical Right in Hungary," in *The Radical Right in Central and Eastern Europe Since 1989*, ed. Sabrina P. Ramet (University Park: The Pennsylvania State University Press, 1999), 139.

28. Cited in Kovács, "Antisemitic Discourse," forthcoming.

29. On "Holocaust trivialization" see Michael Shafir, "Between Denial and 'Comparative Trivialization': Holocaust Negationism in Post-Communist East Central Europe," in *ACTA (Analysis of Current Trends in Anti-Semitism)* 19 (Jerusalem: The Vidal Sassoon International Center for the Study of Anti-Semitism, The Hebrew University of Jerusalem, 2002); and *Între negare øi trivializare prin comparaflie: Negarea Holocaustului în flările postcomuniste din Europa Centralœ øi de Est* (Between denial and comparative trivialization: Holocaust negation in post-Communist East Central Europe) (Iaşi: Polirom, 2002).

30. Cited in Ivan T. Berend, *"Jobbra át!* (Right Face!): Right-Wing Trends in Post-Communist Hungary," in *Democracy and Right-Wing Politics in Eastern Europe in the 1990s*, ed. Joseph Held (Boulder: East European Monographs, 1993), 122.

31. Ibid., 123.

32. These were in Zebegény, Debrecen, and Nagykainza. AP, June 4, 2000; and *RFE/RL Newsline*, August 9, 2001; AP, August 12, 2001; and *Magyar Hírlap, Népszabadság, Magyar Nemzet*, August 13, 2001.

33. Cited in Randolph L. Braham, "The Reinterment and Political Rehabilitation of Miklós Horthy," in *Slavic Almanach*, vol. 2, eds. H. Mondry and P. Schveiger (Johannesburg: University of the Witwatersrand, 1993), 140.

34. See Katherine Verdery, *The Political Lives of Dead Bodies: Reburial and Post-socialist Change* (New York: Columbia University Press, 1999), 16–17.

35. Cited in ibid., 133.

36. István Deák, "A Fatal Compromise? The Debate over Collaboration and Resistance in Hungary," in *The Politics of Retribution in Europe*, eds. István Deák, Jan T. Gross, and Tony Judt (Princeton, NJ: Princeton University Press, 2000), 55–56.

37. Randolph L. Braham, "Assault on Historical Memory: Hungarian Nationalists and the Holocaust," in Randolph L. Braham, *Studies on the Holocaust: Selected Writings* (New York: Columbia University Press, 2001), II, 198.

38. Karsai, 234.

39. Braham, "Assault on Historical Memory," 199.

40. Ibid., 213–14, and 218n.; and Karsai, 234.

41. Berend, 132.

42. Janos, 292–93.

43. James F. Brown, *Hopes and Shadows: Eastern Europe After Communism* (Durham: Duke University Press, 1994), 88.

44. Janos, 225.

45. James F. Brown, "A Challenge to Political Values," in *RFE/RL Research Report* 1:40 (1992): 23–25.

46. Cited in ibid., 23.

47. Berend, 132.

48. Cited in Deák, "Anti-Semitism and the Treatment of the Holocaust in Hungary," 114–15.

49. Cited in Vladimir Tismaneanu, *Fantasies of Salvation: Democracy, Nationalism and Myth in Post-Communist Europe* (Princeton, NJ: Princeton University Press, 1999), 42.

50. Michael Waller, "Adaptation of the Former Communist Parties of East-Central Europe: A Case of Social-Democratization?" *Party Politics* 1:4 (1995): 481–82.

51. Braham, "Assault on Historical Memory," 198.

52. Deák, "Anti-Semitism and the Treatment of the Holocaust in Hungary," 111.

53. Tony Judt, "The Past is Another Country: Myth and Memory in Postwar Europe," in *The Politics of Retribution*, 309.

54. Kovács, "Antisemitic Discourse," forthcoming.

55. The KDNP won twenty-one seats in the 1990 elections and joined the Antall-led coalition. In 1994 it captured twenty-two seats and the party went into opposition. Most members wanted to create a bloc with FIDESZ and the MDF, but a substantial part of rank-and-file membership sought to involve the extremist MIŽP as well. As a result, the center-right group split off from the KDNP, forming the Christian Democratic Union, which then joined FIDESZ. The KDNP failed to enter parliament in 1998 and disappeared from the parliamentary scene. See Janusz Bugajski, *Political Parties of Eastern Europe: A Guide to Politics in the Post-Communist Era* (Armonk, NY: M. E. Sharpe, 2002), 357–58.

56. Kovács, "Antisemitic Discourse," forthcoming.

57. Csurka admits that he had been coerced into signing a statement agreeing to act as an informer for the secret services, but claims his reports never harmed anyone. See Edith Oltay, "Hungary," in "The Politics of Intolerance," *RFE/RL Research Report* 3:16 (1994): 59; and Karsai, 145. Antall produced evidence showing that the FKGP leader (a flourishing lawyer under the previous regime) had intimate relations with the secret services (Oltay, 59; and Karsai, 145). In November 1995, SzDSz leader Gábor Kuncze, who was interior minister in the cabinet of Gyula Horn, sent a document—which seemed to indicate that Torgyán had indeed been a collaborator of the AVH—to the lustration panel of judges that examines the past of all parliamentary members. In August 1998, however, the panel determined that the AVH had threatened and repeatedly tried to recruit Torgyán in 1957 and that, although he managed to avoid collaboration, the AVH registered him as a secret agent under a code name. Having secured a false diagnosis, Torgyán subsequently spent some time in a psychiatric institute in an attempt to fend off further harassment by the secret police, the panel said, concluding that his name had been removed from the register in May 1958. Some three weeks before the panel made public the results of its inquiry, several former members of Torgyán's party told reporters that the FKGP leader's code name in the files of the former secret police had been Lajos Szatmári, and that the information had been provided to the FKGP by Antall, who was by now dead (*RFE/RL Newsline*, 27 June and 15 August 1997; see also Tökés, 395).

58. Tökés, 420, 425.

59. See Tökés, 409, 428; Schöpflin, *Nations, Identity, Power*, 85, 372; and András Bozóki, "The Hungarian Socialists: Technocratic Modernization or New Social Democracy?" in *The Communist Successor Parties of Central and Eastern Europe*, eds. András Bozóki and John T. Ishiyama (Armonk, NY: M. E. Sharpe, 2002), 100.

60. Csilla Kiss, "From Liberalism to Conservatism: The Federation of Young Democrats in Post-Communist Hungary," in *East European Politics and Society* 16:3 (2002): 740–41.

61. Tökés, 330; and Ash, *The Magic Lantern*, 51.

62. Máte Szabó, "Adaptation and Resistance: Institutionalization of Protest Movement (1999–1994)," in *Democratic Legitimacy in Post-Communist Societies*, ed. András Bozóki (Budapest: T-Twins Publishers in cooperation with the International Center at the Tübingen University, 1994), 143.

63. Jeffrey Stevenson Murer, "Challenging Expectations: A Comparative Study of the Communist Successor Parties of Hungary, Bulgaria and Romania," in *Communist Successor Parties in Post-Communist Politics*, ed. John T. Ishiyama (Huntington, NY: Nova Science Publishers, 1999), 194.

64. Szabó, 143.

65. Kovács, "Jewish Assimilation," 116.

66. Kiss, 745.

67. Cited in Judith Pataki, "Hungary: Young Democrats Prepare for 1994 Elections," *RFE/RL Research Report* 1:12 (1992): 9.

68. Michael Waller, "Party Inheritance and Party Identities," in *Stabilising Fragile Democracies: Comparing New Party Systems in Southern and Eastern Europe*, eds. Geoffrey Pridham and Paul G. Lewis (London: Routledge, 1996), 40.

69. Szabó, 143.

70. Kiss, 743; and Szabó, 143–44.

71. Judith Pataki, "Hungary's Leading Opposition Party Torn by Dissension," *RFE/RL Research Report* 2:50 (1993): 25 (emphasis added).

72. Ibid., 25.

73. For the electoral outcome, see Bugajski, *Political Parties of Eastern Europe*, 374.

74. Kiss, 745.

75. Ken Jowitt, *New World Disorder: The Leninist Extinction* (Berkeley: University of California Press, 1992), 91.

76. See Tökés, 196–200.

77. See Klara Kingston, "The Hungarian Status Law," *East European Perspectives* 3:17 (2001), at http://www.rferl.org/eepreport/.

78. Cited in Michael Shafir, "Hungarian 'Bundism': Can It Work?" *RFE/RL Newsline*, September 1, 1999.

79. Schöpflin, *Nations, Identity, Power*, 373.

80. Michael Shafir, "Varieties of Antisemitism in Post-Communist East-Central Europe: Motivations and Political Discourse," *Jewish Studies at the CEU* 3, forthcoming.

81. Kiss, 757.

82. George Schöpflin, "Hungary's Elections: The Dilemma of the Right," *RFE/RL Newsline*, April 29, 1998.

83. See George Schöpflin, "The Hungarian Elections and Beyond," *RFE/RL's Newsline*, April 24, 2002; "New-Old Hungary: A Contested Transformation," *East European Perspectives* 4:10 (2002), at http://www.rferl.org/eepreport/; and "Western Media, Image making and Hungary," *RFE/RL's Newsline*, February 21, 2002.

84. Braham, "Assault on Historical Memory," 207.

85. *RFE/RL Newsline*, September 9 and 10, 1999.

86. Ibid., October 28, 1999; and Braham, "Assault on Historical Memory," 212–13.

87. *Magyar Hírlap*, November 12, 1999; and *Napi Magyarország*, November 13, 1999, both cited in *Antiszemita Kšzbeszéd Magyarországon 2000-ben* (Anti-Semitic discourse in Hungary in 2000), eds. András Gerî, László Varga, and Mátyás Vince (Budapest: B'nai B'rith Elsî Budapesti Kšzšsség, 2001), 213, 153, respectively; see also Braham, "Assault on Historical Memory," 210.

88. *RFE/RL Newsline*, November 16, 1999.

89. Michael J. Jordan, "Terror Museum in Budapest Frightens some Hungarian Jews," Jewish Telegraph Agency, July 21, 2002.

90. See Alan S. Rosenbaum, "Introduction," in Alan S. Rosenbaum, *Is the Holocaust Unique? Perspectives on Comparative Genocide* (Boulder, CO: Westview Press, 1996), 2; and Vladimr Tismaneanu, "Communism and the Human Condition: Reflections on the Black Book of Communism," *Human Rights Review* 2:2, 125–34.

91. See for example, André Gerrits, "'Jewish Communism' in East Central Europe: Myth Versus Reality," in *Vampires Unstaked: National Images, Stereotypes and Myths in East Central Europe*, eds. André Gerrits and Nancy Adler (Amsterdam: Royal Netherlands Academy of Arts and Sciences, 1995), 159–77; Victor Karádi, "Les Juifs et la violence stalinienne," *Actes de la Recherche en Sciences Sociales* 120 (December 1997): 3–31; and Stanisław Krajewski, "Jews, Communism and the Jewish Communists," in *Jewish Studies at the Central European University: Public Lectures 1996–1999* (Budapest: Central European University, 1999), 115–30.

92. See Shafir, "Between Denial and 'Comparative Trivialization'," 60–75; and *Între negare şi trivializare prin comparaţie*, 105–32.

93. Braham, "Assault on Historical Memory," 208.

94. Leon Volovici, "Antisemitism in Post-Communist Eastern Europe: A Marginal or Central Issue?" in *ACTA (Analysis of Current Trends in Antisemitism)*, No. 5 (Jerusalem: The Vidal Sassoon International Center for the Study of Antisemitism, The Hebrew University of Jerusalem, 1994), 16–17.

95. Interview with Csurka on Hungarian Television 2 in *BBC Summary of World Broadcasts-Eastern Europe*, November 19, 1999; and *RFE/RL Newsline*, January 17, 2001.

96. Murer, 203n.

97. See *RFE/RL Newsline*, September 21, 2001.

98. Cited in Gábor Schweitzer, "'Exclude Them, Or If You Don't...'," in *Antiszemita Közbeszéd Magyarországon 2001-ben: Jelentés és dokumentáció* (Anti-Semitic discourse in Hungary in 2001: Report and documentation), eds. András Gerö, László Varga, and Mátyás Vince (Budapest: B'nai B'rith Elsî Budapesti Kšzšsség, 2002), 227–28 (emphasis in Hegedüs's original).

99. Personal communication from Hungarian friend who asked to remain anonymous.

100. *Magyar Hírlap* and *Népszabadág*, November 29 and 30, 2001, December 10, and 19, 2001, June 17, 2002, December 7, 2002, and November 7, 2003; *RFE/RL Newsline*, November 29 and 30, 2001, December 10, and 19, 2001, June 17, 2002, December 9, 2002, and November 9, 2003. Hegedüs was charged with incitement, after having voluntarily renounced his parliamentary immunity, and received a suspended sentence of eighteen months in December 2002. On appeal, however, the sentence was quashed on grounds that his article did not represent incitement.

101. Eric Beckett Weaver, "Hungary's Politics of Disappointment" (2003), unpublished, cited with permission.

102. *Magyar Hírlap* and *Népszabadság*, November 29, 2001, and December 7, 2002.

103. *Magyar Hírlap*, November 15, 2001; *Népszabadság*, January 11, 2002, July 19, 2002; *RFE/RL Newsline*, November 15, 2001; July 19, 2002; Reuters, February 19, 2002; *Antiszemita Kšzbeszéd Magyarországon 2001-ben*, 323.

104. *RFE/RL Newsline*, July 29, 2002.

105. *Magyar Hírlap* and *Magyar Nemzet*, December 7, 2003; *RFE/RL Newsline*, December 9, 2003.

106. *Antiszemita Kšzbeszéd Magyarországon 2000-ben,* 188n.

107. Is Lovás a case of the self-hating Jew? He also happens to be a former colleague of mine at Radio Free Europe/Radio Liberty.

108. All citations from the station's broadcasts in *Antiszemita Kšzbeszéd Magyaror-szágon 2000-ben,* 169–72.

109. *Népszabadság,* May 15, 2003.

110. *RFE/RL Newsline,* January 30, 2002.

111. Ibid., April 11, 2001.

112. *Népszabadság, Magyar Hírlap, Magyar Nemzet,* and *RFE/RL Newsline,* November 5, 2001.

113. Miklós Harászti, "The Gulf That Must Be Bridged, Even If The Other Side Does Not Reach Out," *Budapest Business Journal,* April 29, 2002.

114. See Bugajsli, 374; *Népszabadság, Magyar Hírlap, Magyar Nemzet,* April 8, 2002.

115. See Harászti, "The Gulf."

116. *Magyar Nemzet,* April 22, 2002.

117. Mediafax, June 7, 2003.

118. Kossuth Radio, November 30, 2003, BBC Monitoring.

119. Schöpflin, "New-Old Hungary."

120. George Schöpflin, "Rumanian Nationalism," *Survey* 2–3 (1974): 77–104.

121. Anthropologist Livia Jaroka managed to be elected on the FIDESZ lists, becoming the first Romany deputy elected to the European parliament. (See AFP, June 13, 2004.) FIDESZ gained twelve out of the twenty-four seats, followed by the MSzP (nine seats) and the MDF (one seat). With turnout at a record low of 38.47 percent, it is unclear what significance this election has for the 2006 elections.

122. *Népszabadság, Magyar Hírlap,* and *Magyar Nemzet,* October 27, 2003.

123. *Népszabadság* and *Magyar Hírlap,* October 30, 2003.

124. *RFE/RL Newsline,* November 10, 2003.

125. *Magyar Nemzet,* October 30, 2003.

126. Ibid., and *Népszabadság,* November 3, 2003.

127. *Népszava,* November 3, 2003. Koestler died in 1983 so these "attacks" must have been fairly old. There is no mention of Irving in David Cesarani's detailed biography, *Arthur Koestler: The Homeless Mind* (New York: The Free Press, 1998).

128. See *RFE/RL Newsline,* April 10, 16, 17, and 18, 2003.

129. *Népszabadság,* April 2, 2003.

130. See Tökés, 419.

131. See AFP, December 8, 2004; and *The New York Times,* December 19, 2004.

132. See Attila Pók, "Why Was There No *Historikerstreit* in Post-Communist Hungary?" elsewhere in this volume.

Transylvanian Jewry during the Postwar Period, 1945–1948

Zoltán Tibori Szabó

Forced Labor, Deportations, and the Victims

According to the census figures, 183,000 inhabitants of the Jewish religion in 1910, and 192,000 in 1930,[1] lived on the territory of present-day Transylvania.[2]

As a result of the Second Vienna Award on August 30, 1940, the northwestern part of Transylvania—an area of 43,000 square kilometers with 2.5 million inhabitants—was re-annexed by Hungary. The 1941 census organized by the Hungarian regime in this region counted more than 151,000 inhabitants of the Jewish religion and in that year 41,000 Jews lived in the southern part of Transylvania and in the Banat.[3] In both areas, Christians of Jewish origin were also persecuted.[4] If these latter are included, at the time of the Second Vienna Award, Northern Transylvanian Jewry numbered 164,000,[5] and that of Southern Transylvania 42,000.

Consequently, on the territory of Transylvania in the period before the Holocaust there were at least 192,000 and perhaps as many as 206,000 inhabitants who were considered Jews under the racist legislation of the period.

As early as the autumn of 1940 and continuing the following year, the Jewish community of Northern Transylvania lost several thousand people as a result of deportations. The start of the forced labor programs in 1942 and the 1944 deportations to the German death camps dramatically decreased the number of persons in the Jewish community.

In September 1945 the number of Jews on the territory of Northern Transylvania numbered between 23,000 and 30,000.[6] This includes the Jews who actually returned home from labor service and the camps and those who moved from Southern Transylvania and other parts of Romania, as well as those who fled from Bucovina and Bessarabia. Not included in these figures are the approximately 8,000 to 10,000 people who had survived the death camps and gone directly to Western countries.

On May 6, 1946, the Nationality Department of the Police Director- ate in the Romanian Ministry of Home Affairs prepared a report regard- ing the balance between the number of deported and returned Jews.[7] According to this report, an overall number of 127,377 persons were deported, of whom only 19,764 had returned by May 1946. Hence, the number of those who did not return was 107,613. The reliability of these data is questionable due to an inconsistency regarding the number of Jews deported from Maramures (Máramaros in Hungarian) County: according to the report, 8,500 Maramures Jews were deported, while according to the Kassa (Košice) register, nearly 33,600 Jews were trans- ported to Auschwitz from Maramures County.

An account prepared by the World Jewish Congress in January 1947 estimated that approximately 44,706 Jews lived in Northern Tran- sylvania at that time, while the religious communities of Southern Transylvania and Banat reported a total of 45,738 Jews.[8]

Thus, an accurate estimate of the number of victims is still to be achieved. Circumstances that make this assessment even more difficult are as follows: the lack of reliable registries, the still unmapped postwar movement of the population within Transylvania, the incomplete infor- mation concerning those foreign refugees who fled to Palestine through Romania, and the fact that there are no accurate data regarding the Tran- sylvanian Jews who emigrated from the country.

Nevertheless, we know that between 1942 and 1944 as many as 15,000 Northern Transylvanian Jewish men were taken to forced labor camps, and that, according to the Kassa (Košice) railway commandant's annotations in May and June 1944, nearly 134,000 persons were deported to Auschwitz from Northern Transylvania.[9]

Based on professional and judicious scholarly studies that have managed to avoid the obstacles of speculative data, we can say that the number of Northern Transylvanian Jewish survivors is between 35,000 and 40,000.[10]

Jews were also deported from Southern Transylvania and sent to Transnistria by Romanian authorities in 1942. Very few of them made it back to their homeland. According to statistics provided by the press reports of the time, the number of victims was one thousand at most.[11] After Romanian authorities ended the "Final Solution" program (which resulted in more than 270,000 victims) and made emigration to Palestine possible, between 1943 and 1944 approximately 7,000 Jewish refugees from Northern Transylvania, Hungary, and other countries fled to Romania. Most of them headed to Bucharest, and then on to Constanţa en route to Palestine. A few hundred of them, however, found temporary refuge in Southern Transylvania.[12] As a result, in Southern Transylvania approximately 40,000 Jews survived the deportations.

It follows that approximately 85,000 to 90,000 Transylvanian Jews survived the Holocaust if one includes those who were able to escape to Western countries. Thus the overall number of Transylvanian victims is close to 120,000. Three quarters of Northern Transylvanian Jewry and two thirds of the entire Jewish Transylvanian population were exterminated.[13]

Homecoming and the Reorganization of Community Life

Some of the Jewish men who survived the forced labor camps returned with the Soviet Army. The survivors of the death camps, however, were obliged to wait longer for their return—most of them were released only in the summer of 1945 or later. After coming home, many of them found it difficult to find a place to live[14] and the majority came back exhausted and suffering from various illnesses.[15] The persecution, torture, and familial destruction endured by these persons had ultimately weakened their psychological and physical condition. As a result, the first community institutions created were hospitals and canteens.

The Transylvanian media began dealing with the tragedy of Transylvanian Jewry as early as the autumn of 1944.[16] It can be seen from these early articles that the authors were unaware of the fact that the Jewish population was deported not to regular concentration camps, but to death camps. Nor did the leaders of the Democratic Jewish People's Community (*Demokratikus Zsidó Népközösség* – DJPC), formed in October 1944, know about the scale of the deaths. Although those who returned from the death camps in February 1945 related the circumstances, neither the media, nor the DJPC leaders paid any further attention to their accounts.[17]

On November 19, 1944, the Romanian Division of the World Jewish Congress (WJC) completed its report on the situation emphasizing the assessment of the survivor numbers. The results were published in two separate volumes in 1945 and in 1947. In November 1944 the American Jewish Joint Distribution Committee (the Joint), the Jewish Agency, and the Bucharest branch office of the International Committee of the Red Cross formed a commission, headed by the former editor of the Cluj-based *Új Kelet* (New East) daily newspaper, to visit Northern Transylvania. The purpose of this visit was twofold: to evaluate the number of survivors and to ascertain what measures needed to be taken. According to the WJC report, the delegation found 7,200 Jews living in Northern Transylvania.[18]

Gradually, the Jewish communities in the area came back to life: Jewish hospitals were re-established and the returning refugees were placed in housing centers run by various organizations.[19] On November 26, 1944, the Central Orthodox Office of the Transylvanian and Banat Jewish Communities (*Erdélyi és Bánsági Központi Ortodox Iroda*) was formed. The Neolog (Conservative) communities later established the Association of Jewish Communities of the Western (Neolog) Rite (*Nyugati Szertartású [Neológ] Izraelita Hitközségek Szövetsége*). Through these organizations Transylvanian Jewry was supposed to join the United Federation of Jewish Communities in Romania (*Federaţia Uniunilor de Comunităţi Evreieşti din România*).

The Northern Transylvanian Jewish communities encountered difficulties resulting from the lack of rabbis, cantors, and mohels. According to some reports, over seventy rabbis from the region were exterminated during the Holocaust.[20] The new regime was eager both to draw the communities under the influence and control of the Communist Party and to diminish their spiritual essence and functions. The emergence of the Communist ideology and the lack of charismatic, highly regarded religious leaders made this a relatively easy task.[21]

Between November 14, 1944, and March 9, 1945, Northern Transylvania enjoyed administrative independence. Since the future affiliation of Transylvania was still uncertain, the provisional leaders—both Romanians and Hungarians—tried to tilt the balance in their own interests by convincing the Jewish survivors to support them. The Romanians hoped that as a result of the atrocities suffered during the Holocaust, Transylvanian Jewry—Hungarian by mother tongue and culture—would be totally and forever disillusioned with the Hungarian regime. Also, since a number of Jews had already sympathized with left-wing principles between the two World Wars, Romanian leaders believed that they could draw them in as well.

Jewish survivors faced great difficulties in getting back their houses and only in special cases did they retrieve some of their movable goods (mostly furniture). In the spring of 1945 the trade unions and the Association for the Protection of People (*Népvédelmi Egyesület*) had proposed a solution according to which help for the survivors would be provided from the assets of leaders and followers of the former Fascist regime.[22] The restitution of the real estate and other immovable goods was hindered by the fact that many houses had been destroyed during the war, and their inhabitants moved by the authorities into Jewish dwellings. Movable goods of great value were appropriated by Hungarian and German military officers, civil servants, and clerks; the remaining goods were taken by the local population; and Jewish furniture was pilfered by the Soviets as well.[23] But the left-wing forces that came to power urged the Jews to have patience. Furthermore, fear of a renewal of anti-Semitism caused Jewish leaders to discourage requests for restitution.

A few Jews served in the provisional administrative agencies in postwar Transylvania, which made the representation of Jewish interests in general somewhat easier there. For instance, the city council of Cluj (Kolozsvár) formed on October 13, 1944, had seventeen Romanian, eleven Hungarian, and one Jewish member. [24] On October 21, also in Cluj (Kolozsvár), the Democratic Council of Northern Transylvania (*Észak-Erdélyi Demokratikus Bizottság*) was formed, with the express purpose of promoting the peaceful cohabitation of Romanians, Hungarians, and Jews. The organizations represented on the Council were the Northern Transylvanian Communist Party (*Kommunisták Észak-Erdélyi Pártja*), the Social Democrats of Cluj, the Alliance of Hungarian Workers (*Magyar Dolgozók Szövetsége* – MADOSZ), the Ploughmen's Front (*Ekésfront - Frontul Plugarilor*), the DJPC, and the united trade union representatives.[25]

In the larger cities of Transylvania, the DJPC was formed immediately after the entry of the Soviet Army. The DJPC's policy called for it to establish a new social and political order in cooperation with Romanian and Hungarian democratic forces. Its leaders believed that the Jewish population had experienced the greatest sufferings of the war, but stipulated that "individual revenge is not the goal of the Jews." At the same time, they argued that "the leaders of the anti-Jewish actions have to be punished," the ownership rights and the rule of law had to be reinforced, Jewry had to be compensated, and its integration in the country's industry and commerce had to be pursued within the limits of the national economic program. Moreover, they expressed their aim to undertake measures for the return of the deported. They requested the Allied governments to exercise influence on the Romanian government to insist that the deported persons be sent back from Germany, and, should the request be rejected, to order arrests and internment of Romanians of Saxon and Swabian heritage for as long as the German authorities refused to repatriate those Jews still in Germany.[26]

In February 1945 the DJPC held a meeting in Cluj (Kolozsvár) to create a program for the return of the deported, and requested material and moral support for implementing this program. The organization demanded that the Soviets take "serious and effective measures" to bring home the deported "from the already liberated territories." The left-wing parties, which had been consolidated into the National Democratic Front (*Frontul Naţional Democrat* – NDF, in Romanian; *Országos Demokrata Arcvonal* – ODA, in Hungarian), wanted to give credit for the return of the survivors to the Communist Party (CP). According to Miklós Goldberger, the Northern Transylvanian activist of the CP Central Committee, the return of the deported was an important item on the NDF's agenda; in return, Jewry had an obligation to support the NDF.[27]

On March 6, 1945, the pro-Communist government led by Petru Groza came to power, in part through the electoral success of the NDF. The DJPC held its Northern Transylvanian conference in Cluj the same week. It made a decision to organize aid expeditions in order to locate the persons who were trying to return from the liberated territories, to provide them with on-the-spot medical aid, and to transport them home. For this purpose the DJPC requested "more effective support" from the Romanian, Soviet, and Polish governments, which had not been providing it in substantial amounts. In the beginning, the aid expeditions planned automobile caravans "for the immediate aid of the elderly, the sick and children"; it was apparent that the reality of the death camps remained as yet a blurred concept. Later the DJPC asked for special trains for the transportation of survivors. The conference adopted decisions about preserving and maintaining the property of the deported, making arrangements for the reception of the returned, setting up housing centers and canteens, and measures regarding the founding of the Northern Transylvanian DJPC Central Office in Cluj (Kolozsvár).[28]

In March 1945 the Romanian government made trains available for the return of the survivors. Beginning on March 25 and continuing until the end of June, these trains circulated between Oradea (Nagyvárad in

Hungarian) and Krakow, and between Cluj and Prague.[29] The majority of the deported came back either within this period or in a second larger wave in the summer and autumn of 1945. In the summer of 1945, *Deportált Híradó* (News of the deported) newspaper was set up based in Satu Mare (Szatmárnémeti in Hungarian) to provide information for this group.

New Waves of Anti-Semitism

The demands for the restitution of survivors' possessions generated conflicts between the Hungarian and the Jewish peoples. Immigration of Jews from Bukovina, Bessarabia, and Moldavia also caused much tension, some incidents of which ended with violence and casualties.[30]

At the beginning of October 1945, Vasile Luca, a member of the CP Central Committee, observed that "in Moldavia there is a growing anti-Semitic current" that "is no less important than the same trend in Transylvania." He believed that this phenomenon is caused by the fact that "the masses of people are poisoned with anti-Semitism." Luca, originally from the Sekler Land, insisted that the shirker, "reactionary" Jews should be organized into labor brigades and be marched to the coal mines of the Jiu Valley.[31]

At the end of October, Vasile Luca and another member of the Central Committee, Iosif Chişinevschi, presented the Party's opinion on the "Jewish question" at a meeting held in Bucharest. Luca said that the Party "is not against emigration." In his speech, Chişinevschi, a leading Communist of Jewish origins, attacked the "Jewish reaction" and its exponent, Wilhelm Filderman, the chairman of the Federation of Jewish Communities. He stigmatized those Jews who, according to him, "have not learned anything from the Jewish tragedy" and announced that "Jewish chauvinism is as dangerous as the Romanian-Hungarian or any other kind of chauvinism."[32]

To be sure, it was not only Communist leaders who saw things from an anti-Semitic point of view; hatred against Jews was deeply rooted in both the Romanian and Hungarian populations. This is evident from most of the contemporary police, gendarmerie, and security reports, though the authorities often camouflaged the inter-ethnic tensions by referring to them as "class struggles."[33]

The general economic difficulties, the lack of food, and the drought in 1946 also fostered the upsurge of anti-Semitism. In the same year, alarmist rumors started to surface according to which Jews who had lost their children in the death camps were kidnapping and murdering Hungarian children. The Jewish press categorically rejected the accusations, and said that the "Fascist provocation" must be eliminated through the endorsement of the "inter-ethnic people's democracy."[34]

Between 1945 and 1948 the Joint allocated tens of millions of U.S. dollars for the support of the impoverished Jewish population. In order to avoid trouble from the anti-Semites, Gentiles received Joint assistance as well. Even so, on February 18, 1949, the Communist Party expelled the Joint from Romania. Following that decision, many Jews left the country and emigrated to Palestine.[35]

Immigration, Emigration, and Internal Population Fluctuations

In the second half of 1945 and especially in 1946, many refugees from the Soviet regimes in Northern Bukovina and Bessarabia fled to Transylvania. They believed that it would be easier to emigrate to Palestine or to Western Europe through Hungary. Consequently, most of them rushed to the rapidly tightening border, by then almost completely closed, while a smaller number settled down in various regions of Transylvania.

In 1946 and 1947 Romanian police reports gradually drew attention to the presence of refugees from Bucovina and Bessarabia in the country.[36] In 1947 the majority of the Jews who wanted to escape to Hungary came from Moldavia, the eastern part of Romania. In April 1947, according to a report of the Oradea police, the number of Jews from Old Romania[37]—mainly from Moldavia and Bucharest—who tried to cross the border each day reached between one and two thousand.[38]

Several reports of the Romanian Secret Police in August 1947 make it clear that Jews from Roman, Galați, Tecuci, and other cities, after selling all their possessions in exchange for gold and foreign currencies, headed for Carei (Nagykároly in Hungarian) and other Partium cities near the border.[39]

The eagerness to emigrate surely inspired the Transylvanian Jews as well. In 1946 and 1947 the Transylvanian Jews, especially the young, were trying to reach the British-American occupied areas of Austria and Germany. The creation of the State of Israel in 1948 considerably increased the number of those who wished to emigrate.

The Jews who fled from Bucovina and Bessarabia informed those in Transylvania about the repressive character of the Soviet regime, thus intensifying their misgivings about communism. Security units recorded that Jews showed an "almost sick tendency to emigrate," not as much to Palestine, but to South America "from where they hope to enter the United States." According to some reports even the leaders of the Democratic Jewish Committee were planning to leave the country.[40]

The leading personalities of the Jewish communities were also making a case for emigration. One of the main reasons for that was the central authorities' decision on June 1, 1949, according to which all Orthodox, Neolog, Status Quo Ante, and Sephardic communities were unified under the "Mosaic faith" community controlled by the Communist Party. In the two years following the creation of the unified community, 80 percent of the Romanian rabbis and mohels emigrated to Palestine.[41]

Based on information from various sources on the population movements during the relevant period, several main population trends can be outlined:

1. People moved from Southern Transylvania and other parts of Old Romania to Northern Transylvanian cities. There is no information on the scale of this migration; however, according to circumstantial evidence and survivors' testimonies, the number of these migrants was no more than several thousand.

2. People fled Northern Bucovina and Bessarabia from the end of 1945 onwards following the Soviet accession to power. They went to almost every large city in Transylvania. Their overall number was no more than ten thousand and the majority emigrated legally or illegally in 1946 and 1947.

3. People came from Hungary and other Eastern European countries in the autumn of 1944 and in 1945. The majority of these headed to Bucharest in order to emigrate to Palestine, but some of them lived temporarily in Transylvania. Their number in February 1946 was approximately 20,000, of whom about 13,000 were from Hungary, 6,500 from Poland, and 1,000 from Austria, Germany, and Czechoslovakia.[42]

4. The Jews from Old Romania (especially from Moldavia and Bucharest) illegally escaped to Hungary through Northern Transylvania in the summer of 1946 and from there fled to the

British-American controlled areas. There are no available data on the accurate number of these migrants; however, it can be estimated that they were no less than ten thousand and no more than fifteen thousand. This information is confirmed by certain Zionist reports, according to which, between 1944 and 1948, 25,000 to 30,000 Jews had left the country illegally.[43]

5. Jews (approximately ten thousand) illegally emigrated from Transylvania to Hungary, and then to Western Europe, the United States, and Palestine between 1946 and 1948. This route was discontinued in 1948.

6. Survivors returned from the German death camps. According to community registries their number was estimated at 15,000 to 20,000. Among them were Jews from Hungary and Slovakia as well as Western-European (Dutch, French) Jews who could not return to their home countries because of the ongoing war. The Western European Jews also headed to Bucharest, but spent some time in the Northern Transylvanian housing centers where they could rest and heal.[44]

7. Some Transylvanian Jews moved to Bucharest (to further emigration efforts to Palestine or for other reasons) between 1944 and 1946. They accounted for no more than two or three thousand people.

In the summer of 1947 strict measures were adopted at the Romanian-Hungarian border. The frontier police were empowered to shoot without warning anyone who tried to cross the border illegally. The purpose of this measure was to put an end to the large-scale illegal trafficking of persons and goods across the border.

At the end of 1947, a few weeks before the deposal and expulsion of King Michael I, Romanian authorities authorized the departure to Palestine of 15,000 Jews, most of whom were foreign refugees. At the end of 1948, various Zionist organizations helped another 4,000 Jews to leave the country.[45] The following year, however, the Romanian government outlawed the Zionist organizations, confiscated their property, and imprisoned their leaders.

Consistent with the survey results of the Jewish communities, in 1948 there were 36,613 Jews in historic Transylvania, 12,453 in the Banat, and 27,709 in Partium and Maramures, a total of 76,815. To this number must be added another four to five thousand people, who dropped any connection with the Jewish religious community and chose the path of atheist communism. Hence, approximately 80,000 Jews were living in Transylvania at that time. Assuming that the number of Jews who came from Old Romania and the Soviet territories was 10,000 and that the number of Holocaust victims was 120,000, it follows that between 1945 and 1948 approximately 10,000 Hungarian Jews emigrated from Transylvania.

At the time of the expulsion of King Michael on December 30, 1947, two of the prominent leaders of the Old Romanian Jewry fled the country: Alexandru Şafran, the nation's chief rabbi, left in December and in the spring of the following year Wilhelm Filderman, known for his democratic beliefs and his war-time Jewish-rescue actions, emigrated. These events had a considerable impact on the views of Transylvanian Jews. The new chief rabbi, Moses Rosen, was appointed in 1948, a man many believed to have been a Communist Party sympathizer.[46]

Transylvanian Jews and Communism

The survivors of the Holocaust had several expectations of the new authorities: the abolition of anti-Semitic legislation, the return of their movable and immovable possessions, compensation for non-returnable goods, and a contribution to the reorganization of community life. Some of these requests were fulfilled, but the restitution of property encountered many obstacles and proved to be a difficult process.

Because of the war-time circumstances there was a general lack of goods in the region and many of the returnees restarted their commercial and handcraft businesses. These entrepreneurs were almost immediately labeled as "speculators" taking advantage of the unfortunate circumstances, and thus engaged in the "class struggle."

The authorities disseminated rumors about Jews, according to which their activities were related to nothing but "the black market." The prime minister himself refused some of the survivors' requests on the grounds that "the Jews cannot ask for privileges just because they are Jews." He called upon the Jewish leaders to put an end to the "outrageous lifestyle" of the Jews. "The café bars are filled exclusively with Jews," said Petru Groza, expressing the fear that this would reactivate the ostensibly obliterated chauvinism and anti-Semitism.[47] This was how the prime minister attempted to defend himself against accusations of being a Jew-sympathizer.

On December 19, 1944, the *Monitorul Oficial* (Official Gazette) published Law No. 641, which abolished all racial legislative measures and re-instated the civil rights of Jews. Although this was a major positive step in reestablishing Jewish rights, the Statute of Nationalities, enacted at the same time with this law, did not acknowledge Jewry as a nationality. This question was also debated in the leading organs of the Communist Party, but without a positive outcome. The determination of the Communists to transform Jewry into an exclusively religious community succeeded and remained in effect for a long time.[48]

Between February 12 and 14, 1945, the so-called "Parliament of Northern Transylvania," the Northern Transylvanian National Democratic Front (NDF) congress, was held in Cluj. The newly formed Central Executive Committee consisted of nine Romanians, eight Hungarians, one German, and four Jews. During the negotiations, the Democratic Jewish Peoples' Community put forward its demands and strategies: the DJPC supported the coming into power of the NDF, the annihilation of fascism, and the exposure of Fascist criminals. It also demanded the indictment and punishment of the illegitimate possessors of deported peoples' rights and property, the "retroactive abolition" of Fascist and despoiling legislative measures, compensation for damages suffered, and the restitution of Jewish means of production. It called for the punishment of those responsible for the Jews' tragedy, the return of the deportees, the guaranteeing of Jewish women's rights, the accomplishment of agrarian reform, and the absolute liberty of conscience and religion. It further called for the protection of the right to unhindered emigration to Palestine and other countries, and for Jewish representation in the country's administration, judicial, and education systems, as well as in political, public, central, and local structures. At the same time, it promised that Jews would fight against the emergence of the black market.[49]

Because the Communists and the NDF were the only political actors in the early postwar period that pledged to solve the nationality problem, many Jews enrolled in the Communist Party. The disillusionment that later surfaced was a result of the eradication of free commercial and handicraft business activities through the passage Communist laws and resultant actions, which left many Jews without any means of subsistence.

Since the Communists had not managed to draw the DJPC entirely under their influence, in August 1945 the Jewish Democratic Committee ("the Committee"; *Demokrata Zsidó Komité,* in Hungarian; *Comitetul Democratic Evreiesc,* in Romanian) was formed. Entirely controlled by the Communist Party, in the beginning the Committee was successful in solving certain fundamentally important issues for Jews. For instance, in February 1946 several favorable decisions were reached: time spent in forced labor or death camps was to be taken into account for determining the length of military service, the widows and orphans of the deported were to be provided with the same facilities as war widows and war orphans, 10,000 square meters of canvas were provided by the Public Supply Office for the housing centers, Jewish possessions were excluded from the list of the Agency for Handling Enemy Assets (CASBI), and a fund was established from the assets of the deported for the support of Jewish institutions. The Committee also managed to persuade Prime Minister Groza and the Allied Control Council to support a memorandum written to the Soviet authorities for the immediate release of Jewish prisoners of war.[50] This was required because the prisoners of war in Soviet hands included not only Hungarian and German soldiers but also the Jewish men from the forced labor service units. However, this question was not immediately resolved and two years after the first memorandum, the Committee's branch office in Cluj (Kolozsvár) was compelled to write a second document on the same subject.[51]

Although some said that in Transylvania and Romania communism was brought in by the Jews, this is far from being the case. While it is true that in the beginning many Jews were active in the government, central authorities, police forces, security police of the country, and the leading organs of the Communist Party in numbers well above those corresponding to their national proportion (Ana Pauker, Leonte Răutu, Iosif Chişinevschi, Miklós Goldberger, Valter Roman, Gizella Vass, and others), it is nonetheless evident that the majority of the Jews—craftsmen, merchants, members of the industrial and financial bourgeoisie, doctors, lawyers, and scientists with liberal beliefs, as well as many workers and unemployed people—were extremely wary of Communist ideas.[52]

On August 23, 1944, the very day Romania turned against Germany, 300 of the 1,000 members of the Communist Party were undeniably Jewish. Nevertheless, three years later, on June 1, 1947, only 4.16 percent of 703,000 members of the Communist Party were of Jewish nationality, almost 80 percent were Romanian, and 12.32 percent were Hungarian.

After the 1949 reduction in the membership, the proportion of Jews in the Communist Party was even smaller.[53] In February 1949, 10 percent of the employees of the secret police were Jewish while the Romanian staff (83 percent) dominated the organization and the Hungarian presence was only 6 percent.[54]

On May 9, 1946, the first issue of the Hungarian-language weekly publication *Egység* (Unity), subtitled "The Central Magazine of Transylvanian Jewry," appeared in Cluj. Its stated purpose was to support the Communist Party and the struggle against bourgeois forces. Part of this struggle was the elimination of cooperation between the Jewish population on the one hand, and the religious communities and bourgeois forces on the other. Although the local Democratic Jewish People's Communities continued their work for the next few months, their role gradually diminished and the Jewish Democratic Committee took their place.

Egység was more than eager to follow the Communist Party line on these subjects. In shocking reports, it described the hopeless situation of the *aliyah* groups that left from Italy,[55] the misery of those who waited in the Palestinian emigration centers of Western Europe,[56] the ignorance of the real situation on the part of those trying to escape to Hungary, and the tragedy of the Jews who had already reached Budapest.[57] More optimistically, it published an appraisal of the first-rate conditions in Birobidzhan,[58] the Soviet Jewish "homeland."[59] Starting in 1947 *Egység* published an increasing number of articles urging the Jews to join in productive labor and the formation of the new society.[60] It also printed open letters attempting to prove that anyone who decided to emigrate would be committing suicide.[61]

Communist influence became even more apparent in 1948. By the end of the year the furious fight repression of all Zionist organizations had begun, dissolving these organizations and imprisoning their leaders. *Egység*—which changed its name in March 1949 to *Új Út* (New route)— was intended to lead "the working masses" and illuminate "the Zionist fallacies" for them.[62] Finally, Zionism was proclaimed "the twin brother of anti-Semitism."[63] This propaganda had a considerable negative effect among the Jews and their tendency to emigrate became even stronger.

The ultimate disillusionment of Jewry concerning Communist ideology came with the so-called re-stratification program, which followed the general nationalization of private property. The "re-stratification" strategy affected approximately 60 percent of the Jewish community: 35 percent of it was engaged in handicraft, 25 percent in commercial activities, 10 percent consisted of liberal professionals, and another 10 percent were of unidentified professions.[64] After their "re-stratification," all of them were supposed to be employed by the now state-owned industrial and agricultural enterprises.

By June 11, 1948, the regime had nationalized 1,609 enterprises. Some Jews were appointed as "worker directors" of these companies. For instance, in Cluj (Kolozsvár) and in Cluj (Kolozs) County there were forty-four nationalized enterprises, with thirty-two Hungarian, seven Romanian, and three Jewish "worker directors."[65] Later on of course Jews began to be excluded from leading positions. The last Transylvanian Hungarian Jew working in the central administration, Sándor Jakab, undersecretary of the Ministry of Finance, was fired from his position in March 1952 and was sent to prison[66] for twenty years as part of the Ana Pauker-Vasile Luca-Teohari Georgescu purges, which were also extended to Luca's main collaborators in the Finance Ministry. Jakab was amnestied in 1964. Luca himself was sentenced to death in November 1954. His sentence was commuted to life imprisonment, and he died in his Aiud jail cell in 1963.

Another shock suffered by the Jewish community was the decision on August 3, 1948, to nationalize all Jewish schools—along with the other denominational educational institutions—and to dissolve some of them.

These measures led to the official emigration to Israel of 110,000 Jews between 1950 and 1952.[67] At least one third of them were from Transylvania. The large number of officially permitted emigrants offers evidence of the failure to integrate the Jews into the Communist state-controlled structures of Romania. This has to be acknowledged as a fact, even though in December 1948 and January 1949 Communist leaders tried to disguise the Jewish departures as "red aliyah" emigration programs,[68] whose adherents were supposed to disseminate Communist ideology in Israel and were even officially "trained" for this purpose.

The November 29, 1947, United Nations General Assembly resolution concerning the partition of Palestine and the creation of the State of Israel in the following year were at first welcomed by Romanian Communists. The Party leadership hoped that the new nation would come under Soviet influence. For Transylvanian Jewry, however, the State of

Israel had a much deeper meaning: the unrestricted and unequivocal acknowledgment of national identity and its free exercise.

The People's Tribunals, Intra-Community Accusations, and Inquiries

On April 21, 1945, the Ministry of Justice issued Decree No. 312 creating the People's Tribunals. The trials brought to justice not only the persons directly related to the anti-Jewish measures, but also those who the new regime regarded as war criminals (a group that included investigative journalists as well as politicians and other persons who had illegitimately appropriated Jewish possessions).[69]

In Old Romania and Southern Transylvania, the People's Tribunals tried 187 cases in 1945 and 1946.[70] While twenty-nine defendants were sentenced to death, King Michael commuted most of the sentences to life imprisonment. In Northern Transylvania 481 cases were decided: 100 were sentenced to death and 163 to life imprisonment. Of those sentenced, 370 were Hungarians, eighty-three Germans, twenty-six Romanians, and two were Jews.

The Northern Transylvanian People's Tribunal seated in Cluj (Kolozsvár) began its work in July 1945.[71] The first trial was held in early March 1946. The defendants were sixty-three persons charged with crimes against Romanians and Jews on the occasion of the 1940 entry of the Hungarian forces into Transylvania.[72] The second trial took up the cases of 195 persons officially involved in the implementation of the anti-Jewish measures in Northern Transylvania. The indictment and the testimonies brought to light the atrocities of the Holocaust in Northern Transylvania, the depredation of the Jews, and their persecution and deportation.[73] The verdict of the second trial was delivered on May 22, 1946.

The most important of the accused were convicted *in absentia*, as they had already left the country along with the departure of the Hungarian army and administration. The Tribunal condemned thirty persons to death, fifty-two to hard labor for life, eighteen to imprisonment for life, fifteen to twenty-five years of hard labor, three to twenty years of hard labor, eight to twenty years of imprisonment, one to fifteen years of hard labor, thirteen persons to twelve years of imprisonment, and others for shorter periods of incarceration.[74] The sentences added up to 1,204 years.[75] Not one of the thirty condemned to death was executed. Beginning in 1950, those condemned to prison time were gradually released because the "newly arisen, Soviet-type people's democracy"[76] had a need for some of them.

On August 22, 1947, several of the Tribunal's cases were reopened and forty-seven Hungarians were brought to justice. At the same time, the survivors brought several charges against their fellow deportees who had functioned as doctors or supervisors ("Kapos") in the death camps. Some of these accusations were brought before the court; others were tried by the so-called honor-tribunals of the DJPC.

The survivors as a group believed that the leaders of the Jewish communities in Cluj (Kolozsvár) had betrayed their people. On May 2, 1944, the day before the ghettoization of the Jews, the Neolog chief rabbi, Mózes Weinberger (later Moshe Carmilly-Weinberger), while urging his believers to remain in their homes and abide by the authorities' measures, fled with his wife to Romania. Other members of the so-called Jewish Relief and Rescue Committee (the *Vaadah*) crossed the border to Romania as well. Separately, the members of the local Jewish Council also escaped. Rezső (Rudolf) Kasztner, a lawyer from Cluj (Kolozsvár), made the arrangements directly with Adolf Eichmann to emigrate with his family and others. The Germans transported this group to the Bergen-Belsen concentration camp en route to Switzerland; they formed part of a Jewish refugee transport of 1,684 persons, mostly people Kasztner and his associates thought were "valuable biological material" should there ever be a national homeland for them. The wealthy members of the Kasztner group had paid large amounts of money subsidizing the escape of the others. The list of the 388 Transylvanian refugees included in the Kasztner group was compiled in the ghetto of Cluj (Kolozsvár), while the rest of the community members—who had no knowledge of the plan—were encouraged to wait patiently and not to attempt escape to Romania. They were also told that the Jews in the ghetto would be taken to Kenyérmező in Western Hungary (which later was proved to be a nonexistent place) to perform agricultural labor. Keeping the Kasztner transport secret was a matter of life and death. In 1945 the DJPC set up a council with the purpose of inquiring into the facts of the Kasztner case. The council found Kasztner guilty and also condemned the behavior of most of the Jewish community leaders of Kolozsvár.[77]

Self-Determination Strategies and Identity Dilemmas

One of the main expectations of the Transylvanian Jewish population in the postwar period was that the new regime's assimilation strategy would permit them to fully integrate into the society, a possibility that they had never totally exercised before. Between 1920 and 1944 almost all of Transylvanian Jewry formed a religious minority in the Hungarian population, even though at that time Transylvania was a part of Romania. Although the local authorities compelled them to send their children to Romanian schools, the majority of the Transylvanian Jews remained loyal to their Hungarian mother tongue and culture. Moreover, in the political arena, their support went mainly to Hungarian parties. The fact that after 1940 the Hungarians betrayed these Jews contributed to their trauma.

For the survivors of the Holocaust, the reiterated acceptance of their own "double minority"[78] status became completely impossible. The old assimilation dilemmas came back to life, the uncertainties so characteristic of repressed communities grew even stronger, and minority-status neurosis caused serious psychological crises. For many Jews the solution was the abandonment of their Jewish identity. There were four main alternatives: 1) to blend in with "the democratic masses of people" by taking advantage of the proclaimed internationalism and equality of rights; 2) to assume Romanian identity and entirely give up the past; 3) to emigrate to Palestine and become a "Jewish Jew"; and 4) to emigrate to a foreign country, especially in the West.

In the early postwar period, many Jews chose one of the first two alternatives or a combination of them. Many of them totally rejected the use of the Hungarian language and talked even to each other in Romanian. The Neolog Jews chose to write their epitaphs in Romanian. The fact that the majority of the Jews from Romanian-ruled Southern Transylvania survived the Holocaust, while almost all the Jews from Hungarian-ruled Northern Transylvania were exterminated, served as an incentive for the adoption of these two alternatives.

For a certain segment of Transylvanian Jewry, "communism became the most radical way of everlasting integration."[79] Since the Romanian regime viewed the Hungarian Jews as the most ferocious enemies of Hungarian nationalism and revisionism they were granted important Party appointments.

According to the late professor Ernő Gáll, "all these considerations and viewpoints have played a part in many abuses and mistaken cadre appointments and, on the whole, have created revulsion." Furthermore, "the persecuted often became excessive persecutors, those who endured hundreds of years of injustice also engaged in committing wrongs or remained passive towards the injustices suffered by others."[80] Another factor that deepened the gap between the Jews and the Hungarian population was the arrival of the Soviet Army: for Jews it meant rescue, for Hungarians it brought the loss of national independence, Soviet domination, and difficult minority status.[81]

The relevance of the third and fourth alternatives appeared later when the Jews realized several things: that Romania did not wish to acknowledge the existence of a Jewish nationality, that anti-Semitism had not diminished and in fact was occasionally evident in the higher spheres of the Communist Party, and that the new "re-stratification" strategy had left most of the Jews without any means of income.

Alternatively, there were Jews who tried to overcome their psychological traumas and retain their Hungarian identity. Many of them were active in the left-wing-oriented Jewish organizations. This option was characteristic of the Transylvanian Jewish intellectual elite, who had based its self-determination strategy on the spiritually enriching coexistence of multiple parallel identities.

Conclusions

Some of the main dilemmas facing Transylvanian Holocaust survivors included the question of homecoming against the alternative of emigration; the quest for missing family members; the struggle against the traumas caused by the Holocaust; the repeated self-destructive examination of the reasons of the tragedy; the attitude towards those responsible for the atrocities; their position towards the transformed political, social, and economical situation of the country; the recovery of assets that had been confiscated; the review and reconstruction of community life; accommodation with the new realities; and various identity dilemmas.

In the beginning, many of the survivors enthusiastically supported the emergence of the new regime. In their view, the Soviet Army brought them back to life and afforded them liberty. Later on, however, many Jews realized that the new Soviet-type society would never find an adequate solution to their nationality question. Nationalist and racist intolerance, chauvinism, and anti-Semitism, although reshaped, were still active, regardless of the repeated denials of the left-wing political forces that acceded to power in Romania and Northern Transylvania following the Soviet occupation. The final result was that the majority of the Hungarian-speaking Transylvanian Jews preferred to emigrate as the only possibility to put an end to their long lasting struggles, sufferance, and humiliation.

Certainly other choices were made as well, such as to totally accept the Communist ideology and lifestyle, to assimilate unconditionally, to deny any national affiliation, and so on, but all these examples were only characteristic of particular sub-segments of the Transylvanian Jewish community.

The difference between the various concepts and alternatives was due not only to the politically, economically, and socially heterogeneous nature of the community, but also to the fact that while the measures enforced against the Jews of Northern Transylvania on one hand and Southern Transylvania on the other were similar in their purposes, they were quite distinct in their overall effects.

Notes

1. According to Bárdi-Veres, the overall number of Jews in Transylvania in 1910 was 182,495, and in 1930 it was192,833. Nándor Bárdi and Péter Veres, eds., *Fizionomia etnică și confesională fluctuantă a regiunii carpato-danubiene și a Transilvaniei* (The fluctuating ethnical and confessional physiognomy of the Carpato-Danubian area and Transylvania) (Odorheiu Secuiesc: Haáz Rezső Cultural Association, 1996), 133. However, according to Stark, on the basis of the Romanian census of 1930, 190,945 Jews were living in Transylvania. Tamás Stark, *Zsidóság a vészkorszakban és a felszabadulás után, 1939–1955* (Jewry during the Holocaust and after the liberation, 1939–1955) (Budapest: MTA Történettudományi Intézete [Institute of History of the Hungarian Academy of Sciences], 1995), 65 (hereafter, *Zsidóság*). See also his *Hungarian Jews During the Holocaust and After the Second World War, 1939–1949: A Statistical Review* (Boulder CO: East European Monographs, 2000), 97. The inconsistencies might be the result of the seventeen settlements that are not part of present-day Transylvania and the five settlements that were sliced in two as a result of setting up the Romanian-Hungarian border in 1940.

2. In the present study "Transylvania" consists of the historic Transylvania, the Banat, the Criş-area (Körös-vidék), and the parts of the Partium and Maramures that are in present-day Romania.

3. According to Stark, 151,125 Jews were living in Northern Transylvania, and 40,937 in Southern Transylvania. *Zsidóság*, 65. However, Rotariu indicates that consistent with the figures of the 1941 Hungarian census, 153,462 Jews lived there. Traian Rotariu,

Recensământul din 1941: Transilvania (The 1941 census: Transylvania) (Cluj-Napoca: Editura Presa Universitară Clujeană, 2002), 333. According to the Romanian Division of the World Jewish Congress, in 1942 there were 39,628 persons "of Jewish-blood" in Southern Transylvania. *Populația evreească în cifre: Memento statistic* (The Jewish population in figures: Statistical memento) (Bucharest: Congresul Mondial Evreesc. Secțiunea din România, 1945), 41–42. [Note: Cluj, also known in Romanian as Cluj-Napoca since 1974, is known as Kolozsvár in Hungarian and as Klausenburg in German. In this study it will be identified as Cluj.]

4. In Northern Transylvania on January 31, 1941, 1,710 persons were covered by the definition of Jew under the second Jewish law, although they were not of Jewish religion. By including them we reach a total of 155,162 persons in Transylvania who were covered by the Jewish laws. Rotariu, 333.

5. Randolph L. Braham, *A népirtás politikája: A Holocaust Magyarországon* (The Politics of Genocide: The Holocaust in Hungary) (Budapest: Belvárosi Könyvkiadó, 1997), 74 (hereafter, *A népirtás*).

6. *Zsidóság*, 69.

7. Ion Calafeteanu, et al., eds., *Emigrarea populației evreiești din România în anii 1940–1944: Culegere de documente din arhiva Ministerului Afacerilor Externe al României* (The emigration of the Jewish population from Romania between 1940 and 1944: Documents from the Archive of the Romanian Ministry of Foreign Affairs) (Bucharest: Editura Silex, 1993), 244–45.

8. *Așezările evreilor din România: Memento statistic* (Jewish settlements in Romania: Statistical memento) (Bucharest: World Jewish Congress. Romanian Division, 1947), 31–32.

9. According to the notes of the Kassa (Košice) railway commandant, 133,913 persons were deported from Northern Transylvania to Auschwitz. See *A népirtás*, 1357–359.

10. Béla Vágó, "The Destruction of the Jews of Transylvania," in *Hungarian Jewish Studies*, ed. Randolph L. Braham (New York: World Federation of Hungarian Jews, 1966), 171–222; see also, *Zsidóság*, 64–70.

11. *Szabad Szó*, Timișoara, (November 16, 1944); *Szabadság* (Arad), I (142) (October 19, 1945), 3.

12. Zoltán Tibori Szabó, *Élet és halál mezsgyéjén: Zsidók menekülése és mentése a magyar-román határon 1940–1944 között* (Between life and death: Escape and rescue of Jews on the Hungarian-Romanian border between 1940 and 1944) (Kolozsvár [Cluj-Napoca]: Minerva Művelődési Egyesület, 2001), 148 (hereafter, *Élet és halál*).

13. According to Romanian sources the percentage of the Northern Transylvanian survivors was less than 20. See for instance, J. Alexandru, et al., eds., *Martiriul evreilor din România 1940–1944: Documente și mărturii* (The martyrdom of the Romanian Jews, 1940–1944: Documents and testimonies) (Bucharest: Editura Hasefer, 1991), 264.

14. *Igazság* (Kolozsvár/Cluj), I (13) (June 3, 1945), 5; ibid., I (14) (June 10, 1945), 3.

15. *Világosság* (Kolozsvár/Cluj), II (77) (April 5, 1945), 3.

16. Ibid., I (16) (November 5, 1944), 5; I (19) (November 10, 1944), 3; and I (23) (November 15, 1944), 2.

17. Ibid., II (41) (February 21, 1945), 3.

18. Quoted in *Zsidóság*, 67–68.

19. *Erdélyi Szikra* (Kolozsvár/Cluj), I (3) (March 22, 1945), 7.

20. *Remember: 40 de ani de la masacrarea evreilor din Ardealul de Nord sub ocupația horthystă* (Remember: 40 years since the massacre of the Northern Transylvanian Jews under the Horthyite occupation) (Bucharest: Federația Comunităților Evreiești din Republica

Socialistă România. Secţia de documentare, 1985), 69–70; from this source seventy-six spiritual leaders can be identified, most of them are rabbis, but there are also several mohels.

21. Liviu Rotman, "Romanian Jewry: The First Decade After the Holocaust," in *The Tragedy of Romanian Jewry*, ed. Randolph L. Braham (New York: Columbia University Press, 1994), 306 (hereafter, *Romanian*).

22. *Erdélyi Szikra*, I (5) (April 5, 1945), 3.

23. Arhivele Statului Bucureşti (ASB). Direcţia Generală a Poliţiei. Dosar 44/1945, 20. Quoted in Andreea Andreescu, Lucian Nastasă, and Varga Andrea, eds., *Minorităţi entoculturale. Mărturii documentare: Evreii din România (1945–1965)* (Ethno-cultural minorities. Documentary testimonies: The Jews of Romania 1945–1955) (Cluj: Centrul de Resurse pentru Diversitate Etnoculturală, 2003), 20 (hereafter, *Minorităţi*).

24. *Világosság*, I (18) (November 9, 1944), 4.

25. Gábor Vincze, "A romániai magyar kisebbség történeti kronológiája: Kiegészített változat" (The historical chronology of the Romanian Hungarian minority: Updated version), (Szeged: Manuscript) (hereafter, "Kronológia").

26. *Világosság*, I (16) (November 5, 1944), 5.

27. Ibid., II (40) (February 20, 1945), 2.

28. Ibid., II (57) (March 11, 1945), 5; *Igazság*, I (14) (June 10, 1945), 5; and ibid., I (72) (December 14, 1945), 2.

29. *A népirtás*, 1251; See also Dániel A. Löwy, *A téglagyártól a tehervonatig: Kolozsvár zsidó lakosságának története* (From the brickyard to the freight train: The history of the Jewish population of Cluj [Kolozsvár]) (Kolozsvár [Cluj-Napoca]: Erdélyi Szépmíves Céh, 1998), 209–10; and *A tegnap városa: A nagyváradi zsidóság emlékkönyve* (The city of yesterday: The memorial book of the Oradea [Nagyvárad] Jews) (Tel Aviv, 1981), 183.

30. ASB. Inspectoratul General al Jandarmeriei. Dosar 144/1946, 1–2, 16, and 139; see also, *Minorităţi*, 183–85.

31. Ibid., CC al PCR. Cancelarie. Dosar 86/1945. Quoted in *Minorităţi, 21.*

32. *Igazság*, I (40) (October 23, 1945), 4.

33. Victor Neumann, *Istoria evreilor din România* (The history of the Jews of Romania) (Timişoara [Temesvár]: Editura Amarcord, 1996), 250 (hereafter, *Istoria*).

34. *Egység*, I (3) (May 23, 1946), 1.

35. Hary Kuller, *Evreii în România anilor 1944–1949: Evenimente, documente, comentarii* (The Jews in Romania between 1944 and 1949: Events, documents, commentaries) (Bucharest: Editura Hasefer, 2002), 61 (hereafter, *Evreii*).

36. ASB. Inspectoratul General al Jandarmeriei. Dosar 64/1946, 171; ibid., Direcţia Generală de Poliţie. Dosar 151/1946, 131. 1.; ibid., Ministerul de Interne. Diverse. Dosar 2/1946, 34. Printed in *Minorităţi*, 231–38.

37. The Romanian Kingdom before 1918.

38. ASB. Direcţia Generală a Poliţiei. Dosar 74/1947, 9. Printed in *Minorităţi*, 335.

39. ASB. Ministerul de Interne. Diverse. Dosar 4/1947, 73; ibid., Inspectoratul General al Jandarmeriei, Dosar 70/1947, 100 and 121. Printed in *Minorităţi*, 352–54.

40. Arhiva SRI (Romanian Intelligence Agency Archives). Fond "D." Dosar 9049, vol. 3, 179–80. Printed in *Minorităţi*, 370–71.

41. *Evreii*, 386.

42. Ibid., 62.

43. Ibid., 59.

44. István Somos, ed., *Auschwitz!... Hazatért deportáltak megrázó elbeszélései az auschwitzi, majdaneki, birkenau és lublini német halállágerek borzalmairól* (Auschwitz! ...

The returned accounts of the atrocities in the German death camps of Auschwitz, Majdanek, Birkenau and Lublin) (Kolozsvár/Cluj, 1945); see also, *Igazság* (Kolozsvár/Cluj), I (17) (July 1, 1945), 5; and ibid., I (23) (August 9–15, 1945), 5.

45. *Evreii*, 69.

46. Later it was discovered that Chief Rabbi Moses Rosen supported the emigration of the Jews and, within the limits of the contemporary circumstances, acted accordingly.

47. ASB. Preşedinţia Consiliului de Miniştri. Stenograme. Dosar 10/1945, 36–37. Quoted in *Minorităţi*, 20.

48. *Istoria*, 250.

49. *Erdélyi Szikra*, I (2) (March 15, 1945), 6.

50. *Igazság*, II (35) (February 14, 1946), 3.

51. *Romanian*, 292.

52. *Istoria*, 237.

53. *Evreii*, 28–30.

54. *Minorităţi*, 26.

55. *Egység*, I (16) (August 23, 1946), 7.

56. Ibid., II (65) (August 1, 1947), 4.

57. Ibid., II (67) (August 15, 1947), 3.

58. Birobidzhan (Birobidjan) was the Jewish autonomous territory in the USSR.

59. *Egység*, I (25) (October 25, 1946), 9.

60. Ibid., II (38) (October 24, 1947), 4.

61. Ibid., III (86) (January 2, 1948), 3.

62. Ibid., III (133) (December 10, 1948), 3; III (134) (December 17, 1948), 3; IV (138) (January 14, 1949), 5; IV (139) (January 21, 1949), 2; *Új Út*, IV (146) (March 11, 1949), 4; and IV (158) (June 10, 1949), 5.

63. *Új Út*, IV (175) (October 7, 1949), 1.

64. *Evreii*, 65.

65. "Kronológia..."

66. *Romániai Magyar Szó* (Bucharest) (March 6, 1952).

67. *Evreii*, 69, l; only 90,000 of these persons arrived in Israel. The others went to different European, African, South-American countries, the United States, or Australia.

68. *Romanian*, 315, l.

69. *Igazság*, I (17) (July 1, 1945), 1.

70. "Kronológia..."

71. *Igazság*, I (18) (July 5–11, 1945), 4; I (19) (July 12–18, 1945), 7; I (22) (August 2–8, 1945), 5; I (24) (August 16–22, 1945), 4.; I (25) (August 23–29, 1945), 3; I (40) (October 23, 1945), 2; I (72) (December 14, 1945), 4; and II (68) (March 25, 1946), 3.

72. *Világosság*, III (73) (April 1, 1946), 1 and 5.

73. *Igazság*, II (83) (April 12, 1946), 2; II (123) (June 2, 1946), 5; *Egység*, I (3) (May 23, 1946), 4; and I (4) (May 30, 1946), 1–2.

74. *Igazság*, II (124) (June 3, 1946), 3; *Egység*, I (5) (June 6, 1946), 3.

75. Randolph L. Braham, *Genocide and Retribution: The Holocaust in Hungarian-Ruled Northern Transylvania* (Boston and The Hague: Kluwer-Nijhoff Publishing, 1983), ix–x.

76. *A népirtás*, 1273–274.

77. *Élet és halál*, 50–51. For further details on the Kasztner case in Cluj and Israel, see Randolph L. Braham, *The Politics of Genocide: The Holocaust in Hungary* (New York: Columbia University Press, 1994), 1068–112.

78. Ernő Gáll, "Kettős kisebbségben" (In double minority status) in *Korunk* (Kolozsvár/Cluj), III/II (8) (August 1991), 957–69; see also his, "Kisebbség a kisebbségben" (Minority within the minority), in *The Holocaust in Hungary: Fifty Years Later*, eds. Randolph L. Braham and Attila Pók (New York: Columbia University Press, 1997), 641–60 (hereafter, "Kisebbség").

79. *Istoria*, 249.

80. "Kisebbség," 656.

81. *Istoria*, 249.

From the Periphery to the Center:
The Holocaust in Hungary and Israeli Historiography
Raphael Vago

In this paper I describe the destruction of Hungarian Jewry during the Holocaust as reflected in Israeli historiography. I discuss the changing role and place of the subject over the past fifty-five years, and trace its shift from near the periphery to the center of Israeli research. Neither a survey nor a guide to the subject, this study focuses on the various trends in research, the methods pursued by Israeli historians, and is an attempt to evaluate the contribution of Israeli historiography to the understanding of the Holocaust in Hungary. While in such a reflection on historiography the presence of outside scholars in Israeli publications is vital, this study will only make references to such scholars and their studies in passing: the main subject here is Israeli historians who have published in both Israel and abroad, and the Israeli viewpoint.

The last years of the previous century and the first years of the new one offer an opportunity to summarize and reach some conclusions about the sources and the vast amount of published material on the subject, and by extrapolation to look at the future.

Recent years have seen the publication of Yehuda Bauer's *Rethinking the Holocaust*, and several works by Dan Michman on the current stage of Holocaust research.[1] Changes in Israeli society, changing perceptions in Israel and elsewhere about notions such as "resistance" and "heroism," changing views on the role of the Jewish Councils—all of these phenomena have influenced and shaped recent Holocaust historiography. These developments and others are well reflected in Israeli historiography of the Holocaust in general, and specifically of the Holocaust in Hungary.

Some initial methodological remarks are essential in order to place the topic in its chronological and analytical framework.

History and Historians

The history of Holocaust research passed through several stages of development that reflected a variety of factors: available documentation,

conceptual developments, methodological tools (such as inter-discipli-
nary approaches), and, a factor not often treated, the involvement of
professional scholars in the field (or more to the point, the lack of
professionals working on the subject following 1945). One of the main
reasons for the slow emergence of an Israeli historiography on the Holocaust in Hungary was the fundamental absence of scholars from within
or outside of the academic establishment. Only in the early sixties did
research on the Holocaust in Hungary develop in parallel to the
Eichmann trial, which itself was a turning point in Israeli historiography,
motivated in part by the prominent place of the Holocaust in Hungary at
the trial proceedings. Prior to the establishment of Yad Vashem (and
other Holocaust centers in the early and mid-fifties) and an institutional
framework for Holocaust studies, Israel had few "Hungarian representatives" engaged in research on Hungary. Although Professor Randolph
Braham was associated from the beginning with Yad Vashem and participated in its work, Professor Braham, the dean of Holocaust in
Hungary studies, did not live in Israel. Thus, the complaint that the
Holocaust in Hungary was underrepresented in Israeli Holocaust studies
can be explained by the lack of scholars in Israel working and focusing
specifically on Hungary.

The Institutional Framework and Research
on the Holocaust in Hungary

The various centers either affiliated with political ideologies, especially through the Kibbutz movement, such as Lohame Hagettaot
(Ghetto Fighters' House), Massuah, Yad Mordechai, and of course, Yad
Vashem, which is a special case in itself, focused on public events,
documentation, and research related to the specific movements in which
the place of Hungary had a rather low priority as compared with, for
example, Poland or Lithuania. Among its founders and first generation
of scholars who formulated its scientific agenda, Yad Vashem lacked
people directly involved with the Holocaust in Hungary, and thus Hungary remained on the periphery of its Holocaust research. On the other
hand, the Holocaust in Hungary played a prominent role in the public
sphere, as a politicized event often taken out of the historical context, for
example the debates surrounding the Kasztner Affair, ranging from
Kasztner in Budapest through Brand mission, and the contacts with the
Yishuv leadership, to Kasztner and the judicial system, and Kasztner as

the victim of a political assassination. In a sense, the Holocaust in Hungary became a topic of "targeted research" in which everything related to Kasztner, the negotiations with the Germans, and the role of the Jewish leadership became the main focus. Furthermore, the intensive debate on Kasztner in the Israeli media and political discourse diverted attention from both a serious scholarly examination of the affair in its full complexity, and from the overall picture of the Holocaust in Hungary.

The Role of Hungary in Israeli Historiography

As in the other former Communist countries, Holocaust research in the context of academic contacts and access to documentation in Hungary was greatly influenced and even shaped by the nature of Israeli-Hungarian relations. The miniscule contact that existed before 1967 broke down after the severance of diplomatic relations following the Six-Day War just as the subject began to engage the serious interest of Israeli researchers. This left Israeli scholars without access to Hungarian archives until a gradual thaw in the mid-eighties. Thus Israeli research on the events in Hungary proper atrophied, forcing scholars to use foreign documentation, mainly German and British. Western research on the Holocaust in Hungary was also limited until the early sixties when the publications of Randolph Braham brought the topic closer also to the attention of the Israeli academic community.[2]

The Role of Non-Academic Publications

The Hungarian-language media played a prominent role in Israel, especially the daily *Új Kelet* (New east), periodical newsletters and publications by various local organizations, and the growing number of community memorial books that provided material on local history and the fate of the Jewish communities at a time when archival materials were not accessible. For years *Új Kelet* and other Hungarian-language publications printed personal memoirs, testimonies, documents, and articles, usually connected with anniversaries, aimed at the Hungarian-reading public and thus filled the gap when full-scale studies were rare.

Thus, the Hungarian-language media in Israel—particularly during the period of mass emigration of Hungarian-speaking emigrants to Israel—could be seen as a substitute for academic research, in which the authors, often from academia, conveyed to the Hungarian-reading public the tragedy of Hungarian Jewry.

The Holocaust in Hungary Perceived as Separate Case Studies

In one of the most significant Israeli contributions to the historiography of the Holocaust, Roni Stauber analyzed the issue of the Holocaust and heroism in the Israeli public discourse in the 1950s.[3] In a chapter on the *Judenräte* and the resistance movements, Stauber dates the intensification of the public debate, which replaced and even dislocated more serious scholarly publications, to mid-1955 following the Kasztner trial. The debate focused on the question of whether during the Holocaust there were two separate and opposite ways to respond to the Nazi policy of extermination: Kasztner's road and that of the *Judenräte*, in other words, either criminal cooperation leading to extinction or the armed resistance of the fighting youth movements.[4] The complex emotional debates surrounding the Kasztner affair shifted attention from the fate of Hungarian Jewry overall, and the matter transformed into a political battle among various sectors of the Israeli left, and between the Israeli left and right.

Kasztner became the symbol of the passivity of Hungarian Jewry, and of the paralyzing effect of Jewish leadership there. Hundreds of articles, speeches, public discussions, and debates in the Knesset and the Israeli media shifted attention from the history of the Holocaust in Hungary to the failure of the leadership, emphasizing "cooperation" with the Nazis in comparison with the heroic resistance in the ghettoes. The fate of Hungarian Jewry was not presented in its overall context, but mainly, often only, through the prism of the so-called "Kasztner type" mentality and its subsequent effects on Israeli political culture. In the eyes of the weekly *Ha'olam Haze* (This world), Kasztner represented a Diasporic mentality of "stadlanut," of attempting to change the views of the murderer instead of fighting against him. This picture of the fate of Hungarian Jewry portrayed the Jews as victims of their leaders, led as lambs to the slaughter. The emphasis in Israel was on resistance and leadership, two aspects in which Hungarian Jewry failed. The dominant notion in the public discussion was that Hungarian Jews had made no attempts at self-defense or resistance. In this distorted and partial picture, the saga of the Zionist youth movements was ignored only to appear roughly twenty years, or almost a generation, later, in the seventies.

Thus, the narrative in the fifties focused on action, or rather on inaction, and on criticizing a Diasporic mentality rather than understanding the Holocaust in Hungary in all its complexity. There was no general picture or historical survey, except the polemical one provided by the warring factions in the Israeli public debates. Those wishing to learn about the Holocaust in Hungary found more publications on the Israeli Labor Party's policies, in which Kasztner was active in Israel until his assassination in 1957, than on the Holocaust in Hungary itself. The events in Hungary gradually became a case study for understanding the dangers of the "Kasztner mentality," and in fact by the late fifties there was still no comprehensive attempt to study the Holocaust in Hungary.

The Kasztner case and its impact on Israeli society and politics became a topic of serious academic research in the nineties. In 1995 Yehiam Weiz, a prolific researcher of the Kasztner case, published a study entitled "Between Warsaw and Budapest: On the Questions of Fighting in the Kasztner Trial." Weiz wrote that for years the members of the Hungarian Halutz resistance movement believed that an incorrect and even distorted presentation of the problem of resistance did an injustice to the underground movement in Hungary.[5]

Another case study related to Hungary was the heroic story of the parachutists from Eretz Israel, in which the dominant figure was, and is, Hanna Senesh (Szenes). But here too we face another failed attempt to understand and describe the overall picture. Hanna Senesh's fate became not so much the story of the Holocaust in Hungary, but rather contributed to an emerging topic of research, especially for the younger generation, the policies of the Yishuv leadership (for example, Dina Porat's groundbreaking work).[6] But this occurred in the early eighties and nineties when Israeli historiography started in earnest to cope with the Yishuv and the Holocaust; in the fifties the Hanna Senesh mission was the leading narrative story of heroism and attempts at rescue.

To a large extent, the Hanna Senesh legend became the story of the Yishuv and the volunteer parachutists' personal readiness to sacrifice; Hungary was the location of the drama and not the focus of the saga itself. Hungary remained in the background as Hanna Senesh entered the pantheon of Israeli heroes, and her story became not so much the story of the Holocaust in Hungary, but an example of heroism and personal sacrifice.

Yad Vashem and the Holocaust in Hungary: The First Decade

There is no doubt about Yad Vashem's crucial role in shaping Israeli historiography on the Holocaust and in forming an Israeli collective history. Since its founding in early 1954 all major projects—including taking oral histories, collecting testimonies and documents, and publishing projects such as the Pinkas Hakehilot—aimed at providing in-depth research on the fate of communities and other aspects of the Holocaust. This effort reflected a national attempt to cope with a legacy and to formulate the building blocks of a "national," supra-political narrative of the Holocaust.

A brief presentation of the work on the Holocaust in Hungary in the first decade or so after Yad Vashem's founding reveals the slow development of Holocaust research on Hungary by Israeli historians. In this period Yad Vashem published two major periodicals—*Yediot Yad Vashem* (Yad Vashem news) beginning in April 1954, a bi-monthly newsletter (often with irregular and double issues), and from 1957 first a Hebrew and then an English version of its annual *Yad Vashem Studies.*

Yediot Yad Vashem reflected an early attempt to provide the public—both the academic and educational community—with short articles and information. One striking feature of its content is the absence of the Holocaust in Hungary, or its very marginal treatment as compared to other countries, especially to Poland, the Baltic States, and the Soviet Union. But in the mid-1950s lack of knowledge about the Hungarian case was a reflection of a more general ignorance of the Holocaust. For example, a short item in January 1956 mentioned that the "Israeli journalist Zeev Laqueur," later better known as Walter Laqueur, published an article in the German monthly *Der Monat* about the Kasztner affair in which he noted that the Israeli public was widely ignorant of the Holocaust and that so-called "sensational" items in the Israeli press, such as Kasztner's testimony on behalf of Kurt Becher, were already known and published in the proceedings of the Nuremberg Trials in 1947–48.[7]

Some references to Hungary appeared in reviews of publications, but not as original research. Thus, Yehuda Komlos reviewed Arthur Geyer's *A magyarországi fasizmus zsidóüldözésének bibliográfiája, 1945–1958* (Bibliography of Jewish persecutions by Hungarian fascism, 1945–1958), and Nathanel Katzburg published a serious review of C.A. Macartney's *October Fifteenth.*[8] Katzburg's review did not comment on the state of Israeli Holocaust historiography, but it presented to the Israeli reader a rare review of one of the major studies of the time about Hungary and the fate of Hungarian Jewry.

One of the few articles devoted to Hungary was that of Yehuda Komlos entitled "About the Activities of the Jewish Underground in Hungary," in which he wrote, "Our knowledge about the revolt—using the Hebrew term 'meri'—of Hungarian Jewry is very limited." He praised Yad Vashem's activities in collecting testimonies from members of the youth movements, and provided a coherent general overview of rescue activities in Hungary. The work of the underground, he wrote, "is a story of bravery and boundless heroism." The short study relied on the testimonies available at Yad Vashem, suggesting the research potential of such sources. The author was well aware that no other studies on the subject existed, and he noted that, "this brief review does not pretend to be complete, its aim is to provide some characteristics of the topic, based especially on testimonies from the Yad Vashem Archives."[9] For years following this early appraisal of the activities of the Zionist youth organizations, no attempt was made to write the history of the Zionist youth movements, except for chapters published by the organizations themselves, such as *The Book of the Jewish Partisans* published by the Hashomer Hatzair,[10] until Asher Cohen's pioneering publication in 1986.[11]

While a comparative study situating Hungary in context with the other European states would require additional parameters and analysis than is possible in a brief remark, it should be noted that Slovakia, for example, was fully covered by *Yediot Yad Vashem* in articles by Livia Rothkirchen. Judging from the names of the authors writing on Hungary—very few in the first years of *Yediot Yad Vashem*—and from the emerging studies during the early and mid-sixties, the lack of Israeli historians on Hungary and the Holocaust in Hungary is blatantly evident. A major reason for the non-treatment, if not the ill-treatment, of the Holocaust in Hungary was the absence of Israeli experts on that country.

The early sixties witnessed a gradual change, though this was scarcely evident from Yad Vashem's publications: in the first four volumes of *Yad Vashem Studies* published between 1957–1961 there were no specific studies devoted to Hungary. Only in the fifth volume was there a translated study by Jenö Lévai entitled, "New Discoveries on Hungary in the Light of the Eichmann Trial."[12] An opening footnote referred to the article as a part of a forthcoming study on Hungarian Jewry during the Horthy period "under preparation for Yad Vashem" that apparently was never published. The Eichmann trial and its voluminous proceedings on the fate of Hungarian Jewry were widely covered by the Israeli media, including the Hungarian-language press, especially the daily *Új Kelet* and the weekly *A Hét* (The week). However scholarly studies continued to be limited due to a combination of two factors: the lack of Israeli historians engaged in relevant research, and the failure until the Eichmann trial for the impact of the nature, the speed, and the extent of the devastation of Hungary's Jewry to enter more intensely into Israeli historiography.

It also should be emphasized that the rather small circle of Israeli universities and research institutions in the fifties did not enable the development of Holocaust-related documentation and research beyond certain limits and these generally focused on certain political movements, especially the youth organizations. Nonetheless, new research centers, some of them just emerging and defining their aims and prospects, such as the Ghetto Fighters' House, Massuah, Yad Mordechai, and Givat Haviva, have prepared the groundwork for the next period of expansion in Holocaust studies and research to make use of a growing body of documentation from Israeli sources, such as personal testimonies. These sources are now available to the gradually increasing number of students and researchers working on themes related to the Holocaust in Hungary. The increase in Israeli research on the Holocaust was also linked to the maturing of the younger generation who survived the Holocaust, and understood that as yet not enough had been written or done to preserve the recent past.

The Boom of the Sixties and Seventies

Studies on the Holocaust in Hungary proliferated in the sixties and the seventies. From the mid-sixties on, practically each volume of *Yad Vashem Studies* contained an essay on Hungary, while at the same time new publications included articles on the Hungarian experience. Furthermore, with the expansion of Israeli academic and scientific life, Yad Vashem and other institutions began to organize symposia and conferences on the Holocaust, in which Hungary became one of the principal topics. Parallel to these developments came an increase in translations into Hebrew of work appearing outside Israel. Indeed, the most prominent author to be translated was Randolph Braham, who had engaged in cooperative ventures with Yad Vashem since its establishment, and who was in fact the first one to urge more intensive research on Hungary. Braham actively participated in most of the major conferences on the Holocaust (not only in those dealing directly with Hungary) that took place in Israel. These conferences, especially those at Yad Vashem and at the Strochliz Institute for Holocaust Studies at Haifa University, contributed much to the proliferation of studies focused on Hungary. Braham also played a leading role in fostering the publications of Israeli scholars abroad. His three-volume *Hungarian Jewish Studies* published between 1966 and 1973, and in other volumes he edited and published outside Israel, included studies by Israeli authors such as Nathaniel Katzburg, Bela Vago, and several from the younger generation including the late Asher Cohen and Raphael Vago.

The topics covered by the Israeli historians since the mid-sixties broadened the range of research into several major fields:

1. Jewish leadership during the Holocaust;

2. Diplomatic activities to rescue Hungarian Jewry;

3. Resistance and rescue activities, especially by the Zionist youth movements;

4. Aspects of Hungarian-Jewish relations, including Hungarian antisemitism in the inter-War period and the Hungarian right wing; and

5. Regional and local history—especially Northern Transylvania.

These fields reflected not only the personal research and activities of those involved, but also the available primary sources. These topics also interested the wider public beyond academia.

The use of Israeli documentation, especially the testimonies available at Yad Vashem, increased. For example, Bela Vago's study of the political and diplomatic activities aimed at the rescue of North-Transylvanian Jews, including aspects relating to Romania, was based largely on material from Israeli archives.[13]

The opening of the British archival documents in the Public Record Office (PRO) relating to the war years enabled several researchers to tackle crucial aspects of the Hungarian situation using fresh documentary materials. For instance, Bela Vago's work on the intelligence aspects of the Brand mission was largely based on documents from the

PRO, which shifted the focus from a politicized debate on the Kasztner affair to an analysis of various aspects of the Nazi offer.[14]

New publications and periodicals on the Holocaust and on general topics related to modern Jewish history opened new possibilities and channels for the publication of studies on Hungary. *Yalkut Moreshet* published by the Moreshet-Mordechai Anilevich Study and Research Center associated with the Hashomer Hatzair movement first appeared in late 1963, and it included numerous studies on Hungarian Jewry. Among *Yalkut Moreshet*'s early editors, Yehuda Bauer and Israel Gutman wrote methodological and historiographical studies about aspects of the Holocaust in Hungary. Perhaps the publication's most important contribution to the research of the Holocaust in Hungary was its special volume in May 1994 dedicated to the 50th anniversary of the events. The 400-page volume became one of the most extensive contributions on Hungary in Israeli historiography. A new volume on the 60th anniversary was published in April 2004.

Yalkut Moreshet also printed reviews on Hungary-related topics. Thus, Zvi Erez, who became a major contributor to studies on the Hungarian events in the pages of *Yalkut Moreshet* and in other publications, reviewed a long essay by Livia Rothkirchen entitled "The Development of Anti-Semitism and the Persecution of the Jews 1920–1945," which served as an introduction to Moshe (Sandberg) Zanbar's book *Year Without an End*.[15] Writing in summer of 1967 Erez mentioned that "to the best of our knowledge Rothkirchen's study on the history of Hungarian Jews before and during the Holocaust is the first of its kind to be published in Hebrew."

Yalkut Moreshet's contribution to Hungary-related topics was crucial: between 1963 and 2002 more than sixty articles directly related to Hungary were published, while only four were published on Greece, thirteen on France, and one on Latvia. Such comparisons may be taken out of context, but still they indicate a major boost in Hungarian-related work. Among the authors in *Yalkut Moreshet* with several publications each Erez and Sari Reuveni stand out; and the journal also published several testimonies by members of the Hehalutz youth movements.

Another significant publication that started in the seventies, *Massuah* was launched in 1973 at the Holocaust Memorial Center of the Ha'Noar Hatzioni youth movement in Kibbutz Tel-Ithzak. While not matching *Yalkut Moreshet*'s coverage of Hungary, *Massuah* did publish more than a dozen studies including the 1983 lectures delivered at the Kibbutz on the Zionist youth movements. In its first issue it carried a study by Moshe Biderman called "On the Ha'Noar Hatzioni in Hungary," one of several studies focusing on the activities of the youth movements, especially the Ha'Noar Hatzioni. The study presented a chronological development of the movement, emphasizing its pre-war activities and the continuity with the underground activities during the Holocaust. Focusing on the rescue activities of the youth movements, *Massuah* printed several studies, such as those by David Margalit, Moshe Gonda, Gabriel Horowitz, and Hava Eichler on the Ha'Noar Hatzioni in Hungary, and by Roni Stauber on rescue activities organized in Hungary related to other Nazi occupied areas.[16] Thus, *Massuah* became a major forum for research on the Zionist youth movements and other aspects of the Holocaust.

The founding of the Strochliz Institute for Holocaust Research at Haifa University in 1976 provided a new and dynamic forum for Holocaust research, conferences, symposia, as well as beginning in 1978 the annual publication of *Dapim Le'heker Tkufat Ha-Shoah* (Studies on the Holocaust period), which included in nearly every issue articles related directly to the Holocaust in Hungary. The first volume included studies by Asher Cohen (who emerged in the mid-seventies as one of the important new scholars on the youth movements) on Peter Veres' racism and antisemitism, and by Bela Vago on "Jewish Leadership Groups in Hungary and Romania—Their Reactions to Nazi Politics."

Likewise, the two volumes published following international conferences held at Haifa University on Jewish assimilation and Jewish-non-Jewish relations in Eastern Europe provided new studies on Hungarian-Jewish relations during the twentieth century, such as those written by Nathaniel Katzburg, Bela Vago, George Schöpflin, George Barany, and others.[17]

In the early seventies Yad Vashem began a series of international historical conferences usually devoted to a specific topic. The second conference, held in April 1974, dealt with rescue attempts during the Holocaust; Bela Vago's study about the British government and the fate of Hungarian Jewry in 1944 represented Hungary. His sources were for the most part the British documents in the PRO, again an indication that new primary sources were being utilized by Israeli scholars. The proceedings were published in 1977.

To sum up this dynamic period, and I have of course mentioned only a sample of the work done then, the sixties and the seventies were the period of maturing for Israeli historiography, witnessing an expansion both in quality and quantity. New institutions and research facilities, such as the Strochlitz Institute at Haifa University working together with the Ghetto Fighters' House, expanded the collecting of documents and also provided the opportunity for a relatively small number of new researchers to pursue topics linked directly to the Holocaust in Hungary and the Hungarian Jewish experience in the twentieth century. In marked contrast to the fifties and even early-sixties, the Holocaust in Hungary became a major topic in Holocaust studies and research.

Surveys of the Holocaust appeared gradually, especially with the publication of the *Pinkas Hakehilot* series by Yad Vashem, in which the volume on Romania included long introductory chapters on Transylvania, the Holocaust in Northern Transylvania, and the fate of the Jewish population in Southern Transylvania. In the early nineties Yad Vashem published the first comprehensive Hebrew-language account of the Holocaust in Hungary authored by Randolph Braham and Nathanael Katzburg.[18]

The two major developments in Israeli historiography at this point related to debates and to the culture of collective memory in Israel: the issue of the behavior of Jewish leaders in Hungary during the Holocaust and the activities of the Zionist youth movements.

Jewish Leaders and the Zionist Youth Movements as Primary Subjects

Numerous publications reflected several important emerging aspects of the Israeli historiography on these subjects. One of the most important was the gradual de-politicization of sensitive Holocaust issues; another was the changing conception of resistance and heroism that allowed a new perspective and evaluation of the activities of the youth movements. This meant a gradual demise of movement-centered narratives in the "it was us and not them who succeeded where others have failed" style. The expanding scholarship on the youth movements' rescue activities moved toward a more consensual approach: after publishing its own history, each movement could present a more comprehensive account in a kind of "united front," which was more "virtual reality" than reality. It was not the case of "inventing history," but rather the ability to see the larger picture of the youth movements' activities, rather than to focus on one specific movement's history during the period.

The new perceptions of resistance in its wider forms—not only armed actions, but all acts aimed at opposing the Nazis and their collaborators' operations to exterminate the Jews—allowed a more balanced view and analysis of rescue activities and of the very nature of resistance under the conditions existing in Hungary.[19]

For years Israeli historians had tackled the problem of the Jewish leadership. But the gradual change occurred with regard to the demonization of the leadership from the emotionally laden years of the Kasztner affair to a more objective, less emotional debate, which still left open a wide spectrum for critical analysis. Yad Vashem's Third International Historical Conference in 1977 was devoted to "Patterns of Jewish Leadership in Nazi Europe 1933–1945." The tone on Hungary was set by Randolph Braham, who stated that "We must attempt to re-construct the historical situation in which these leaders operated as faithfully and exactly as available sources will permit."[20]

Most of those who presented papers at the conference phrased their views and opinions cautiously, and some wondered whether they should be working on the subject at all. The dilemmas continued to confront Israeli historians, as was evident some twenty-six years later when Zvi Erez wrote that he would abstain from judging the actions of the Jewish Council in Budapest because, he noted, the role of the historian is "only to point out and shed light on the motivations and the actions of forces and individuals to the best of his ability."[21]

In fact, prior to this conference, Yad Vashem devoted a one-day meeting in 1975 to the "Leadership of Hungarian Jewry in the Test of the Holocaust." The papers were published in 1976, and they included one study by Randolph Braham on ways to evaluate the activities of the "Jewish Councils." The authors of this small volume included most of the Israeli researchers working on aspects of the Holocaust in Hungary, including Yehuda Bauer (who treated the problem of the Jewish leadership in Hungary and the Kasztner affair in a variety of publications), Livia Rothkirchen, Nathaniel Katzburg, Bela Vago, and Joseph Shefer (whose article on the leadership of the underground youth movements was one of the first attempts to outline the "patterns of leadership"). If this brief conference had a thesis it was the understanding that it was still difficult to evaluate objectively the functioning of the Hungarian Jewish leadership during the Holocaust. Gideon Hausner's closing remarks summed up the various arguments: the eminent jurist, who had been Eichmann's prosecutor, quoted from the various participants on the difficulties of the topic, and reached a "verdict" on the behavior and actions of the leaders. Perhaps the long-term impact of the Yad Vashem volume was in the clearly outlined "division of labor" between the Zionist and the Jewish leaders, as well as the differences in mentality among the various factions in the leadership. The stress on their mistakes, mistaken assumptions, and tactics to hide the truth from the Jewish community indicates that the historians' negative judgments continued, but they were to become in subsequent years more cautious and more sympathetic to the complex realities of the period.

The saga of the history of the youth movements is one of the indicators in the development of Israeli historiography. For the purposes of this paper I shall limit the discussion to some of the major trends and developments.

The first comprehensive, groundbreaking work on the topic was written by Asher Cohen and published in English in 1986, followed by editions in Hebrew and Hungarian.[22] He used the term "resistance" in the title as a clear indication that, unlike previous definitions of the term and its relevance to Hungary, the youth movements' underground activities were in fact a clear case of active as opposed to passive or spiritual "resistance." This terminological usage was important to place the youth movements' actions on their proper base and conceptual framework.

Cohen's work was written at a time when studies related to the Zionist youth movements in Hungary had begun to appear more often in various anthologies, symposia, and conferences. While for years the subject was underrepresented in Israeli historiography, and for that matter in collective memory, the early eighties witnessed a new trend as the activists of the period increasingly presented their own experiences. Gradually a more complex picture emerged as deeper analytical inquiry moved forward into a variety of subjects, such as the motives behind the organizations' activities, the relationship between the Zionist parties and their youth wings, and the relationships among the various youth movements and their relations with the small Hungarian underground formations.

Over the years various publications and public meetings brought forth the stories of various movements, which perhaps justly could claim that they had been underrepresented or even absent from Israeli historiography, for example B'ne Akiva. By the early eighties all the youth movements had their various "official" histories written, which in turn generated more public attention, including from the second generation.

The Zionist underground in Hungary became a topic on the agenda of numerous meetings. For example, in December 1982 Masuah held a conference on "The Ha'Noar Hatzioni and Akiva in Times of Crisis" to mark the occasion of the publication of Asher Cohen's book in Hebrew.

In June 1987 a conference was held at the University of Haifa and the Ghetto Fighters' House on the "Zionist Youth Movements during the Holocaust." The published papers comprised the first Israeli academic publication to deal with the more universal aspects of rescue and resistance activities during the Holocaust, including a prominent discussion of the subjects in their Hungarian contexts, in addition to the activities of the youth movements in Poland, the Baltic States, and elsewhere.

The topic was not exhausted, however, and a wave of new publications followed Asher Cohen's integrative work. In the early nineties, Hava Eichler published *Under the Shadow of Death—Zionist Youth in Times of Trial*, narrating the history of the Ha'Noar Hatzioni. Several memoirs published by members of the youth organizations in recent years have added significantly to our understanding of the motives, the personalities, and the ways and means of action of these organizations. The latest publications indicate that this generation, now in their late seventies and early eighties wishes to pass on their legacy to the third generation.

The Past Twenty Years

In March 1984 Randolph Braham hosted at the City University of New York a major conference on the Holocaust in Hungary. This gathering was followed by the largest international conference held on the subject in Israel at the University of Haifa. Unfortunately the Haifa conference's organizer, Bela Vago, fell ill at the New York venue and could not participate in Haifa. The published papers of the two conferences became classic texts for the study of the Holocaust.[23] The presence of historians from Hungary at the Haifa conference added to its significance, indicating the beginning of a gradual thaw in Hungarian-Israeli academic relations.

The papers presented gave an overview and in a sense summed up our knowledge of the Holocaust forty years after the event. This trend was also reflected in Nathaniel Katzburg's *Hungary and the Jews*, which dealt with the political and legal history of the inter-war period until 1943.[24] Likewise, Yehuda Don's studies highlighted the less well-documented economic and social consequences of the anti-Jewish legislation, which led to the pauperization of Hungarian Jewry before the deportations. However, there is no doubt that Braham's *The Politics of Genocide* provided the main source and road-map for understanding the Holocaust in Hungary. It appears that researchers in Israel often first checked Braham's volumes to find under-researched subjects. Since the late eighties new sources have gradually become available from Hungarian archives.

A special edition of *Yalkut Moreshet* in 1994 was devoted to the Holocaust in Hungary and represented yet another major venture in Israeli historiography.[25] With a combination of original research, analysis, documents, and personal testimonies, the volume became a valuable tool for students and professors alike. Various periodicals continued to publish studies related to Hungary, for example, Roni Stauber's work on rescue missions from Hungary published in *Yalkut Moreshet*.[26]

Israeli scholars made significant contributions to a conference in London on the Holocaust in Hungary held in April 1994, the papers from which were published in 1997.[27] Among the participants, Yehuda Bauer, Dina Porat, Asher Cohen, Yehuda Don, Shlomo Aronson, and Robert Rozett presented a wide spectrum of topics that reflected the state of Israeli historiography both from a comparative viewpoint and from their own research experience. The unanswered questions highlighted at the conference indicated the necessity for continued research and analysis of one of the most tragic and dramatic chapters of the Holocaust.

The trend to reflect critically on some previous work in light of new documents or interpretations has not been absent from Israeli historiography. For example, Sari Reuveni's study on Horthy and the Jews presents a critical summary of our knowledge of Horthy's policies by examining the earlier work of Israeli and other historians.[28]

Comprehensive studies of Hungarian Jewish history, including the Holocaust, were rare in Israeli historiography. The most prominent exception was Yitzhak Perri (Friedman), who was not only active in organizing public events on the topic, but who published a series of volumes that traced hundred of years of Hungarian Jewish history, including several volumes on Transylvania. His narratives about the richness of Hungarian Jewish life further reinforced the tragic loss of their traditions during the Holocaust. Perri's specific studies on the Holocaust present an overall analysis of the issues involved while also focusing on local history, such as his work on the Jewish community of Marosvásárhely (Târgu Mures in Romanian).

Other historians, for example Michael Silber, even though not focusing directly on the Holocaust have provided through their academic work valuable contributions to the knowledge of the Hungarian Jewish past, especially in terms of social history.

At this sixtieth anniversary of the Holocaust in Hungary several academic and public events in Israel commemorated the event. *Yalkut Moreshet* devoted half of its April 2004 issue to Hungary, in which Zvi Erez published a useful chronology of the Holocaust. Likewise, the 2004 volume of *Yad Vashem Studies* devoted the majority of its contents to the Holocaust in Hungary.

In the early twenty-first century, Israeli historians face several issues and problems. It is true that since 1989 newly available documentation enables further research on both the macro and micro levels. Yet it seems that the possibility exists for a slowdown in Israeli historiography. A new generation of Hungarian historians is enthusiastically and actively at work taking the place of those from other countries for whom access to sources is open, but they do not live in Hungary. Some historians, for example Robert Rozett, are utilizing the excellent material available at Yad Vashem. Nonetheless, the number of historians from the new Israeli generation is rather low. There are of course some younger scholars of note, such as Guy Meron and others, who specialize on Hungarian Jewry, if not directly on the Holocaust, and they may fill in the ranks in the years to come. It is certain, however, that Israeli historiography will face a diminution in the profile of academic research unless a new generation is supported both morally and materially to engage in the subject. There are several masters' theses and perhaps Ph.D. dissertations in progress—but often these students complain that there are no more subjects to research. Perhaps this statement compliments the previous generations, but there remain a variety of issues and subjects that can and should be explored.

Now that research is becoming more "globalized" in the sense that Hungarian researchers spend time in Israel and in America at the United States Holocaust Memorial Museum, and Israeli scholars now have access to sources in Hungary, we can perhaps hope that the opportunity exists to negate the more pessimistic remarks above. All of us want the legacy of the first generation of scholars passed on to the following generations.

Notes

1. Yehuda Bauer, *Rethinking the Holocaust* (New Haven, CT: Yale University Press, 2001); and Dan Michman, *Hashoah V-Hikra* (The Holocaust and Holocaust research) (Tel-Aviv: Moreshet, 1998).

2. Randolph L. Braham, ed., *Hungarian Jewish Studies*, vols. 1–3 (New York: World Federation of Hungarian Jews, 1966–1973).

3. Roni Stauber, *Ha-Lekah le-Dor* (Lesson for this generation: Holocaust and heroism in Israeli public discourse in the 1950s) (Jerusalem: Yad Ben Zvi Press, 2000).

4. Ibid., chapter 6.

5. The essay "Bein Varsha le-Budapest" appeared in *Dapim Le-Heker Tkufat Ha Shoah* 12 (1995).

6. Dina Porat, *The Blue and Yellow Star of David* (Cambridge: Harvard University Press, 1990).

7. *Yediot Yad Vashem* 6–7 (January 1956).

8. N. Katzburg, "Hungaria Beshnot ha-sloshim ve-haarbaim," *Yediot Yad Vashem* 19–20 (May 1959); Yehuda Komlos, "Bibliografia al redifat yehudei Hungaria," *Yediot Yad Vashem* 21–22 (December 1959).

9. Ibid., 25–26 (February 1961).

10. *Sefer Hapartizanim Hayehudim* (The book of Jewish partisans) (Merhavia: Sifriat Hapoalim. 1958).

11. Asher Cohen, *The Halutz Resistance in Hungary 1942–1944* (New York: The Rosenthal Institute for Holocaust Studies of the City University of New York, 1986).

12. *Yad Vashem Studies* 5 (1962).

13. Bela Vago, "Political and Diplomatic Activities Relating to the Rescue of the Jews of Northern Transylvania," *Yad Vashem Studies* 6 (1967).

14. Bela Vago, "Intelligence Aspects of the Yoel Brand Mission," *Yad Vashem Studies* 10 (1974).

15. Zvi Erez, "Sefer al Redifat Hayehudim Be-Hungaria" (A book on the persecution of the Jews in Hungary), *Yalkut Moreshet* 4:4 (1967); *Shana Le-ein Ketz* (Year without end) (Jerusalem: Yad Vashem, 1966).

16. David Margalit, "Mivtzaey Ha-hatzala be-Hungaria" (Rescue actions in Hungary), *Massuah* 2 (1974): 90–96; Moshe Gonda, "Ha'Noar Hatzioni Be-Hungaria Be-tkufat Ha-shoah" (The Na'Noar Hatzioni in Hungary during the Holocaust), *Massuah* 2 (1974): 96–100; Gabriel Horowitz, "Edut Zikharon al-peilut Ha'noar Hatzioni" (Memories of the

Ha'Noar Hatzioni), *Massuah* 17 (1989). Hava Eichler's two Hebrew-language articles, both titled "Ha'Noar Hatzioni be-Hungaria" (The Ha'Noar Hatzioni in Hungary), appeared in *Massuah* 16 (1988): 118–25, and *Massuah* 30 (2002): 281–90; and Roni Stauber's essay, "Peulot Ezra ve-Hatzala me-Hungaria Be-sithey ha-shlita ve-hahaspaa he-germanit" (Rescue and aid activities from Hungary into areas under German control and influence), appeared in *Massuah* 19 (1991): 63–94.

17. Bela Vago and George Mosse, eds., *Jews and Non-Jews in Eastern Europe, 1918–1945* (New York: Wiley, 1974); and Bela Vago, ed., *Jewish Assimilation in Modern Times* (New York: Westview Press, 1981).

18. *Hungaria* (Hungary) (Jerusalem: Yad Vashem, 1992).

19. Raphael Vago, "The Concepts of Resistance and Heroism in Israel Historiography and Public Opinion," *Studia Iudaica* X (2001).

20. Randolph L. Braham, "The Official Jewish Leadership of Wartime Hungary," in *Patterns of Jewish Leadership in Nazi Europe 1933–1945* (Jerusalem: Yad Vashem, 1979).

21. Zvi Erez, "Ha-Moatzah ha-Yehudit ha-Ahrona be-Europa" (The last Jewish council in Europe), *Yalkut Moreshet* 76 (October 2003).

22. See footnote 11 above.

23. The Haifa conference papers are in *Dapim Leheker Tkufat HaShoah* 4 (1984), and those from the CUNY conference in Randolph Braham and Bela Vago, eds., *The Holocaust in Hungary: Forty Years Later* (New York: Columbia University Press, 1985).

24. Nathaniel Katzburg, *Hungary and the Jews: Policy and Legislation, 1920–1943* (Ramat-Gan: Bar-Ilan University Press, 1981).

25. See Arieh Yaari, Zvi Erez, David Gur, and Eli Netzer, eds., *Yalkut Moreshet* 57 (May 1994).

26. Roni Stauber, "Peulot Ezra ve-Hatzala me-Hungaria Be-sithey ha-shlita ve-hahaspaa he-germanit" (Rescue and aid activities from Hungary into areas under German control and influence), *Massuah* 19 (1991): 63–94.

27. David Ceserani, ed., *Genocide and Rescue: The Holocaust in Hungary* (Oxford and New York: Oxford University Press, 1997).

28. Sari Reuveni, "Horti ve-ha-Yehudim" (Horthy and the Jews), *Yalkut Moreshet* 74 (November 2002).

Postwar
Art and Literature

Trauma and Distortion: Holocaust Fiction and the Ban on Jewish Memory in Hungary*

Zsuzsanna Ozsváth

As soon as World War II ended, and the survivors of the camps, death marches, and labor-service companies returned to Hungary, and those who had been ghettoized or in hiding resurfaced, there emerged memoirs and fictional accounts about the Holocaust. Most authors of these accounts were Jews, driven by the desire to register and preserve the record of their unprecedented ordeal.[1] At first, neither the general public nor the leadership of Hungary's new political system, including writers on the left, showed great interest in the events of the Holocaust. For the most part, they were more involved in determining their own place in the new world than analyzing the past from the "Jewish point of view." Nor did most non-Jewish writers and poets pay much attention to the Shoah, believing that World War II and "Hungary's tragic fate at Trianon" were the factors responsible for the nation's enormous losses. And because a number of these literati had earlier been involved in right-wing, populist, nationalist, even anti-Semitic agitation, they were slow to change gears. Small wonder that the first chroniclers of the Shoah did not have large, sympathetic audiences listening to their tales.[2] Yet they felt urged to write them down.

As a result, Holocaust literature was born immediately after the war and displayed a wide range of heretofore unimaginable personal and communal anguish. This trend continued until 1948, when the Soviet government and the newly organized Hungarian Communist Party— with the blessings of its cultural-commissars—began to deny the particularly Jewish aspect of the Shoah, generalizing and universalizing this unprecedented assault on Jewish life and tradition. An anti-Semitic campaign initiated in Moscow further encouraged the hostility of Hungarian officialdom towards the Jews, by defining "Jewish mentality" as the source of "rootless cosmopolitanism," and by persecuting and suppressing "Hebrewism" and Jewish religious and cultural institutions.[3]

---

* In memory of my friend Éva Szabolcsi.

Under the weight of such political and existential pressures on authors and readers alike, the depiction of Hitler's war on the Jews changed shape and structure in Hungarian culture. The change, in fact, started to appear in tales and "testimonials" indicating that this "inhumanity" had been created by the same "capitalist-imperialist interests" that had brought about the war. According to these views, the oppressors of the Jews were also oppressors of working people everywhere. The distortion of Holocaust remembrance and Jewish history intensified in the late 1940s and early 1950s, after Stalin attacked some of the greatest Soviet-Yiddish writers and artists. In 1953, he accused a group of Jewish doctors of participating in "Zionist conspiracies" designed to overthrow the Kremlin. As a result of these campaigns, hundreds of Jews were arrested and indicted under the Soviet criminal law system. Some of them "died" in prison, others were executed or condemned to hard labor in the Gulag.[4] Likewise, in Hungary, scores of prominent Jews were arrested, tortured, and sentenced.[5]

Anti-Semitic agitation in the Communist world, however, did not end with Stalin's death, nor later with the collapse of the Rákosi government in Hungary. While more open to reform and granting more freedom for the expression of Jewish religious life than the previous government, the Kádár regime carefully watched and regulated Jewish participation in Hungarian public life.[6] In addition, it decided to go further and erase the "Jewish-question" altogether, ending such perennially sensitive issues as "Jewish identity" and "Jewish memory."

The pressure on the Jews "to forget their past" (or at least not to stress it too intensely) was, of course, not new in Hungarian-Jewish history. In fact, it had been the driving force behind the enormously successful nineteenth-century assimilation processes that turned hundreds of thousands of Jews into passionate Magyar patriots in less than a few decades.[7] Small wonder then that they fought heroically and died by the thousands in the Great War for their beloved fatherland. They hoped for reconciliation even after the White Terror murdered 5,000 to 6,000 Jews, and even after the new anti-Jewish laws stripped them of their economic, political, and civil rights in the late 1930s and early 1940s. The ensuing German occupation of 1944, however, erased all hope for a while: most Hungarian Jews were killed in the Holocaust.

After the Shoah, the wider world changed a great deal. Some survivors left the country; others stayed because they were too tired to run, or because once more many hoped to take root and become part of the nation, a process that they believed would ultimately eradicate *all* differences between Jews and Hungarians including their ancient religion and the past, which some now eagerly wished to forget.[8] In this way, much of Hungarian literature and contemporary media that dealt with the events of the "war years"—even during the 1960s, 1970s, and 1980s— either suppressed or portrayed the Shoah as having only coincidentally Jewish features. Jews were portrayed as alienated, often grotesque characters, bereft of both the consciousness of selfhood and Jewish collective memory. At the same time, even during those years and under those circumstances, a few texts emerged that did not capitulate to the state-imposed ban on Jewish memory or even follow their authors' determination to forget the past. Rupturing the layers of repression, these texts recalled, repeated, and expressed the events of the Shoah, bearing witness to the immensity of the trauma it created.[9]

István György's 1945 book, *Fegyvertelenül a tüzvonalban*, is one of the first eyewitness accounts of the Jewish labor service to appear in Hungary's post-Holocaust period.[10] Using documentary representation and historical narrative techniques, György focuses on his experience on the Russian front. Force-marched in rain, snow, and freezing weather across cities, towns, and the mud-drenched fields of the Ukraine, deprived of sleep, warm clothes, food, and water, the servicemen died by the thousands or were massacred by their guards.[11] Unlike most of his comrades, György survived this ordeal and returned home in the fall of 1943. But then, in the spring of 1944, he was again drafted and taken to Bor, a Serbian mining town in Yugoslavia. Broken physically and psychologically by starvation, hard work, and the ever-present vermin, and put under the pressure of constant and brutal attacks by the guards, the servicemen suffered through the summer of 1944. Then, in late August, when the German army started to evacuate the Balkans, the Jewish labor-service companies were ordered to begin their march back to Hungary. Of the two contingents organized for the march, György was placed in the second. While many people in the first contingent were massacred at Cservenka, the second was later captured by partisans in Hungary and liberated.[12]

Writing immediately after the war, György remembered every detail of his ordeal and created a memoir that most scholars of the field view as one of the major testimonies of the Hungarian labor-service experience. Yet the text offers more than documentary representation. It makes use of literary juxtapositions that assault the reader's senses. The descriptions of the snow fields, life-rending hunger, and brutal murder clash over and over against the servicemen's remembrance of home with their beloved ones, creating heart-breaking tales of suffering and loneliness. As for the victims and their tormentors, we encounter no difficulty identifying them. The servicemen are unquestionably Jewish, their murderers are mostly ordinary Hungarians. The anguish the narrator encounters does not explain anything about "class war" or the "human condition." It demonstrates the murder of the Jews, shifting into focus a world that emerges more brutal than anything previously encountered.

Another early major text is Béla Zsolt's 1946–47 novel, *Kilenc koffer*.[13] Like György, Zsolt had first been a slave laborer on the Russian front for a year and a half. But as the novel starts, he is a prisoner amid thousands of Jews in the ghetto of Nagyvárad. From the horrors he had already experienced in the Ukraine, and the images of a terrifying death hovering over him in the ghetto, Zsolt's narrator concludes there is no hope for survival. Using documentary representation, conventional narrative, and flashbacks, the author interconnects the servicemen's torture on the front with the surrealistic world of the ghetto, where the displacement of life by death has already started, where the familiar has already lost its meaning, and where a grotesque and harsh reality dissolves all previously known experience about the world.

Like György, Zsolt shows no hesitation in revealing that the servicemen in the Ukraine as well as those in the ghetto are Jews, and that their murderers are Hungarians. Nor does he portray the Shoah as part of a general war upon humanity. Revealing his knowledge of the ghetto's impending demise, he gives a penetrating account of a world where gas is waiting for the living, murder replaces life, love has become harmful and treacherous, and even the deepest human relationship turns fragile in the face of atrocity.

On the other hand, Tibor Déry's short account, *Emlékeim az alvilágból*, written within the "realist tradition" of the Party guidelines, gives words to an experience significantly different from that of György or Zsolt.[14] Déry, who has become one of the great writer-heroes of the 1956 Hungarian Revolution, was accused of treason, sentenced to nine years, and imprisoned for three under the Kádár government. Clearly he suffered brutal reprisals for his heroic stance. But he could not resist the

Party line regarding the "Jewish question." Or was he not yet ready to give up his innermost hopes for equality and a better, more just world, for which he had been yearning for so long? His narrator, hiding during the German occupation, rarely mentions the word *Jew*; nor does he struggle with the problem of the ancient tradition of hatred turned against the Jewish people. Cryptic and pensive, he sees the violence but avoids examining its significance. In fact, he claims that the war is responsible for the ongoing murder. The war destroys people's inhibitions; the war creates killers (a stance that he immediately contradicts, however, by admitting his own incapability to take a pistol in his hand). Also, unlike most literary characters of Holocaust novels or memoirs, whose lives are limited to near survival, Déry's procrustean narrator helps others to resist the Germans and is, in turn, helped to survive by his comrades. Alienated from the persecuted Jews and their killers, he places his hopes in the coming world of the Soviet Republic and in his own future as a Hungarian Communist writer.

But then, despite state-controlled attempts to erase the memory of the Holocaust from both Jewish history and Hungarian culture, suddenly, and almost inconceivably, a few new scholarly and literary works appeared in the late 1950s and early 1960s that struggled against this suppression. Among them was the novel, *Elysium*, written in 1958.[15] Perplexingly, its author was Imre Keszi, one of the country's cultural commissars. Simply disregarding the restrictions on Jewish memory—restrictions that Keszi had obviously approved and practiced for many years—the novel interweaves documentary narrative, representation, and historical trauma. It gives account of the heart-wrenching calvary of a thirteen-year-old boy in the *universe concentrationaire*, his arrest by the Hungarian gendarmerie, deportation to Auschwitz, and the unimaginable torture he endured as one of the victims of the Nazis' medical experiments. Inexplicably, if we consider its time and space, the novel is not about universal suffering or universal evil, but rather about the fate of the Jews in the twentieth century.

In the decade following the publication of Keszi's book, other texts have appeared, puncturing the ban on open discussions of the Shoah in Hungarian culture.[16] Moreover, by the early 1970s, a slow but steady flow of artistic writing began to be published, demonstrating that the trauma the Jewish genocide created is ongoing, a force that does not diminish, but rather grows over time. One of the first literary pieces contributing to this flow was István Gáll's novel, *Napimádó*.[17] Interweaving dream images, flashbacks, and conventional representation, the text revolves around a couple, Juli and Robi, living in different worlds that cannot be easily integrated. Juli, a child during the Holocaust in Hungary, has lived ever since with horrific memories festering in her mind. In fact, her life has been traumatized by the Shoah. Ten years old, abandoned, running away from Germans, Hungarians, and the bombardment of Budapest, she finally finds her place in a children's home, under the auspices of the Red Cross. A fourteen-year old boy, Kisgyuri, cares about her and shares with her everything he has: his food, his bed, and his love. One day, to the accompaniment of their barking dogs, the Germans kill him.

Juli survives and grows up. She even overcomes her parents' neglect. And there is nothing "remarkable" in her way of life except two seemingly "strange" habits. She is obsessed with playing games (word-games, poetic and metaphorical games, games for acting out and using poetry, games that interweave reality and fantasy). In this way, she re-lives her past in the "ghetto house" where she had played these games day and night for months. Her other "habit" involves a remarkable kind of insomnia. As soon as she goes to bed at night, she remembers her days of hiding as a child: she looks for Kisgyuri, hears the Germans yelling and their dogs barking. Re-living this scene again and again in her dreams, Juli reinforces Freud's observation regarding the need for repetition caused by trauma.[18] She also echoes Primo Levi's uncanny question, "Why is the pain of every day translated so constantly into our dreams, in the ever-repeated scene of the unlistened-to story?"[19] The significance of her urge to re-live that pain and repeat that experience is further emphasized by the narrator's three-fold, verbatim reiteration of her arrival in the children's home, Kisgyuri's care of her, and his murder. Her memory of horror need not be retrieved: it is ongoing, over-shadowing her nights, her thoughts, her relationships, her dreams, collapsing the time between past and present. The trauma she experienced, and which will forever remain part of her "unlistened-to story," determines the ways in which she lives and feels and acts.

On the other hand, Robi, a child of "Christian Hungarians," comes from another world. He was never homeless, never separated from his parents. Although he, too, suffered as a child, as did many ordinary Hungarians during and after the war, he was not a Jew, singled out, abandoned, threatened by torture and murder, and, ultimately, by the erasure of his family and community. In this way, the rift between the couple is vast. On the one hand, it reveals the un-healable trauma, on the other, it is paradigmatic of Jewish existence in Hungary. In fact, it demonstrates that traumatic memory occupies a space in the human mind and seems unable to be assimilated into ordinary life.

György Gera's novel, *Terelö út*, also deals with the fragmentation and power of repressed memory, all of which Gera juxtaposes against a number of factual reports, newspaper articles, and laws of the time.[20] Deported as a child to a concentration camp in Austria, the narrator travels to Vienna as an adult, where he suddenly finds himself drawn into a search for the camp's remains. He leaves the main road behind, partly rides and partly walks across byways, gets lost again and again, but through flashbacks, narrative memory, and hallucinatory visions he locates it.[21] But what he finds no longer resembles the past he remembers: the people who were there deny its existence; the camp site is disguised and covered-up. What was once reality can no longer be recognized. Contrary to the speaker's traumatized memory, layers of changes have altered the world, revealing that present life and wounded memory can never be integrated.

Instead of ending the novel at this point, however, Gera finds another solution. His narrator meets a Jewish doctor, someone who *can* reconstruct the camp. In fact, over the years, the doctor has gathered every bit of information he could find and kept all the records of the perpetrators. Now he invites his visitor to join him in the process of bringing the murderers to justice. At this point, the narrator makes an argumentative, political decision: it is not *this* he was searching for. If reconstructing the past means acting upon it, he is willing to forget and accept the consequences of his decision.

On the other hand, Maria Ember's *Hajtü kanyar* shows no intellectual-moral desire for eliminating the community's wounded memory.[22] The novel takes us directly into the terrain of the Holocaust and explores the trauma the main character, "the boy," has suffered. Ember's task, of course, is almost unbearably difficult. To remember and sculpt the details of the chamber of horrors as sharply and as clearly as she does thirty years after the event demonstrates that she has never lost sight of this experience—that the trauma has remained lodged in her mind. Using military orders, documents, decrees, reports, newspaper articles, records of evidence, and correspondence that constantly interrupt but also frame the narrative, the story illuminates a grotesquely murderous world. With his father interned and probably killed, the boy and his mother are thrown into the ghetto with thousands of crazed Jews. Beaten, tortured, humiliated, and at the end deported to Strasshof, the main character finds himself in a new world, in which the abnormal defeats the normal, and hunger, thirst, brutality, and death replace life, a world that can never be forgotten by those who saw—or by those who heard about it. In this way, despite the ever-present political pressures of the 1970s in Hungary, *Hajtü kanyar* bears out the permanent damage the camps meted out to Jews, afflicting their sense of life and their future.

These novels were followed by several new ones, each defying the government's policy to suppress Jewish memory. Among them, Imre Kertész' novel, *Sorstalanság,* was published in 1975.[23] Caught by mere coincidence, from one fatal moment to another, arrested and deported to Auschwitz, fifteen-year-old Gyuri Köves is thrown into unimaginable chaos, into a world lying in wait to catch, collect, and kill every Jew. Attempting to make sense of its rules and nature, the boy must first understand that he cannot trust his own eyes, nor his own senses in the camp. Indeed, the camp he sees defies human experience and every bit of logic. At first, he believes he will play soccer in Auschwitz; is relieved when he sees the "well-dressed, orderly, nice German officers"; finds Dr. Mengele a "sympathetic, well-meaning gentleman"; and thinks the smell of the crematorium comes from a leather plant. As his experience in the "real" world cannot help him understand Auschwitz, so does the camp fail to offer him any knowledge of the outside world. These two realms cannot be assimilated and Gyuri, like the rest of the prisoners, will remain traumatized for the rest of his life. His memory can never be erased, no matter what the political system in power might offer or threaten. He has, as the novel testifies, not forgotten anything.

Finally, even in 1984, when György Somlyó's novel *Rámpa* was published, the state-supported, massive denial of the Holocaust still lay heavily on Hungary's media, school system, and the country's cultural and political scene.[24] Somlyó's book, like those before it, explodes the taboo and demonstrates the omnipresence of the trauma Jews experienced directly or vicariously in the Shoah. Using his main character's permanently stained memory of fear, atrocity, and murder, Somlyó dissolves the separation between past and present, even among the layers of the ancient and recent past. He also produces a highly crafted, unbroken flow of perceptions, merging them with streams of the speaker's conscious and unconscious thoughts, mental images, flashbacks, and free associations. With this approach, he sculpts the book's dominant image, the narrator standing on a ramp with thousands of Jews behind him, all destined for torture and destruction. His look is fixed at once on the past and the present, on the inside and the outside, on his early childhood, youth, family, intellectual interests, sexual experience, and the physical torture and death laying before him. Standing between the boxcar and an escape route, he is suddenly allowed to leave by chance, by the means of Raoul Wallenberg's "protected pass." But having seen what he has, he will not be able to leave behind that ramp for as long as he lives; in fact, he will forever repeat and re-live that experience.

Breaking the ban on Jewish memory and imagination, novelists and writers revealed that the trauma Hungarian Jews suffered during the Shoah did not disappear under the pressure of dictatorships, anguish, or self-denial. In fact, it has become a permanent part of the Hungarian-Jewish experience for both those who were there and those who have been touched by it. As Primo Levi foresaw the problem many years ago, "...for us even the hour of liberty rang out grave and muffled...because we felt that...now nothing could ever happen good and pure enough to rub out our past, and that the scars of the outrage would remain within us for ever, and in the memories of those who saw it, and in the places where it occurred, and in the stories that we should tell of it."[25]

Notes

1. For a discussion of Hungarian Holocaust literature, see Anna Földes, "A Holokauszt a magyar (proza)irodalom tükrében" (The Holocaust in the mirror of Hungarian [prose] fiction), in *Tanulmányok a Holokausztról, I* (Studies in the Holocaust, I), ed. Randolph L. Braham (Budapest: Balassi Kiadó, 2001), 73–122.

2. On the Hungarian writers and the "Jewish question," see Gyula Juhász, "A barbár korhullám (A magyar szellemi élet és a zsidó kérdés a második világháború elött és alatt, 1938–1944)" (The barbaric tide of the age [Hungarian intellectual life and the Jewish question before and during the second world war, 1938–1944]), *Új Írás* (New writing) (July 1984), 64–96; Zsuzsanna Ozsváth, "Can Words Kill? Anti-Semitic Texts and Their Impact on the Hungarian Jewish Catastrophe," in *The Holocaust in Hungary: Fifty Years Later*, eds. Randolph L. Braham and Attila Pók (New York: Columbia University Press, 1997), 79–116; and Zsuzsanna Ozsváth, *In the Footsteps of Orpheus: The Life and Times of Miklós Radnóti* (Bloomington: Indiana University Press, 2000), 25–52.

3. Arno Lustiger, *Stalin and the Jews* (New York: Enigma Books, 2003), 199–211.

4. Lustiger, *Stalin*, 218–45; Anne Applebaum, *The Gulag: A History* (New York: Doubleday, 2003), 474–75.

5. Paul Lendvai, *Anti-Semitism without Jews: Communist Eastern Europe* (New York: Doubleday, 1971), 311–12; Eugene Duschinsky, "Hungary," in *The Jews in the Soviet Satellites*, eds. Peter Meyer et. al. (Westport: Greenwood Press: 1953), 483–85.

6. See the Soviet stance regarding Jewish participation in the Rákosi era, in Tamás Aczél and Tibor Méray, *The Revolt of the Mind: A Case History of Intellectual Resistance Behind the Iron Curtain* (New York: Frederick A. Praeger, 1959), 159.

7. On the issue of Jewish assimilation, see Viktor Karády, "Egyenlőtlen elmagyarosodás, avagy hogyan vált Magyarország magyar nyelvű országgá?" (Uneven magyarization: Or how did Hungary become a Magyar-speaking country?), in *Zsidóság, Modernizáció, Polgárosodás: Tanulmányok* (Jewry, modernization, embourgeoisement Studies) (Budapest: Cserépfalvi, 1997), 151–95.

8. Viktor Karády, "Traumahatás és menekülés: A zsidó vallásváltók szociológiája 1945 elött és után" (Trauma and escape: Sociology of the converted Jews before and after 1945) in *Önazonosítás, sorsválasztás: A zsidó csoportazonosság történelmi alakváltozásai Magyarországon* (Self-identity and life choice: Historical character changes of Jewish group identification in Hungary) (Budapest: Új Mandátum, 2001), 263–95.

9. Of course, many additional outstanding texts did not conform to the ban on Jewish memory than I discuss in this paper.

10. István György, *Fegyvertelenül a tüzvonalban* (Unarmed in the battlefield), 4th ed. (Budapest: Cserépfalvi Kiadás, 1945).

11. On the torture of the servicemen in the army, see also Gábor Mermelstein, "A Jew in a Motorized Unit of the Hungarian Army," and Zoltán (Csima) Singer, "History of Labor Service Company 110/34," both in *The Wartime System of Labor Service in Hungary: Varieties of Experiences*, ed. Randolph L. Braham (New York: Columbia University Press, 1995), 1–14, 15–54.

12. On Bor and Cservenka, see Randolph L. Braham, *The Politics of Genocide: The Holocaust in Hungary*, revised and enlarged edition (New York: Columbia University Press, 1994), I, 343–52; György Nagy, "History of Labor Service Company 108/84 of Bor," in Braham, *The Wartime System*, 55–127; and Nathan Eck, "The March of Death from Serbia to Hungary (September 1944) and the Slaughter of Cservenka (Story of a Survivor of the Death Pit)," in *Yad Vashem Studies on the European Jewish Catastrophe and Resistance* (Jerusalem: Yad Vashem, 1958), II, 255–94.

13. Béla Zsolt, *Kilenc koffer* (Nine suitcases) (Budapest: Magvetö, 1980).

14. Tibor Déry, *Emlékeim az alvilágból* (My memories of the underworld), drawings by István Zádor (Budapest: National Council of Peace, 1955).

15. Imre Keszi, *Elysium* (Budapest: Magvetö, 1958).

16. Among them appeared the important historical documentary of the labor service in Hungary, see Elek Karsai, ed., *"Fegyvertelen álltak az aknamezökön . . ." Dokumentumok a munkaszolgálat történetéhez Magyarországon* (Unarmed they stood on the minefields. . ." Documents on the history of labor service in Hungary) (Budapest: A Magyar Izraeliták Országos Képviselete, 1962).

17. István Gáll, *Napimádó* (The sun-worshiper) (Budapest: Szépirodalmi Könyvkiadó, 1970).

18. On this topic, see Joshua Hirsch's excellent study, *After Image: Film, Trauma, and the Holocaust* (Philadelphia: Temple University Press, 2004).

19. Primo Levi, *Survival in Auschwitz: The Nazi Assault on Humanity*, trans. Stuart Woolf (New York: Simon & Schuster, 1996), 60.

20. György Gera, *Terelö út* (Byways) (Budapest: Magvetö, 1972).

21. Similar methods are used by the protagonist of Alain-Fournier's *Le grand meaulnes* (1913) in his journey to find the "lost domain." While the two domains are essentially different from one another, the main characters' desire for repetition and their urge to recover the past are quite similar.

22. Maria Ember, *Hajtü kanyar* (U-turn) (Budapest: Szépirodalmi Könyvkiadó, 1974).

23. Imre Kertész, *Sorstalanság* (Fateless) (Budapest: Magvetö, 1975).

24. György Somlyó, *Rámpa* (Ramp) (Budapest: Szépirodalmi Könyvkiadó, 1984).

25. Primo Levi, *Reawakening*, trans. Stuart Woolf (New York: Collier Books, 1961), 54.

Imre Kertész's *Fateless* on Film:
A Hungarian Holocaust Saga[1]

Catherine Portuges

In the spring of 2004 on the eve of European Union expansion to include Hungary, the sixtieth anniversary of the Holocaust in that country was commemorated. These two events of profound resonance were accompanied by an intense consideration of Hungary's past and a preoccupation with the question of how people remember the past, how memory works in the present. Hungarian memory at this crucial turning point turned to examine the massacre of the country's Jewish population in 1944, which, by virtue of having been concentrated into the last months of that year, constituted the most intensive process of extermination in the Nazis' war against the Jews. Yet despite the proliferation of publications in recent years, it is important to remember the repression that once surrounded discourse of the Shoah in Hungary, and its virtual disappearance from the public scene after 1948.[2]

In order to account, albeit briefly, for the stages that led to the end of that silence, it is useful to consider a major development in the realm of artistic expression: over the course of the 1970s, the memory of the Shoah appeared to return to public discourse primarily in the form of literary texts produced by a generation of writers who had personally experienced the persecution as adolescents.[3] Among them was Imre Kertész, who engaged the question of the role of the Holocaust in Hungarian literature in his lecture "Long Dark Shadow," printed in *A Holocaust mint kultúra: Három előadás* (The Holocaust as culture: Three lectures), suggesting that

> nothing would be simpler than to collect, name and evaluate those Hungarian literary works that were born under direct or indirect influence of the Holocaust.... However, in my view that is not the problem. The problem...is the imagination. To be more precise: to what extent is the imagination capable of coping with the fact of the Holocaust? How can the imagination take in, receive the Holocaust, and, because of this receptive imagination, to what extent has the Holocaust become part of our ethical life and ethical culture.... This is what we must talk about.[4]

The novelist was awarded the Nobel Prize in Literature in 2002 mainly on the basis of *Sorstalanság* (Fateless), first published in 1975, and in general for his work that "upholds the fragile experience of the individual against the barbaric arbitrariness of history." In the novel, he draws upon the "barbaric arbitrariness" of his own tragic experience as a fifteen-year-old Hungarian Jew in Auschwitz.[5] In the aftermath of the Nobel Prize, and following years of relative invisibility, Kertész was catapulted into the forefront of media attention, generating acclaim as well as ambivalence and hostility. Born in Budapest, he considers himself to be part of a generation whose life can be characterized by several key dates: 1944, 1945, 1948, 1953, and 1956. After his liberation from Buchenwald, Kertész made his living in Budapest as a journalist, opera librettist, and occasional factory worker, subsequently receiving prizes for his collected works (published in Germany in 1999 by Rowohlt-Verlag). The author considers the original English translations of *Fateless* and *Kaddish for a Child Not Born* as "a disgracefully bad English translation, a fact I consider utterly unethical...."[6] He believes his publisher "acted disreputably," and insists that the translations "have nothing to do with what I wrote. The language, yes, that's all that connects me to Hungary.... How strange. This foreign language is my mother tongue...."[7] (Both texts have since been published in new translations by Tim Wilkinson: *Kaddish for an Unborn Child*, Vintage Books, November 2004; and *Fatelessness,* Random House, December 2004.)

Although *Fateless,* narrated from the perspective of a young boy's nightmare in the camps, was written between 1960 and 1973 and published in 1975, it received wide recognition only after 1990, ultimately earning first place on the Amazon.com bestseller list. Kertész' *Kaddish for a Child Not Born*, an interior monologue from the point of view of the same narrator who, now an adult, reflects on the relationship between his Holocaust experience and his refusal to sire children, was published on the fiftieth anniversary of the liberation of Auschwitz. Kertész writes in *Kaddish*: "Auschwitz must have been hanging in the air for a long, long time, centuries, perhaps like a dark fruit slowly ripening in the sparkling rays of innumerable ignominious deeds, waiting to finally drop on one's head...." Yet in interviews, he has characterized himself as "a non-believing Jew. Yet as a Jew I was taken to Auschwitz, as a Jew I was in the death camps and as a Jew I live in a society that does not like Jews, one with great anti-Semitism. I always have the feeling that I was obliged to be Jewish. I am Jewish, I accept it, but to a large extent it is also true that it was imposed on me."[8]

In a September 2003 interview, "I Felt the Nobel Prize to be a Distracting Flight," Kertész states,

> Germany was from the very first moment forced to confront its past and could not do so in any way other than self-examination. This was not an easy process—it lasted a long time, and actually only after the student movements of 1968...did the breakthrough take place.... In Hungary as well, after the war some kind of clarification began, but soon afterwards this whole group of issues was suppressed. So Hungary has not yet had its turn in coming to terms with the past. It is true that Hungary indeed suffered a great deal of national pain, it was a threatened country, and one has to understand that it is more sensitive to suffering. But the time will come, even if the nation does not yet have the power or solidarity or generosity (*nagyvonaluság*) to complete the process.... Membership in the European Union now gives the country *carte blanche* to do so.[9]

The Nobel Academy considered *Fateless* disturbing for the book's "lack of moral indignation." Perhaps this assessment has more than a little to do with a specifically Central European meta-language not easily deconstructed by others. Indeed, Kertész might well have anticipated this aspect of the Academy's response when he declared, in an interview broadcast on Hungarian radio in 1991,

> I was not brought up as an observant Jew and I did not become a believer later on; at the same time, I find that Judaism is an absolutely decisive moment of my life, one I am attached to because, on account of it, I lived through a great moral test. But is it possible to rise above the experiences one lives through in such a way that we don't exclude them and at the same time manage to transpose them to a universal level? ... My country has yet to face up to the skeleton in the closet, namely awareness of the issue of the Holocaust, which has not yet taken root in Hungarian culture, and those writing about it [still] stand on the sidelines.... I think it is a success if my book has made even a slight contribution to this process.[10]

A significant gesture toward this process of re-inscribing Hungarian Holocaust memory was the Hungarian Motion Picture Foundation's February 2003 decision to provide funding for a film adaptation of *Fateless*—the very Foundation that, two years earlier, had allocated the majority of its budget to productions many considered nationalist epics, *Bánk Bán* (2003) and *Hídember* (Bridge man, 2003).[11] That a new film from such a different perspective and sensibility was actually produced, based on the author's screenplay published in both Hungarian and German, suggests that both Kertész and the Hungarian government embraced the opportunity afforded by his new status to make just such a contribution.

The production in fact marked the directorial debut of Lajos Koltai, the renowned cinematographer and veteran of more than seventy features, including distinguished films such as István Szabó's Oscar-winning feature *Mephisto* (1982), as well as his Oscar-nominated *Confidence* (*Bizalom*, 1979), *Colonel Redl* (1984), *Hanussen* (1988), *Meeting Venus* (1991), *Taking Sides* (1999), and *Sunshine* (1999).[12] Nonetheless, given Kertész' much-publicized critique of published translations of his books, one wonders whether his personal invitation to Koltai to direct the adaptation from book to screen—also a form of translation—will in time meet a more auspicious fate. Koltai discussed his perspective in a recent documentary, *Koltai Napló* (Koltai's diary) screened at the Hungarian Film Week, known as the *Szemle* (Review), in February 2004.[13] In one documentary sequence, Kertész expresses his reservations concerning previous Holocaust-related films.

> Many directors have tried to deal with the theme of the concentration camps. But few have done so in an authentic way. After the war, in 1946–47, I saw a film about Auschwitz by a Polish woman director, which I found stunning. The first few scenes are astonishingly authentic: it is raining, early morning in Birkenau. The women prisoners are very tired, they start to move slowly back and forth, in a totally credible way. What Spielberg does [in *Schindler's List*], in contrast, is inauthentic: inmates call to each other across barbed wire...this would have been totally impossible...the whole picture lacks credibility....[14]

However, it should be noted that the sharp increase in the number of Holocaust films produced may be attributable to the 1993 release of *Schindler's List*; among other factors, public debate surrounding the film led to the creation of Spielberg's Survivors of the Shoah Visual History Foundation, which has become a major site of international archival, oral history, film, video, and digital research and preservation.

In my first interview with Koltai in February 2003, and again a year later in Budapest, the director referred to numerous failed attempts to secure funding for the project, long before the Nobel Prize was awarded to a Hungarian writer for the first time in history.[15] Koltai began our conversation by asserting that, "this has been a living project for years, and not merely a sudden urge to capitalize on the Nobel." Explaining that his preparation of the film was based on the author's own scenario, he conceptualized it as "a Hungarian work of art...a Central European co-production involving slightly more than 50 percent of Hungarian funding." The film's total budget was $11.7 million (2.5 billion forints), the largest budget ever allocated for a Hungarian production. The director agreed with Kertész that, in his words, "this story would not be worth making into a film except under the most perfect conditions...the best advertisement for the film would be the star quality of Kertész himself...when, the other day, he read aloud to me some parts of his latest novel, I saw again that not only is he a highly unique thinker but also a great performer."[16]

The cast includes a Hungarian youth portraying the principal role of György Köves, and the film was to be made in Hungarian and dubbed or subtitled in English and German.[17] The film, Koltai added, was shot in color, "but completely matte on the screen; although it might be adequate in black-and-white; that technique was already used by Spielberg in *Schindler's List*. I will try for an effect somewhere between color and black-and-white." The director's vision invites comparison with the visual strategies of recent large-scale Holocaust-centered films such as Roman Polanski's *The Pianist* (2002), based on the memoirs of Ladislaw Szpilman, a young musician in the Warsaw ghetto. That film's star, Adrien Brody, won an Oscar for best actor, as did Polanski for best director at the 2003 Academy Awards, for a work that also addresses Polanski's own experience as a child of the Holocaust.[18] Films as diverse in approach and conceptualization as Liliana Cavani's *The Night Porter* (Italy, 1974), Roberto Benigni's *Life Is Beautiful* (Italy, 1998), and Claude Lanzmann's *Shoah* (France, 1985) still elicit debate over representational strategies adequate to convey what many survivors consider to be unrepresentable.[19]

For *Fateless*, Koltai created a simulacrum of the camps on location near the Hungarian capital to re-imagine the texture and look of Auschwitz, Buchenwald, and Zeitz, the camps Kertész survived as an adolescent deportee.

> [The film] will be linear, with no major dramatic point, tracing the path of a boy who in the end is totally destroyed by his experience. The opening sequence will be set in the beautiful colors of a magnificent central

> European autumn, and gradually fade to black-and-white over time as we
> see the consequences of his experience inscribed in his psyche.

The complex logistics include the deployment of 150 actors and 12,000
extras and the use of digital technology to graft the protagonist onto
authentic wartime film footage. The director received numerous offers of
help from Hungarian Holocaust survivors; one presented a collection of
previously unpublished photographs taken inside the camp with a hidden
Agfa camera. A quite different response to the production was noted by
the Hungarian daily *Népszabadság* in an article entitled "*Sorstalanság*:
Víszály a díszlet miatt" (*Fateless*: Conflict over the set décor) concerning public reaction to the filming.

> Scenes from the Nobel prize-winning novel by Imre Kertész that take
> place in the Buchenwald concentration camp will be shot at a location
> that is under the control of the Interior Ministry. The people of Piliscsaba
> themselves offered this opportunity to the director. However, the daily
> *Magyar Nemzet* reported protests to the effect that Pilis is a sacred
> location, an ancient, protected, and endangered site, suggesting that it
> might disturb the peace of the landscape if a death camp were to be built
> there. One protestor drew a parallel between the construction of this set
> and the Israeli Prime Minister Sharon's visit to the Temple Mount ... but
> he did not say exactly what kind of conflict might erupt in twenty-first-
> century Hungary ... some seem to detect a hidden anti-Semitism behind
> these published objections.[20]

This reaction raises the question of witnessing and testimony: to
what extent do differences exist between films written and directed by
direct witnesses and victims, and those based on memoirs, historical
accounts, photographic documents, or, as in this case, autobiographical
novels, adapted or "translated" to another medium by those without
direct experience of the Holocaust? While a full account of this important issue lies beyond the scope of this paper, we must consider the ways
the internal, often inchoate language of psychological experience is
translated into the more specific, graphic language of cinema. The case
of *Fateless* is complex, involving on the one hand a witness/victim—
Kertész, the writer and screenwriter—and a non-witness—Lajos Koltai,
the director/translator.[21]

A cinematic meditation on fate and its absence, on the trauma
survived by a very young protagonist, disposes of a variety of modalities
depending upon the protagonist's (and the filmmaker's) conception of

the term: it may be represented as dramatic, quotidian, random, inevitable, or pre-ordained, in narrative and experimental genres, as documentary or fiction, in feature-length or short formats. Additionally, as previously theorized in psychoanalytic and structuralist film scholarship, the film medium is supremely capable of evoking immediacy and intimacy, recurrent temporality, or repetition and timelessness. In genres from tragedy to melodrama to comedy, cinematic fate has variously been portrayed as a universal existential condition common to all human beings, for example Robert Bresson's French provincial protagonists in *Mouchette* (France, 1967) and the prisoners in his *Un condamné à mort s'est échappé* (A condemned man escapes, France, 1956), or Michelangelo Antonioni's upper-middle-class urban Italians in *L'Avventura* (Italy, 1960). One of Hungary's most innovative directors, Béla Tarr, visualizes fate "as emanating from below, so to speak, rather than from above," as portrayed in his seven-hour masterpiece *Sátántangó* (1994) and his surreal epic *Werkmeister Harmoniák* (2001), insuring that "no one may claim that [my] films represent only the misery of the poor.... In [my] world deconstruction is slow but unstoppable, and finds its way everywhere. The question therefore is not how to stop or avoid this process, but what we do in the meantime."[22] As director, Koltai also invites the audience to ponder this question. To do so, requires a filmic sense of temporality adequate to Kertész's literary style through which the reader follows his protagonist's odyssey into the *univers concentrationnaire*.

The saga of *Fateless* invites comparison with other Hungarian films that address this profoundly challenging subject, thus opening a space for discussion of cinematic representation of the Holocaust in Hungary sixty years later. Production files, interviews with writers, directors, producers, literary, and film historians become part of this very public text-in-the-making, which is inescapably situated within the small but important genre of Hungarian films that—whether semi-autobiographical or wholly fictional, if indeed such a construct exists—constitute a valuable history of Holocaust representation. These works simultaneously interrogate and articulate the unresolved question of intergenerational transmission of Jewish identity and its traumatic sequels upon successive generations.[23]

The debates surrounding *Fateless* may be illuminated by the concept of "post-memory,"[24] which has usefully theorized visual representation as a powerful medium through which the connection to an object or source is mediated not through recollection but through imaginative investment and re-creation. This empathic projection characterizes the experience of survivors whose own stories are considered of less importance to the subjects than those of a previous generation shaped by traumatic events. The reader's engagement with the text, like that of the film viewer's with the screen image, thus becomes part of a dialectical process in which the necessary work of mourning can occur.

Let us return for a moment to Koltai's statement that "this film will be different from other Holocaust movies," by recalling selected Hungarian films, both semi-autobiographical and wholly fictional, produced after the Holocaust. One of the most relevant to this discussion is perhaps *Apa* (Father, 1966) directed by István Szabó. The film focuses on a twenty-year period from the early 1940s to the early 1960s, and deploys a narrative technique based on flashbacks in which factual and imaginative material are interspersed in a familiar modernist cinematic approach.[25] *Hideg Napok* (Cold days, 1966), directed by András Kovács, is a fictionalized version of a much-debated historical event—the massacre by Hungarian soldiers of several thousand Jewish and Serbian inhabitants of Novi Sad in 1942—that may be read today as a courageous filmic intervention at a time when uncomfortable silence had long engulfed the question of Hungary's role in World War II.[26]

Budapesti Tavasz (Spring comes to Budapest, 1955), directed by Felix Máriássy, vividly reconstructs the last days of the German occupation in 1944 with scenes of horrifying immediacy that include the mass shooting of Jews on the banks of the Danube and the defeated Fascists using civilians as hostages against the advancing Russians.[27] Zoltán Fabri's 1961 feature film *Két félidő a pokolban* (Two half-times in Hell) concerns a group of Hungarians in a German labor camp in the Ukraine, where the inmates are ordered to stage—and, not unexpectedly, lose—a soccer match with their guards in honor of the Führer's birthday. The earliest film on the subject is *Valahól Europában* (Somewhere in Europe, 1947), directed by Géza Radványi, in which a group of children aged from five to eighteen, orphaned by the war or separated from their parents, band together to survive by raiding untended farms and fields. The first half of the film quietly and without sentimentality chronicles the process whereby they become progressively more hardened and anarchic, stealing boots from the bodies of men hanged by the wayside, and eventually even accepting death and deprivation as their normal lot in life. Finally, one must mention the Polish production *Otatni Etap* (The last stage, 1947), directed by Wanda Jakubowska, herself a survivor of Auschwitz, shot on the exact locations where the filmmaker herself had been a deportee, a courageously groundbreaking film that has influenced others of this genre.

István Szabó's *Apa* illuminates through the monologue of a young female protagonist Kertész's own profoundly conflicted and ambivalent stance toward Jewish identity and assimilation, a particularly complicated stance characteristic of Hungarian Jewish writers, artists and intellectuals. The film is a compelling tribute of a son, Takó, active as a student in the uprising of 1956, to his father who died in World War II. It begins with the statement, "I confront your failure, you who look human." In one powerful scene, a teacher asks his class of young boys how many lost a father during the war; nearly three-quarters of the class stand up in a silent testimony to the toll of the war on Jewish families. A later sequence addresses the question of Jewish identity somewhat more directly when Takó, now a university student, walks along the Danube with Anni, a student friend, who confesses to him:

> It's awful, you know. For years I denied that my father died in a concentration camp. I'd make up a story rather than admit I was Jewish. I finally realized the futility of it and I faced reality. I even went to Auschwitz with an excursion group and I took pictures. All I got were pictures of well-dressed tourists milling around. Sometimes I still feel ashamed and pretend not to be Jewish. I am Hungarian, am I not? The forgotten past of my ancestors doesn't count. And I can't overcome it. I want to be proud of that Jewish past for which my parents gave their lives. I simply can't behave normally. I just don't know where I belong, where I want to belong, what I am, or where I should belong. The Pope at last forgave the Jews for their sins. That means that they were guilty of crucifying Christ 2000 years ago. And those who twenty years ago let six million Jews be gassed and burned? How soon will they be absolved? You see how maddening this can be, and how idiotic this Auschwitz thing is! Part of me is there. My parents and relatives perished there. But I can't go on harping on it just to get sympathy. I feel ashamed for belonging to those who were slaughtered like sheep. I always feel as if I had to prove something....[28]

It is all the more remarkable that this brilliant monologue was produced in 1966 when such questions were rarely addressed in Hungarian or, for that matter, in East-Central European cinema. Clearly both documentary and narrative cinema are powerful means of enacting memory and mourning, enabling filmmakers and viewers alike to work through trauma. Both are forms of witnessing and testimony and both are capable of addressing voyeurism, violence, comedy, and propaganda, as well as historical research. Since 1989 Hungarian cinema has undergone dramatic and traumatic changes in, among many other aspects, filmmakers' sense of obligation with respect to their audiences. A number of films made in the 1990s have, whether directly or obliquely, invoked the Holocaust in Hungary, including Krisztina Deák's *Eszter könyve* (The book of Esther), Robert Koltai's *Sose halunk meg* (We'll never die), Judit Elek's *Tutájosok* (The rafters), and *Ébredés* (Awakening), to mention only a few. The past fifteen years have thus witnessed the return of Hungarian Jewish history to the center of the cinematic stage through ambitious historical frescoes as well as intimate, moving narratives.

Where once Hungarian cinema was seen as "the most important art," whose purpose was to bear witness to political realities, today's industry is far more dependent upon profits and market shares, although legislation enacted in 2004 promises to restore much-needed stability to Hungarian film production.[29] That the Hungarian government allocated half the national film budget to the producers of *Fateless*, with the balance to come from international co-producers in Holland, Germany, and Italy, suggests at the very least an opportunity to use Kertész' celebrity to promote a national narrative of the Holocaust. Nonetheless, Koltai's task was monumental, perhaps not unlike that Art Spiegelman faced with regard to his illustrated book, *Maus*, a highly sophisticated representation of the interplay of animal figures with masked humans that enabled him to portray Holocaust events and memory without showing them directly—depicting, as the author says, "the masking of these events in their representation."[30] This concern might well address the responsibilities of present and succeeding generations through its exhortation to measure up to the psychological and historical challenges posed by those who survived and subsequently sought, often at great personal cost as in the case of Kertész, representational strategies commensurate to a seemingly impossible project.

Fateless was produced by the Budapest-based production company MagicMedia and producer Péter Barbalics, who had held the rights to Kertész's screenplay adaptation for a number of years. Earlier plans to

film in English were abandoned, according to the director, after he realized that a central narrative element lies in the linguistic confusion and
isolation of the Hungarian Jews upon their arrival in camps largely
populated by Polish inmates. Reference to Wanda Jakubowska's *The
Last Stage* might prove useful in resolving such linguistic concerns: the
main protagonist is a translator, who thus serves as a cornerstone for the
multi-lingual inmates whose native languages include Polish, Greek,
Hungarian, French, Portuguese, and many others.[31] Koltai gives the
impression of having a passionate—if not always clearly articulated—
vision of the project. With a score by the award-winning Italian movie
composer Ennio Morricone, and a shooting schedule of seventy days, the
film was scheduled to complete production by the end of March 2004,
and was meant to premiere in conjunction with Hungary's accession to
the European community in 2004, thereby marking the Hungarian film
industry's début as a European entity. However, production delays due
to financing problems resulted in the postponement of the film's release
until 2005, when it premiered at the Thirty-Sixth Annual Hungarian Film
Week in Budapest on February 8.

By linking Koltai's contemporary project with earlier films, I suggest that cinematic representations of the Shoah may be readable in light
of those that have preceded them. This speculative mode of analysis may
enable us to engage in a kind of interactive, imaginative exercise with
the work in progress, an inter-textual dialogue with the multiple
discourses of individual and collective memory. My wish is at once to
honor and, in some sense, facilitate Koltai's and Kertész' interest in
communicating with survivors and others who may have experiences,
ideas, or materials to contribute to their project.

Post-Nobel Prize interest in Kertész was undoubtedly enhanced by a
number of factors, not least of which was the desire to illuminate a great
national literature suffering from a perceived linguistic isolation that
often relegated it to minor or marginalized status. The Nobel Laureate's
new novel[32] is set in Budapest after the fall of the Iron Curtain, about
which he has remarked, "This book will be the last glance I will personally cast on the Holocaust."[33] Such a statement, while understandable in
terms of the vast literature of the Shoah, nonetheless gestures toward the
layered process of remembrance characteristic of those who have made
writing—and filmmaking—their duty in order to bear witness and
memorialize. One can hope that the retrospective glance cast by the film

version of *Fateless* will be mapped onto the topography of cinematic representations that sustain the intergenerational work of memory transmission at a time when the desire to forget—the very gesture *Fateless* so persuasively rejects—is too common.

Epilogue

Sorstalanság (the costliest film in the history of the Hungarian film industry) was first screened in competition on February 15, 2005, at the 55th Berlin International Film Festival at the Berlinale Filmpalast to strong critical acclaim. One *New York Times* reviewer wrote that "the harrowing *Fateless* centers on a Jewish teenager and death-camp inmate for whom heroics is beside the point of survival,"[34] while another noted: "With the help of other prisoners and sheer good fortune, Köves survives near-starvation, disease and the fearsome 1944–45 winter. Yet his greatest shock comes when he finally returns to Budapest and discovers his father is dead, his home has been occupied by another family and even surviving Jews tell him he must move on. Köves no less than Mr. Kertész finds himself looking back at the solidarity of life in the camps with nostalgia."[35] According to *Variety*, *Fateless* is "exquisitely modulated and superbly mounted…a genuine way of looking at the Holocaust that is markedly different in tone from other such stories including *Schindler's List* and *The Pianist*,"[36] while another critic commented: "This is an extremely powerful film that has captured the imagination…."[37] "*Fateless* shows us a vision of the Holocaust that has never before been portrayed on screen…. It is a remarkable adaptation of a great novel, and the fact that Kertész himself has played such an important role in its genesis makes it all the more meaningful an experience."[38] In conjunction with its presentation at the Toronto International Film Festival on September 8, 2005, the catalogue reads:

> The directorial debut of virtuoso cinematographer Lajos Koltai, *Fateless* is destined for worldwide critical acclaim and a lasting place in the hearts of international audiences. Although he deftly handles sprawling themes, Kertész knows it is not grand gestures but private, intimate details that make this story visceral and potently devastating. Koltai expertly renders these through an atmospheric use of colour and lighting and an assortment of memorable, eccentric—even oddball—supporting characters that challenge the shopworn cinematic clichés of epic tragedy. *Fateless* offers an incisive, unflinching view of personal despair and tenacious perseverance.[39]

Hungary has selected *Fateless* as its entry for consideration for the Best Foreign Language Film of the year at the 2006 Academy Awards in Hollywood.

Notes

1. An earlier version of this essay was presented for the panel "Imre Kertész: From the Holocaust to the Nobel Prize," American Hungarian Educators Association Conference, Columbia University, New York City, April 24, 2003 (co-sponsored by the Hungarian Cultural Center and Columbia University Institute of East-Central Europe). I am grateful to Professor Randolph Braham and the organizers of "The Holocaust in Hungary: Sixty Years Later" for inviting me to participate in the March 2004 Washington D.C. conference jointly sponsored by the Center for Advanced Holocaust Studies, United States Holocaust Memorial Museum, and the Rosenthal Institute for Holocaust Studies.

2. Peter Kende, *Le Défi hongrois: De Trianon à Bruxelles* (Paris: Editions Buchet-Chastel, 2004). According to Kende, this repression was the result of a convergence of factors, among which was the arrival of the Soviets, a development that was more immediately important in the eyes of Christians, and the fact that the Communists did not wish to compromise their internationalism by crediting the complaints of any particular national group.

3. See Susan Suleiman and Eva Forgács, eds., *Contemporary Jewish Writing in Hungary: An Anthology* (Lincoln NE: University of Nebraska Press, 2003), for an excellent selection of texts by writers including István Örkény, György Konrád, Péter Nádas, György Spiró, and Mária Ember.

4. *A Holocaust mint kultúra: Három elöadás* (Budapest: Századvég 1993). This excerpt is cited by Suleiman and Forgacs, 171, in a translation by Imre Goldstein. The lecture was originally given on October 23, 1991, as part of a colloquium on "Hungarian-Jewish Coexistence (1848–1991)." Kertész's other publications include the novels *A kudarc* (Fiasco, 1988), *Az angol lobogó* (The English flag, 1992), and three lectures on the Holocaust, *A Holocaust mint kultúra* (The Holocaust as culture).

5. Imre Kertész, *Fateless*, trans. Christopher C. Wilson and Katharina M. Wilson (Evanston, IL: Northwestern University Press, 1996). The book has also been translated into Czech, French, Dutch, German, English, Norwegian, Portuguese, Spanish, Danish, Hebrew, Italian, Swedish, and Slovak, among other languages, yet Kertész is rarely mentioned in the North American press, and then often only in passing.

6. Reported by Lajos Koltai to the author, Budapest, October 2002.

7. "A Nobel-díjat zavaró repülesnek éreztem" (I felt the Nobel Prize to be a distracting flight), *HVG-HetiVilag* (September 6, 2003), 47–48.

8. *The Jerusalem Report* (November 4, 2002).

9. "A Nobel-díjat...." My appreciation to Prof. László Dienes for the translation.

10. Alan Riding, "Nobel for Hungarian Writer Who Survived the Death Camps," *The New York Times* (October 11, 2002), A7–8.

11. *Bánk Bán*, a screen adaptation of a classic opera by Ferenc Erkel, is set in medieval Hungary and features Eva Marton, Andrea Rost, and Attila Kiss B. in what some regard as the most important musical drama of Hungary's national cultural heritage. Photography was by Oscar-winning cinematographer Vilmos Zsigmond, who fled Hungary in 1956.

12. In addition to his work with Szabó, Koltai has collaborated with acclaimed directors such as Péter Gothár (*Megall az Idö* [Time stands still], 1982), Pál Gábor (*Angi Vera*, 1978), and Márta Mészáros (*Örökbefogadás* [Adoption], 1975), and he has worked for more than a decade in Hollywood with other eminent directors.

13. *Koltai Napló 2001–2003*, produced by András and Klára Muhi, Hungary, 2004, premiered in Budapest on February 7, 2004. The author is grateful to the producers for providing a video copy of this film.

14. Kertész is referring to *Otatni Etap* (The last stage), directed by Wanda Jakubowska (Poland, 1948), discussed below. I thank László Dienes, professor of comparative literature at the University of Massachusetts, for invaluable collaboration in translating these excerpts.

15. "Sorstalanság: viszály a díszlet miatt" (Fateless: Conflict over the décor), in *Népszabadság* (August 3, 2003).

16. Koltai added, "It would not be elegant to make such a film without Hungarian participation. After all, it is Hungary's first Nobel Prize for literature." All citations of Lajos Koltai are based on the author's conversation with him, Budapest, February 2003 and February 2004.

17. "There are no star roles.... Even if someone were to contribute additional funding, I would not want one," the director insists.

18. Polanski first discovered *The Pianist* when it was republished in Polish in 1998 under its new title, two years before the author's death: "I had searched for decades for a model parallel to my life, which I couldn't film myself.... Szpilman's book was the text I was waiting for—a testimony of human endurance in the face of death, a tribute to the power of music and the will to live, and a story told without the desire for revenge." Through Szpilman's book, Polanski could finally represent the trauma he, too, had suffered. See Catherine Portuges, "Review of *The Pianist*," *American Historical Review* 108:2 (Summer 2003): 622.

19. See André Pierre Colombat, "Claude Lanzmann's *Shoah*," in *The Holocaust in French Film* (London: The Scarecrow Press, 1993), 299–344.

20. Quoted in *Népszabadság* (August 3, 2003) (my translation).

21. Joshua Hirsch develops this distinction in his chapter on post-traumatic autobiography in *Afterimage: Film, Trauma, and the Holocaust* (Philadelphia: Temple University Press, 2004), 112 ff.

22. I am grateful to András Kovács, Eötvös Loránd Tudományegyetem, Budapest, for sharing with me his essay, "The World According to Béla Tarr," catalogue copy published for the Museum of Modern Art's New York City retrospective.

23. See Hirsch, *Afterimage*, for a critical analysis of post-traumatic cinema and the politics of representation.

24. A concept elaborated by Marianne Hirsch in *Family Frames: Photograph, Narrative and Postmemory* (Cambridge: Harvard University Press, 1997).

25. Graham Petrie, *History Must Answer to Man* (Budapest: Corvina Kiadó, 1978), 114–20.

26. Ibid., 185–86.

27. Ibid., 10–11.

28. *Apa*, author's transcription from the film's subtitles.

29. Legislation for a new Hungarian Film Law was enacted and approved in January 2004, assuring foreign investors of appropriate revenues and enabling co-productions to reap the benefit of their investments. I am grateful to Magyar Filmunió for inviting me to be pre-

sent at the February 2004 *Filmszemle* (Film review) in Budapest where press conferences were held to disseminate this information.

30. Art Spiegelman, *Maus: A Survivor's Tale* (New York: Pantheon Books, 1986).

31. Hanno Löwy, "The Mother of all Holocaust Films? Wanda Jakubowska's Auschwitz Trilogy," DEFA Film Library Lecture, University of Massachusetts Amherst, September 2003. I am grateful to Professor Löwy for subsequent exchanges on this topic.

32. Imre Kertész, *Feslzámolás* (Liquidation), trans. Tim Wilkinson (New York: Knopf, 2004).

33. Cited in "Thorny prose in little language wins literary distinction," ABC News Online (Friday, October 11, 2002) at http://abc.net.au/news/indepth/featureitems/literature.htm.

34. Manohla Dargis, *New York Times* (February 21, 2005).

35. Alan Riding, *New York Times* (February 16, 2005).

36. Ed Meza, "'Heights' takes fall: Terrio pic pulled from Berlin Competition," *Variety* (Wednesday, February 9, 2005).

37. Peter Bradshaw, *The Guardian* (Wednesday, February 16, 2005).

38. *ThinkFilm* (April 19, 2005).

39. Michèle Maheux, *Toronto International Film Festival Official Catalogue* (at www.e.bell.ca/filmfest).

Jewish Literary Renaissance in Post-Communist Hungary

Ivan Sanders

After reviewing the changes in Hungarian cultural life in the past decade and a half, one could confidently conclude that one of the more conspicuous changes we have witnessed has been the renewed interest in things Jewish. Caution is in order, however. "Interest in things Jewish" is a deliberately inclusive, ambiguous, and loaded formulation, for it includes not only numerous publications of Jewish interest: historical, literary, and sociological works, including penetrating, often controversial reassessments of events, issues, and problems touching on the Hungarian Jewish experience, but also a veritable flood of explicitly and often crudely anti-Jewish writings ranging from Holocaust denials to conspiracy theories, and the warmed over clichés of traditional religious anti-Judaism. This type of "Jewish-related literature" appeared in Hungary soon after the regime change in 1989, and fifteen years later it still has a prominent place in the far-right press and other media. All one has to do is consult the many items under the heading "Anti-Semitism" in the bibliography of Jewish topics appended to each issue of the journal *Múlt és Jövő*, or the annual "roundup" published by the Hungarian chapter of the B'nai B'rith under the title *Anti-Semitic Discourse in Hungary*. Fortunately, my topic is not this hate literature but another kind of literary revival, that of the literature dealing with Hungarian Jewry and with Jewish topics and themes in general. I would venture to say that more books of Jewish interest have been published in each of the past fifteen years than in the previous forty-year period.[1]

If we focus on literature, the volume of material is not quite so substantial, though even here the quantitative tally is impressive. In his rather somber and chastening postscript to an anthology of post-Holocaust Hungarian Jewish writing published in Budapest in 1999, János Kőbányai, who as editor, publisher, and writer has played a major role in making past and present Hungarian Jewish literature better known, points out that "only one tradition of closed-ended Hungarian Jewish assimilation survived the great destruction, and that is the rejection of tradition."[2] And at the end of his essay, he notes, perhaps even more bitterly, that "the names of several authors that by right should be present [in such an anthology] are missing. Interestingly, paradoxically, in similar anthologies published only abroad, we encounter a very different roster of names."[3] I don't think I would be giving away any secrets if I revealed that Kőbányai is obliquely referring to the fact that while such prominent contemporary Hungarian writers of Jewish origin as Péter Nádas, Mihály Kornis, György Spiró, and Péter Lengyel have contributed to an anthology of Hungarian Jewish writing published recently in English translation by the University of Nebraska Press,[4] they did not wish to be included in the volume compiled by János Kőbányai in Budapest. (We should note that other major Hungarian writers—Imre Kertész and György Konrád—had given permission to have pieces reprinted in Kőbányai's collection.)

Why this selective reluctance on the part of some Hungarian writers of Jewish origin to be labeled as Jewish writers, or to have their works considered a part of Jewish literature? It is an old story, of course, as old as the process of assimilation itself, in particular the assimilation of European Jews. For a number of Hungarian writers of Jewish extraction, what the poet Miklós Radnóti wrote in a now famous letter in the early forties remains the definitive pronouncement on the subject. Radnóti's letter was addressed to Aladár Komlós, a noted critic who did believe that there is such a thing as Hungarian Jewish literature. Komlós had asked Radnóti to contribute poems to an anthology he was then editing of works by Hungarian writers considered Jewish by the new law of the land, and who therefore found it increasingly difficult, if not impossible, to place their writings in non-Jewish Hungarian publications. Radnóti, who considered himself a Hungarian poet to the end, refused to enter this "denominational ghetto." "I never denied my Jewishness," he writes in his letter to Aladár Komlós,

> but I do not feel Jewish. I was never taught to be religious, I do not feel a need for it, I don't practice it. Race, blood ties, unseverable roots, ancient pangs quivering in every fiber—I consider such things utter nonsense, and not the defining characteristic of my intellectuality, my spirituality, or my poetry. Even in the social sense I see the "community of Jews" as a bogus designation. This has been my experience. Perhaps it isn't so, but this is how I feel, and I could never live a lie. My Jewishness has become the problem of my life, but it is circumstances, laws, the world that have made it so. The problem was forced on me. Otherwise I am a Hungarian poet; my relatives I have already spoken about....[5]

Earlier in the letter, Radnóti refers to two pictures hanging in his study, reproductions of portraits of János Arany and Ferenc Kazinczy, two greats of nineteenth-century Hungarian literature. Radnóti relates to Komlós that when "uninitiated" visitors, looking at the pictures, ask, "Are they relatives of yours?" he answers, "Yes, they are."[6]

A great many Hungarian artists of Jewish descent, perhaps the majority, still espouse Radnóti's credo. Let me provide a personal example. A number of years ago I wrote an essay on Péter Nádas's great novel, *Book of Memories*, in which I offered a Jewish reading of the work, and argued that in the social and historical context of the novel, its central hero has to be Jewish.[7] Nádas found my essay deeply offensive, and though we were good friends—I was also his translator—this put a strain on our relationship, which remains to this day. Let me hasten to add that Péter Nádas, like Radnóti, has never denied his Jewish origins, though like other Hungarian artists in such a situation—the well-known film director István Szabó comes to mind—Nádas finds it easier to talk about his Jewishness abroad in a language other than his native Hungarian. Moreover, Nádas, like Szabó, has treated Jewish subjects in his other works. But as tolerant and liberal-minded a person as he is, he felt that even as a literary critic I did not have the right to speculate about a fictional character and call him a Jew, although Nádas left that question entirely open. He was offended by the fact that I exposed him, "outed" him as it were, as the author of a Jewish novel, which he had no intention of writing.

We should stress that it is not because of a sense of shame or inferiority, a desire to gloss over certain parts of their heritage, or out of some misplaced, exaggerated nationalist feeling that Péter Nádas and other authors are reluctant to consider themselves anything but Hungarian writers, and view any other designation as inappropriate, parochial, retrograde, even degrading. They insist on being only Hungarian because they have a vivid historical memory. Of course, the real culprits here are pernicious ideologies and the tragedies to which they led. There are quite a few Hungarian artists and intellectuals who, though they are too young to remember the years of persecution, are well aware of the fact that their predecessors, or family members, were herded first into symbolic and then actual ghettoes, and who therefore do not wish to enter a "denominational ghetto" voluntarily.

One might say this is not a completely satisfying explanation. After all, Hungary has been a democracy for fifteen years, and though anti-Semitism has reared its ugly head during this time, the kind of stigmatization many Hungarian Jews, not only artists, instinctively fear is a thing of the past. But we also know that the peculiarities of Hungarian Jewish assimilation, quite apart from historical traumas, have left an ambiguous legacy. Let me try to illuminate this with another example. It has been pointed out, most recently by literary historian Eva Reichmann,[8] that two histories of Hungarian literature were published around at the same time in the 1930s: Gyula Farkas's *Az asszimiláció kora a magyar irodalomban (1867–1914)* (The age of assimilation in Hungarian literature—1867–1914) and Antal Szerb's broader *Magyar irodalomtörténet* (History of Hungarian literature). Farkas's highly controversial book examines the work of authors active during the period in question purely from the point of view of their being assimilationists, and his conclusions are rather devastating. He thinks that after 1867 Hungarian literature declined, the Hungarian character receded, and an alien spirit took over. The literary history of Antal Szerb, a critic and essayist of Jewish descent who died as a forced laborer in early 1945, is thoroughly modern and European in approach, revealing the influence of the *Geistesgeschichte* school of criticism. For the record, Gyula Farkas's book is a historical curiosity, a period piece, which nobody reads anymore, while Szerb's *Irodalomtörténet* is still used, still delightfully readable, and one of the finest works of its kind in Hungarian. Nevertheless, in one sense Szerb's book also represents an extreme position. While Farkas's interest is exclusively in the ethnic and religious origins of the authors he discusses and the effect of these origins on their works (mostly negative in his estimation), Szerb virtually ignores this aspect and is especially silent on the subject when it comes to assimilated Hungarian Jewish writers, including those writers (József Kiss, for example) in whose works Jewish influences are not at all irrelevant. So, in a sense, we are dealing with distortion and repression on both sides. And this is the highly ambiguous tradition to which contemporary Hungarian writers are heir.

There have been writers who responded to the challenge of this legacy by masking, universalizing, and submerging their Jewish themes; Jewishness in these works becomes a subtext that must be decoded, deconstructed, in a manner of speaking. This is what Péter Nádas does in his *Book of Memories*, and my essay on the novel is an exercise—so unwelcome by the author—in decoding. Others have noted this tendency and have written about it. For example, in a much quoted essay aptly titled "De-Judaization in Hungarian Jewish Literature," the philosopher Ágnes Heller discusses the phenomenon with regard to three Hungarian writers: Ferenc Molnár, Tibor Déry, and Péter Lengyel, and comes to the conclusion that this concealment, or obfuscation, though it may stem from a degree of self-denial or even self-hate, can make a work resonant, suggestive, and of course it can also impoverish it.[9] In a literary text, oblique allusions and ambiguous hints—whether they refer to politics, religion, or something else—can always add excitement, turn the reader into a detective, a fellow conspirator, though the feeling that something is missing is also always present.

Let me illustrate with a couple of simple, even trivial examples. The *topos* of the wanderer's return to his original home is common enough in literature. In modern Hungarian literature, because of the many dislocations caused by historical upheavals, the return of the exile or emigrant to his or her native country or city is an especially ubiquitous theme. In the early sixties, Ferenc Karinthy wrote a short story called "Túl az operencián" ("Beyond the seven seas"), in which an elegant, middle-class Budapest lady returns to her native city that she left in the late 1940s and visits her former maid and her family. She is received with great cordiality by the hard-working and prospering working-class family. Their hospitality is unexceptionable, the conversation polite, though it soon falters, and after all the pleasantries have been exchanged there is not much more to say. The social gap that had always been there seems wider now. The lady leaves the house of her former maid tired and disappointed. "Túl az operencián" is a typical story of the period, yet there is a tentativeness and awkwardness not only about the story itself but also about the manner of presentation, as though the author couldn't decide what to reveal and what to withhold. We learn that before they left, she and her husband had been makers and purveyors of fine china, they have a German-sounding name, and are now comfortably settled in New York. They might be Jewish; then again they might not be. The number of things left unsaid makes Karinthy's story vague and indefinite—a torso.

Transylvanian-born Zsófia Balla's much more recent story, "A nagyapám háza" (My grandfather's house), included in János Kőbányai's previously mentioned anthology, is also about a return—a family from Israel paying a visit to their Transylvanian hometown after an absence of forty-nine years. In this story, nothing is glossed over: the author details the visitors' contradictory feelings about their hometown, the mixture of nostalgia and bitterness, and the locals' lingering resentment of the one-time victims whom they now see as rich Westerners throwing their weight around. Zsófia Balla's story is also modest in scope, a sketch really, but at least it is forthright and honest. We might cite a counterexample from the same collection of Hungarian Jewish stories: György Dalos's marvelous vignettes about growing up Jewish in Communist Hungary, "Anecdotes from Childhood," were first published in 1978, during the Kádár era. Wry, subtle, written with a gentle touch, these anecdotes nevertheless focus on the absurdities of life in Hungary in the early Communist years, as seen by an orphaned Jewish boy who is raised by his tenacious grandmother. A sequel to these little gems, entitled "Anecdotes from Adulthood," lack the sharpness and poignancy of the earlier collection. Written in a period of far greater freedom, they are long-winded, explicit, and obvious.

All this is not to say that the fall of communism and the years of change did not have a liberating effect on all Hungarians. In her reminiscences, Ágnes Heller recalls the moment in her youth when she embraced communism and snapped out of her previous existence, forgetting her Zionist past, her Jewish past, and also her Hungarian self—for years she was in the thrall of an ideology. Her reawakening, her return to her roots, she says, happened early, during the 1956 Revolution; she realized then that she was both Hungarian and a Jew.[10] But it is a fact that as a thinker and writer Ágnes Heller began to rediscover Jewish literature and history only after 1989. Since then all of her books are published by Múlt és Jövő, the most important publisher of books on Jewish subjects in Hungary today. Her example may be exceptional and conspicuous, but it does say something important about spiritual reorientation in post-1989 Hungary. For many the historic changes meant a moment of truth; they could say and do things they had not dared for years. For example, the well-known psychologist and writer Tamás Vekerdy published a slim volume entitled *Zsidó könyv* (Jewish book) several years ago, in which more than once he writes the simple sentence, "I am a Jew."[11] One senses the relief, the exhilaration accompanying such a public declaration. Another dramatic and cathartic utterance can be heard in a Hungarian film made in 1989, at the very cusp of the changing era. The film is *Tutajosok* (*The Memories of a River* in English), made by Judit Elek and based on the famous Tiszaeszlár blood libel case. In the film's final scene, after all the defendants have been acquitted of the charge of ritual murder, the prosecution's star witness, Móric Scharf, the adolescent son of one of the accused (who, partly because he had been "prepped" by the examining magistrate and partly because he rebelled against his authoritarian father, testified against him in open court, rejecting his family, his community, his faith), in a contrite but unnatural gesture, kneels before his father and in very proper Hungarian begs for forgiveness. But then, in a sudden, heart-rending outburst, the boy sobs, in Yiddish, "Tate, harget mich!" (Father, kill me!), after which József Scharf lifts the boy from the kneeling position and embraces him. Now this is a fictional scene. Nothing in the available historical record shows that something like this actually took place.[12] But I cannot help feeling that this anguished outcry springs from a deep need—present in the director and perhaps in many other Hungarians of Jewish background—to atone, indeed to be punished, for allowing themselves to be duped, led astray, brainwashed into denying an important part of their being, just as the young boy was brainwashed by his handlers in what was planned by the prosecution as a sort of show trial. (The film suggests in a number of ways that the Tiszaeszlár trial prefigured the political show trials of the late 1940s and early 1950s—except that in 1883 justice and reason ultimately prevailed, and the compelling arguments of a liberal Hungarian aristocrat, Károly Eötvös, succeeded in staving off the forces of unreason.)

Since the 1989 watershed, Hungarian Jewish literature has enjoyed a kind of renaissance. For the first time in a long time, works of fiction appeared about Jewish characters and Jewish life situations that did not have to resort to indirect or coded, euphemistic language. Writers emerged in the new era who were either too young to publish before (Gábor T. Szántó), or turned to belles-lettres rather late (István Gábor Benedek), or were under publication ban before 1989 (György Dalos). Certain hitherto sensitive, painful, even taboo subjects could be treated more freely: Jewish religious life during the Communist years, Jews in the Communist secret police in the late forties and early fifties, collaboration between community leaders and the security apparatus, and so on.

Published in the mid-to-late nineties, these works aimed at a larger readership, and some of the new writings, especially István Gábor Benedek's books, achieved considerable popularity.[13] But they are popular fictions, often sentimental, melodramatic, offering the reader colorful "ethnic" characters, earthy language, and plots with unexpected twists and turns. Generally they lack the depth, seriousness, and stylistic innovations of earlier examples of Hungarian literature on Jewish themes. But readers in the nineties, it seems, were no longer interested in oblique, parabolic representations, in playing detective or reading between the lines—they were interested in anecdotal realism, which is certainly not a new tradition in Hungarian literature. It is worth noting that in the post-1989 period, the best-selling foreign Jewish writer in Hungary has been Chaim Potok, who during the Communist era was not published in Budapest, probably because he was considered "too Jewish," but also because he was not deemed literary enough. During the same period many works by such renowned American Jewish authors as Saul Bellow and Bernard Malamud were published in Hungary—works which, in the fifties and sixties at least, were seen both in this country and abroad as the best that American literature had to offer.

The family novel has been seen as a particularly suitable genre for conveying the Hungarian Jewish experience, if only because it is a story of rather rapid assimilation through several generations. We need only think of works by Tamás Kóbor, Lajos Hatvany, András Komor, Károly Pap, and Illés Kaczér to realize that the ups and downs of Hungarian Jewish history has been told to a large extent through family novels. In recent decades, a new generation of writers produced post-Holocaust examples of family or generation novels, but these, as Rita Horváth, a student of the genre, points out, are attenuated, fragmented versions with mythic beginnings, abrupt breaks, and uncertain endings.[14] This trend continued in the nineties, and even in the more popular kind of Hungarian Jewish fiction referred to earlier we get brief synopses of the genre. For example, in one of István Gábor Benedek's stories, we read the following:

> Then he came out with it. The familiar story. The grandfather who was still an observant Jew. The son who already changed his name and pursued happiness in more worldly ways. Thus Deutsch became Derczei, the casino replaced the synagogue, Jewish fellowship gave way to hobnobbing with the gentry. But then came the war, the deportations, and

sobering forced labor. And here stands a member of the third generation, a disgusting specimen, a smiling interviewer among the interrogators, whose questions are usually punctuated with slaps in the face.[15]

This brief outline of a Hungarian Jewish family's history in the twentieth century will be familiar to those who saw one of the most famous Hungarian films of recent years: István Szabó's *Sunshine,* an elaborate cinematic version of a family novel. The film tells an important and thus far neglected story, which in many ways is unique in the annals of Jewish history. Though making some concessions to Hollywood-style filmmaking, *Sunshine* incorporates themes, characters, and episodes from a number of Hungarian-Jewish sources. Szabó's film met with unexpected success in Hungary and (there is much anecdotal evidence for this) it had a positively cathartic effect on many Hungarian Jews.

More recent films focusing specifically on the Holocaust in Hungary are worrisome because they are formulaic, inauthentic, and sensationalist. I am thinking of films like *Gloomy Sunday* (*Szomorú vasárnap*), a German film actually, shot in Budapest based on a Hungarian story and using a number of Hungarian actors, and Andor Szilágyi's *Rose's Songs* (*A Rózsa énekei*). The latter is a particularly glaring example of cinematic kitsch. It may work as wish fulfillment, but it strains credibility to the utmost. The film is derivative in many ways; let me cite just one example. Supposedly based on a true story, *Rose's Songs* is about a group of Hungarian Jews taking refuge in a Buda villa in late 1944, their spirit being kept up by a famous Jewish opera singer whose house this is. A young boy, the son of the film's main character, does his turn as a peeping tom, climbing up a tree and catching glimpses of a pretty young girl taking a shower, and on one occasion of a wig-wearing Orthodox Jewish lady, one of those hiding in the house; he happens to look when the lady's wig slips, exposing her bald head. The boy is so taken aback, he falls off the tree. The scene is highly reminiscent of a recurring memory in Imre Kertész's novel *Kaddish for a Child Not Born*, whose first-person narrator recalls that on a visit to observant relatives in the country, he once opened the bedroom door and saw not a sheitel-wearing aunt but "a bald woman in a red gown in front of a mirror."[16] He is dismayed, and the image stayed with him. But whereas in Kertész's novel the image becomes a potent symbol Jewish vulnerability and shame, in Andor Szilágyi's film it is simply a grotesque moment, one of many in the film whose sole aim is to shock, without carrying any real meaning.

Imre Kertész, with or without the Nobel Prize, has achieved something very important in modern Hungarian literature, and specifically in the literature about the Holocaust, in that he has combined the reach for universality, the distilled, mythic truth of a parable, with the concreteness of realist fiction. György Köves, the hero of *Fateless*, is not simply a victim, one of the persecuted who gains insight into his own fatelessness, but a very real Jewish boy from Budapest who tells his story. Kertész has always insisted that in *Sorstalanság* he did not intend to write a Holocaust novel, or indeed a novel in the conventional sense. "The greatest danger for me lay in the temptation of giving way to anecdotal digressions, intriguing, colorful but inessential details, singularly interesting little stories," he said in a 1999 interview. "The action had to follow a clearly devised structure, it had to be reduced to essentials. The story of Auschwitz has become part of the repository of European knowing and European memory. I had to fashion my story as a collective myth."[17] Indeed, each scene, each episode and character in the novel is at once concrete and emblematic; each detail used is crucial and representative.

Fateless is a universally valid meditation on evil in the twentieth century, an existentialist novel in which an absurd universe appears in the guise of a totalitarian system that strips one of his or her real self and imposes a role, a fate. Yet there is nothing abstract about the novel—for Kertész, lived reality is too important. He is a survivor who bears witness, but he is also a writer. Implicit in *Fateless* (as well as in Kertész's other works) is the belief that there is—there must be—art after Auschwitz. All of Kertész's literary works, not just *Fateless*, are the painful and risky undertakings of a writer who turns the material of his own life into serious fiction. The result is stirring and also disquieting, because for his characters transforming lived reality into words on paper is too often an obsessive rather than redemptive act.

All writers who deal with the Hungarian Jewish experience face such risks, even those whose works are not autobiographically inspired. But only the most courageous and gifted can, like Kertész, shy away from easy answers, facile dénouements, and suggest that sudden insights and epiphanies may light the way but for an instant, after which one feels lost again.

Notes

1. Here is a representative sample of Hungarian Judaica published in recent years: Aladár Komlós, *Magyar-zsidó szellemtörténet a reformkortól a holocaustig* (Hungarian Jewish history of ideas from the age of reform to the Holocaust), 2 vols. (Budapest: Múlt és Jövő, 1997); Kinga Frojimovics, et al., eds., *A zsidó Budapest—Emlékek, szertartások, történelem* (Jewish Budapest—monuments, rites, history), 2 vols. (Budapest: MTA Judaisztikai Kutatócsoport, 1995); Petra Török, ed., *A határ és a határolt—Töprengések a magyar-zsidó irodalom létformáiról* (Boundaries and limits—Meditations on Hungarian Jewish literature) (Budapest: Yahalom, 1997); Gábor Hamp, Özséb Horányi, and László Rábai, eds., *Magyar megfontolások a Soáról* (Hungarian reflections on the Shoah) (Budapest: Balassi Kiadó, 1999); János Pelle, *Az utolsó vérvádak* (The last blood libels) (Budapest: Pelikán, 1995); Viktor Karády, *Zsidóság, modernizáció, polgárosodás* (Jews, modernity, and the rise to middle class) (Budapest: Cserépfalvi, 1997); and Alan Unterman, *Zsidó hagyományok lexikona* (Lexicon of Jewish lore and legend) (Budapest: Helikon, 1999).

2. János Kőbányai, ed., *Budapesti aggadák—A holocaust utáni irodalom* (Budapest Aggadot—Post-holocaust literature) (Budapest: Múlt és Jövö, 1999), 334.

3. Ibid., 338.

4. See Susan R. Suleiman and Éva Forgács, eds., *Contemporary Jewish Writing in Hungary—An Anthology* (Lincoln: University of Nebraska Press, 2003).

5. Miklós Radnóti, *Napló* (Diary) (Budapest: Magvető Könyvkiadó, 1989), 210.

6. Ibid., 209.

7. See Iván Sanders, "Metakommunikáció haladóknak—Nádas Péter *Emlékiratok* könyvének zsidó olvasata" (Meta-communication for advanced students—A Jewish reading of Péter Nádas's *Book of Memories*), in Török, 373–85.

8. See her essay, "Vád alá helyezett szerzők?" (Authors under indictment?), in Török, 230–45.

9. Ágnes Heller, "Zsidótlanítás a magyar zsidó irodalomban" (De-Judaization in Hungarian Jewish literature), in *Pikareszk Auschwitz árnyékában* (Picaresque in the shadow of Auschwitz) (Budapest: Múlt és Jövő, 2003), 7–25.

10. See Ágnes Heller, "A zsidóság vonzásában" (Drawn to Judaism), in *Zsidó szellem ma* (The Jewish spirit today) (Budapest: Múlt és Jövő, 1999), 23–62.

11. Tamás Vekerdy, *Zsidó könyv* (Jewish book) (Budapest: Ursa Minor, 2002), 10–11.

12. See Judit Elek and Mihály Sükösd, *Tutajosok—A tiszaeszlári per dokumentumai* (The rafters—Documents of the Tiszeszlár trial); and Judit Elek, *Tutajosok— Filmforgatókönyv* (The rafters—The screenplay) (Budapest: Magvető, 1990).

13. See for example Gábor T. Szántó, *Mószer* (Snitch) (Budapest: Magvető, 1997); *Keleti pályaudvar, végállomás* (Eastern station: End of the line) (Budapest: Magvető, 2002); István Gábor Benedek, *A komlósi tóra* (The torah scroll of Tótkomlós) (Budapest: Dan Könyvkiadó, 1994); *Az elégett fénykép* (The burned photograph) (Budapest: Magyar Könyvklub, 1997); György Dalos, *A körülmetélés* (The circumcision) (Budapest: Magvető, 1990); and Dalos, *Az istenkereső* (The God-Seeker) (Budapest: Magvető, 1999).

14. Rita Horváth, "A Changing Genre: Jewish Hungarian Family Novels After the Holocaust," in *The Treatment of the Holocaust in Hungary and Romania During the Post-Communist Era*, ed. Randolph L. Braham (New York: Columbia University Press, 2004), 201–15.

15. István Gábor Benedek, *Az elégett fénykép*, 231–32.

16. Imre Kertész, *Kaddish for a Child Not Born*, trans. Christopher C. Wilson and Katharina M. Wilson (Evanston, IL: Northwestern University Press, 1997), 19.

17. "A vizsgálódó mondat" (The inquiring sentence), *Élet és Irodalom* (Life and literature) (November 12, 1999), 3.

Contributors

Jean Ancel is affiliated with the Yad Vashem Institute in Jerusalem. He is the author and editor of numerous works on the Holocaust and the history of Romania and Romanian Jewry, including *Documents Concerning the Fate of Romanian Jewry during the Holocaust* (1986), *The History of the Holocaust: Romania* (2002), and *Transnistria, 1941–1943: The Romanian Mass Murder Campaigns* (2003).

Ivan T. Berend is Professor of History and Director of the Center for European and Russian Studies at the University of California, Los Angeles. A former president of the Hungarian Academy of Sciences (1985–1990), he is the author or co-author of many works, including *Economic Development of East Central Europe in the Nineteenth and Twentieth Centuries* (1974), *Hungarian Economic Reforms, 1953–1988* (1990), and *Central and Eastern Europe, 1944–1993: Detour from the Periphery to the Periphery* (1996).

Randolph L. Braham is Distinguished Professor Emeritus of Political Science at The City College and the Doctoral Program at the Graduate Center of the City University of New York, where he also serves as Director of the Rosenthal Institute for Holocaust Studies. He is the author and/or editor of numerous works, including *The Politics of Genocide: The Holocaust in Hungary* (1994).

Brewster S. Chamberlin is former Director of Archives and International Programs at the United States Holocaust Memorial Museum in Washington. He has written extensively on Holocaust-related documentation in archives around the world and on the history of modern Germany and the city of Paris. His most recent book is *Mediterranean Sketches: Fictions, Memories and Metafictions* (2005).

Holly Case is Assistant Professor of History at Cornell University. Her doctoral dissertation, titled "A City between States: The Transylvanian City of Cluj-Kolozsvár-Klausenburg in the Spring of 1942," focused on inter-ethnic relations in Hungarian Northern Transylvania during the Second World War.

Tim Cole teaches history at the University of Bristol in Britain. A former Pearl Resnick Postdoctoral Research Fellow at the Center for Advanced Holocaust Studies at the United States Holocaust Memorial Museum in Washington, Professor Cole is the author of *Selling the Holocaust: From Auschwitz to Schindler: How History is Bought, Packaged and Sold* (1999) and *Holocaust City: The Making of a Jewish Ghetto* (2003).

Dan Danieli is affiliated with the Survivors of the Shoah Visual History Foundation. A specialist on the Hungarian labor service system, he is the author of *Captain Ocskay: A Righteous Man* (1996).

Alice Freifeld is Associate Professor of History at the University of Florida, specializing in twentieth-century Central Europe, the Habsburg Monarchy, and the Jews of East-Central Europe. She is the author of *Nationalism and the Crowd in Liberal Hungary, 1848–1914* (2000) and co-editor of *East Europe Reads Nietzsche* (1998).

Paul Hanebrink is Assistant Professor of History at Rutgers University. He is the author of *In Defense of Christian Hungary: Religion, Nationalism, and Anti-Semitism in Hungary, 1890–1944* (forthcoming). He also authored "Continuities and Change in Hungarian Antisemitism, 1945–1948," published by the U.S. Holocaust Memorial Museum in an occasional paper titled "Hungary and the Holocaust: Confrontation with the Past" (2001).

Radu Ioanid is Director of the International Archival Programs Division of the Center for Advanced Holocaust Studies at the United States Holocaust Memorial Museum in Washington. A specialist on the Holocaust in Romania, he is the author of several monographs, including *The Sword of the Archangel: Fascist Ideology in Romania* (1990), *The Holocaust in Romania: The Destruction of Jews and Gypsies under the Antonescu Regime* (2000), and *The Ransom of the Jews: The Story of the Extraordinary Secret Bargain between Romania and Israel* (2005).

Gábor Kádár, a Budapest-based historian, is co-creator of the permanent Hungarian exhibition in the Auschwitz-Birkenau State Museum. He is the author of several studies on the Hungarian chapter of the Holocaust. He is the co-author of *Self-Financing Genocide: The Gold Train, the Becher Case and the Wealth of Hungarian Jews* (with Zoltán Vági, 2004).

Victor Karády is Professor of Sociology at the Central European University of Budapest. Retired from the Centre National de la Récherche Scientifique, Paris, he is the author of numerous scholarly works in many languages in history, demography, and sociology. His most recent work in English is titled *The Jews of Europe in the Modern Era: A Socio-Historical Outline* (2004).

László Karsai is Professor of History at the University of Szeged, Hungary. An expert on the history and historiography of the Roma and Jewish Holocaust, he is the author of several monographs, including *The Gypsy Question in Hungary, 1919–1945* (1992) and *Holocaust* (2001). He also co-edited several volumes relating to war crimes trials, including *A Szálasi per* (with Elek Karsai, 1988) and *Az Endre-Baky-Jaross per* (with Judit Molnár, 1994).

Ferenc Katona is an archivist at the United States Holocaust Memorial Museum. A former editor at the Publishing House of the Hungarian Academy of Sciences, Mr. Katona has contributed essays and articles to a number of Hungarian-language periodicals, including *Irodalomtörténet* (Literary history) and *Új Élet* (New life), both of Budapest.

András Kovács is Professor of History and Sociology at the Central European University of Budapest. An expert on Jewish identity and postwar antisemitism in Hungary, he is the author of numerous sociological studies published in collective works and scholarly journals. He co-edited *New Jewish Identities* (with Zvi Gitelman and Barry Kosmin, 2003), contributing an essay titled "Jewish Groups and Identity Strategies in Post-Communist Hungary."

Daniel A. Lowy is a research scientist working at the U.S. Naval Research Laboratory in Washington, D.C. Formerly on the faculty of the University of Memphis, in addition to authoring 45 research papers in electrochemistry, Dr. Lowy also published several books on the Holocaust, including *From the Brickyard to the Freight Train: The History of the Jews of Kolozsvár* (1998) and *Kolozsvár Engraved in Stone* (co-authored, 1996).

Judit Molnár is Associate Professor of Political Science at the University of Szeged, Hungary. She is the author of several books, including *Jewish Fate in 1944 in the Fifth (Szeged) Gendarmerie District* (in Hungarian, 1995). She co-edited *The Endre-Baky-Jaross Trial* (in Hungarian, with László Karsai, 1994). Her scholarly articles have appeared in journals such as *Történelmi Szemle, Kritika, Múlt és Jövö,* and *Szombat.*

Zsuzsanna Ozsváth is Leah and Paul Lewis Chair of Holocaust Studies at the University of Texas at Dallas. A specialist in Holocaust literature and poetry translations, she is the author of several books, including *In the Footsteps of Orpheus: The Life and Times of Miklós Radnóti* (2000), *Attila József: The Iron-Blue Vault* (with Fred Turner, 1999), and *Foamy Sky: The Major Poems of Miklós Radnóti* (with Fred Turner, 1999). Her essays have appeared in *Judaism, Partisan Review, The Hungarian Quarterly,* and other journals.

Attila Pók is Deputy Director of the Institute of History at the Hungarian Academy of Sciences and of the "Europa Institut" of Budapest. A specialist on modern East Central European political and intellectual history, he is the co-editor of *The Holocaust in Hungary: Fifty Years Later* (with Randolph L. Braham, 1995) to which he contributed an essay titled "The Search for Scapegoats and the Holocaust" (in Hungarian). He also contributed chapters to *Challenges of Economic History: Essays in Honor of Ivan T. Berend* (János Buza, ed., 1996) and *The Nazis' Last Victims: The Holocaust in Hungary* (Randolph L. Braham with Scott Miller, eds., 1998).

Catherine Portuges is Director of the Interdepartmental Program in Film Studies and Professor and Graduate Program Director in Comparative Literature at the University of Massachusetts, Amherst. She is the author *Screen Memories: The Hungarian Cinema of Márta Mészáros* (1983) and co-editor of *Cinema in Transition: Post-Communist Central Europe* (forthcoming). Her essays have appeared in journals such as *American Historical Review, Spectator, Slavic Review,* and *The Moving Image.* She has also contributed chapters to *The Cinema of Central Europe* (2005), *Comparative Cultural Studies and Central European Culture Today* (2001), and *Nationalisms and Sexualities* (1992).

Ivan Sanders is Professor Emeritus of English at Suffolk Community College/SUNY, and Adjunct Professor at Columbia University's East Central European Center. He is the prize-winning translator (Füst Milán Prize, Tibor Déry Prize, Soros Translation Award) of works by George Konrád, Péter Nádas, Péter Esterházy, and others. His studies on Jewish literary topics have appeared in many journals, including *Judaism*, *Jewish Social Studies*, *Soviet Jewish Affairs*, and *The Hungarian Quarterly*.

Michael Shafir is Coordinator for European Affairs, Online Journalism, at Radio Free Europe/Radio Liberty in Prague, where he also serves as editor of *East European Perspectives*. He is the author of *Romania: Politics, Economics and Society. Political Stagnation and Simulated Change* (1985) and *Between Negation and Comparative Trivialization: Holocaust Denial in Post-Communist East-Central Europe* (2002). He has contributed chapters to several books published in Austria, the Czech Republic, Great Britain, and the United States. Dr. Shafir has published a large number of articles in a variety of languages in many countries.

Zoltán Tibori Szabó is a Cluj-based correspondent for the Budapest daily *Népszabadság* and a columnist for *Szabadság,* the Hungarian-language daily of Cluj (Kolozsvár). A Pulitzer Prize-winner for Hungarian-language journalism, he is the author of several Holocaust-related works, including *Between Life and Death: The Escape and Rescue of Jews Across the Hungarian-Romanian Border between 1940–1944* (in Hungarian, 2001). He has also published a large number of articles on the fate of Romanian and Transylvanian Jewry.

Zoltán Vági is co-creator of the permanent Hungarian exhibition in the Auschwitz-Birkenau State Museum and a member of the group of historians appointed to design the content of the Hungarian Holocaust Museum in Budapest. He is the author or co-author of several studies on the Holocaust in Hungary, including *Self-Financing Genocide: The Gold Train, the Becher Case, and the Wealth of Hungarian Jews* (with Gábor Kádár, 2004).

Raphael Vago is Senior Lecturer in History at Tel Aviv University, where he is also associated with the Cummings Center for Russian and East European Studies and the Stephen Roth Institute for the Study of Contemporary Anti-Semitism and Racism. His major areas of research include extremist movements, anti-Semitism, the Holocaust, and post-Communist affairs. He is the author of *The Grandchildren of Trianon: Hungary and the Hungarian Minority in the Communist States* (1989). Dr. Vago has also contributed chapters to several collective works, including *Hungarian-Jewish Studies* (1973), *Points of View: Studies and Research in the Problems of Soviet and East European Studies* (in Hebrew, 1977), and *The Holocaust in Hungary: Forty Years Later* (1985).

Elie Wiesel is Andrew W. Mellon Professor in the Humanities at Boston University. The winner of the Nobel Peace Price in 1987 and former chairman of the United States Holocaust Memorial Council, he is the author of a large number of books translated into many languages.

Index